Contents at a Glance

Table of Contents

Part III: Getting to Know Keys, Modes, and Chord Progressions 91

Introduction

Music theory is the study of how music works. *Guitar theory* focuses on understanding music from a guitar player's perspective. Makes sense, right? With a good working knowledge of guitar theory, including the use of scales, chords, progressions, modes, and more, you can easily figure out why a song is put together the way it is and how you can improvise and compose your own music.

About This Book

This book aims to explain how you can play popular music on the guitar fretboard, as well as why certain elements of music go together the way they do. Specifically, it covers what types of scale patterns guitarists use and how they form chords, assemble chord progressions, and apply modes.

Note: By *popular music,* I mean the types of songs you regularly hear on Top 40 and classic rock radio stations, including music by Chuck Berry, The Beatles, Eric Clapton, Led Zeppelin, the Eagles, Guns N' Roses, Dave Matthews Band, and U2, just to name a few. Throughout this book, you discover important details of songs like "Johnny B. Goode," "Purple Haze," "Tears in Heaven," "Stairway to Heaven," "Sweet Child O' Mine," "With or Without You," and many more.

Instead of taking a traditional approach to music theory, which usually emphasizes reading and writing standard musical notation, this book takes a hands-on approach that emphasizes playing on the guitar fretboard and using guitar tablature and neck diagrams. For example, it shows you how to play scale patterns used for riffing and jamming guitar music, as well as how to build the same chord shapes on the fretboard that famous guitarists use. It also shows you how to play through common chord progressions that you hear in the most popular radio hits. Perhaps most importantly, though, it explains how all these components work together.

With the primary focus being on scales, chords, and progressions, this book doesn't cover much in the way of note reading, rhythm, and technique. It also doesn't teach many of the classic music theory terms and concepts that are normally part of a formal music curriculum. So although you may not be able to pass a music theory exam at a music school after reading this book, you will know how familiar guitar songs are put together and how you can compose and improvise songs on your own.

Rhythm and technique are very important to good guitar playing, but these topics fall outside the scope of this book. If you're new to guitar, you can train your fingers to become a lean, mean guitar-playing machine by working with *Guitar For Dummies, Guitar Exercises For Dummies, Rock Guitar For Dummies, Blues Guitar For Dummies,* and *Classical Guitar For Dummies* (all written by Mark Phillips and/or Jon Chappell and published by Wiley). You can also learn about basic rhythms by working with a beginner-level note-reading course like *Mel Bay's Modern Guitar Method, Hal Leonard Guitar Method,* or anything else that is similar.

Here's what sets this book apart from other guitar resource materials:

- **The practicality and efficiency of the content:** If you don't need to know a certain topic or technique to play guitar and understand popular music, I don't present it here. On the flip side, I cover many concepts that don't typically show up in traditional music theory courses but that are important for guitar players to learn.
- **The number of familiar song references:** Say goodbye to learning abstract ideas without knowing how they apply to the music you know and love! I refer to some of the most popular songs and famous guitarists of all time in the pages that follow.

As you work your way through this book, keep in mind that sidebars and Technical Stuff icons are skippable. A few other things to note are

- All the information applies to both acoustic and electric guitar unless otherwise noted.
- I use six-string guitars and standard tuning in all examples and figures unless otherwise noted.
- You can apply much of the information in the book to bass guitar, too.
- I use a right-hander's perspective throughout the book.
- You have to look up and practice popular song references on your own. I don't include the music here.

Within this book, you may note that some web addresses break across two lines of text. If you're reading this book in print and want to visit one of these web pages, simply key in the web address exactly as it's noted in the text, pretending that the line break doesn't exist. If you're reading this as an e-book, you have it easy — just click the web address to go directly to the web page.

Foolish Assumptions

Before you dive in, I need to make one thing clear right now: This book is not for beginners! It's for guitar players who already know the basics and can play but who want to take their knowledge and skills to the next level. Perhaps you've been playing for years but have never really understood what you're doing. Whatever the case may be, to get the full benefit of this book, you need to know and be able to play and read the following:

- Open chords and open chord songs
- Power chords and power chord songs
- Barre chords and barre chord songs
- Some melodies, riffs, and simple solos
- Guitar tab and neck diagrams

You don't need to be an expert on these concepts; you just need a working knowledge of them. You don't have to know how to read standard musical notation, either, because tablature is the preferred notation method here. If you still need to learn the basics and acquire the skills I list here, I suggest you start with *Guitar For Dummies,* by Mark Phillips and Jon Chappell (Wiley).

Icons Used in This Book

In order to highlight different types of information, I've marked certain paragraphs with the following icons:

This icon points out tips, tricks, shortcuts, and more that make your life as a guitar player a little easier.

This icon points out especially important concepts that you don't want to miss or forget.

This icon highlights technical information (go figure!) that you can skip if you're short on time (or if you just want to focus on the need-to-know stuff).

This icon points out the audio tracks and video clips I've recorded to illustrate various scales, patterns, and so on throughout the book.

Beyond the Book

As if all the great information in this book weren't enough, you can go beyond the book for even more!

I've recorded numerous audio tracks and video clips so that you can view and listen to various scale patterns, chord progressions, and more throughout the book. Go to `www.dummies.com/go/guitartheory` to access these files.

Also be sure to check out the free Cheat Sheet at `www.dummies.com/cheatsheet/guitartheory` for all sorts of super-handy info, including a fretboard diagram showing notes along the 6th and 5th strings, sample major scale patterns, a chart of Roman numerals and the scale degrees and major/minor chord qualities they represent, and mode names.

Where to Go from Here

As with all *For Dummies* books, you don't have to read this book from beginning to end. You can certainly try starting anywhere you like. However, because musical concepts build on top of one another, you won't be able to fit all the pieces together and see the big picture until after you've completed most of the chapters. That being said, I suggest starting with Chapters 1 and 2 in Part I. From there you can decide whether you want to focus more on chords or scales. If you're primarily a rhythm guitar player, you may find Parts II and III the most useful. If you're primarily a lead guitarist, you may want to focus on Part IV.

As you work through this book, work with each concept one at a time. Take breaks from the text to practice and rehearse what you read about. Your goal is to commit every skill to both your mental memory and your hand memory before reading on and playing more. You may learn some concepts after only a few minutes of practice; others may take hours. Take as much time as you need to practice playing and rehearsing the topics I cover here. This isn't a race. Enjoy the process and make everything stick — that is, work with the concepts until they become a permanent part of your playing.

Remember: It's not enough to play a new chord shape or scale pattern off a page in this book. You need to play each shape or pattern in context (that is, in actual songs) to really understand what to do with it. That's why I reference so many songs throughout this book. You don't need to look up and learn every single song I mention, but try to play through a few examples every time you learn a new concept. You don't have to learn every song in its entirety, either. If I reference a song because it features a guitar riff using a particular scale, then just focus on playing that riff. If my focus is on the chord progression, then just play through the chord changes. (If you're not sure where to find the music for a given song referenced in the text, check out `www.musicnotes.com`, `www.sheetmusicplus.com`, or `www.musicdispatch.com`.)

Part I

Getting Started with Guitar Theory

getting started with guitar theory

For Dummies can help you get started with lots of subjects. Visit `www.dummies.com` to learn more and do more with *For Dummies.*

In this part . . .

- Discover exactly what guitar theory is and why it's so valuable to learn. See how focusing on elements of popular music and familiar songs can help you better apply theory to your own music. Prepare yourself to play scales, chords, progressions, modes, and more.
- Get familiar with a guitarist's perspective and a hands-on approach to music theory. See how the fretboard is a grid and get to know the basic concepts, such as intervals, whole steps, half steps, flats, and sharps, that all guitarists use to find their way around the fretboard. Visualize shapes and patterns on the neck. Explore the benefits of using guitar tablature and neck diagrams over standard musical notation.

Chapter 1

Guitar Theory in a Nutshell

In This Chapter

- Understanding why guitar theory is important
- Getting to know the fretboard with the help of guitar tabs and neck diagrams
- Surveying the different scales guitarists need to know
- Building chords and chord progressions

So you want to find out more about guitar theory? Well, you've come to the right place. This chapter gives you a quick overview of guitar theory and explains why this information is so useful for guitar players to know. It also introduces you to some of the elements you'll encounter throughout this book, like guitar tabs, neck diagrams, scales, and chords. Be sure to take the quiz at the end of this chapter to see what you already know about guitar theory. Then dive in to the rest of the book to find out what you don't know.

To hear an audio example that explains why guitar theory is so important and demonstrates the sound of some of the material presented throughout this book, listen to Audio Track 1.

Why Learn Guitar Theory?

Music theory is the study of music — how it's written, notated, discussed, thought of, and played. As you may have already guessed, *guitar theory* is the study of how music theory specifically applies to the guitar fretboard. It usually focuses on how the different components of songs, such as scales, chords, and progressions, fit together to create something great. Guitar theory is a topic best suited for players at the intermediate level and above who already know the basics of playing chords and who want to take their knowledge to the next level and learn to navigate the fretboard like the pros.

You can study music from many different angles. For instance, you can study notation, technique, rhythms, scales, chord construction . . . the list goes on and on. While all musical topics have their benefits, scales, chords, and progressions top the list of must-knows for guitarists. After all, every guitarist, beginner to advanced, strums chords, follows progressions, and plays melodies, riffs, solos, and bass lines with scales.

But what's the point of learning all this theory stuff? Can't you just randomly plunk away on your guitar and progress to guitar-hero status with enough practice? Well, I suppose that if you're blessed with enough raw talent, you can probably go pretty far without learning much about music. As for the rest of us, though, we need to put some thought and effort into learning about guitar theory to get what we want out of playing.

If you've ever heard a player who seems to know what's coming next the first time through a song, you've seen what understanding a little theory can do. Knowing how music is composed before you start learning a new song can help you pick up on that song a whole lot quicker. And if you want to improvise, compose, or just understand the music you play better, you need to know the theory behind it. Plus, learning about music can be as enjoyable as playing it.

Navigating the Fretboard

Guitar players navigate the fretboard in a few ways. First, they know the location of some key notes. For example, they often know the notes along the 6th and 5th strings well and use them to track chord shapes and scale patterns. Second, they identify notes on other strings by tracing them to the 6th and 5th strings with simple octave shapes. I cover these notes and octave shapes in detail in Chapter 2; here, I introduce you to the fretboard with neck diagrams and guitar tabs.

Seeing the fretboard as a grid

Remember when you had to match shapes in kindergarten? Now you can put that skill to good use. With the way that guitar strings and frets run perpendicular to each other and the way that they're all numbered, the fretboard is like a grid. Instead of concentrating on the pitches and note names of the scales and chords you play, focus on how they fit into the grid.

Everything you play on your guitar makes a shape or pattern. You get to know important relationships in music by arranging and connecting these shapes and patterns. This grid-like arrangement is what separates the guitar from other instruments such as the piano and is why you don't need to know how to read standard musical notation to develop a good working knowledge of guitar theory. Instead, you focus on the fretboard by using guitar tablature and neck diagrams.

Viewing neck diagrams

Neck diagrams are a great way to map out chord shapes and scale patterns. They allow you to see a bird's-eye view of the guitar neck. Figure 1-1 shows three vertical neck diagram examples. For each diagram, you're looking at the face of the fretboard straight up and down. Here's what you see in each diagram:

- The first diagram shows a sample G major scale pattern with the letters representing the notes.
- The second diagram shows a G major barre chord shape with the numbers representing fingerings.
- The third diagram shows a combination of both, with all the circles representing the scale pattern and the black dots specifically outlining the barre chord. Also, in this example the numbers represent neither notes nor fingerings but rather intervals (which you get to know in Chapter 2).

The numbers to the left of each diagram indicate fret numbers: 3fr. is short for 3rd fret, 5fr. is short for 5th fret, and 7fr. is short for 7th fret.

Figure 1-2 shows the same examples as Figure 1-1 but this time in a horizontal neck diagram format. Here, you're looking at the face of the fretboard longways and upside down. The top line represents the 1st string, and the bottom line represents the 6th string. This is how you see the guitar neck when you hold a guitar to play it and lean over to view the fretboard in your hands. Notice that the fret numbers appear below the horizontal diagrams.

As you see, a lot of information can be displayed in fretboard diagrams from scales to chords, notes to intervals, fingerings to shapes. Diagrams can be displayed vertically or horizontally. You see diagrams used in all these ways throughout the book.

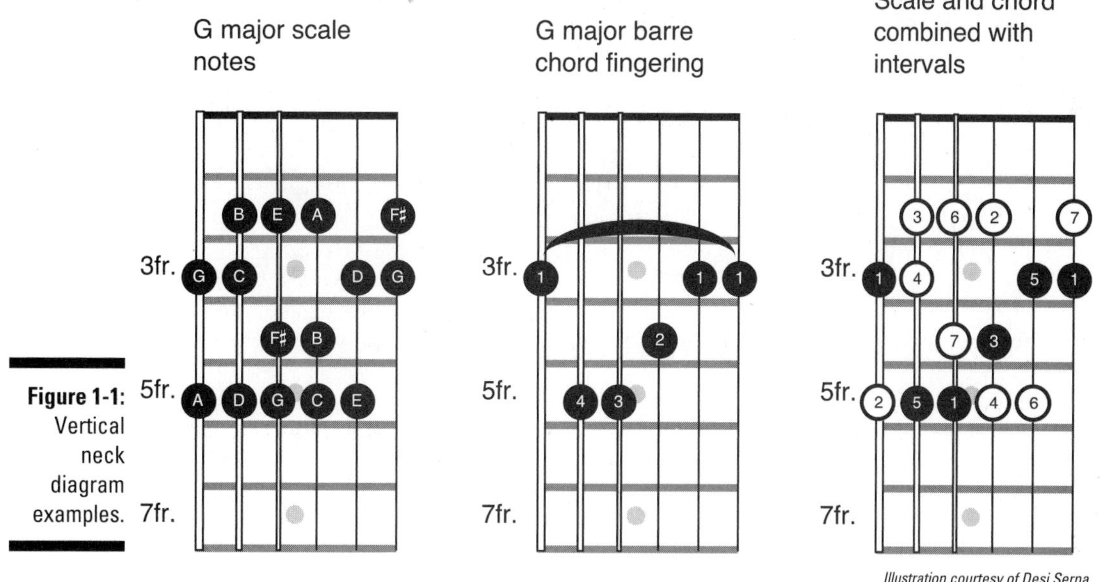

Figure 1-1: Vertical neck diagram examples.

Illustration courtesy of Desi Serna

G major scale notes

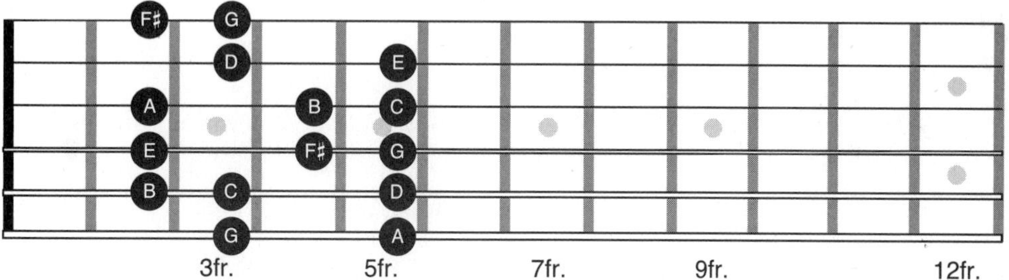

G major barre chord fingering

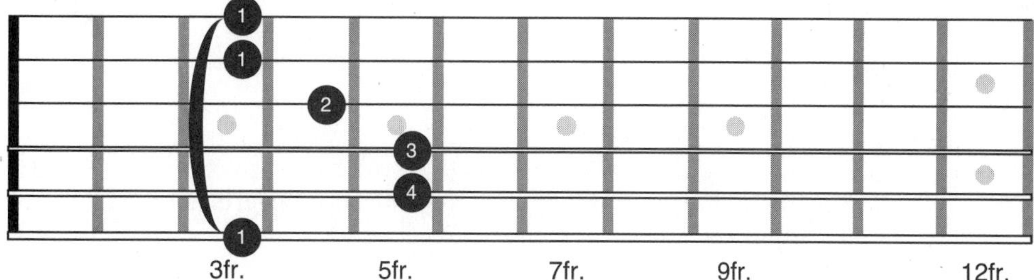

Scale and chord combined with intervals

3fr. 5fr. 7fr. 9fr. 12fr.

Figure 1-2: Horizontal neck diagram examples.

Illustration courtesy of Desi Serna

Reading guitar tablature

Reading music is a skill that requires a lot of study and practice; not to mention, standard music notation only indicates pitches. Because you can play most pitches in several different positions on the neck, and because many of the presentations in this book focus on specific positions, shapes, and patterns, you want to know exactly where to place your fingers for certain pitches. That's where guitar tabs come in handy. Guitar *tablature,* or *tab* for short, is a number system that indicates exactly where to place your fingers on the fretboard. If you can count the strings and frets on your guitar, then you can instantly read tab. Tab is especially handy for writing out examples that you want to play in series, like a scale pattern or a set of chord changes. I use a neck diagram to illustrate what a scale looks like as a pattern and tab to show you how to ascend and descend through the notes of the scale in the proper order.

In Figure 1-3, you see three chords written in standard musical notation. If you know how to read music, then you can easily find these pitches in the first position on the guitar.

Figure 1-3: Three notes in standard musical notation.

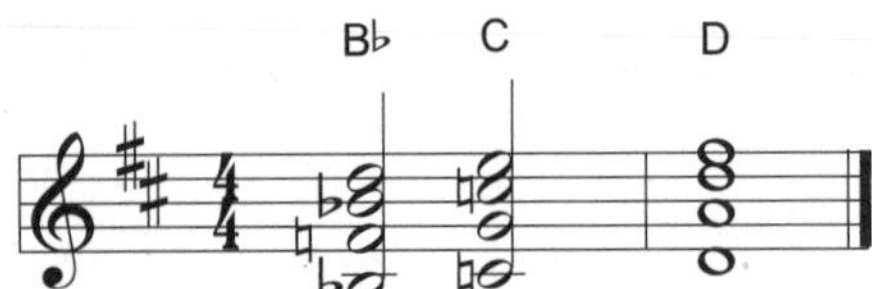

Illustration courtesy of Desi Serna

In Figure 1-4, you see the same three chords in tab. Notice that you can now see two important things that you couldn't see in standard notation:

- These chords aren't all played in the 1st position.
- These chords are all based on the very same shape moved up two frets at a time.

Figure 1-4: Three notes in guitar tab.

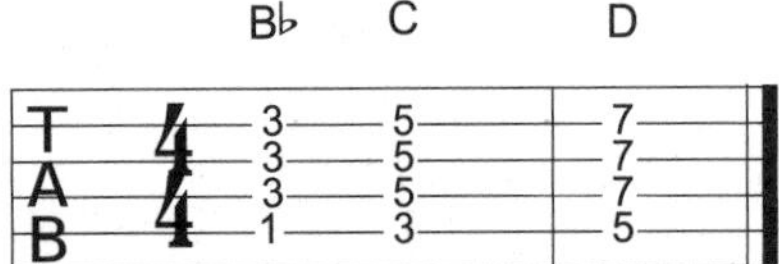

Illustration courtesy of Desi Serna

In Figure 1-5, you see the same chords again but this time with a more complex rhythm. In this case, it's useful to have both forms of notation. Most guitar players look at the tab to finger and fret the notes and look at the music to count the rhythms.

Reading notation and counting rhythms are beyond the scope of this book. But in case you already know how to read music a bit, throughout the book, I occasionally combine the two when I think doing so is helpful. If I don't include music and rhythms, though, it means that they're unimportant and you should just focus on the tab.

Figure 1-6, shows an example of *slash notation,* which I use when you need to play chord changes in time but not in any specific position or voicing. Usually slash notation includes only very basic rhythm marks, allowing you to fill the bar any way you see fit (called *comping*). With this type of notation, chord symbols appear above the staff. Some forms of slash notation don't include note stems like you see in my example, only slashes, hence the name.

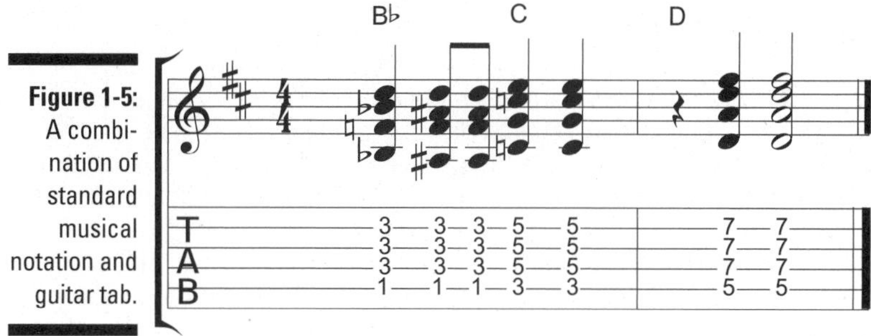

Figure 1-5: A combination of standard musical notation and guitar tab.

Illustration courtesy of Desi Serna

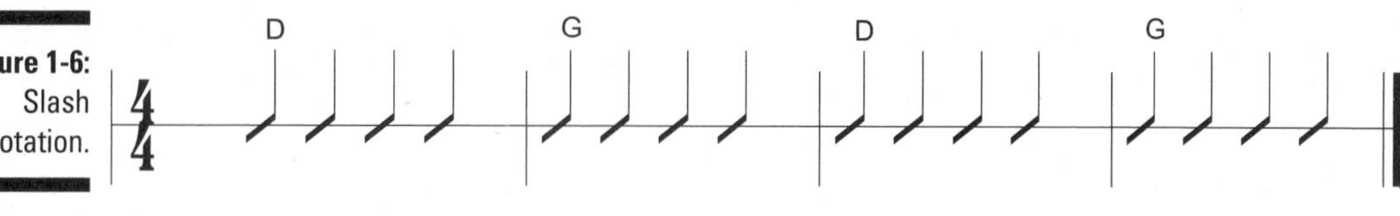

Figure 1-6: Slash notation.

Illustration courtesy of Desi Serna

In Figure 1-7, you see an example of *rhythmic notation,* a method that specifies an exact rhythm in which to play or comp the indicated chords. You don't need to be able to read standard musical notation or rhythmic notations in this book, but I occasionally include them anyway in case you find them helpful.

Figure 1-7: Rhythmic notation.

Illustration courtesy of Desi Serna

Playing Scales

A *scale* is a series of notes played one at a time in an ascending or descending fashion. Guitarists use scales to play melodies, riffs, lead guitar solos, and bass lines. Different types of scales make different patterns on the fretboard that you have to learn and practice. In popular music, the two most commonly used types of scales are the pentatonic scale and the major scale. From the major scale come modes. The harmonic minor is one more type of scale that's useful for guitar players to know.

Pentatonic scale

Pentatonic scales are derived from major scales. As the name implies, the *pentatonic* is a five-tone scale. Because the pentatonic has fewer tones than do major scales (which have seven), its patterns are easier to finger and play on the fretboard. The simple box-shape patterns that the pentatonic scale makes on the fretboard are ideal for getting started with riffing and jamming. Plus, many of the most recognizable guitar riffs of all time are based in pentatonic patterns. Popular pentatonic songs include "My Girl" by The Temptations and "Purple Haze" by Jimi Hendrix. For these reasons, guitar players often learn pentatonic scale patterns first. You get started with this scale in Chapter 11.

Major scale

Guitarists use major scales to riff and jam, too. The more melodic a line is, the more likely it is to use a seven-tone *major scale.* Think "Joy to the World," which is simply a descending major scale. You hear something similar in the opening to "Friend of the Devil" by Grateful Dead and the chorus to "Wild World" by Cat Stevens.

In addition to using the major scale to play melody, guitarists use it to measure intervals, build triads and chords, add chord tones and extensions, chart chord progressions, and determine keys. You could say that everything is drawn from the major scale or relates to it in some way. For this reason, I introduce basic major scale patterns as early as Chapter 2 and use them to help explain fretboard navigation, chords, progressions, and keys throughout Parts I, II and III. You work on covering the whole fretboard with major scales for playing riffs and solos in Chapter 12. Major scale patterns also make minor scales and all the modes.

Modes

Perhaps no other musical topic generates more intrigue and confusion than modes. But the concept is so simple that most musicians miss it. Modes are all the different types of scales that the major scale makes when you change the starting point and pitch center in the scale. This includes the minor scale and also all the modal scales that have Greek names such as Dorian, Phrygian, Lydian, and so on. Far from being an advanced or exotic concept, most music is in some type of mode, and properly identifying a song's mode is critical to understanding its composition and construction. You don't learn new scale patterns to play modes. The modal concept is all based on key centers and how major scale patterns are applied. You get to know both aspects of modes in Chapters 7 and 13.

Harmonic minor scale

The *harmonic minor scale* is an altered minor scale that plays a very important role in music. Its primary purpose is to create a dominant 7th chord that pulls to a minor tonic, a very strong harmonic resolution. If you're not sure what I'm talking about, don't worry! I tell you all about dominant function in Chapter 9 and the harmonic minor scale in Chapter 14. In the meantime, listen to "Smooth" by Santana to get in on the action.

Working with Chords

Chords are built from groups of three notes called *triads*. Understanding how to use the major scale to build triads and recognizing the resultant sequence of major and minor chords are two extremely important aspects to music. You work with triads by stacking the major scale in 3rds in Chapter 3. The information in Chapter 3 then becomes the basis for the remaining chapters on chords and progressions.

CAGED chord system

You can play literally thousands of different chord shapes on the fretboard, but most of them can be traced back to just five common open forms. These forms are C, A, G, E, and D. Together they make up what's called the guitar *CAGED chord system,* which includes arpeggio patterns, chord inversions, and various chord voicings. In Chapter 4, you move up basic open position chords and convert them into barre chord shapes. You then break these barre chords into a variety of other forms that are common in popular music.

Adding chord tones and extensions

In addition to using plain major and minor chords, guitarists add other scale tones to triads to create chords like Cmaj7, Dm7, Gsus4, and Fadd9. See Chapter 5 for more details.

Passing chords

Other types of chords, called *passing chords,* don't stem from the major scale at all. They sound very unusual on their own but create nice voice leading when placed in between the right chord changes. You get to know these types of chords in Chapter 10.

Charting chord progressions

You've probably heard musicians calling out numbers on the bandstand, right? "One . . . four . . . five . . . " — well, get ready to find out what those numbers mean. The numbers refer to the scale degrees and chords that the music cycles through. Recognizing chord movement and playing by numbers can help you chart and remember songs better, which, in turn, enables you to apply scales properly, play by ear, and compose your own music.

Musicians often refer to a chord progression by the way it moves numerically through a scale or pattern rather than by its actual pitches. Fortunately, playing chord progressions and playing by numbers go hand in hand, and the whole concept is easier on the guitar than most other instruments. In Chapters 3 and 6, you use major scales to build chords and map out numbered patterns on the neck. These chord patterns are the basis for most chord progressions used in popular music.

Testing Your Guitar Theory Knowledge

Are you ready to get started? Here's a short quiz to help put your musical gears into motion. If you don't know the answers now, don't worry; you will after you work through this book.

1. What's the difference between a major 3rd and a minor 3rd?
2. What do a root, a 3rd, and a 5th make?
3. Which two chord shapes does Rolling Stones guitarist Keith Richards favor?
4. In chords like Gmaj7, Asus4, and Dadd9, what do the numbers mean?
5. If you had to play chords I, IV, and V in the key of G, what chords would you play?
6. In which mode is "Oye Como Va" by Santana?
7. What does it mean to "borrow" a chord?
8. Fill in the blank: V7 leads to _____.
9. I'm thinking of a type of chord that sounds unusable on its own but perfect in between the right chord changes. What is it?
10. What are the two primary types of scale patterns used in popular music?
11. True or False: Modes are scales with their own unique patterns.
12. What do you call a natural minor scale with a raised 7th?
13. In what way do blues players break the rules of traditional harmony?
14. How do you play licks and phrases and develop your own style?

Answers:

1. One fret (Chapter 2) 2. Major triad/chord (Chapter 3) 3. A form and C form (Chapter 4) 4. They're added scale degrees/intervals. (Chapter 5) 5. G, C, and D (Chapter 6) 6. Dorian mode (Chapter 7) 7. To combine chords from two different scales that both center on the same tonic pitch (Chapter 8) 8. I (Chapter 9) 9. Passing, diminished, or augmented chord (Chapter 10) 10. Pentatonic and major (Chapters 11 and 12) 11. False: Modes are based on major scale patterns. (Chapter 13) 12. Harmonic minor scale (Chapter 14) 13. They use minor pentatonic scales over major chords. (Chapter 15) 14. Learn songs! (Chapters 16 and 17)

Chapter 2

Navigating the Fretboard Like a Pro

In This Chapter

- Memorizing notes along strings 6 and 5
- Getting familiar with whole steps, half steps, sharps, and flats
- Using octave shapes and playing intervals

Believe it or not, mastering the guitar fretboard doesn't require you to memorize every single note on it. Guitar players may play notes all over the neck, but they usually navigate by using shapes and patterns and mainly the notes on strings 6 and 5.

In this chapter, you get to know the natural notes along strings 6 and 5 and then use them to track everything else you play on the fretboard with octaves. You see the difference between a half step and a whole step and find out how to fill in the gaps between natural notes with flats and sharps. Finally, you explore intervals and octaves and discover which songs can help you use them.

Armed with this information, you can begin to make your way around the guitar neck like a pro and set yourself up for mastering the chord shapes and scale patterns I cover in the rest of this book.

Listen to Audio Track 2 to hear notes, steps, octaves, and intervals — the subject of this chapter.

Tracing Everything Back to Strings 6 and 5

Guitar players use the notes along strings 6 and 5 to track other notes on other strings, so the first thing to do is memorize the natural notes on strings 6 and 5. The *natural notes* are the letters A through G without any flat or sharp signs next to them. Figure 2-1 displays all the natural notes on the 6th string between the open position and the 12th fret.

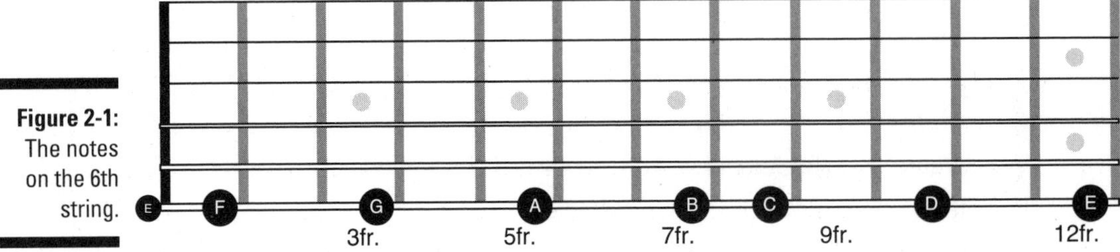

Figure 2-1: The notes on the 6th string.

Illustration courtesy of Desi Serna

You may already be familiar with some of these notes because they're used so frequently, especially as *roots* (the primary pitch from which a chord gets its letter name) to common chords. For example, the open 6th string is E, and it serves as the root of all open E chords, including E and E minor. To help you keep track of these natural notes, consider the following five key points as you look at the group of fretboard diagrams in Figure 2-2:

- The open 6th string is E and the root of an E chord.
- The 1st fret is F and the root of an F chord.
- The 3rd fret is G and the root of a G chord.
- The 5th fret is A; it matches the 5th string open and is used for relative tuning.
- The 12th fret is E, an octave higher than the same string open. (It's specially marked by two inlays on most guitars.)

Instead of looking at the fretboard empty and trying to remember its notes, connect the notes to something familiar, like common chord shapes and other strings. Try playing through the five notes in the preceding list forward and backward, reviewing the associations I lay out for you. Call out the notes as you play them to further cement them into your memory.

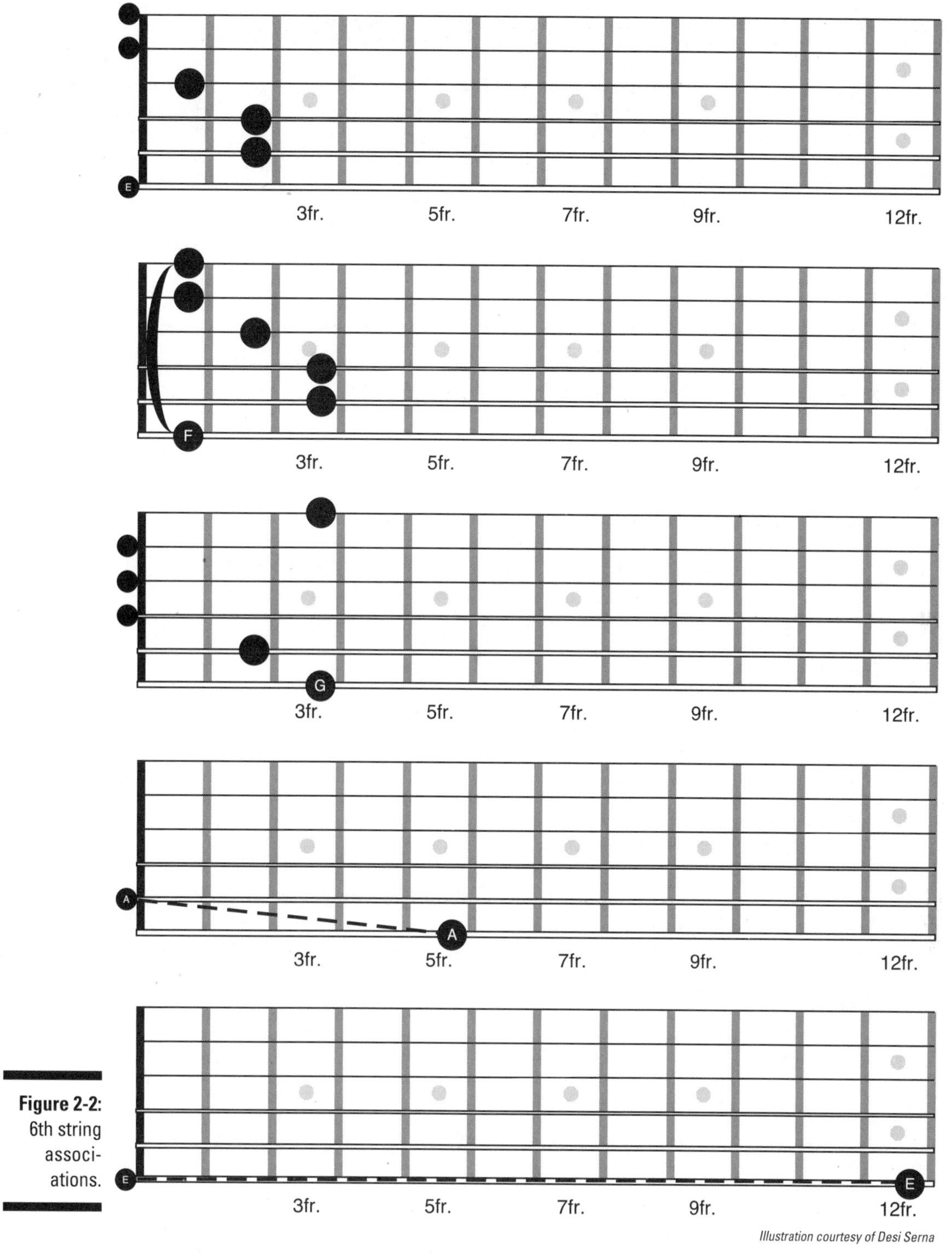

Figure 2-2: 6th string associations.

Illustration courtesy of Desi Serna

Figure 2-3 shows the natural notes on the 5th string.

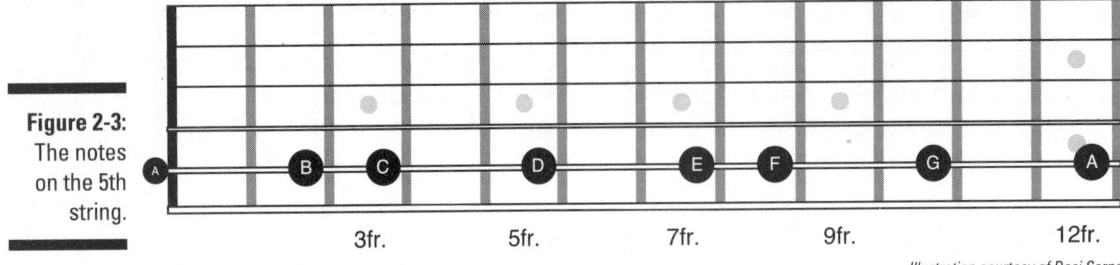

Figure 2-3: The notes on the 5th string.

Illustration courtesy of Desi Serna

Just as you do for the 6th string notes, you can associate the notes along the 5th string with common chords and another string, as I explain in the following list and Figure 2-4:

- The open 5th string is A and the root of an A chord.
- The 2nd fret is B and the root of a B7 chord.
- The 3rd fret is C and the root of a C chord.
- The 5th fret is D; it matches the 4th string open and is used for relative tuning.
- The 7th fret is E, an octave higher than the 6th string open.
- The 12th fret is A, an octave higher than the same string open. (It's specially marked by two inlays on most guitars.)

Moving between pitches with whole steps and half steps

Musicians measure the distance between *pitches* (sound frequencies or notes) with intervals called whole and half steps. (See the later section "Measuring the Space between Pitches with Intervals" for more on intervals.) The distance between one pitch and the next is called a *half step* or *semitone*. On a guitar, a half step is one fret. Two half steps make up a *whole step* or *whole tone,* which is two frets. For example, E-F and B-C are half steps, while F-G-A-B and D-C-E are whole steps. These pitches are always separated by these distances, regardless of where you play them on the fretboard.

E-F and B-C are always a half step apart. All the other notes are separated by a whole step.

Naming the pitches between natural notes: Sharps and flats

The pitches between the natural notes are called flats and sharps. A *flat* is one half step lower than its corresponding natural note and is marked with a musical symbol that looks like a lowercase *b* (♭). A *sharp* is a half step higher and is marked with a symbol that looks like a number or pound sign (♯). (***Tip:*** To help you keep these two terms straight, think of the *lower*case *b* as representing a *lower* pitched note or a *flat* being lower like a *flat* tire.)

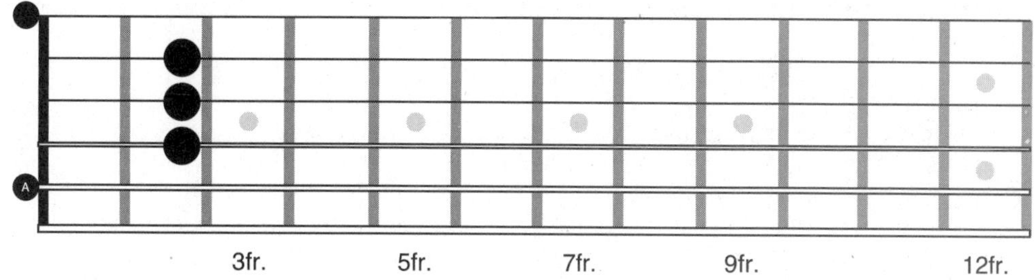

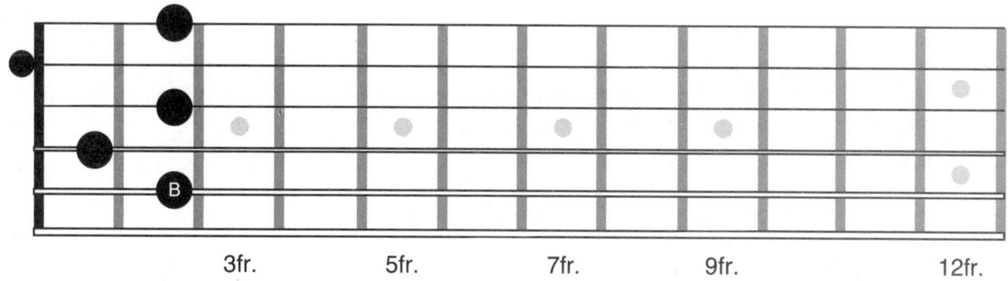

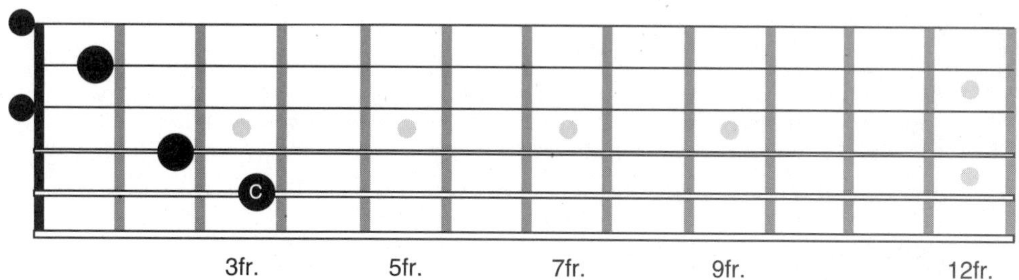

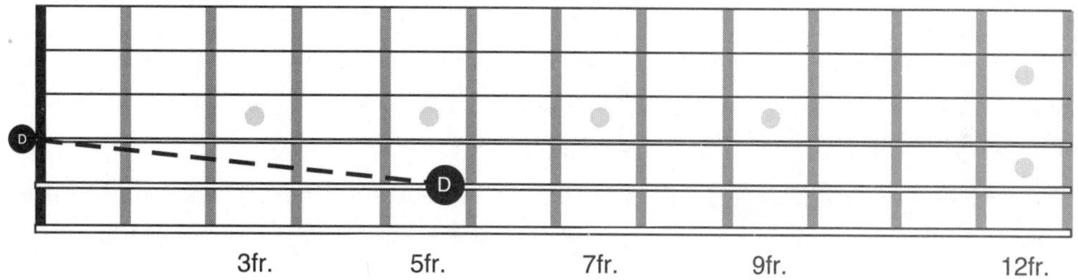

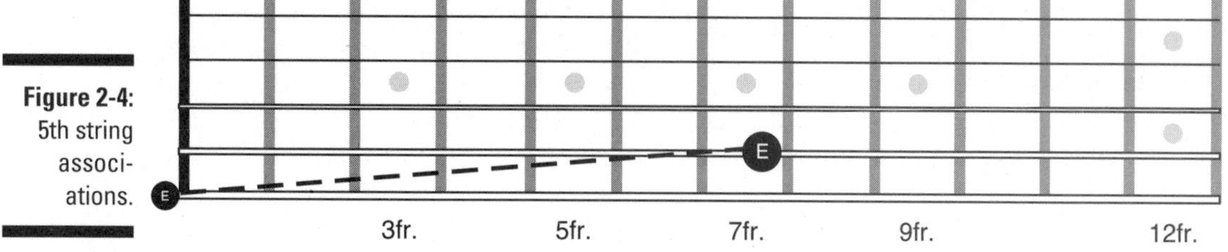

Figure 2-4: 5th string associations.

Illustration courtesy of Desi Serna

How to name a flat or sharp pitch

When naming the pitches between the natural notes, look at the key signature to determine whether a note should be called flat or sharp. For example, in the key of E, you call the pitch at the 2nd fret F♯. The notes of E major are E-F♯-G♯-A-B-C♯-D♯. You don't want to call the second note of the E major scale G♭ because if you did, you'd end up with two Gs in a row and no F (E-G♭-G♯, and so on). Because the first note is E, the second note must be some form of F — hence the name F♯ rather than G♭. In the D♭ major scale (D♭-E♭-F-G♭-A♭-B♭-C), you have to call the same pitch G♭; otherwise, you end up with two Fs in a row and no G (D♭-E♭-F-F♯, and so on).

For example, the pitch in between F and G on the 6th string is either F♯, meaning one half step higher than F, or G♭, meaning one half step lower than G. F♯ and G♭ are *enharmonic,* meaning they're two different note names with the same pitch. Similarly, the pitch in between G and A is either G♯ or A♭.

Grouping notes

To memorize the remaining notes on both strings, think of the notes in groups, as I explain in the following sections. Grouping notes together helps you remember string areas that don't connect easily to a common open chord or open string.

As you review the note groups I cover here, take a few moments to rehearse all the notes in each group, playing through them forward and backward and calling them out as you go. After you have all these natural notes memorized, you can easily fill in the gaps with flats and sharps.

A-B-C

To start, take the first three notes on the 5th string: A-B-C. You can play this same group of notes with the same spacing beginning at the 5th fret of the 6th string, as shown in Figure 2-5.

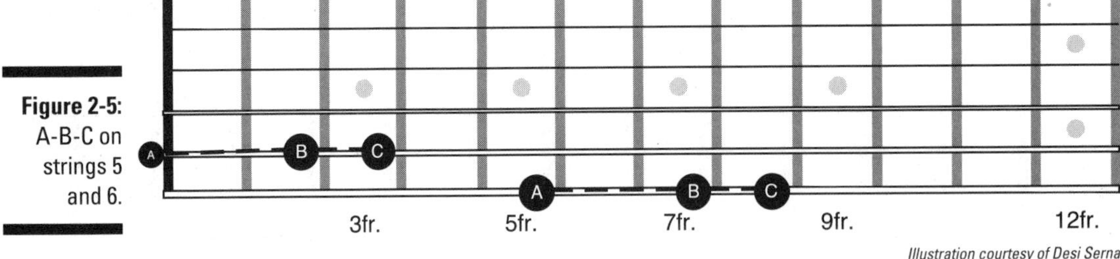

Figure 2-5: A-B-C on strings 5 and 6.

Illustration courtesy of Desi Serna

Wherever you find an A, B is always a whole step higher, and B and C are always a half step apart. If you memorize these notes on the 5th string between the open position and the 3rd fret, then you also know the notes on the 6th string between the 5th and 8th frets — they're the same!

C-D-E

Similarly, you can group the notes C-D-E. These notes are always separated by whole steps. On the 5th string, they're at frets 3, 5, and 7, and on the 6th string, they're at frets 8, 10, and 12 (see Figure 2-6).

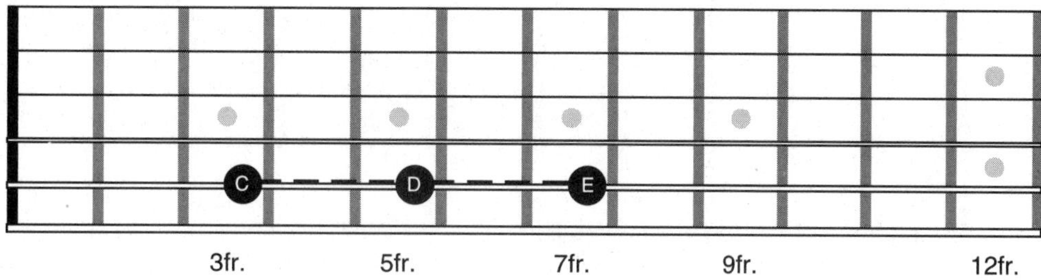

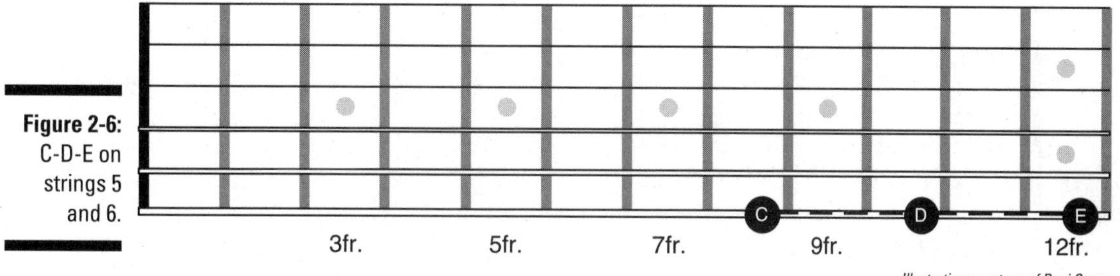

Figure 2-6: C-D-E on strings 5 and 6.

Illustration courtesy of Desi Serna

Whenever you're on a C, you can reach up a whole step to D and another whole step to E. Likewise, whenever you're on an E, you can reach *down* a whole step to D and another whole step to C.

E-F-G

You can also group the notes E-F-G on the 6th and 5th strings, as shown in Figure 2-7. On the 6th string, these notes are between the open position and the 3rd fret; on the 5th string, they're between the 7th and 10th frets.

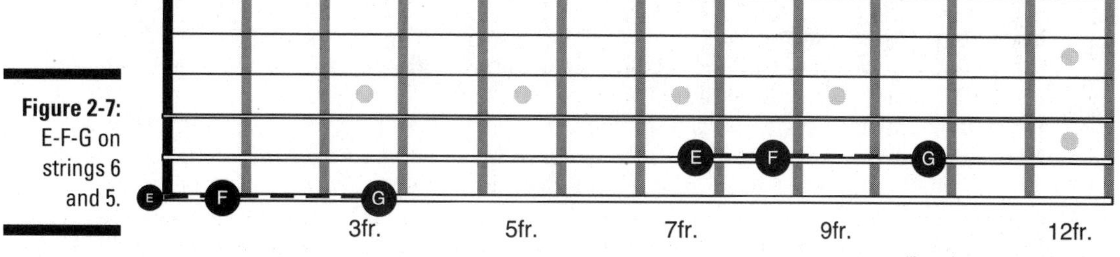

Figure 2-7: E-F-G on strings 6 and 5.

Illustration courtesy of Desi Serna

Wherever you find an E, F is always a half step higher, and F and G are always a whole step apart.

F-G-A

Finally, you can group the notes F-G-A, which are always separated by whole steps. On the 6th string, they're at frets 1, 3, and 5; on the 5th string, they're at frets 8, 10, and 12 (see Figure 2-8).

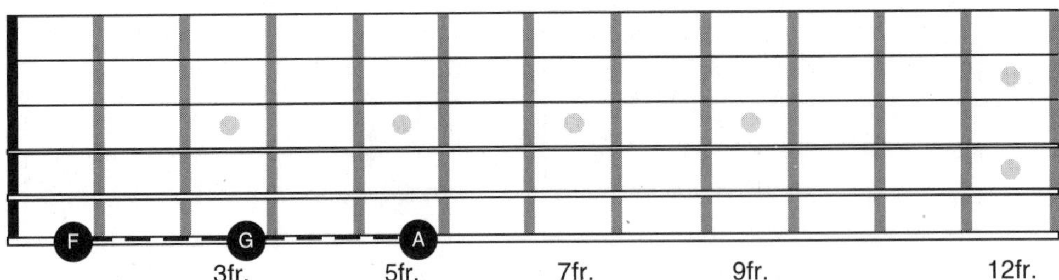

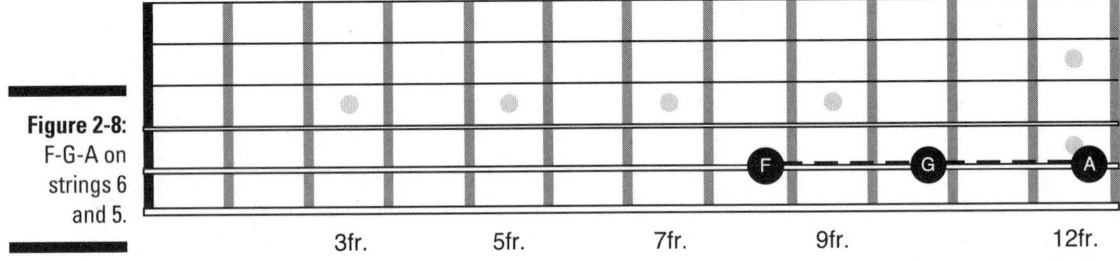

Figure 2-8: F-G-A on strings 6 and 5.

Illustration courtesy of Desi Serna

Whenever your 1st finger is on F, you can reach up a whole step to G and another whole step to A. Similarly, whenever your 4th finger is on A, you can reach *down* a whole step to G and another whole step to F.

Tracking Notes and Playing Songs with Octaves

You can use the notes along strings 6 and 5, which I cover in the preceding section, to track any note anywhere on the fretboard. You do so with the help of octave shapes. An *octave* is the distance between one pitch and another with half or double its frequency. In other words, it's a higher or lower version of the same pitch. You can also think of an octave as the same pitch in a different *register*. Octave pitches are also called *unison pitches.* On the guitar fretboard, octaves follow certain spacings or shapes that you finger in different ways; I explain how to finger these shapes in the following sections.

In music, the word *unison* can mean a couple of things. Firstly, it refers to two identical pitches being sounded by separate or different instruments, including voices. For example, two guitar players both playing their 6th strings open produce unison pitches. Secondly, it can refer to pitches that are the same but separated by an octave or more. For example, one guitarist playing the 6th string open and another playing the 1st string open, both E, produce unison pitches.

Shaping octaves with your 1st finger on strings 6 and 5

The first octave shape you need to know stems off of strings 6 and 5. Place your 1st finger somewhere on the 6th or 5th string and use another finger to reach over two strings and up two frets: You now have the same note an octave higher. Figure 2-9 shows what this octave shape looks like. Notice that you can also play octaves of the open strings.

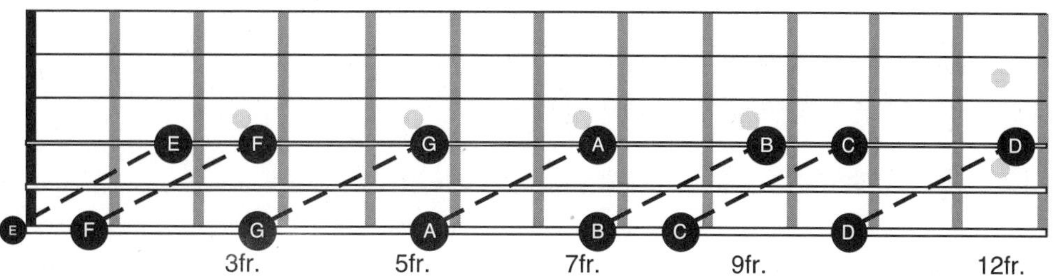

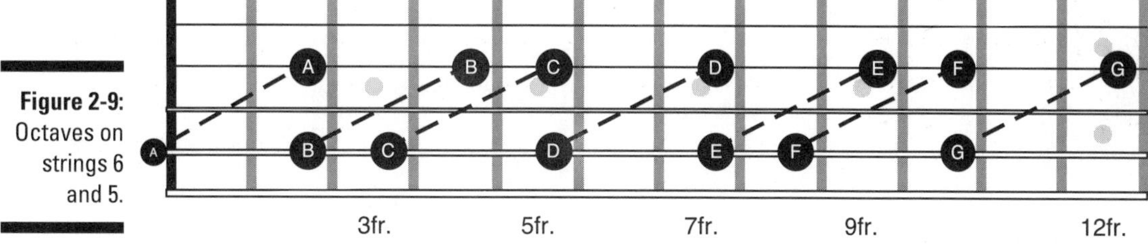

Figure 2-9: Octaves on strings 6 and 5.

Illustration courtesy of Desi Serna

You can finger these octave shapes with either your 1st and 3rd fingers or your 1st and 4th fingers — whichever is more comfortable. You also have the option of picking the strings separately, fingerpicking them together, or muting the unwanted strings as you strum.

Guitar players usually opt to strum octave shapes on strings 6 and 5 by using a pick and leaning their fretting fingers back to touch (but not fret) other strings to prevent them from ringing. This technique creates a raking sound from the muted strings. In fact, jazz guitar legend Wes Montgomery was famous for playing melodies and solos by using octave shapes in this fashion, opting to strum across the strings with the pad of his right thumb for a soft, mellow sound. You hear this technique in his song "Bumpin' on Sunset." Jimi Hendrix strummed the same kind of octave shapes with a pick, using distortion, for his songs "Fire" and "Third Stone from the Sun."

For a demonstration on how to finger and play octave shapes, watch Video Clip 1.

If you need to identify a note on string 4 or 3, use octave shapes to trace it back to the notes you have memorized on strings 6 and 5.

Shaping octaves with your 1st finger on strings 4 and 3

You can play octave shapes with your 1st finger on string 4 or 3 and the octaves on string 2 or 1, although the shapes are slightly different than they are on strings 6 and 5. With the way the 2nd string is tuned (one half step lower), you need to move over two strings and up *three* frets to reach the octave (see Figure 2-10). Remember that you can also play octaves of the open strings.

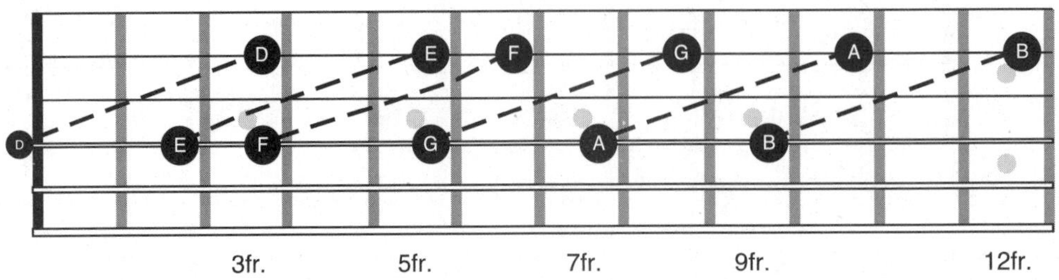

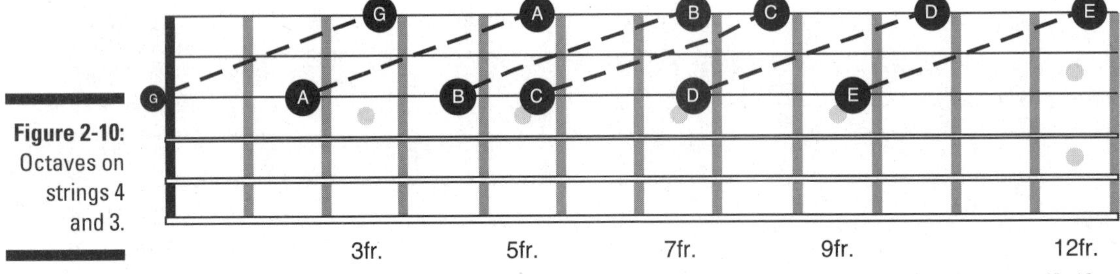

Figure 2-10: Octaves on strings 4 and 3.

Illustration courtesy of Desi Serna

If you have to identify a note on string 2 or 1, use octave shapes to trace it back to strings 4 and 3 and then again to strings 6 and 5. However, keep in mind that the 1st string is E just as the 6th string is E, and the positions of all the notes on both strings are the same.

Shaping octaves that are three strings apart

Another octave shape that's less common but still good to know reaches over three strings and in the direction opposite the previous shapes direction. You can play these octaves by placing your 1st finger on either string 1 or 2 and then reaching over to either string 4 or 5 with either your 3rd or 4th finger, as shown in Figure 2-11. Notice that you can also use the open strings.

Repeating octaves beyond the 12th fret

The preceding sections cover notes between the open strings and the 12th fret, but what about the fretboard area beyond that? Fortunately for your memory, everything — including notes and spacing — repeats at the 12th fret. Hence, all the inlay markers beyond the 12th fret correspond to the inlays before the 12th fret, which is why most guitars specially mark the 12th fret with two inlays. Just as strings 6 and 5 open are E and A, the same strings are E and A at the 12th fret. Just as the first inlay marker past the open 6th string is G, the first marker past the 12th fret is also G. On the 5th string, C is at the first markers in both positions. As you can see in Figure 2-12, the guitar neck between 0 and 12 is identical to the neck between 12 and 24, though your guitar may not have a full 24 frets. Notice the fret numbers indicated below the neck diagrams.

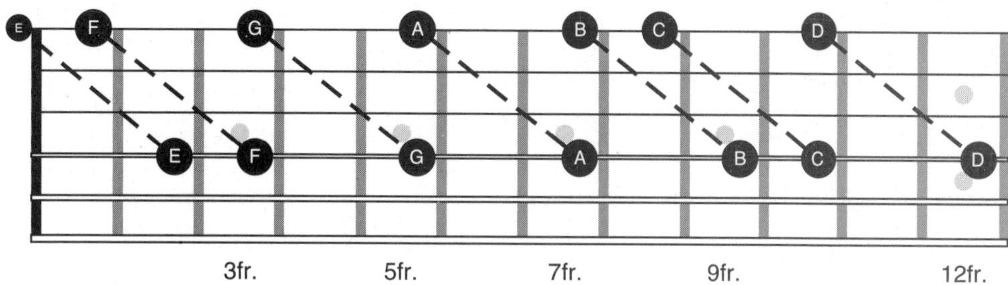

3fr. 5fr. 7fr. 9fr. 12fr.

Figure 2-11: Octaves that are three strings apart.

Illustration courtesy of Desi Serna

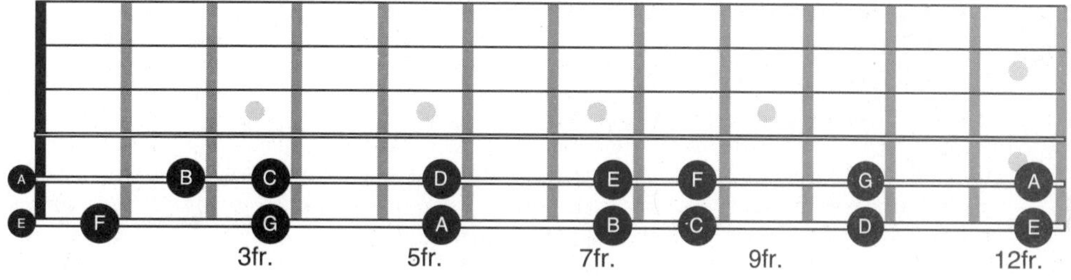

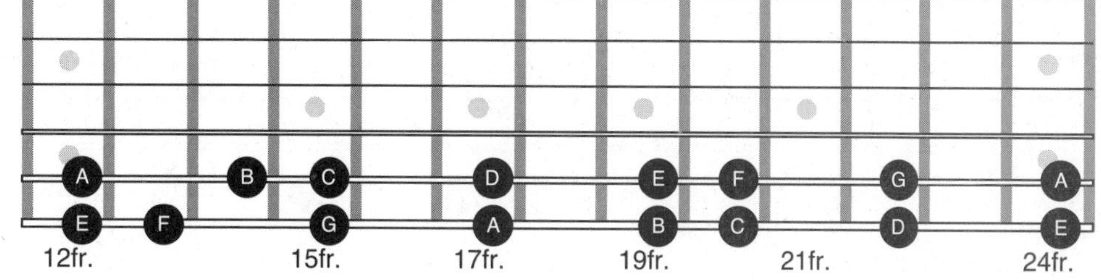

Figure 2-12: Notes open to 12 and from 12 to 24.

Illustration courtesy of Desi Serna

After you can identify any note on the fretboard by using various octave shapes to trace it back to a note you have memorized on string 6 or string 5, I recommend that you practice your skills. Pick a note and track it across the whole fretboard. For example, see how many E notes you can play.

In addition to using octave shapes to identify and track notes, you often hear them being used in music. Here are some popular songs that feature guitar octaves:

"All the Small Things" by Blink 182

"In and Out of Love" by Bon Jovi

"Kashmir" by Led Zeppelin

"Killing in the Name" by Rage Against the Machine

The following songs feature octaves on the bass, with some examples doubled with guitar:

"Higher Ground" by Red Hot Chili Peppers

"Immigrant Song" by Led Zeppelin

"Miss You" by The Rolling Stones

"My Sharona" by The Knack

Measuring the Space between Pitches with Intervals

Just as builders use measurements to identify distances between points, guitarists use *intervals* to identify distances between pitches. Intervals are important to understand because you use them to build scales and chords and to describe musical movement (which is what the rest of this book is all about).

The tape measure used in music is called the *major scale.* The major scale has seven pitches that are separated by a series of intervals known as *whole* and *half steps.* Here's what the major scale formula looks like:

W-W-H-W-W-W-H

The Ws represent whole steps, and the Hs represent half steps. Starting on any note, you can follow this basic step formula to produce the major scale. Figure 2-13 shows what the major scale looks like when you start on G.

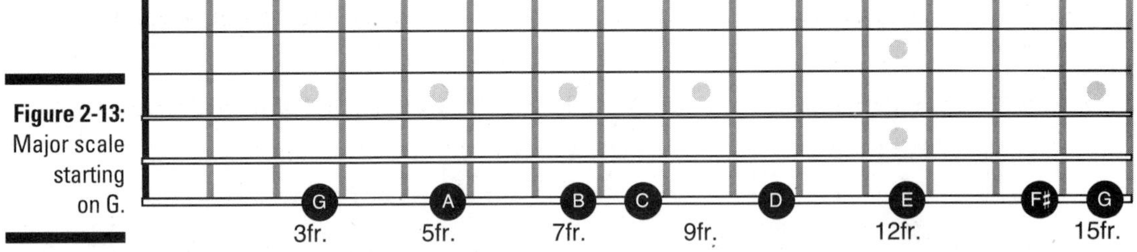

Figure 2-13: Major scale starting on G.

Illustration courtesy of Desi Serna

Note: Before you can look at each interval individually, analyze its steps, and explore how it looks on the fretboard, you need to see the major scale in a few different positions, which I illustrate for you in Figure 2-14. You don't have to memorize these scale patterns right now; they just provide a visual reference for the rest of this section. (Turn to Chapter 12 for details on playing and using major scale patterns.)

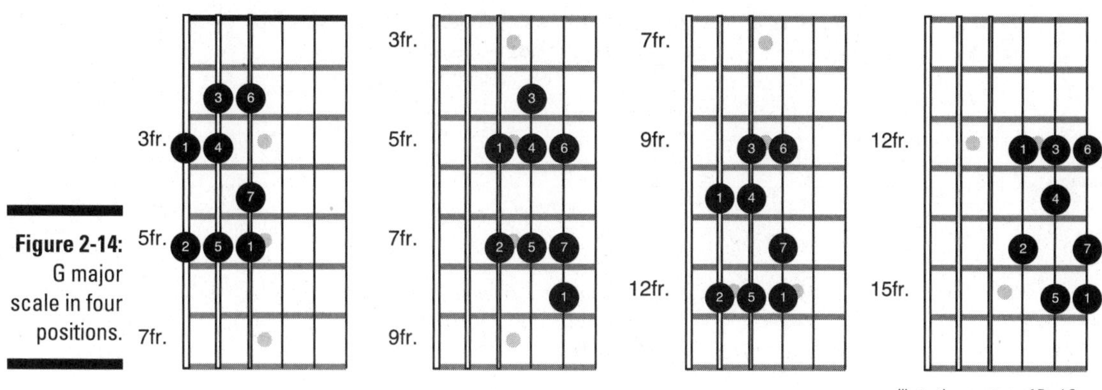

Figure 2-14: G major scale in four positions.

Illustration courtesy of Desi Serna

Playing intervals 1 through 7

The distance from the 1st to the 2nd scale degrees in the major scale is called a *second interval,* from the 1st to the 3rd is called a *third,* from the 1st to the 4th is called a *fourth,* and so on. Here's what makes up each interval:

- **2nd:** A whole step above the 1st scale degree.
- **3rd:** Two whole steps or over a string and back one fret.
- **4th:** Two and a half steps or over one string.
- **5th:** Three and a half steps or over a string and up two frets.
- **6th:** Four and a half steps or over two strings and back one fret. (The same note is also over one string and up two whole steps.)
- **7th:** Five and a half steps or over two strings and up one fret. (A 7th is one half step shy of an octave.)

Whenever you move from string 3 to 2 to play an interval, you need to move up an extra fret because the 2nd string is tuned a half step lower than the others. For example, a 3rd is normally over a string and back one fret, but when moving from string 3 to 2, a 3rd is over a string and in the very same fret. Normally a 4th is over one string, but it's up one fret from string 3 to 2. You see this earlier in the section on octaves where you have to reach up an extra fret between strings 4 and 2 and 3 and 1. Moving from the 6th string to the 1st, everything changes at the 2nd string, and an extra fret is needed. Because the 1st string is tuned to the 2nd string in the same manner that strings 6 to 3 are tuned, intervals between them are normal.

In the following sections you take a closer look at those intervals that typically occur in guitar parts.

3rds

Guitarists often play what are known as *harmonic intervals,* which are really just intervals you play together to create harmony. *Thirds* are a common type of harmonic interval.

To play thirds, play the 1st and 3rd scale degrees simultaneously and then ascend or descend the scale in groups of two with the notes always 3 scale degrees apart. You can do this in five different positions by following the tab in Figure 2-15. You can also hear and see this example in Video Clip 2.

```
T 4
A 4
B
e|-----------------|------------------|-------------------|------------------|-------------------|
B|-----------------|------------------|-------------------|------------------|-------------------|
G|-----------------|------------------|-------------------|------------------|--4--5--7--9------|
D|-----------------|------------------|---------0--2------|--4--5--7--9-----|--5--7--9--10-----|
A|--2--3--5--7-----|--9--10--12--14---|--2--3---2--3------|--5--7--9--10----|-------------------|
E|--3--5--7--8-----|--10--12--14--15--|--3--5-------------|------------------|-------------------|

e|---------------------|--------------|----------------|--7--8--10--12---|--14--15--17--19--||
B|---------------------|--0--1--3--5--|--7--8--10--12--|--8--10--12--13--|--15--17--19--20--||
G|--11--12--14--16-----|--0--2--4--5--|--7--9--11--12--|------------------|-------------------||
D|--12--14--16--17-----|--------------|----------------|------------------|-------------------||
A|---------------------|--------------|----------------|------------------|-------------------||
E|---------------------|--------------|----------------|------------------|-------------------||
```

Figure 2-15: Harmonic 3rds in G.

Illustration courtesy of Desi Serna

Figure 2-15 and the corresponding video clip show just five examples in the G major scale. You can play in 3rds in other keys by starting at a different fret and using the same interval shapes. For example, start on A at the 5th fret of the 6th string to play 3rds in the A major scale.

Many songs feature guitar parts played in 3rds. One of the best examples is the opening to "Brown Eyed Girl" by Van Morrison. The guitar plays the G major scale in 3rds over the G chord and the C major scale in 3rds over the C chord. Here are a few other songs that feature 3rds:

"Heaven" by Los Lonely Boys

"La Bamba" by Los Lobos

"My Best Friend's Girlfriend" by The Cars

"Proud Mary" by Creedence Clearwater Revival

"Rhiannon" by Fleetwood Mac

"To Be with You" by Mr. Big

"Twist and Shout" by The Beatles

"Walk on the Wild Side" by Lou Reed (bass)

"When the Sun Goes Down" by Kenny Chesney

6ths (or inverted 3rds)

Sometimes guitarists invert 3rds by moving the 1st degree up an octave. What was 1-3 becomes 3-1. The interval is inverted, get it? For example, G-B would become B-G. Figure 2-16 illustrates two examples of inverting the 3rd G-B.

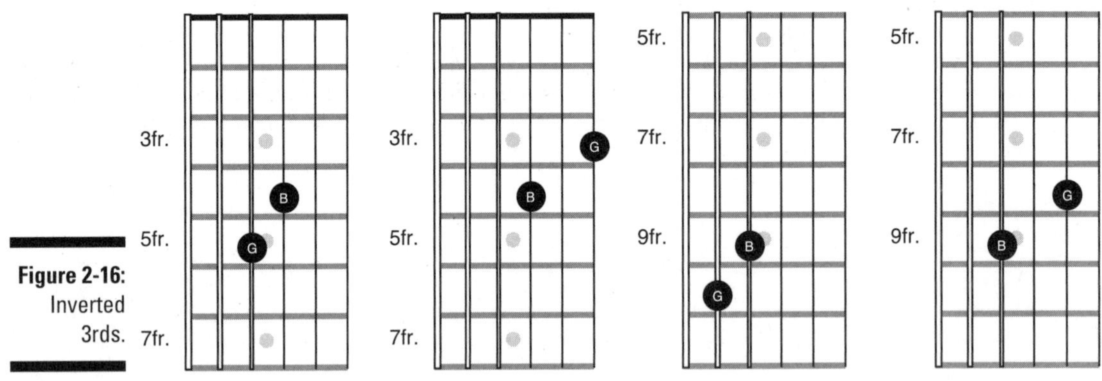

Figure 2-16: Inverted 3rds.

Illustration courtesy of Desi Serna

With intervals, you always count from the note in the lowest position to the note in the highest position. Thus, inverted 3rds are more commonly called *6ths.* G to B is 3 scale degrees (G-A-B, *one-two-three*), so the interval is called a 3rd. B to G, on the other hand, is 6 scale degrees (B-C-D-E-F♯-G, *one-two-three-four-five-six*), so it's called a 6th.

You can play through the whole scale in 6ths in two different positions by following the tab in Figure 2-17. Because you only want to sound the notes in the tab and not the other strings, and because these interval shapes are two strings apart, you need to either fingerpick or apply some left-hand muting technique (like you do with octave shapes).

```
T 4 -3--5--7--8--|-10--12--14--15-|----------------|----------------||
A 4 -------------|----------------|-8--10--12--13--|-15--17--19--20-||
B   -4--5--7--9--|-11--12--14--16-|----------------|----------------||
    -------------|----------------|-9--10--12--14--|-16--17--19--21-||
    -------------|----------------|----------------|----------------||
    -------------|----------------|----------------|----------------||
```

Figure 2-17: Playing in 6ths.

Illustration courtesy of Desi Serna

Harmony-wise, when you play in 6ths, you hear 3rds and roots, but technically, the distance between each pair of notes from low to high is identified as a 6th.

"Brown Eyed Girl" by Van Morrison features 6ths throughout the song, but many other songs, including the following, also use 6ths in various keys:

"The Ballad of John and Yoko" by The Beatles

"Finish What You Started" by Van Halen

"Have You Ever Really Loved a Woman?" by Bryan Adams

"Patience" by Guns and Roses

"Wanted Dead or Alive" by Bon Jovi

"Your Body Is a Wonderland" by John Mayer

"Your Smiling Face" by James Taylor

5ths

By far, the most popular type of harmonic interval among guitar players is the *5th.* After all, a root and a 5th make up the so-called *power chord* that appears in almost every distorted rock song ever recorded. Think about the opening to songs like "Rock You Like a Hurricane" by The Scorpions, "Hit Me with Your Best Shot" by Pat Benatar, and anything by Black Sabbath, Nirvana, Kiss, or the Ramones — just to name a few. (Technically, a power chord isn't a chord because chords have to include three or more notes; see Chapter 3 for more on chord construction.)

A 5th is written as G5, A5, and so on in a chord chart. Figure 2-18 shows the G scale in 5ths in two different positions. Notice that the 7th scale degree has a 5th that's different from all the rest. It naturally occurs one half step lower in the scale and is called a *flat 5th* (see the later section "Filling in the gaps with flats and sharps" for more details).

Figure 2-18: 5ths in G.

Illustration courtesy of Desi Serna

4ths (or inverted 5ths)

Sometimes guitarists invert 5ths by moving the lower note up an octave while keeping the upper note the same. For instance, G-D would become D-G. Figure 2-19 illustrates two examples for you.

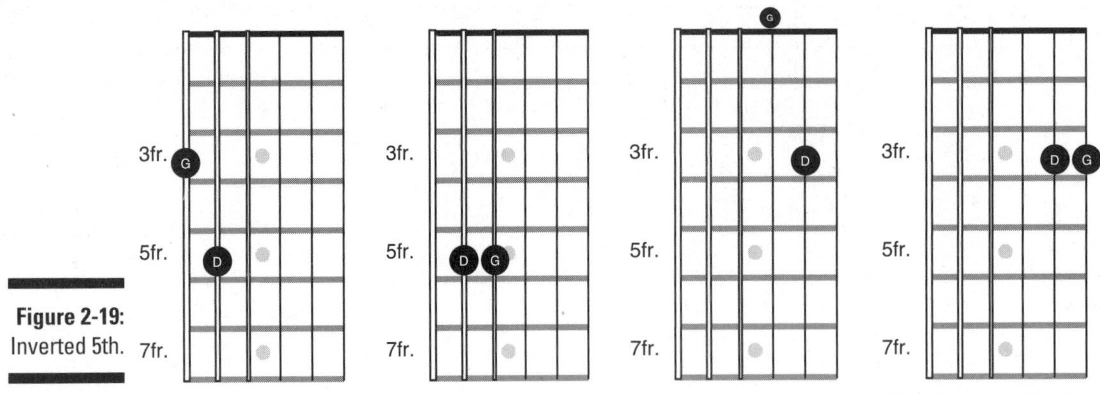

Figure 2-19: Inverted 5th.

Illustration courtesy of Desi Serna

Inverted 5ths are more commonly called *4ths* for the same reason that inverted 3rds are called 6ths. G to D is a 5th (G-A-B-C-D), while D to G is a 4th (D-E-F♯-G).

You can play the G major scale in 4ths by following the tab in Figure 2-20.

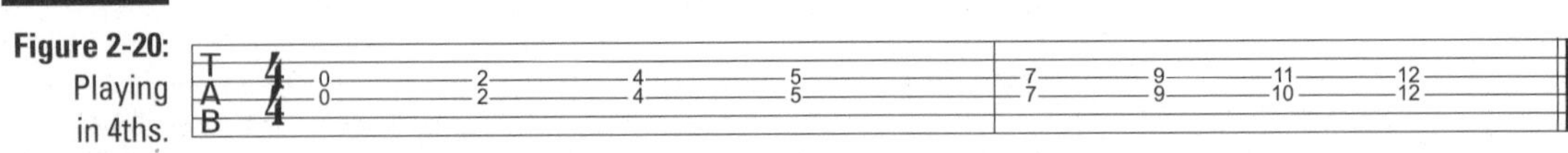

Figure 2-20: Playing in 4ths.

Illustration courtesy of Desi Serna

In harmony, when you play in 4ths you hear the upper note of the interval as the root and the lower one as the 5th, but technically, the distance between each pair of notes from low to high is a 4th.

By far the most famous example of using 4ths is in the song "Smoke on the Water" by Deep Purple. The opening guitar riff uses 4ths in G minor. Other songs include "Money For Nothing" by Dire Straits and "Wish You Were Here" by Pink Floyd.

Filling in the gaps with flats and sharps

Like the spaces between natural notes, the spaces between intervals are filled with flats and sharps. For example, the 1st and 2nd major scale degrees are a whole step apart, meaning they have a pitch in between them. This pitch is called a *flat 2nd* (♭2) because it's one half step lower than a 2nd interval. Here are the rest of the flats that appear between the major scale degrees:

- **Flat 3rd (♭3):** The pitch in between 2 and 3
- **Flat 5th (♭5):** The pitch in between 4 and 5
- **Flat 6th (♭6):** The pitch in between 5 and 6
- **Flat 7th (♭7):** The pitch in between 6 and 7

Figure 2-21 shows flat intervals on the fretboard marked in black.

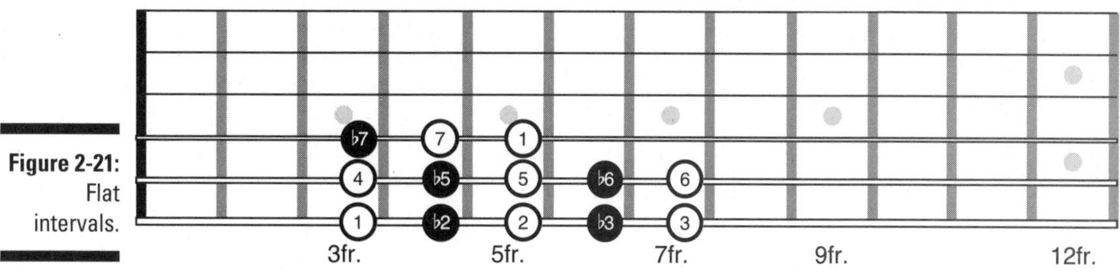

Figure 2-21: Flat intervals.

Illustration courtesy of Desi Serna

Some flats can also be considered sharps. For example, you can also call a flat 5th a *sharp 4th* (♯4). However, musicians usually use the term *flat* in these cases because flats are used to identify minor intervals. For example, a flat 3rd is also called a *minor 3rd,* a flat 6th is also called a *minor 6th,* and a flat 7th is also called a *minor 7th.* Musicians often think in terms of major and minor. More on this in Chapters 7 and 13.

While playing in 3rds, you may notice that some 3rds are one half step lower than others. For example, in the G major scale, G and B (G-A-B) are two whole steps apart, while A and C (A-B-C) are only one and a half steps apart. In music, the distance from G to B is major, while the distance from A to C is minor, which is why the same intervals are called major and minor 3rds.

When you play the major scale in 3rds (see Figure 2-15), notice that three of the scale degrees have major 3rds, while four of them have minor 3rds. Specifically, the formula is major-minor-minor-major-major-minor-minor. They each have what's called a *perfect 5th,* except for the last one (which has a flat 5th).

Interval qualities

In music, intervals are classified by one of five qualities. The five interval qualities in music are

- **Perfect (P):** The perfect intervals are 5ths, 4ths, and 8ths (better known as *unisons* or *octaves*).
- **Major (M):** The major intervals are 3rds, 6ths, and 7ths.
- **Minor (m):** The minor intervals are flat 3rds, flat 6ths, and flat 7ths.
- **Augmented (A):** When you increase a perfect or major interval by one half step, you get an augmented interval, which is also called a sharp interval. For example, G to C is a 4th, while G to C♯ is a sharp or augmented 4th (A4 or ♯4).
- **Diminished (°):** When you decrease a perfect or minor interval by one half step, you get a diminished interval, which is also called a flat interval. For example, G to D is a 5th, while G to D♭ is a flat or diminished 5th (♭5 or °5). G to B♭ is a minor 3rd, while G to B𝄫 is a double flat or diminished third (𝄫3 or °3).

  Decreasing an interval that's already flat, like a minor 3rd, creates a double flat or diminished interval. What's confusing here is that, from a player's perspective, decreasing a minor interval simply puts you on another interval — namely, a 2nd (in the previous example, B𝄫 is enharmonically an A). You may also be wondering whether decreasing a major interval is also considered diminishing. Nope! Decreasing a major interval creates a minor interval.

Part II

Working with Chords from the Ground Up

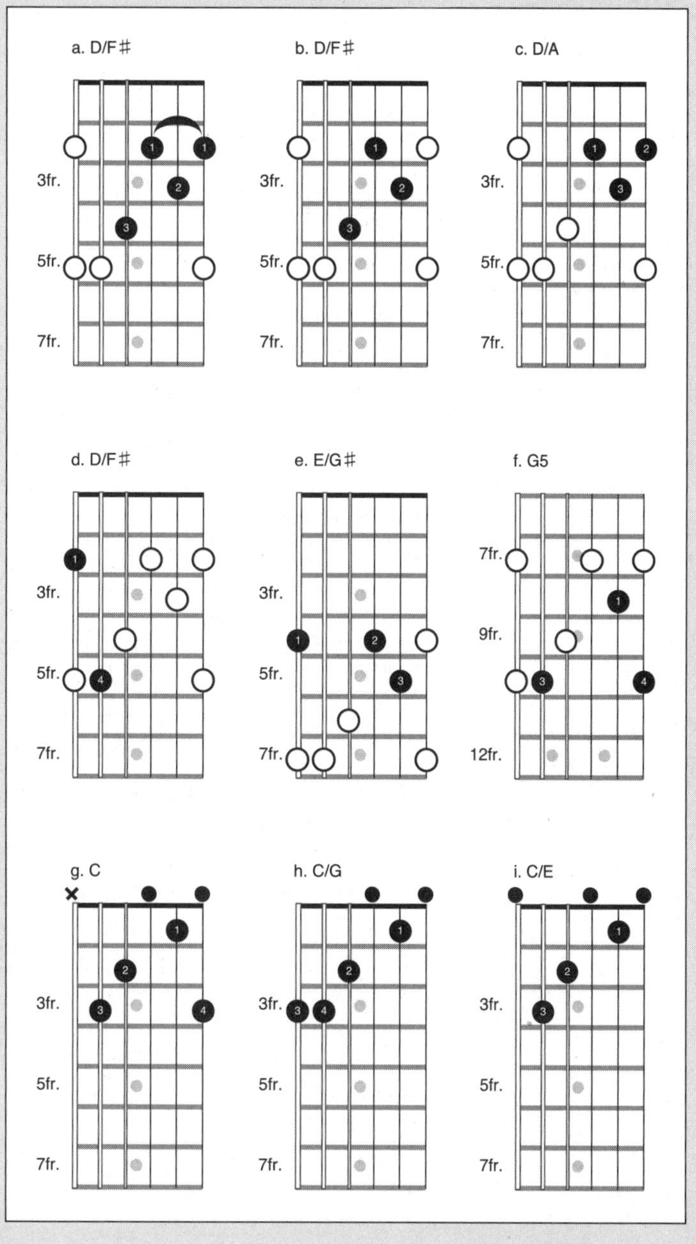

Head to www.dummies.com/extras/guitartheory to take a look at how Keith Richards makes use of the C and A form barre chords from the CAGED system to play the signature chord riffs of the Rolling Stones.

In this part . . .

- Harmonize the major scale to form triads and chords and play through a sequence of major and minor chords. Discover some popular songs that use the seven triads of the major scale.
- Use the CAGED chord system to form moveable chord shapes, including chord inversions and chord voicings. Play arpeggio patterns and analyze how popular songs are played.
- Find out what all the little numbers next to chord names mean. Add chord tones and extensions to basic triads and chords using 2nds, 4ths, 6ths, 7ths, and 9ths to create fuller-, richer-sounding chords.

Chapter 3

Harmonizing the Major Scale to Form Triads and Chords

In This Chapter

- Getting familiar with chord construction
- Building a triad and chord on each major scale degree
- Playing through the harmonized major scale
- Playing songs that use triads

In this chapter, you get started with basic chord construction by stacking the major scale in 3rds to form triads and then playing the notes of these triads simultaneously to sound chords. The basic chords you form here are the platforms on which other types of chords are built in Chapters 4 and 5. The sequence of major and minor chords that the major scale produces — one of the most important patterns in all of music — is used, among other things, to play chord progressions and chart chord changes (which you begin to explore in Chapter 6).

Listen to Audio Track 3 to hear some examples of what you encounter in this chapter, including chord construction, triads, chords, and the harmonized major scale.

Building Triads and Chords

A *triad* is a set of three notes stacked in 3rds. Playing in 3rds means that you start on a scale degree, count it as "1," and then move to the scale degree that is three away, "3." For example, the G major scale is G-A-B-C-D-E-F♯. If you start counting from G, then the 3rd is B (G-A-B, 1-2-3). If you start counting from A, then the 3rd is C (A-B-C, 1-2-3).

A triad is a group of three notes that are all a 3rd apart. For example, in the G major scale, G and B are a 3rd apart and B and D are a 3rd apart. Together all three of these notes are a 3rd apart. You call this two consecutive 3rds. G-B-D make a G triad. You also call the *members* of the triad *root, 3rd,* and *5th* because counting from the starting point, G, B is the 3rd degree and D is the 5th.

G	A	B	C	D	E	F♯
1	2	3	4	5	6	7
G		B		D		
1		3		5		

Harmonizing a root, 3rd, and 5th together (in other words, playing them simultaneously) produces a *chord.* Basically, the difference between a chord and a triad is that a chord is a group of three or more notes, and a triad is specifically a root, 3rd, and 5th.

You build triads on all scale degrees by following a formula of 3rds. Not all triads are the same. Because of the half step and whole step formula of the major scale, some 3rds are closer or farther apart than others. As a result, there are major triads and minor triads. One triad is diminished.

Major triad: Building from the 1st scale degree of the major scale

Building a triad starting from the 1st degree of the major scale produces a major triad. Sounding the notes of this triad simultaneously produces a major chord.

In the first diagram in Figure 3-1, you see all 7 degrees of the G major scale in one sample position. In the second diagram, you see just the root, 3rd, and 5th triad. When you strum all three of these triad notes simultaneously, you play a chord. Specifically, this chord is *G major* — *G* because the root is G and *major* because the distance between the root and 3rd is two whole steps, which make up a major 3rd. The third diagram in Figure 3-1 shows you that the actual note names of the G triad are G, B, and D.

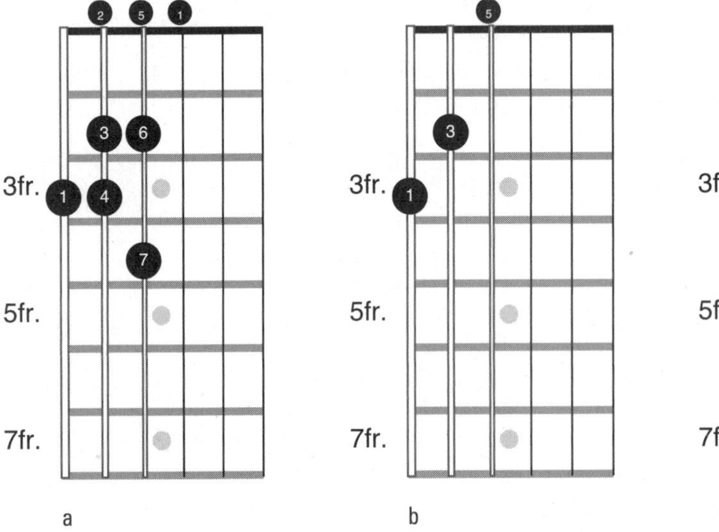

Figure 3-1: G major scale and G triad.

Illustration courtesy of Desi Serna

Need help getting started with building and playing triads? Watch Video Clip 3.

A G major chord is always made from the notes G-B-D; however, you can have more than one occurrence of each note. For example, you can play a G major chord as G-B-D-G or G-B-D-G-B. You can even stack the notes out of order like this: G-D-G-B. Whatever order you play the notes in and however many occurrences of each note you play, all combinations of G-B-D produce harmony that's recognized as a G major chord.

Figure 3-2 shows a handful of common G major chord shapes. Notice that they all use the same notes, although not necessarily in the same number or order. Chords like the ones shown here are considered triads because, technically, they're still based on three pitches even though they vary in the exact number and order of their notes.

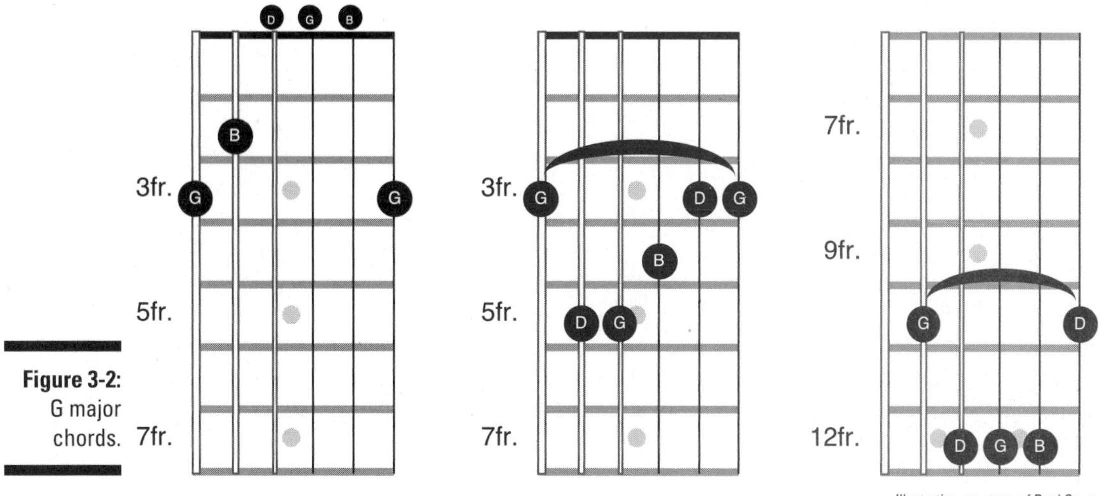

Figure 3-2: G major chords.

Illustration courtesy of Desi Serna

Minor triad: Building from the 2nd scale degree of the major scale

Using the G major scale I introduce in the preceding section, count *one-two-three-four-five* from the 2nd degree, A (A-B-C-D-E), and take every other note, 1-3-5 or A-C-E. This is an *A minor triad* — *A* because the root is A and *minor* because the distance from 1 to 3 is a step and a half, which makes up a minor 3rd or flat 3rd (♭3) interval.

Figure 3-3 shows you how to build a triad from the 2nd major scale degree, A. The major scale used here is exactly the same as the one used for the previous triad, G major. The only difference is that you're now counting from the 2nd scale degree, A, to determine its 3rd and 5th. I left the G note at the 3rd fret of the 6th string blank so that you know not to start on it.

You can play the note A either on the open 5th string or at the 5fth fret of the 6th string. You need to do the latter to play the triad as a chord. From the figure, you can see that the notes of this A minor triad are A-C-E.

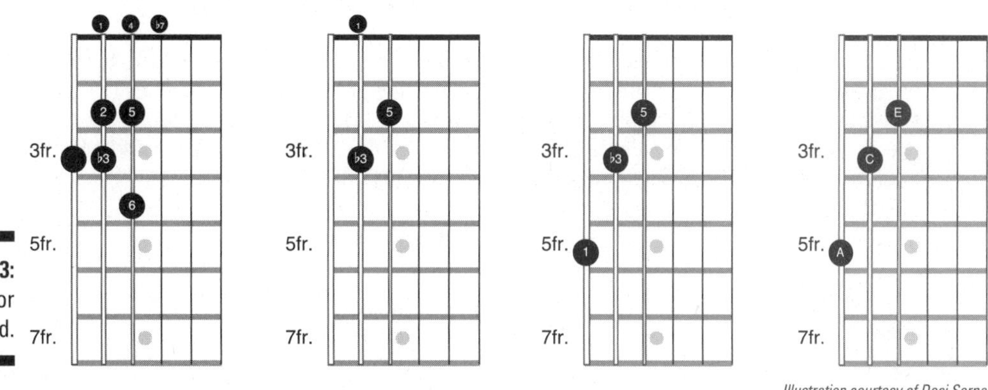

Figure 3-3: A minor triad.

Illustration courtesy of Desi Serna

Figure 3-4 shows a handful of common A minor chord shapes. Notice that they all use the same notes, although not necessarily in the same number or order. (In case you don't know, an "x" at the top of a string indicates that you don't play that string.)

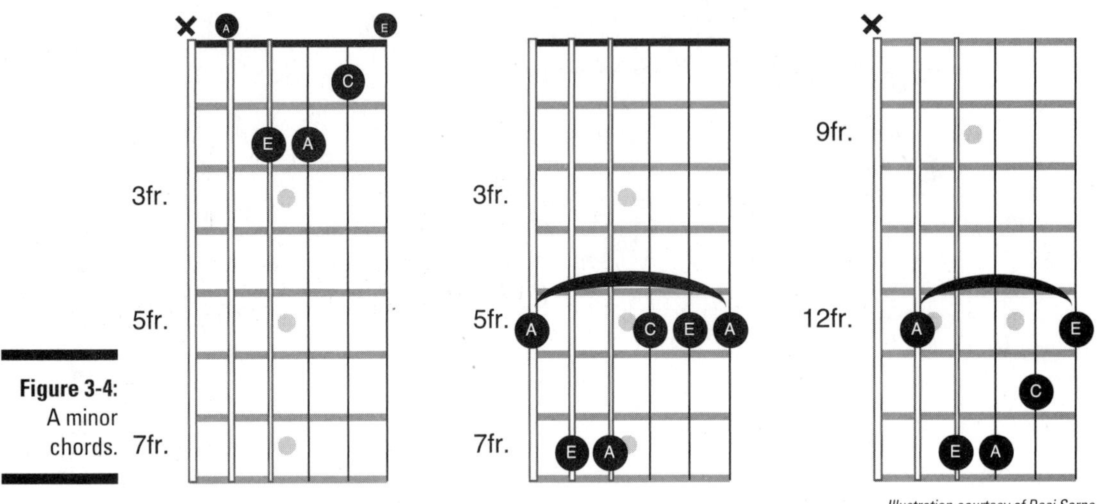

Figure 3-4: A minor chords.

Illustration courtesy of Desi Serna

Playing through the Seven Triads of the Major Scale

After you understand how to build triads (see the preceding section), you can continue to build on each degree in the G major scale (refer to Figure 2-14 in Chapter 2 for G major scale patterns). I encourage you to do this on your own on the fretboard. Here's what the completed scale looks like in triads:

1. G: G-B-D, G major
2. A: A-C-E, A minor
3. B: B-D-F♯, B minor
4. C: C-E-G, C major
5. D: D-F♯-A, D major
6. E: E-B-G, E minor
7. F♯: F♯-A-B, F♯minor♭5 (also called a *diminished triad*)

By following the tab in Figure 3-5, you can play through all seven major triads in three different ways. The first four measures put each interval on a separate string. The next four measures put the 3rd and 5th on the same string. The last four measures put the root and 3rd on the same string. Remember that the triad notes are exactly the same in all three examples; each version just uses some notes in a different location.

Playing triads one note at a time, as shown in Figure 3-5, is often done in riffs and bass lines. Guitar riff examples include

"Centerfield" by John Fogerty

"Manic Depression" by Jimi Hendrix

"Tightrope" by Stevie Ray Vaughan

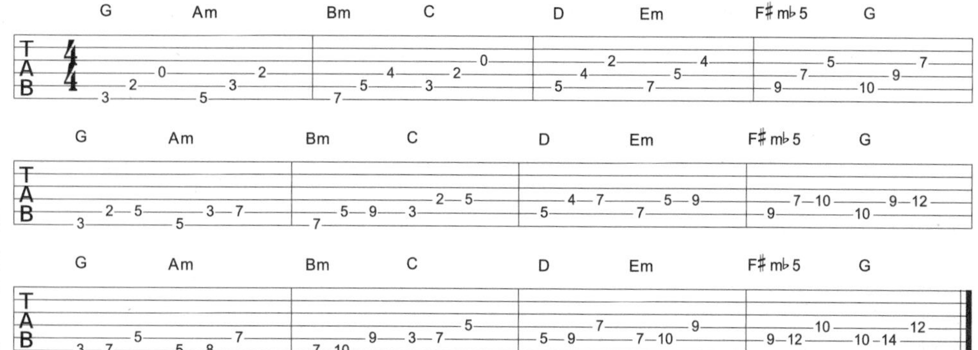

Figure 3-5: Major scale triads in G.

Illustration courtesy of Desi Serna

Bass examples include

"Ob-La-Di, Ob-La-Da" by The Beatles

"Hound Dog" by Elvis Presley

"Stir It Up" by Bob Marley and the Wailers

Playing the Chord Sequence of the Major Scale

If you take each triad from the major scale and play its notes as a common chord shape, you get the seven chords shown in Figure 3-6. The chords are shown first in the open position and then as barre chords that move up the neck along the 6th and 5th strings.

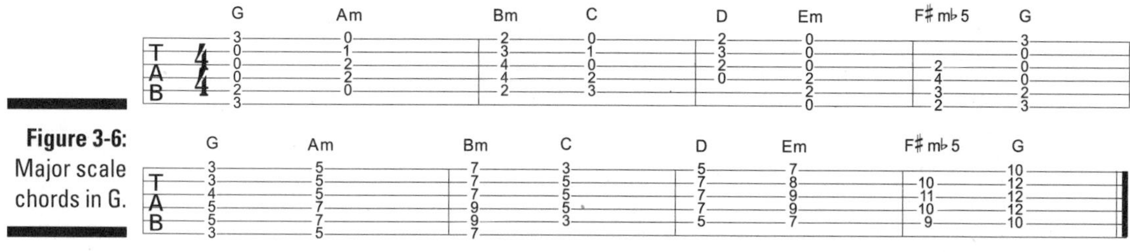

Figure 3-6: Major scale chords in G.

Illustration courtesy of Desi Serna

You can hear and see the G major scale chords by watching Video Clip 4.

Notice how the 1st, 4th, and 5th scale degrees produce major chords, while the 2nd, 3rd, and 6th scale degrees produce minor chords. These six chords are the ones most commonly used in music, so I recommend that you memorize their qualities. From 1 to 6, the sequence is major-minor-minor-major-major-minor.

Say and play that sequence over and over because it's one of the most important patterns in music. After all, you don't just see it in the G major scale. Because you construct every major scale by using the same intervals, all the scales produce the same types of triads and the same major/minor chord sequence. So the 1st degree of every major scale makes a major chord, the 2nd makes a minor, and so on. You get some practice with this sequence in various keys as you play chord progressions in Chapter 6.

Chapter 4

Forming Chord Shapes with the CAGED System

In This Chapter

- Forming and fingering major and minor chord shapes
- Playing chord inversions and voicings
- Visualizing how chord shapes connect to cover the whole fretboard

Guitar uses five basic major chord shapes. In the open position, they are C, A, G, E, and D. What does that spell? *CAGED.* The cool thing about these chords is that you can play each one as a barre chord and move it around the neck, and you can break these barre chords into smaller chord shapes. Also, each chord is taken from a larger arpeggio pattern that you can use to form additional voicings, as you soon see.

In the guitar world, you can apply the CAGED system in a few different ways. This chapter deals with using it to form and finger chords. You literally play every possible major and minor chord. More than that, you get to know the simple concept used to form these chords so that you don't have to memorize a bunch of chord diagrams. You change the ordering and spacing of the pitches by using inversions and voicings. You get away from standard chord shapes and play new chord forms that offer more variety and versatility.

Listen to Audio Track 4 to hear some examples of the CAGED system in action.

Making Chord Inversions and Chord Voicings

Before you can use the CAGED system to create different chord inversions, you need to familiarize yourself with a few terms and concepts.

- A *chord inversion* is a reordering of notes in a chord. A C major chord is C-E-G, root-3rd-5th, with the root, C, placed in the *bass* (lowest) position. If you play the chord with E in the bass as E-G-C (3rd-5th-root), you make what's called the *first inversion.* If you put the 5th in the bass as G-C-E (5th-3rd-root), you make the *second inversion.* In inversions, the chord *members* (the intervals that make up the chord) trade the bottom position. You can see some examples in Figure 4-1. (***Note:*** You don't need to memorize or practice these examples now. They're just here to illustrate what an inversion is.)

With chords, if a note other than the root is played in the lowest (bass) position, you have to specify it with a slash (/). The letter before the slash is the actual chord, and the letter after the slash is the *alternate bass note.*

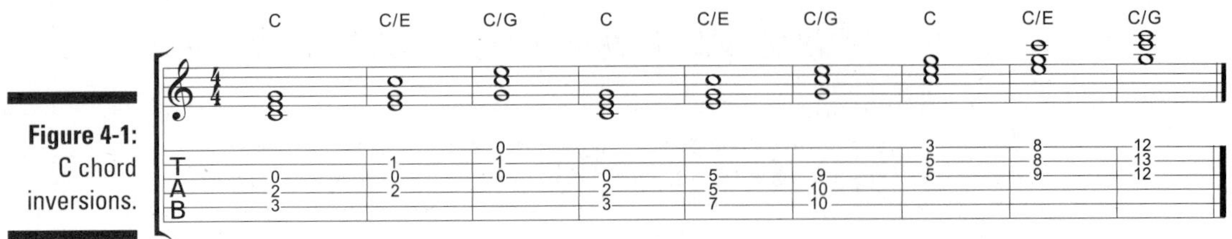

Figure 4-1: C chord inversions.

Illustration courtesy of Desi Serna

- A *chord voicing* refers to the order and spacing of a chord's members. Any combination of C-E-G makes a C chord, but C-E-G sounds different than E-G-C or C-G-C-E. Each inversion in Figure 4-1 is a different voicing.

  Figure 4-2 includes some additional chord voicings for C. Some examples have spacing between their pitches that require you to either mute strings or fingerpick. The way that these chord shapes are *voiced* (in other words, the order of and spacing between the notes) gives them their individual sounds.

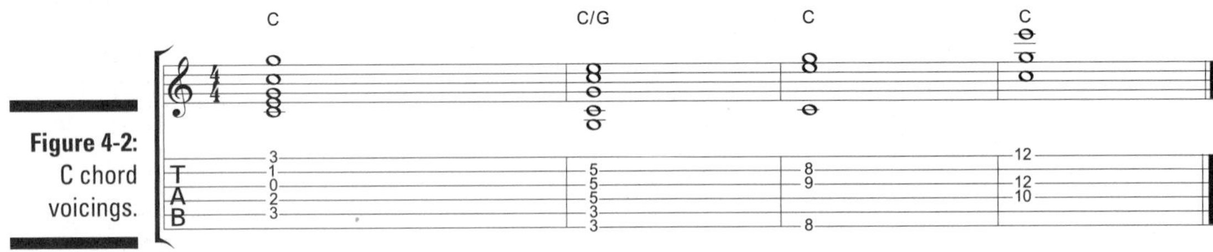

Figure 4-2: C chord voicings.

Illustration courtesy of Desi Serna

Using the C Form

The open C chord is one of the most basic types of chords that guitarists play. You probably learned it early on when you first started with guitar. But did you know the C chord shape doesn't have to be confined to the open position? You can move the shape up and play other major chords with it. Just remember if you move your fingers up, you also have to move up the open strings in the chord shape. You accomplish this move either by placing a *capo* (a device clamped on the fingerboard to raise the open strings) on your guitar or by rearranging your fingers and barring across the neck, which is what I focus on here.

When you move the C shape away from the open position and use it to form chords with other notes, the new chords are no longer C. Instead, they take on new names according to the root pitches that they're formed on. For example, move a C shape up one fret and it becomes C♯, up two frets and it becomes D, then D♯, E, and so on. Although you name each chord by its root, you still think of the shape as a *C form,* (not to be confused with the actual chord name).

In the following sections, you see the open C chord moved up and played as a barre chord, an arpeggio pattern, and then as fragmented chord voicings. After you understand how this process works, you can move through the remaining CAGED forms with less explanation. After you work through all the CAGED forms, you can connect them to cover the whole fretboard and play a sample chord progression.

Using the C form as a moveable barre chord

To use the C form as a moveable barre chord, your 1st finger acts like a capo and lays across (barres) the guitar neck while your remaining fingers form the rest of the chord shape. One way to arrive at this fingering is to play an ordinary open C chord, replace fingers 1-2-3 with 2-3-4 (this puts your 4th finger on C at the 3rd fret of the 5th string), slide your fingers up two frets, and then barre across the 2nd fret with your 1st finger. Figure 4-3 shows you what this chord shape looks like. The numbers indicate the fingering.

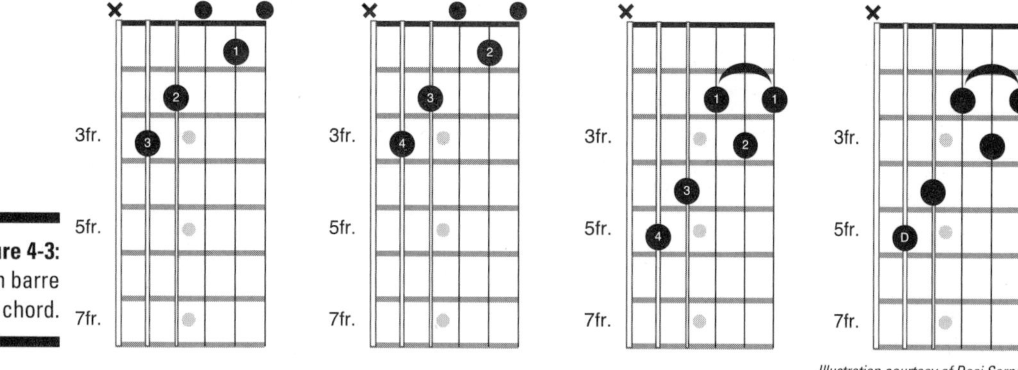

Figure 4-3: C form barre chord.

I demonstrate for you how to get started with fingering and playing your first CAGED form, C, in Video Clip 5.

When everything is in place, this shape actually becomes a D chord. Your 4th finger ends up on the new root D at the 5th fret of the 5th string, as shown in the fourth diagram in Figure 4-3.

Don't fret (no pun intended) if this barre chord is hard to play. This shape is rarely, if ever, used in its entirety. Instead, it's usually broken apart into smaller, more easily fingered pieces. However, to understand where these fragments come from, you need to know the full form. So focus more on visualizing the shape of the C form barre chord and don't worry about playing it perfectly.

If you're having trouble fingering this whole barre chord, don't barre completely across the fingerboard with your 1st finger. The only open strings in a C chord are the 1st and 3rd, so you need to barre only enough to cover those strings when you move the shape up.

Slide this barre chord shape around and play a major chord for any note along the 5th string, as shown in Figure 4-4. Note that the root is always under your 4th finger.

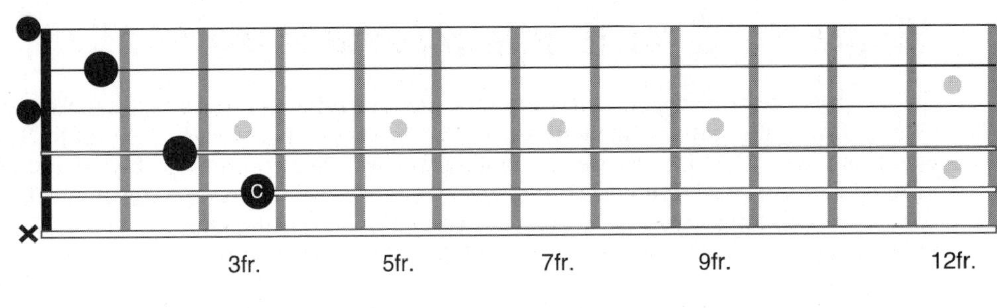

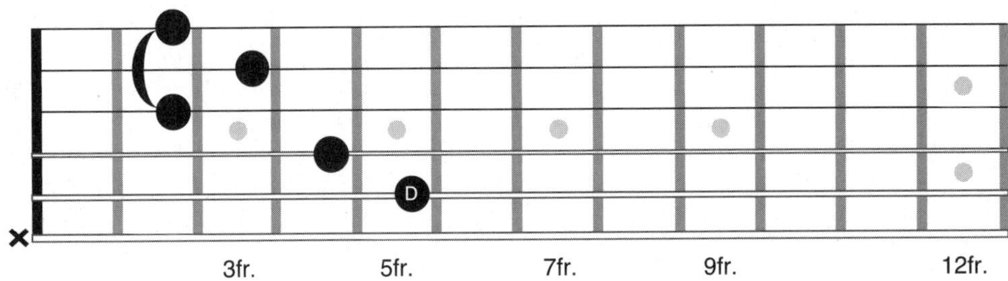

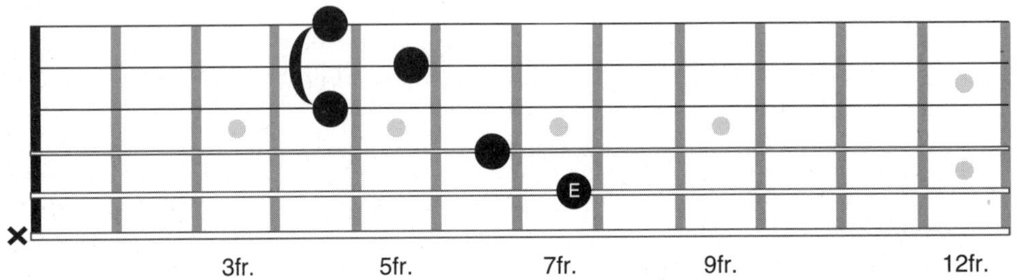

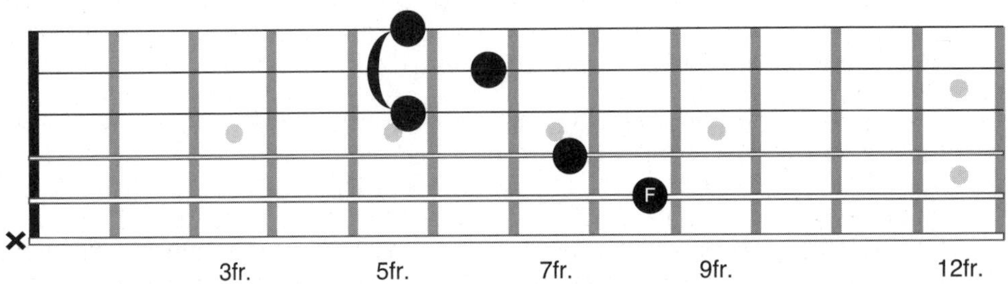

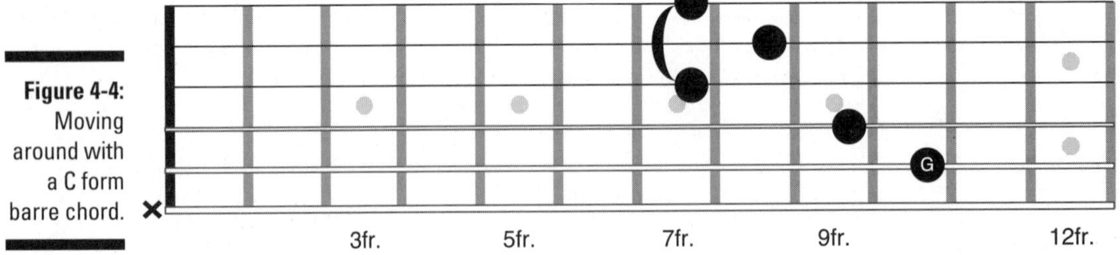

Figure 4-4: Moving around with a C form barre chord.

Illustration courtesy of Desi Serna

Playing a C form arpeggio pattern

Before you break down the C form into smaller and more useable chord voicings, I suggest that you add to it in the form of an arpeggio pattern. An *arpeggio* is a technique in which you play the notes of a chord one at a time like a scale rather than simultaneously as a chord. The term is also used as the verb *arpeggiate* to describe how players pick through the notes of chords individually rather than strumming them all simultaneously (think of the opening to "The House of the Rising Sun" by The Animals or "Everybody Hurts" by R.E.M.).

For example, a D chord is D-F♯-A. Using the position of a C form D chord, you find these notes in the barre chord shape but also outside of it. For instance, you see an F♯ at the 2nd fret of the 6th string, an A at the 5th fret of the 6th string, and another A at the 5th fret of the 1st string. To form a full arpeggio pattern, play through *all occurrences* of these notes in this position from low to high and then high to low like a scale, as shown in the tab in Figure 4-5.

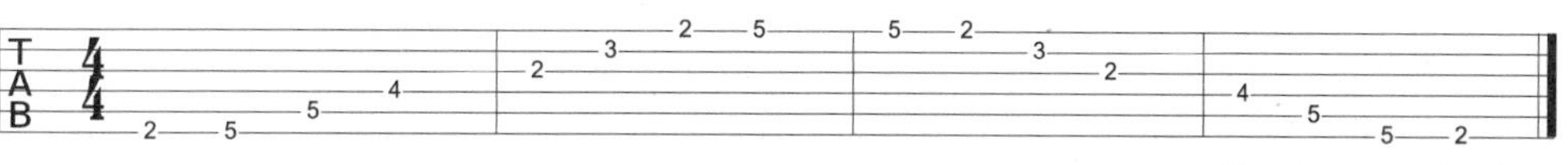

Figure 4-5: C form arpeggio pattern tab.

Illustration courtesy of Desi Serna

Notice that the lowest pitched note available in this position is where the arpeggio pattern begins — on the 3rd of D, or F♯. When mapping out an arpeggio like this, you don't need to start on the root. Instead, touch on all chord members in the position.

Also notice that some strings have more than one chord member on them. When playing notes simultaneously as a chord, you can choose only one note per string, but arpeggios allow you to play multiple notes on a string because you can fret and pick each one individually. For example, when playing a chord, you can use either the F♯ or the A on the 1st string but not both. When playing an arpeggio, you can play both.

In Figure 4-6, you see the shape this arpeggio pattern makes on the fretboard. I include the pattern three times. The numbers in the first diagram indicate the chord intervals, the letters in the second diagram indicate the note names, and the numbers in the third diagram indicate a sample fingering. I put the intervals and note names in to add more perspective, but you don't need to memorize them. Feel free to try my sample fingering or come up with a different fingering that better suits you.

Play through the C form arpeggio one note at a time like a scale, ascending and descending until you have it completely memorized. You can also use this pattern at different frets to play arpeggios for other pitches, as shown in Figure 4-7. I show you just three examples, C, D, and E, but you can position the pattern around any note along the 5th string. Notice that the arpeggio pattern also works for C in the open position.

As you work through this chapter, don't try to memorize all the different chord shapes presented. Instead, focus on memorizing the arpeggio patterns from which each form is taken. Then you can use those patterns to build any shape you want.

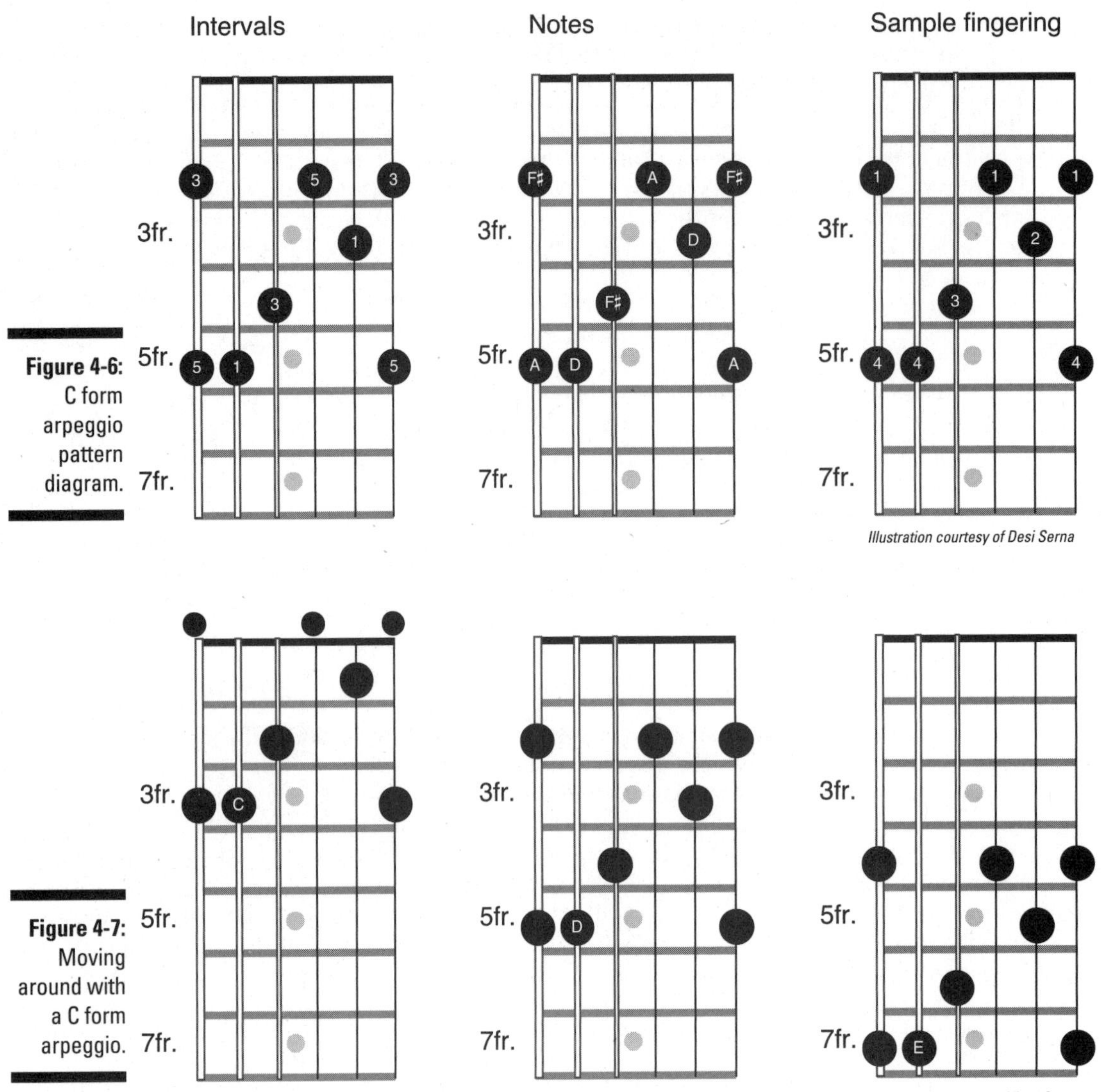

Figure 4-6: C form arpeggio pattern diagram.

Illustration courtesy of Desi Serna

Figure 4-7: Moving around with a C form arpeggio.

Illustration courtesy of Desi Serna

Playing C form chord voicings

Different C form chord voicings are played by breaking down the arpeggio pattern into smaller, fragmented pieces. Figure 4-8 shows you several ways to play partial chord shapes based on the full C form. In these examples, you fret and pick only the black dots. The numbers in the black dots are suggested fingerings. The white dots represent the remainder of the arpeggio pattern that you aren't using. I put everything together like this so you can see exactly how each chord fragment fits into the full form.

- Figure 4-8a is a fragment on strings 1 to 4. This chord shape is used in "Stairway to Heaven" by Led Zeppelin as a D/F♯. It's considered a type of first inversion because the 3rd is in the bass position. You can play it either by barring with your 1st finger across the first three strings (as I show) or by using all four fingers to fret each note individually.

- Figure 4-8b is a fragment on strings 2 to 4 and is used in "Jack and Diane" by John Mellencamp. As shown in the figure, this chord voicing is D/F♯, but in "Jack and Diane," it's played together with the open A string as a D/A. It's also moved two frets higher and used as an E/A.
- Figure 4-8c is a fragment on strings 1 to 3 and is part of an open D chord. It's also moved around the neck as different chords in "Hole Hearted" by Extreme.
- Figure 4-8d is an inverted 3rd interval used in "Stay Together for the Kids" by Blink 182 as a D/F♯. Notice that the root of this chord shape is the note in the top position, D, not the note in the bottom position, F♯, which is the 3rd. Technically, this shape isn't a full chord because it lacks the 5th interval, but roots and 3rds are usually written as major chords anyway.
- Figure 4-8e is an E/G♯. Eric Clapton fingerpicks this chord shape in "Tears in Heaven."
- Figure 4-8f uses notes spaced in a manner that requires you to mute the unwanted strings, fingerpick, or some hybrid of the two. It's used in the song "Cliffs of Dover" by Eric Johnson as a G5. The "5" stands for power chord. Technically, this shape is only a root and 5th and not a full chord.
- Figure 4-8g shows that you can play an open C chord with a high G on top.
- Figure 4-8h is an open C chord with a low G in the bass. Pink Floyd uses this shape in "Wish You Were Here."
- Figure 4-8i is an open C chord with a low E in the bass. Stone Temple Pilots use it in "Plush."

When you use fragmented chord shapes, make sure you still visualize the unused notes so that you can track what the chord name is. For example, when I play the D/F♯ used in "Stairway to Heaven," my eye still sees the full C form barre chord and looks to the 5th fret of the 5th string where my 4th finger would be to identify the chord voicing as a D. Being so close to the open position D chord, you probably easily recognize the D/F♯ as being related to it, but as you move further up the neck it becomes more difficult to identify fragmented chords and more helpful to visualize the root notes of the whole form on the 5th string.

Other songs that use variations of the C form include

"All Right Now" by Free

"Crazy Train" by Ozzy Osbourne

"Cult of Personality" by Living Colour

"Domino" by Van Morrison

"Firehouse" by Kiss

"Flirtin' with Disaster" by Molly Hatchet

"Free Ride" by Edgar Winter Group

"Funk #49" by James Gang

"I'm Bad, I'm Nationwide" by ZZ Top

"Let it Ride" by Bachman-Turner Overdrive

"Snow (Hey Oh)" by Red Hot Chili Peppers

"Take it Easy" by the Eagles

"316" by Van Halen

"What I Like about You" by the Romantics

"You Ain't Seen Nothin' Yet" by Bachman-Turner Overdrive

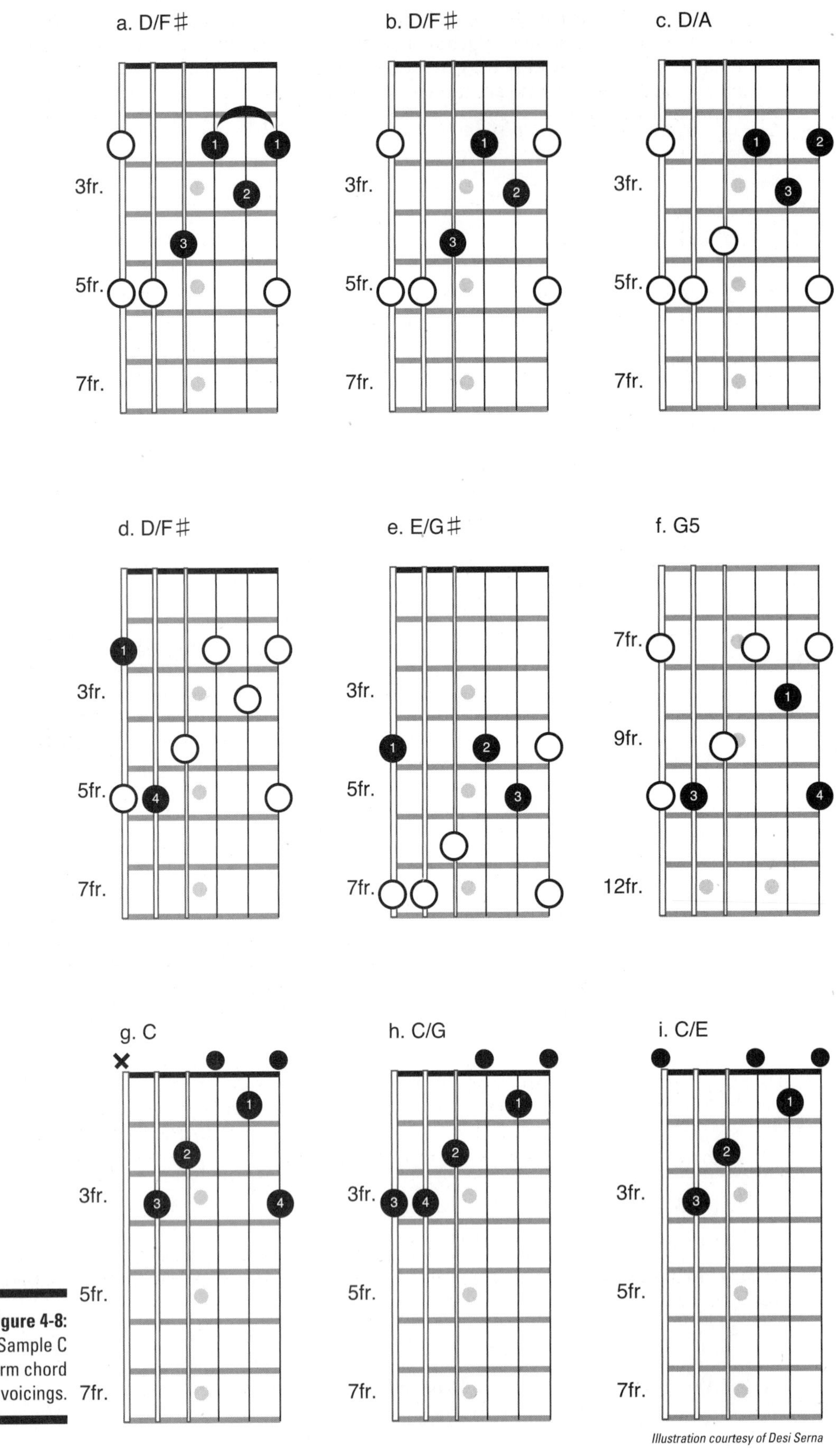

Figure 4-8: Sample C form chord voicings.

Illustration courtesy of Desi Serna

The style of Keith Richards from The Rolling Stones is built almost entirely around the use of a C form barre chord. Although he detunes his 1st and 5th strings and often omits the 6th string completely by not even putting it on, the rest of his strings, 2 through 4, remain the same as standard tuning. These are the strings Richards used to play a partial C form barre chord on so many of his signature songs, like "Brown Sugar," "Start Me Up," and "Honky Tonk Women," just to name a few.

Using the A Form

The *A form* is one of the most commonly used shapes and is typically what comes to mind when guitarists think of barre chords. In Figure 4-9, you move up an open A chord and use it as an A form barre chord to play major chords all along the 5th string. With this shape, the root is under your 1st finger on the 5th string. In the figure, I give you four examples to get you started.

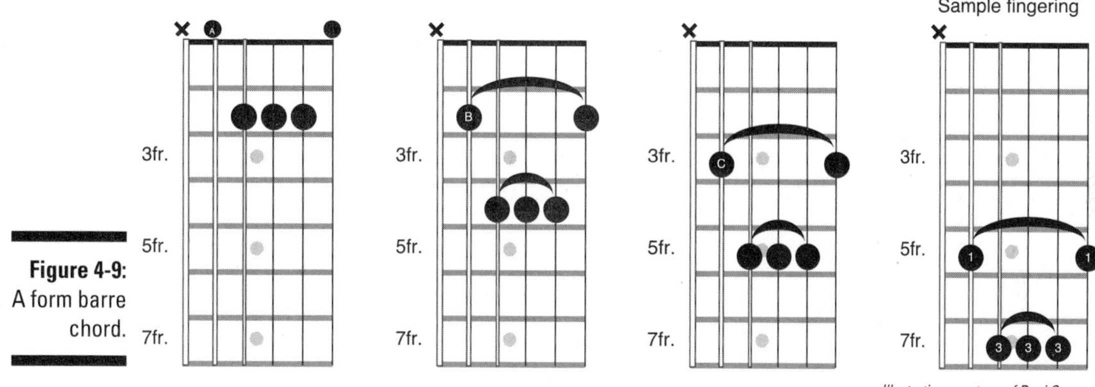

Figure 4-9: A form barre chord.

The most popular fingering for this shape includes barring with your 3rd finger to play strings 2 through 4, but you can also use separate fingers if you prefer. If you barre with your 3rd finger, you may find it necessary to leave out the note on the 1st string because it's difficult not to bump into it. This in turn means that you don't need to barre with your 1st finger because it's only fretting the root on the 5th string. If you should need the note on the 1st string to ring clearly, then skip the barre and use separate fingers to fret each note individually. Some people can barre with their 3rd finger and still get the note on the 1st string to ring clearly. Maybe you can, too. Experiment to see which fingering technique works best for you.

After you play the A form barre chord, play the A form arpeggio pattern as shown in the four examples in Figure 4-10. Remember that you play these notes individually from lowest pitch to highest pitch in an ascending order like a scale; then reverse direction. Use the diagrams in the figure to play major arpeggios for roots along the 5th string. For your reference, I use numbers to show the intervals in the first three diagrams. The fourth example includes a sample fingering.

The A form arpeggio pattern has two additional notes that aren't part of the barre chord. This includes a note on the 6th string and another on the 4th string. Notice that you play two notes in all on the 4th string.

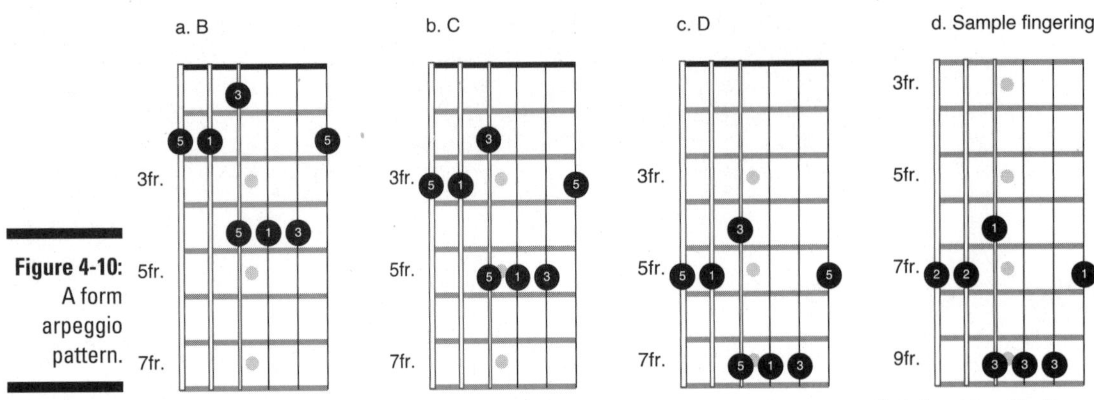

Figure 4-10: A form arpeggio pattern.

Illustration courtesy of Desi Serna

You can break up this arpeggio into various chord voicings, as shown in Figure 4-11. Remember to fret and play only the black dots. The clear dots are only to show where the remainder of the whole form is. Try my suggested fingerings or use your own.

- Figure 4-11a uses only strings 1 through 3. Led Zeppelin uses this shape in the interlude to "Stairway to Heaven" as both a type of C, as shown here, and a type of D two frets higher.
- Figure 4-11b features a shape on strings 2 to 4 that's often used together with a C form on the same strings. You can barre these three notes with your 1st finger to play a C and then add your 2nd and 3rd fingers to play an F in C form, as you hear in "Brown Sugar" by The Rolling Stones.
- Figure 4-11c shows a standard power chord shape that's used on countless songs.
- Figure 4-11d shows one way to incorporate the extra arpeggio note on the 4th string. John Mayer uses this shape in the chorus of "Daughters."
- Figure 4-11e is similar to Figure 4-11d, minus the root D on the 5th string. This D/F♯, which is really only a root and 3rd, shows up in the chorus to "All Right Now" by Free.
- Figure 4-11f uses the extra arpeggio note on the 6th string. It's an F power chord with the 5th, C, in the bass and is used in the opening to "The Wind Cries Mary" by Jimi Hendrix.
- Figure 4-11g is an F played as only a root and 3rd and is used in "Scar Tissue" by Red Hot Chili Peppers. This interval is often called a *10th* because the 3rd is a register above the root, ten steps in the major scale.
- Figure 4-11h is a C and is arpeggiated in the opening to "Cliffs of Dover" by Eric Johnson.

If only the root and 5th are used in a chord, it's considered a *power chord,* and you write it as *C5, F5,* and so on. If only a root and 3rd are used, then you sometimes see it written as *G(no5).* However, most of the time a root and 3rd combo is still considered a major chord and is written as such, even though the absence of the 5th technically makes it incomplete.

Many of the songs I list in the section "Playing C Form chord voicings" also use the A form. Guitarists often combine the two sets of chord voicings by barring the A form on strings 2 to 4 with the 1st finger and then adding the 2nd and 3rd fingers to build a partial C form, as is the case in "Jack and Diane," "Funk #49," "All Right Now," and many others. Keith Richards uses the same technique in most songs by The Rolling Stones.

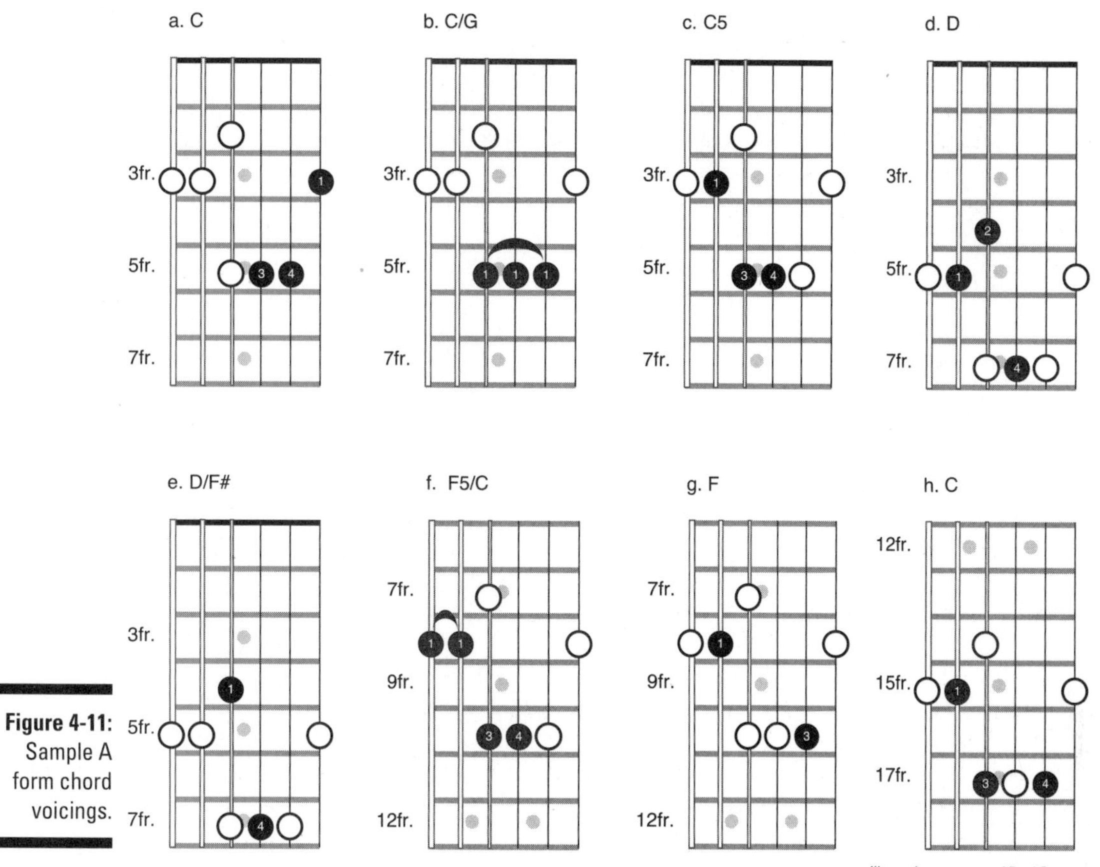

Figure 4-11: Sample A form chord voicings.

Illustration courtesy of Desi Serna

Using the G Form

Figure 4-12 shows you the *G form.* Like the C form, this barre chord is hard to play and rarely, if ever, used in its entirety. Don't worry about being able to play it perfectly because more often than not, you break it down into other, more manageable shapes. You use the G form to form major chords for notes along the 6th string.

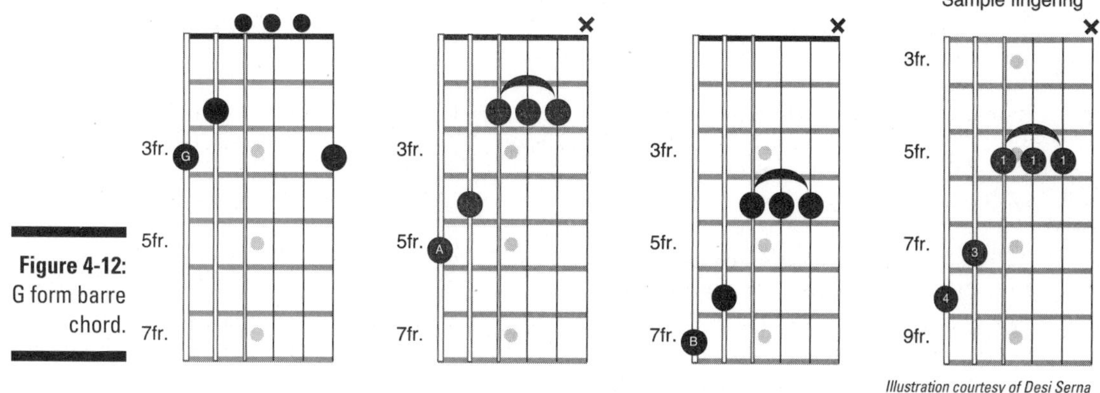

Figure 4-12: G form barre chord.

Illustration courtesy of Desi Serna

Play the full G form arpeggio pattern shown in Figure 4-13. It includes an additional note on the 2nd string. Play it as a scale.

The additional chord tone on the 2nd string explains why you can play an open G chord with either the 2nd string open, B, or the 3rd fret of the 2nd string, D. Both notes are part of the chord.

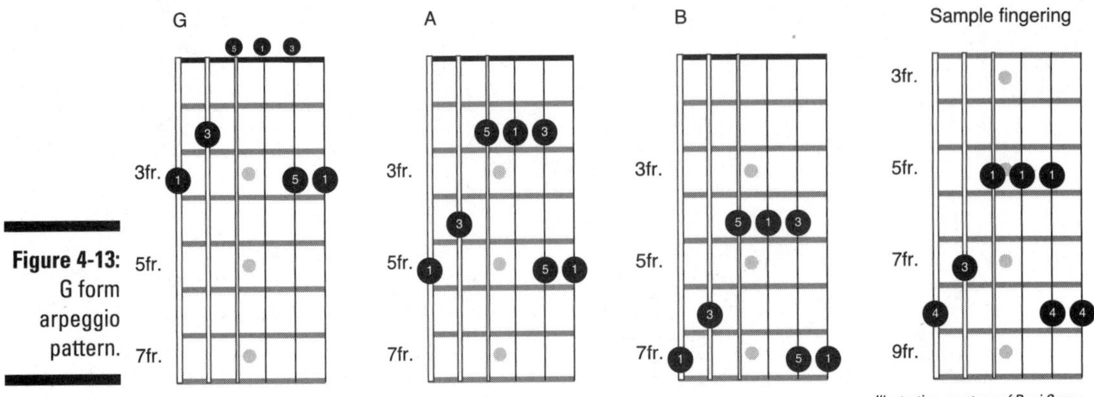

Figure 4-13: G form arpeggio pattern.

Figure 4-14 shows you how to play G form chord voicings.

- Figure 4-14a features a part of the barre chord that's used in the song "Snow (Hey Oh)" by Red Hot Chili Peppers as a B.
- Figure 4-14b shows the C/G used in the opening to "Stairway to Heaven" by Led Zeppelin.
- Figure 4-14c shows the F/A used in the opening to "The Wind Cries Mary" by Jimi Hendrix.
- Figure 4-14d is a very common, open position G/B. Variations of this shape are used in many acoustic guitar songs, such as "Dust in the Wind" by Kansas, "Landslide" by Fleetwood Mac, and "Blackbird" by The Beatles.

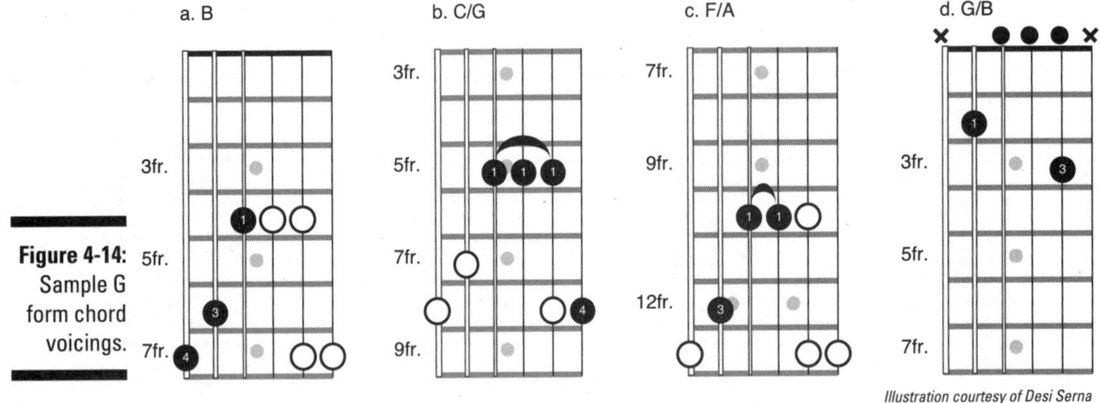

Figure 4-14: Sample G form chord voicings.

Other songs that make use of G form chord voicings include

"China Grove" by The Doobie Brothers

"Fade to Black" by Metallica

"Gimme Three Steps" by Lynyrd Skynyrd

"Tears in Heaven" by Eric Clapton

The G form has three notes in a row on strings 2–4 just like the A form. In fact, the two forms are connected by this group of notes (as you find out in a moment). I mention in the A form section that you can fret this group of notes with your 1st finger and use it together with a partial C form to play in the style of Keith Richards, among others. Now you see that this type of chord change can be viewed as a combination of the G form and C form too.

Using the E Form

Like the A form, the *E form* is a standard barre chord shape. You use it to form major chords for notes along the 6th string, as shown in Figure 4-15. You can form it into some unique chord voicings, especially when you use the extra note found in its arpeggio pattern.

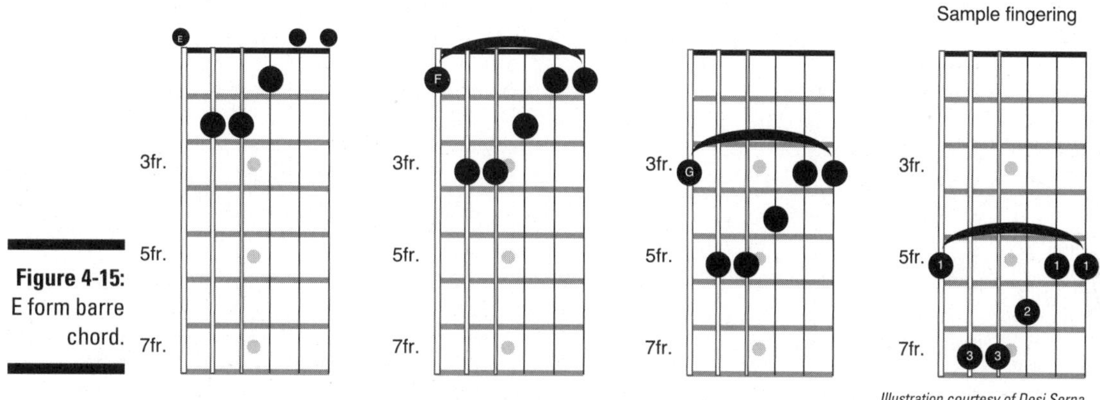

Figure 4-15: E form barre chord.

Illustration courtesy of Desi Serna

You add only one note to the E form shape to complete the arpeggio pattern: a 3rd interval on the 5th string (see Figure 4-16). Play it as a scale.

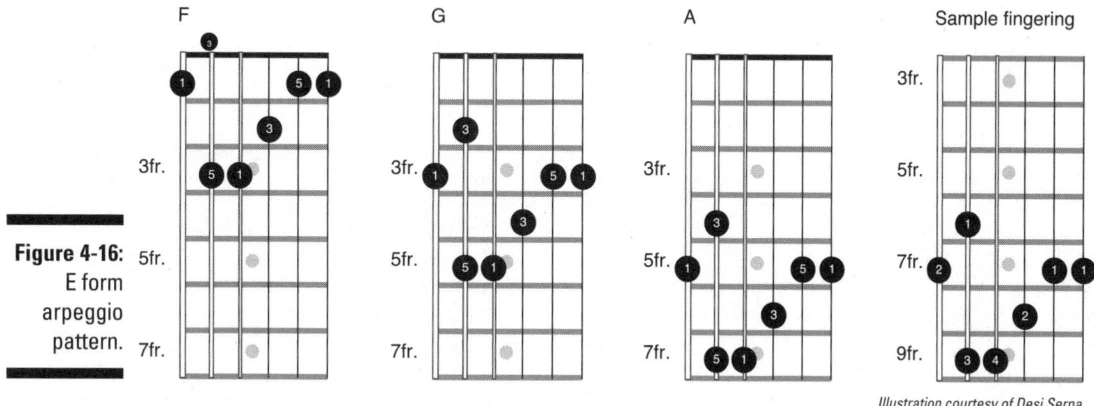

Figure 4-16: E form arpeggio pattern.

Illustration courtesy of Desi Serna

In Figure 4-17, you play some of the E form chord voicings heard in popular music.

- Figure 4-17a is a common F chord that guitarists usually learn together with basic open chords. You can always play a full E form barre chord partially like this, and you can still visually track the root on the 6th string when you do.

- Figure 4-17b is similar to the preceding F shape, but it's reduced even further to include only the first three strings. This E/G♯ is used in "Gloria" by Van Morrison. Even though you're fretting and playing only strings 1 through 3, you can still track the root E on the 6th string with your eye.
- Figure 4-17c is the B♭/F used in the opening to "Johnny B. Goode" by Chuck Berry.
- Figure 4-17d uses a unique spacing of the root and third and is featured in the song "Tripping Billies" by Dave Matthews Band. This interval is often called a *10th* because the 3rd is a register above the root, ten steps in the major scale.
- Figure 4-17e is an inverted 3rd with the root in the top position and the 3rd in the bass. It's used as a B/D♯ and an A/C♯ in the opening to "Hold On Loosely" by 38 Special.
- Figure 4-17f is a G/B with some unique spacing that's arpeggiated in the opening to "Cliffs of Dover" by Eric Johnson.

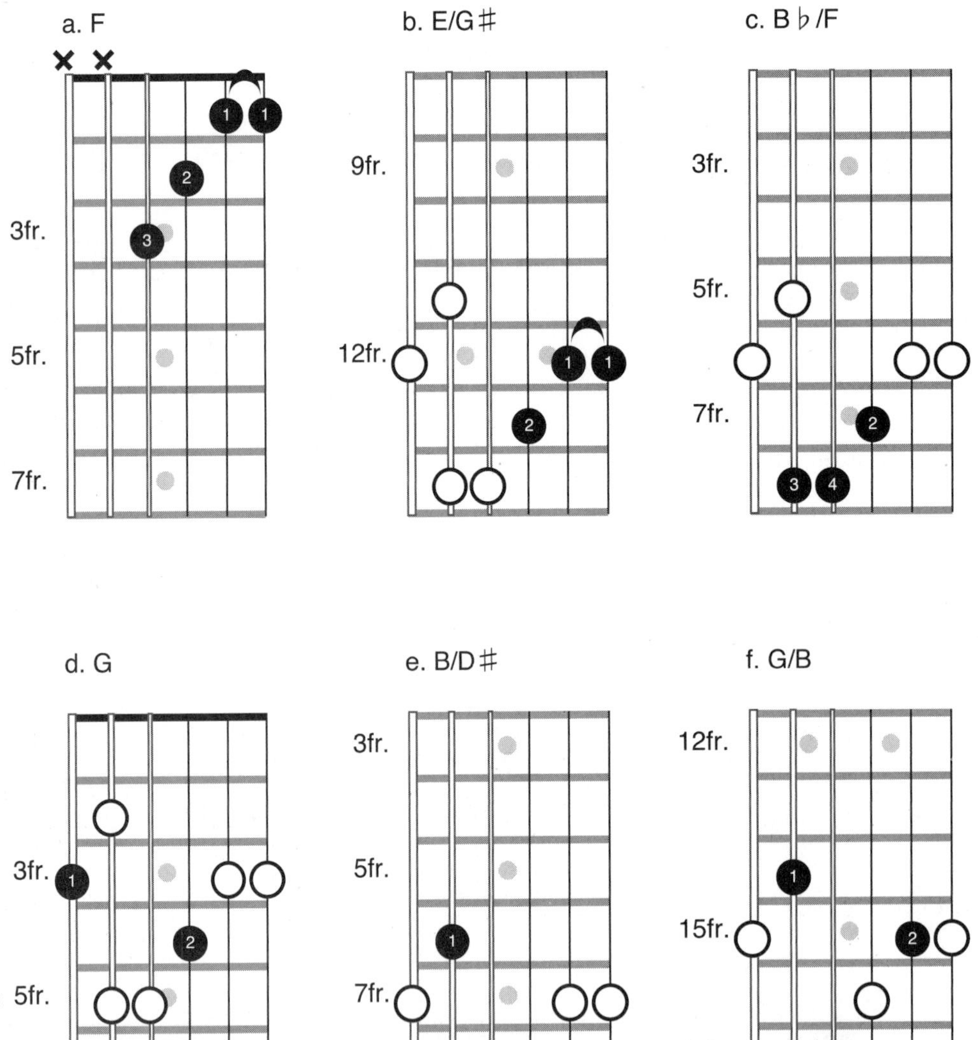

Figure 4-17: Sample E form chord voicings.

Other songs that use chord voicings based on the E form include

"Another Brick in the Wall (Part II)" by Pink Floyd

"Burning Love" by Elvis Presley

"Caught Up in You" by 38 Special

"Domino" by Van Morrison

"Eye of the Tiger" by Survivor

"Good Lovin'" by The Young Rascals

"Life's Been Good" by Joe Walsh

"Me and Julio Down by the Schoolyard" by Paul Simon

"Santeria" by Sublime

"Soul Man" by Sam & Dave.

"Under the Bridge" by Red Hot Chili Peppers

Using the D Form

The D form is unique in that it's the only CAGED form that isn't rooted to either the 6th or 5th string. Instead, its root is on the 4th string (see Figure 4-18). This form is awkward to finger and technically isn't a barre chord. As with some of the other CAGED forms, you don't usually use it in the same way that it appears in the open position.

You may prefer to finger the D form in a different way. For instance, some guitar players swap their 2nd and 3rd fingers. Others can barre the 1st and 3rd strings with their 3rd finger and fret the note on the 2nd string with their 4th finger. Feel free to experiment, but remember, you don't need to play this whole chord perfectly.

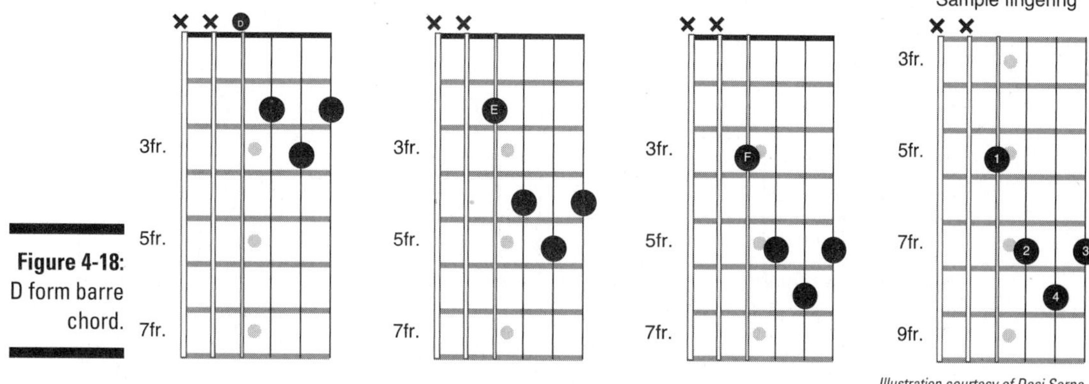

Figure 4-18: D form barre chord.

Illustration courtesy of Desi Serna

You can play the full D form arpeggio pattern in Figure 4-19. Notice that you have a lot more to work with here than what's present in the small D form. Three additional chord members on strings 4 through 6 fit with this form. Play it as a scale.

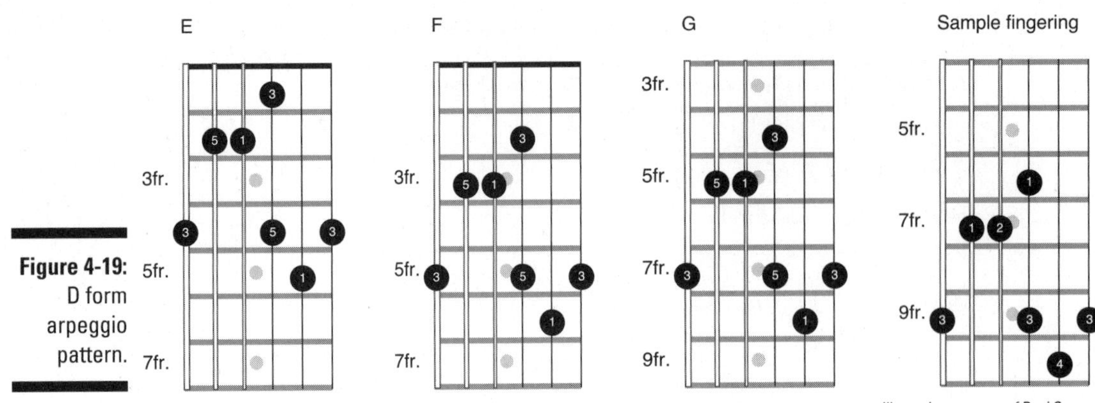

Figure 4-19: D form arpeggio pattern.

Illustration courtesy of Desi Serna

The D form is used less often than the other CAGED forms, but it still has the potential to form some unique and useable chord voicings, as you can see in Figure 4-20.

- Figure 4-20a is a very common version of an open D that puts the 3rd, F♯, in the bass at the 2nd fret of the 6th string. It's often fingered as a regular D chord with the thumb wrapped around the neck to fret the 6th string. You hear variations of this shape used in "Free Bird" by Lynyrd Skynyrd.
- Figure 4-20b is a power chord with the root on the 4th string. This F5 is used in "All the Small Things" by Blink 182.
- Figure 4-20c is an E/G♯ and fits into both a D form and a C form (see the earlier section "Using the C Form"). It's used in "Tears in Heaven" by Eric Clapton. You can finger this shape with your first three fingers or try using your thumb, as I illustrate in the figure.
- Figure 4-20d is another variation on E/G♯. This one occurs in "Crash into Me" by Dave Matthews Band.
- Figure 4-20e is an F♯/A♯ and is used in "Snow (Hey Oh)" by Red Hot Chili Peppers.

The triangular D shape on strings 1 through 3 is often moved around the guitar neck. This shape fits into both the D form and the C form. You trace the root back to either the 4th or 5th string by using these forms.

Most uses of the D form occur in the open position as a D/F♯, as in "Free Bird." Other songs that feature variations on D/F♯ include

"Babe I'm Gonna Leave You" by Led Zeppelin

"Change the World" by Eric Clapton

"Hole Hearted" by Extreme

"More Than a Feeling" by Boston

"More Than Words" by Extreme

"Plush" by Stone Temple Pilots

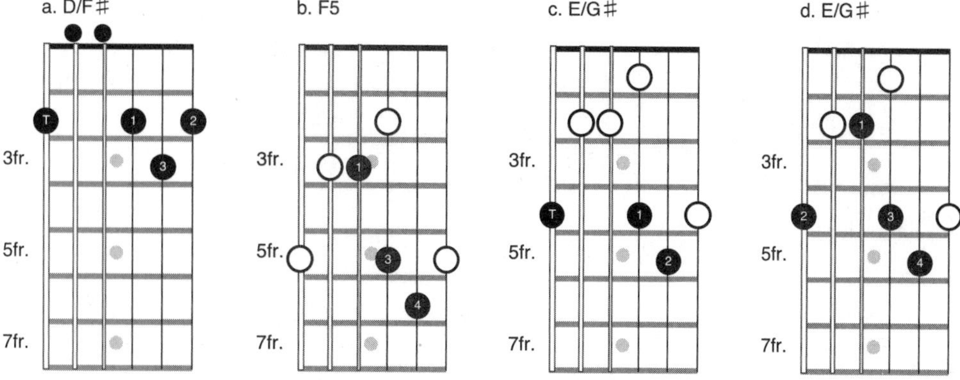

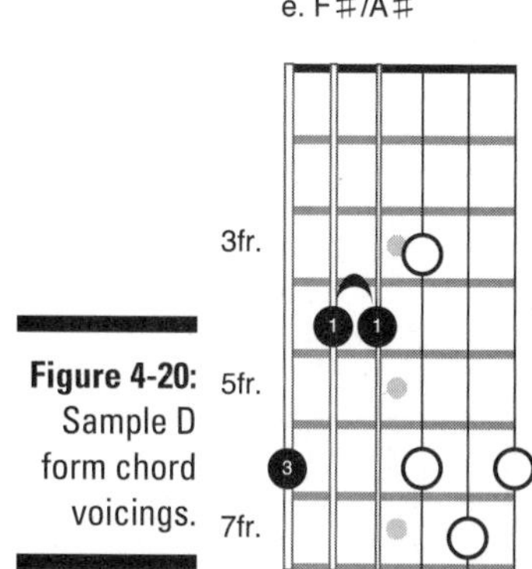

Figure 4-20: Sample D form chord voicings.

Illustration courtesy of Desi Serna

Connecting the Five CAGED Forms

In this section, you connect the five CAGED forms all with the same chord to cover the whole fretboard. For example, play a C chord with every CAGED form. Start with each form in its open position, and then move up the neck by using different forms while staying on the same chord. As you move from position to position, keeping with the same chord, the forms always go in the order of C-A-G-E-D, C-A-G-E-D, and so on.

Starting on C

Figure 4-21 starts with an open C chord and then follows with C chords in different forms in all positions on the neck. To simplify things, I use barre chords in place of full arpeggio patterns. You can expand on the arpeggios from these starting points.

Notice that the second form of C is the A form, the second letter in CAGED. The third form of C is the G form, the third letter in CAGED, and so on. Also notice that each new position uses a portion of the previous form, as shown by the dotted lines in the figure. In this way, all the positions are connected. You can keep connecting the CAGED forms in order like this until you either run out of fretboard or can't reach any higher.

Focus on visualizing how each form connects to the next, as indicated by the dotted lines between individual diagrams. Practice connecting forms both forward and backward.

Watch Video Clip 6 to see how to connect the CAGED forms in Figure 4-21.

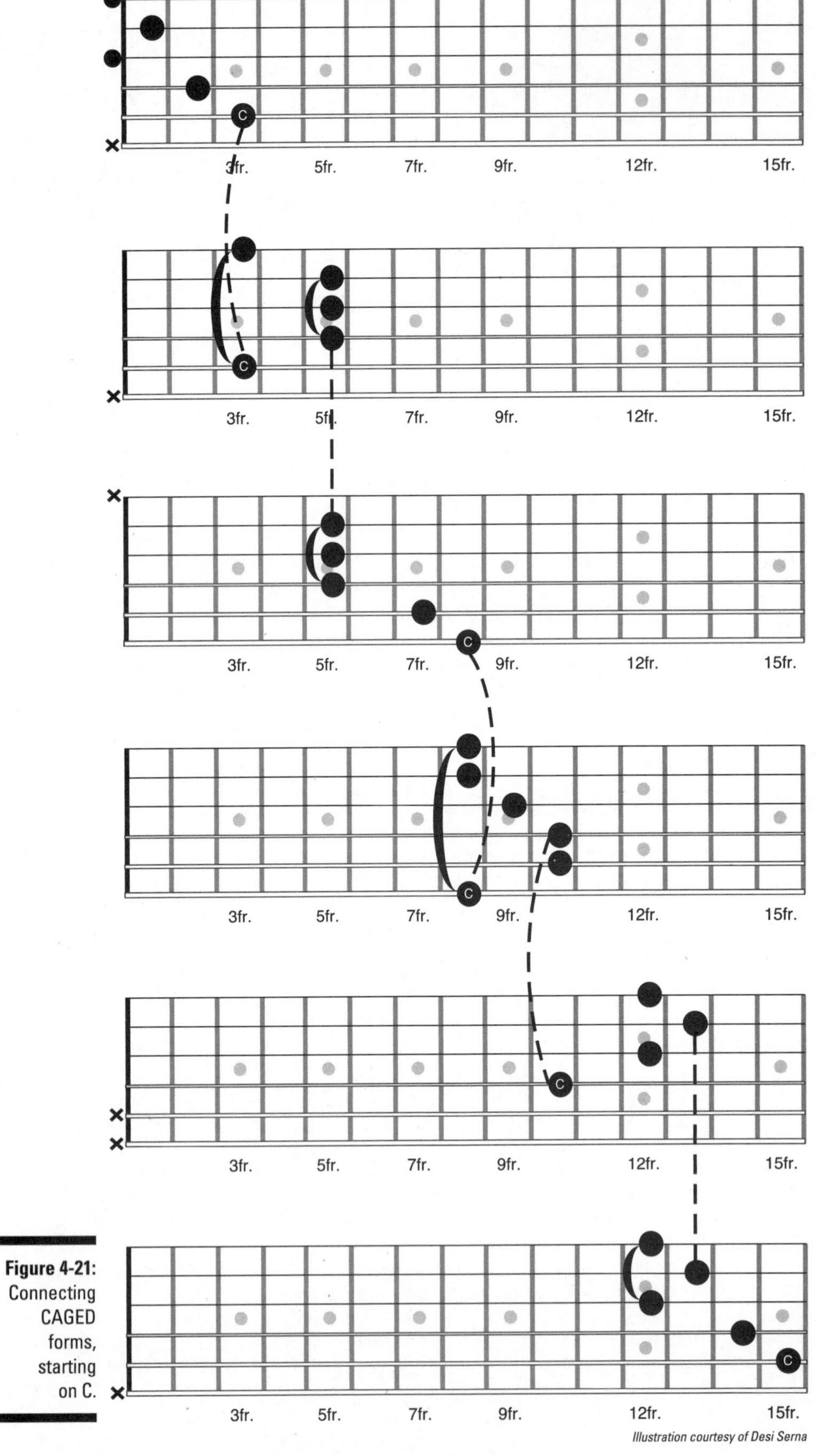

Figure 4-21: Connecting CAGED forms, starting on C.

Starting on A

In Figure 4-22, you start with an open A chord and connect to all its forms on the fretboard. Because you're starting on the second letter in CAGED, A, the next form is the G form, followed by the E form, and so on.

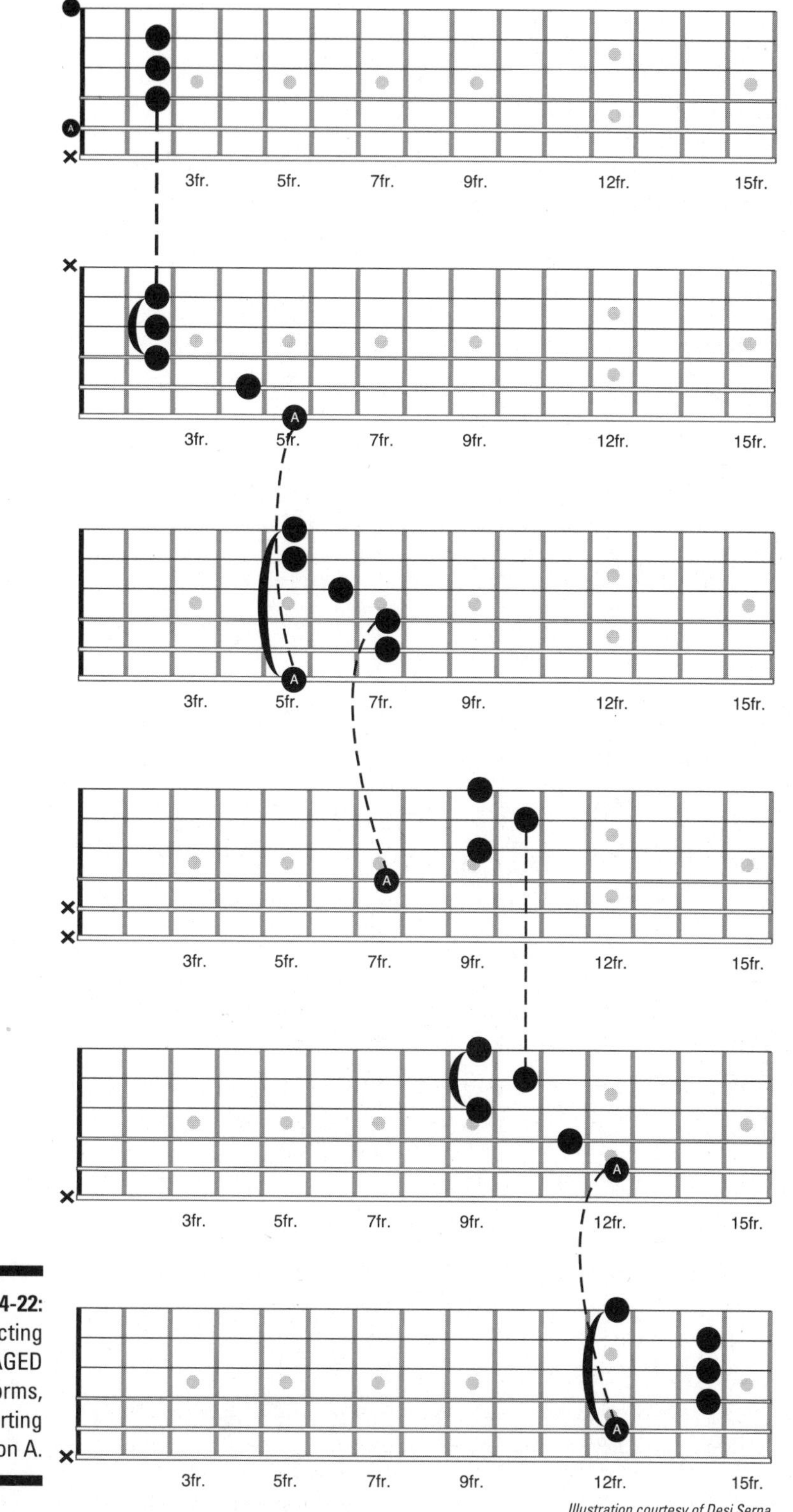

Figure 4-22: Connecting CAGED forms, starting on A.

Illustration courtesy of Desi Serna

Starting on G

With Figure 4-23, you start with a G chord and connect to all its forms.

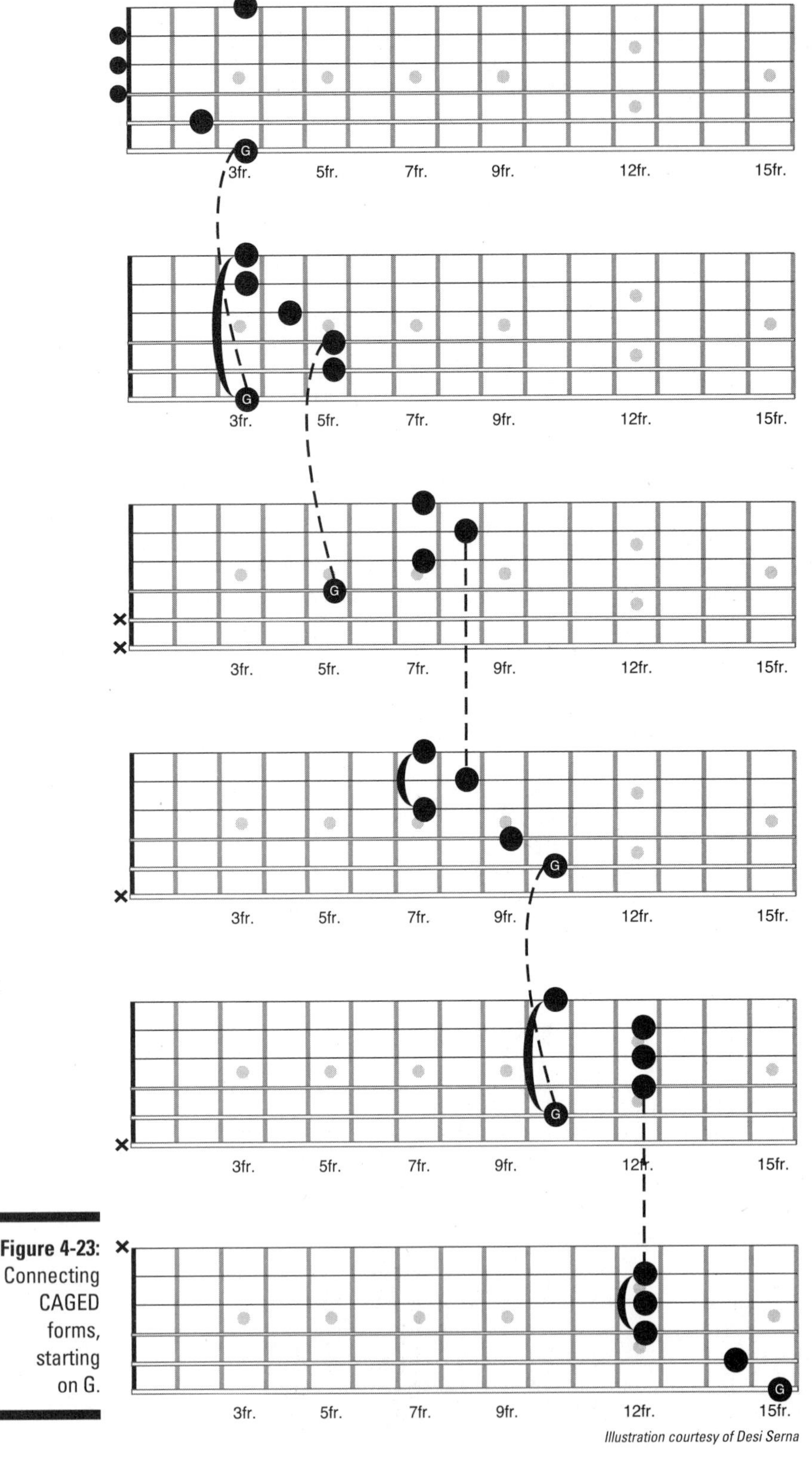

Figure 4-23: Connecting CAGED forms, starting on G.

Illustration courtesy of Desi Serna

Starting on E

Guess what happens in Figure 4-24? Yep, you start with an E chord and connect to all its forms.

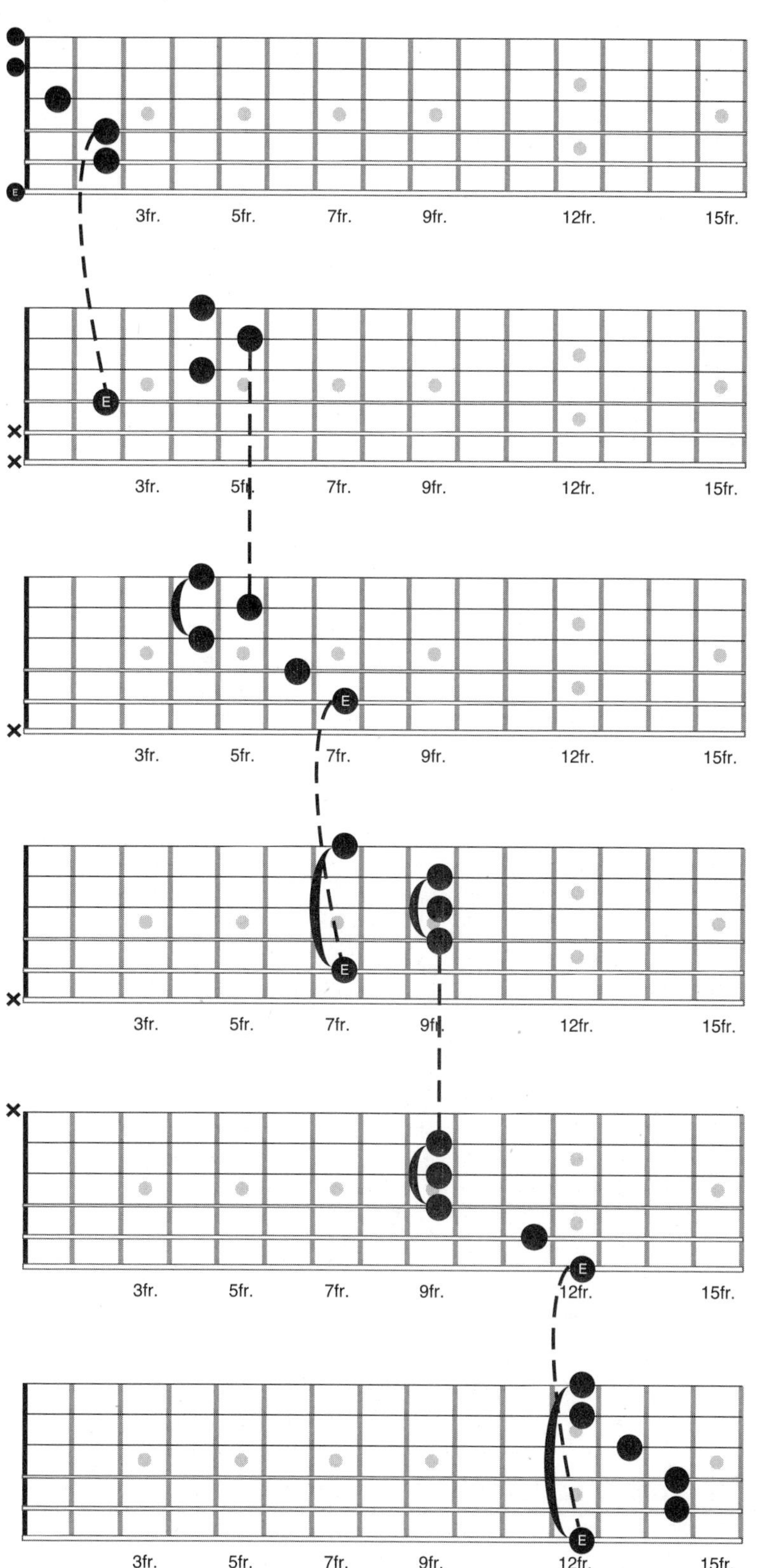

Figure 4-24: Connecting CAGED forms, starting on E.

Starting on D

Figure 4-25 shows the last chord that I start you from in this chapter, D. But don't stop here! Try exploring other possibilities on your own. For example, start on an F, F♯, B, B♭, E♭, and so on. Whichever form you start on, the other forms of the same chord always follow the letters in CAGED. Not to mention, the forms always connect in the same manner that I illustrate for you with the dotted lines between diagrams.

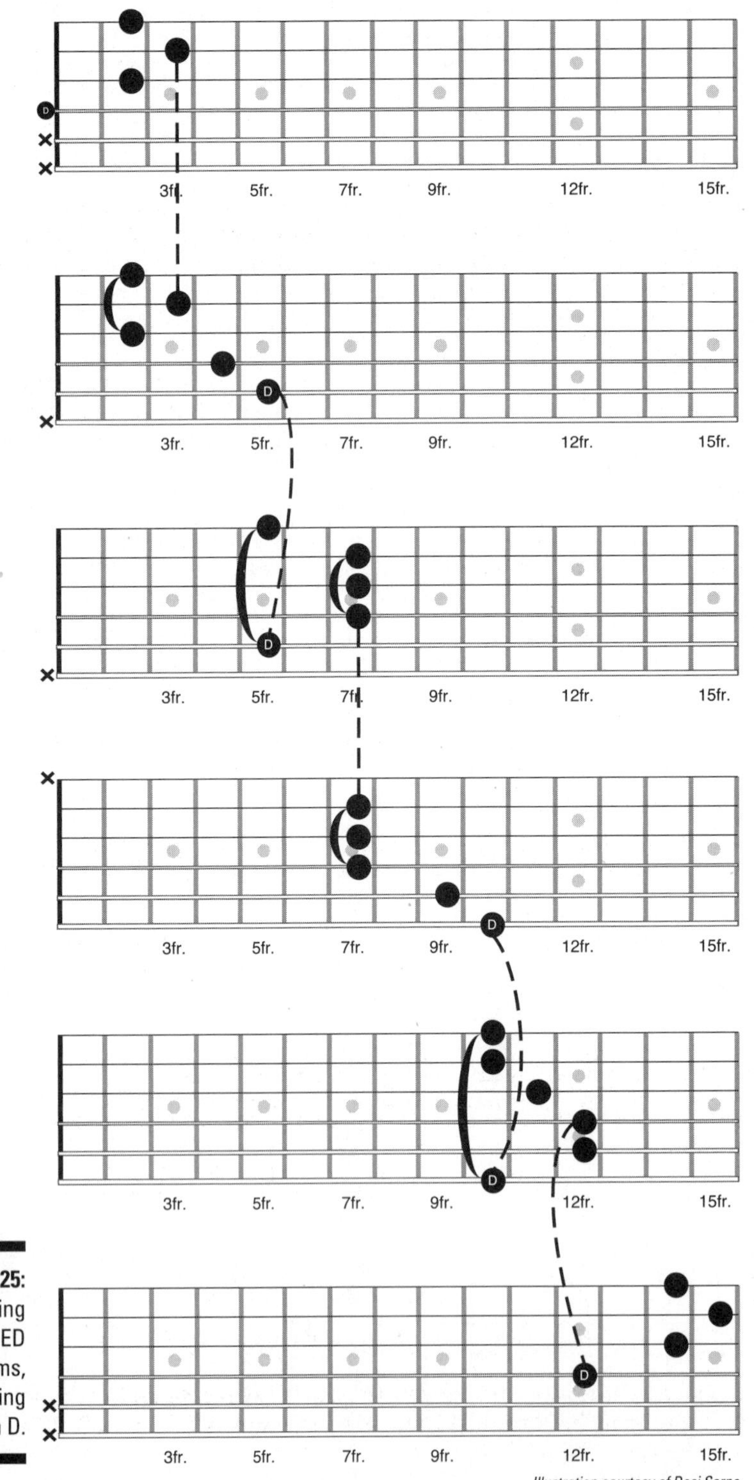

Figure 4-25: Connecting CAGED forms, starting on D.

Illustration courtesy of Desi Serna

Sample CAGED Chord Changes

CAGED forms always appear together with other forms. So after you know how to play all the forms, you're ready to combine them to play a set of sample chord changes. The chord changes you see in this section are based on the chords and progression shown in Figure 4-26.

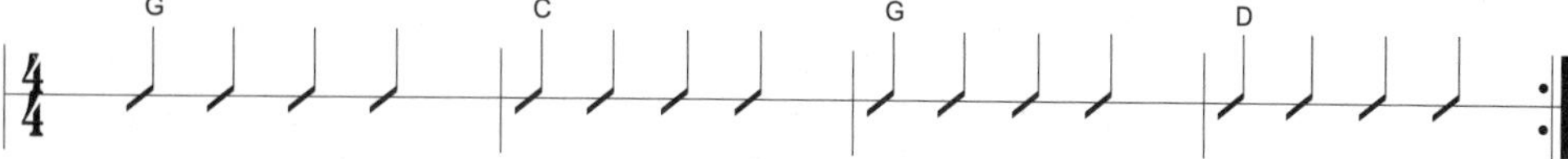

Figure 4-26: G chord progression.

Illustration courtesy of Desi Serna

This figure shows a typical three-chord progression in the key of G. For reference, "Brown Eyed Girl" by Van Morrison is based on a similar chord progression. With the most basic approach, the progression is played using common open chords or standard E form and A form barre chords. Try strumming these chords with one of those options now. Then, move on to the next figure to make it more interesting with different chord voicings.

The following three examples, starting with Figure 4-27, use a variety of CAGED forms for G, C, and D following the chord progression shown in Figure 4-26. Each example covers a different position. Each position has three parts, each one on a different set of strings and each one played differently to add even more variety.

Note: Remember to visualize how chord fragments fit into their full forms.

Figure 4-27: CAGED chord changes — Round 1.

Illustration courtesy of Desi Serna

Watch Video Clip 7 to see how to play through the example in Figure 4-27.

Though each shape is labeled with a chord name that properly reflects its bass note, don't let this information distract you. Instead, just think of everything as G, C, and D. That would be the letters before the slash.

Figure 4-28 shows the same chord progression played in a new position.

Figure 4-28: CAGED chord changes — Round 2.

Illustration courtesy of Desi Serna

Figure 4-29 illustrates one final example in a 3rd position.

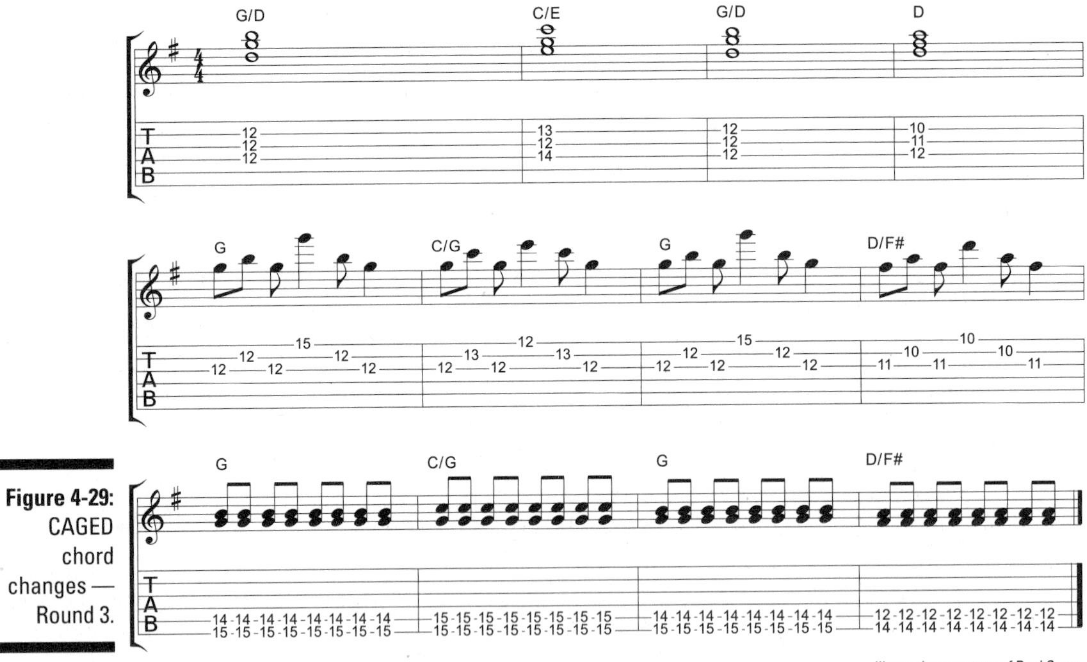

Figure 4-29: CAGED chord changes — Round 3.

Illustration courtesy of Desi Serna

You can certainly find many more ways to play these chords, but these three progressions give you plenty to work on for now. A great way to practice these chord changes is to play right along with a song like "Brown Eyed Girl." You can also make a multi-track recording of yourself playing and combining the different parts.

Playing Minor CAGED Forms

Just as you use the CAGED arpeggios to form major chord voicings (see the preceding sections), you can do the same with minor arpeggios. In this section, you lower all the 3rds in each arpeggio pattern to minor 3rds (♭3rds). This simple adjustment changes everything from major to minor. You then fret and play different kinds of minor chord voicings with each of the five minor CAGED forms.

Adding the minor CAGED forms to the majors is a lot to pile on your plate, especially if all the major forms haven't yet sunk in completely. I suggest working through this next section very slowly, possibly even saving the minor forms for another time.

Playing the C minor form

Figure 4-30a shows the original C form (major). Compare that to Figure 4-30b, which shows the Cm form (the *m* stands for minor). As you can see from the figure, the Cm form uses the same arpeggio pattern as the C form except with minor 3rds. Figures 4-30c and 4-30d show some sample minor chord voicings. Notice that the actual chord in this position is Dm. In fact, Figure 4-30d is part of a basic open Dm chord that's a commonly used shape all over the neck. Remember to only play the black dots in examples like this.

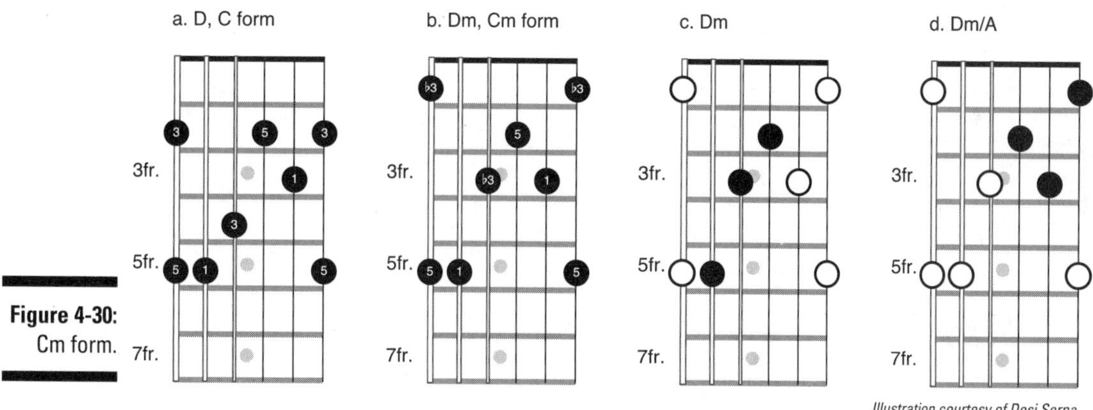

Figure 4-30: Cm form.

Playing the A minor form

Figure 4-31a shows the original A form, while Figure 4-31b shows the same arpeggio pattern with minor 3rds — or the Am form. In this position, the actual chords are C and C minor. Figure 4-31c illustrates a commonly used minor chord voicing. Notice that it's a standard minor barre chord. This barre chord is often reduced to only strings 1 to 3, as shown in Figure 4-31d.

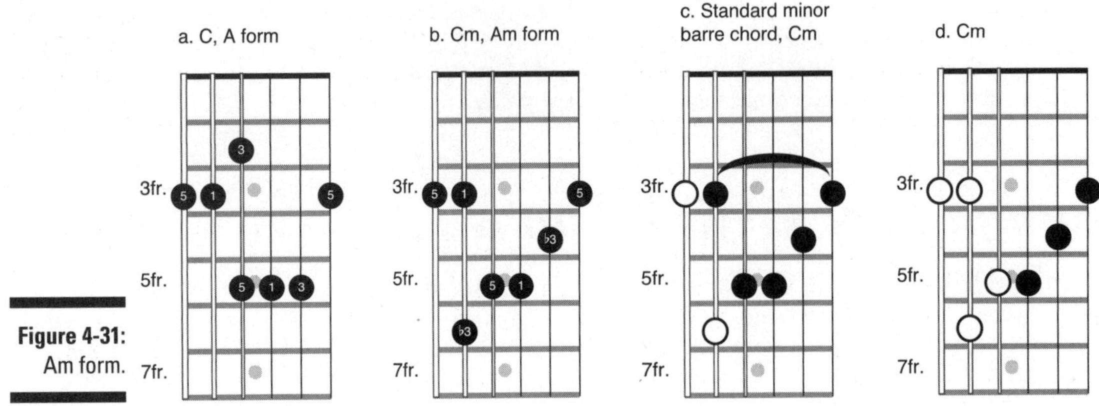

Figure 4-31: Am form.

Playing the G minor form

In Figure 4-32a, you see the original G form, followed by the same arpeggio pattern with minor 3rds (or Gm form) in Figure 4-32b. In this position, the actual chords are A and A minor. Figure 4-32c shows you one way to get a useable barre chord out of it. Figure 4-32d shows a unique Dm in Gm form that appears in the song "So Much to Say" by Dave Matthews Band.

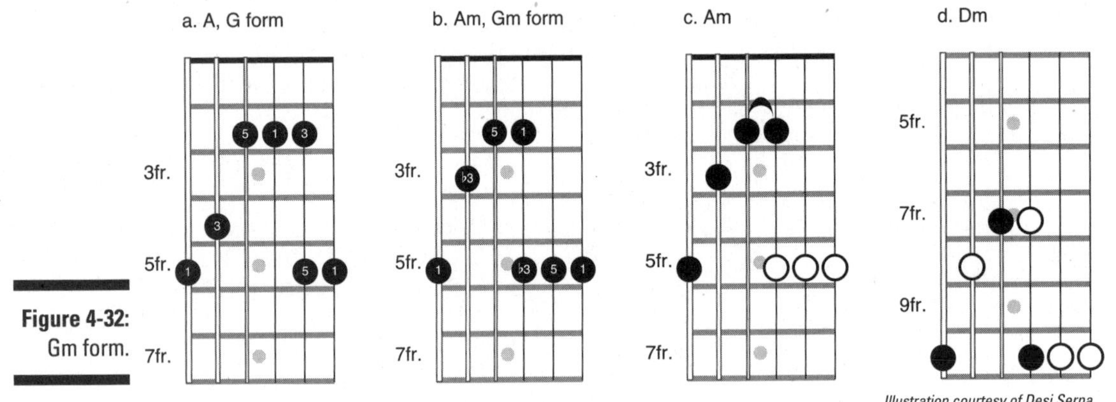

Figure 4-32: Gm form.

Playing the E minor form

Figure 4-33a illustrates the original E form, while Figure 4-33b shows the same arpeggio pattern with minor 3rds (or Em form). In this position, the actual chords are G and G minor. Figure 4-33c shows a sample minor chord voicing, which is a standard minor barre chord. This barre chord is often reduced to just strings 1 through 3, as shown in Figure 4-33d.

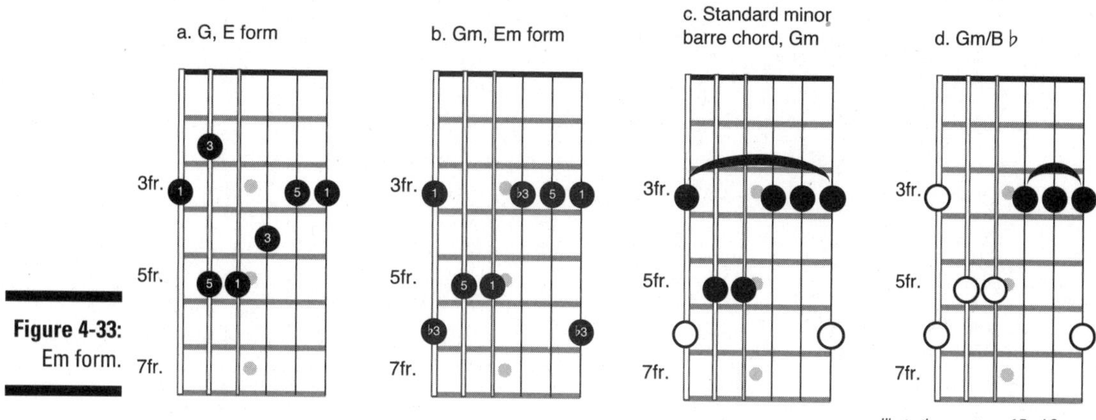

Figure 4-33: Em form.

Illustration courtesy of Desi Serna

Playing the D minor form

Figure 4-34a illustrates the original D form, followed by the same arpeggio pattern with minor 3rds (Dm form), shown in Figure 4-34b. In this position, the actual chords are F and F minor. Figure 4-34c shows a sample minor chord voicing, which is a full Dm shape when played in the open position. Notice that this shape shares a lot in common with the Cm form (see the earlier section for details on the C form).

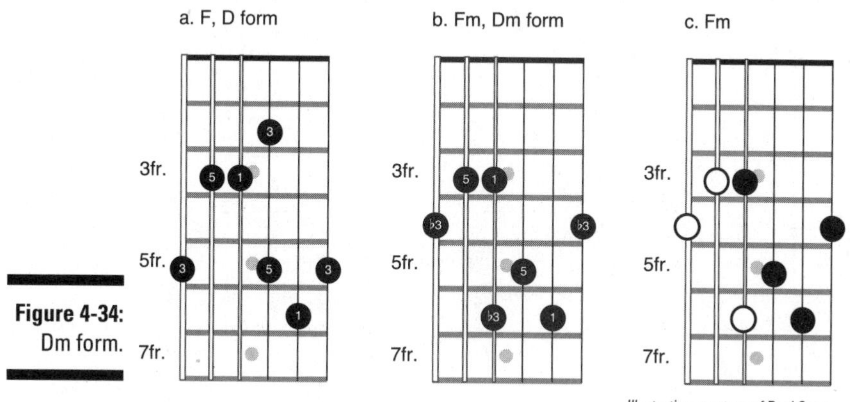

Figure 4-34: Dm form.

Illustration courtesy of Desi Serna

Connecting the Five Minor CAGED Forms

The five minor CAGED forms connect just as the five major ones do (see the section "Connecting the Five CAGED Forms" for details). Figure 4-35 shows one example of how to connect the five minor forms, starting on a Cm form, Dm. Here, the whole minor arpeggio patterns are shown; the black dots indicate the most commonly used chord voicings. Focus on the black dots as you play through this exercise. Then work through the same exercise, starting on other minor chords, on your own.

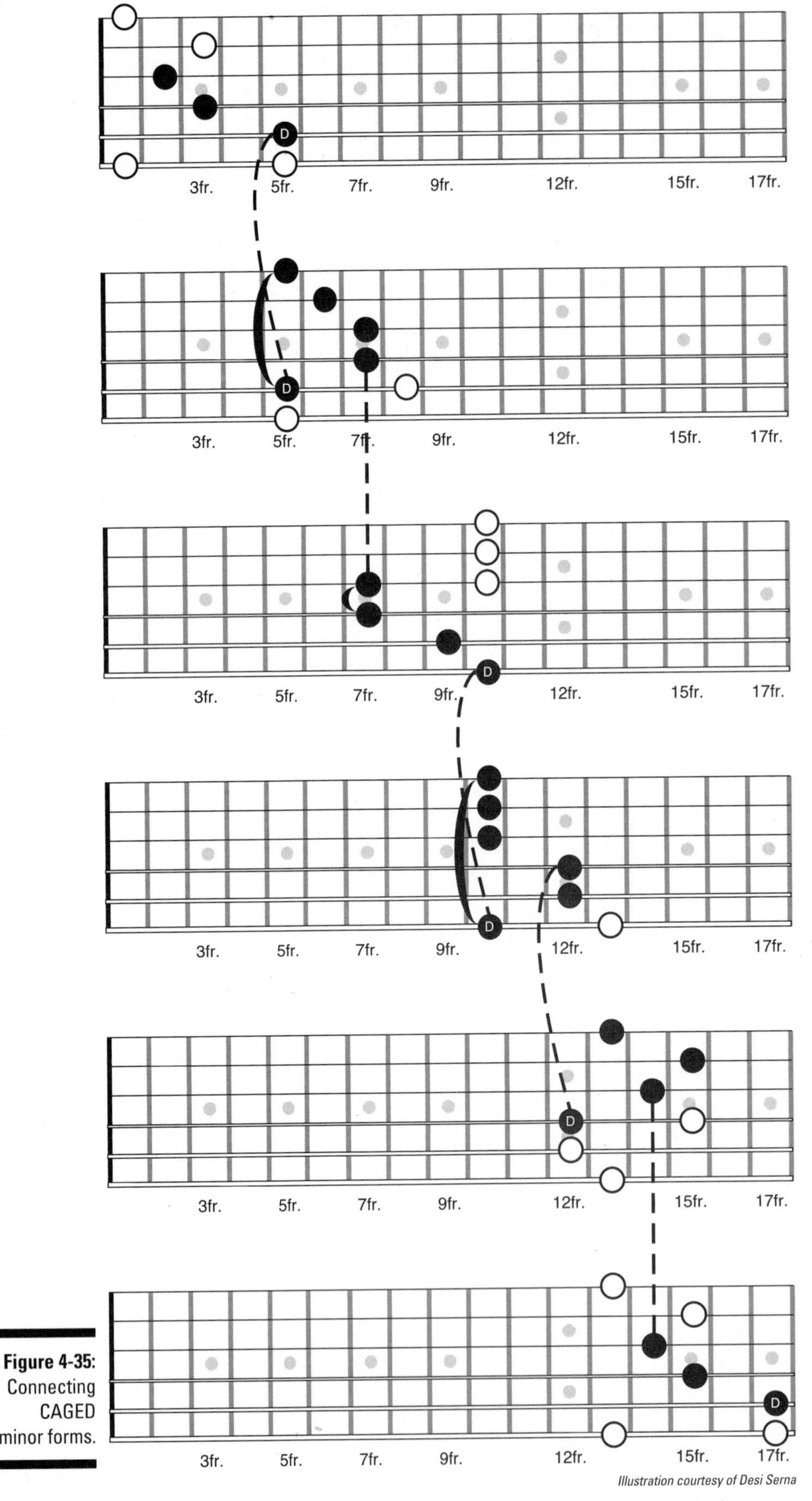

Figure 4-35: Connecting CAGED minor forms.

Illustration courtesy of Desi Serna

Minor CAGED Chord Changes

In this section, you play a sample chord progression that uses different minor CAGED forms (see Figure 4-36). The chord progression is based in the key of A natural minor using the chords Am, Dm, and Em. Every four bars the same chord changes are repeated but in a different position using different voicings. You touch on four positions in all with the fourth one being an octave higher than where you start in the open position. Slashes are used to reflect the alternate bass notes of some of the chord forms, but you can ignore them and just focus on the primary chords written before the slashes.

In terms of using minor chord forms to play chord progressions, you certainly have many more possibilities than what you see in Figure 4-36, and you can mix minor forms with major ones (as many of the songs referenced in this chapter do), but this example is enough to get you started.

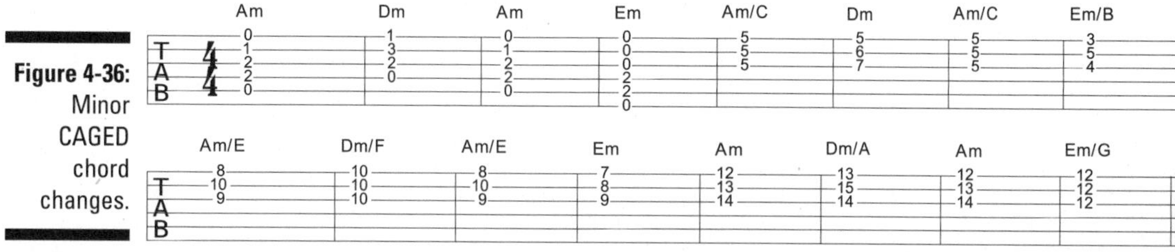

Figure 4-36: Minor CAGED chord changes.

Illustration courtesy of Desi Serna

I recommend that you try playing along with the song "Maria, Maria" by Santana, which is based on a progression using the same chords shown in Figure 4-36. You don't need to learn the actual guitar parts in the song. Instead, just play along with the music by following the chord changes with different minor CAGED forms.

Chapter 5

Adding Chord Tones and Extensions to Chords

In This Chapter

- Discovering added chord tones and extensions
- Getting to know 2nds, 4ths, 6ths, 7ths, 9ths, 11ths, and 13ths
- Playing "sus" and "add" chords
- Using 6ths to play blues shuffles
- Producing harmony with pedal points

Chords are constructed from roots, 3rds, and 5ths. These intervals come from the major scale where the scale degrees produce different triads, some major and some minor (and one diminished). Guitar players add chord tones and extensions to triads by incorporating other degrees from the major scale. These added scale degrees include 2nds, 4ths, 6ths, 7ths, 9ths, 11ths, and 13ths.

In this chapter, you break away from the standard major and minor chords to play new chords with more depth and color. You get to know what the little numbers next to chord names mean and how you can form new chord shapes. Finally, you get some practice playing pedal point, a technique that adds more harmony to chord changes.

Rather than have you play all the chord types that are taught in traditional theory, I use this chapter to focus you on chords that guitarists typically use in popular music. Of course, I don't cover every single chord type that you may come across, but I give you enough examples so that you can begin to make sense of other types of chords when you encounter them.

Listen to Audio Track 5 to hear some examples of chord tones, extensions, and pedal point plus get an overview of what this chapter is all about.

About Chord Tones and Extensions

Before you get started playing new types of chords, some preliminary information about chord construction and naming convention is in order. This is not a comprehensive explanation of the whole subject, but it's enough to prep you for the rest of the chapter where many more details are revealed.

You go beyond playing triad-based chords by adding in the degrees of the major scale other than 1, 3, and 5. These added *chord tones* are the 2nd, 4th, 6th, and 7th.

Sometimes chord tones extend an octave above the 7th. In this case, the chord tones are called *extensions* and are numbered to reflect their position in the register above the first seven degrees of the scale. For example, 2 becomes 9, 4 becomes 11, and 6 becomes 13.

G	A	B	C	D	E	F♯	G	A	B	C	D	E	F♯
1	2	3	4	5	6	7	8	9	10	11	12	13	14

In music theory, 1, 3, 5, and 7 are always counted the same regardless of register. Only 2, 4, and 6 get renumbered when they extend beyond the 7th. And they only get renumbered once. Transpose them up additional octaves and their numbers don't increase.

When an extension like 9, 11, or 13 is present in a chord, then the 7th is supposed to be included too, plus any extensions before the one in the chord name. For example:

G major: 1-3-5, G-B-D

Gmaj7: 1-3-5-7, G-B-D-F♯

Gmaj9: 1-3-5-7-9, G-B-D-F♯-A

Gmaj11: 1-3-5-7-9-11, G-B-D-F♯-A-C

Gmaj13: 1-3-5-7-9-11-13, G-B-D-F♯-A-C-E

But, this isn't always the way it's done, as you soon see.

If an extension is added to a triad, but the 7th and other extensions aren't also included, the term *add* is used. For example:

G: 1-3-5, G-B-D

Gadd9: 1-3-5-9, G-B-D-A

Gadd11: 1-3-5-11, G-B-D-C

Gadd13: 1-3-5-13, G-B-D-E

Moving onto sus chords, because of their proximity to the 3rd, 2 and 4 often replace the 3rd. When this happens, the chord becomes *suspended* and the abbreviation *sus* appears in the name. For example:

G: 1-3-5, G-B-D

Gsus2: 1-2-5, G-A-D

Gsus4: 1-4-5, G-C-D

The lack of a 3rd in sus chords creates an open, unresolved sound.

If a 2 or 4 is added but the 3rd remains, then the term *add* is used. For example:

Gadd2: 1-2-3-5, G-A-B-D

Gadd4: 1-3-4-5, G-B-C-D

But, remember, 2nds and 9ths are the same. So are 4ths and 11ths. So you may see the chords above stacked and written as follows:

Gadd9: 1-3-5-9, G-B-D-A

Gadd11: 1-3-5-11, G-B-D-C

Notice that these chords use the very same notes as the chords before them. The only difference is in how the notes are stacked and the chords named. But guitar players often stack chord members out of order anyway, so it's hard to follow a strict convention. As a result, 2nds and 9ths and 4ths and 11ths are often used interchangeably.

Guitarists not only need to rearrange chord members at times but also leave some out in order to make a chord shape physically playable and pleasant sounding. This is especially true as you add more chord tones and extensions.

For example, a major 13th chord is supposed to be stacked 1-3-5-7-9-11-13. You don't have enough fingers and strings for that! Obviously, something has to go. In cases like this, you at least try to retain the 3rd, the 7th, and the extension that the chord is named after. So a Gmaj13 might be played 1-3-7-13, 1-7-3-13, or some such combination.

Adding 7ths to the Major Scale Chords

You begin playing new chords by adding 7ths to major scale chords. Adding 7ths is a good place to start because it's in keeping with the consecutive 3rds formula that triads follow (1-3-5-7 are all consecutive 3rds). Plus, you can easily add 7ths without needing to suspend a 3rd or interfere with the rest of the triad. Using the G major scale and its basic triads as a starting place, you add a 7th to each chord by counting up seven from each scale degree.

Figure 5-1 includes seven diagrams, all with the same notes from the G major scale. Each diagram counts from a different starting point so you can see the 7th of each scale degree. Starting points and 7ths are shown in black. The starting points are the roots to each triad/chord in the scale. You add the 7ths to the basic triads to create 7th chords.

A 7th is a 3rd above a 5th and keeps with the 3rds sequence used to build the basic triads. In the major scale, counting 1-2-3 is a 3rd, but so are 3-4-5 and 5-6-7. In all, you build a 7th chord by using the intervals 1-3-5-7, which are all a 3rd apart.

There are two types of 7th intervals. One type — the *major 7th* — is almost an octave, missing it by just a half step and named after the type of 7th that occurs in the major scale. You see major 7ths on G and C in Figure 5-1. The other type — a *minor* or *♭7th* — misses the octave by a whole step and is named by the type of 7th that occurs in a minor scale. You see minor 7ths on A, B, D, and E in the same figure. You may be wondering why the 5th scale degree has a minor 7th when it produces a major triad and chord. More on this in a moment!

The following list shows what the basic major and minor triads in G look like after you add 7ths to create 7th chords. The notations in parentheses illustrate the most common ways to write the chord names. (Find out how to use triads to play plain major and minor chords in Chapter 3.)

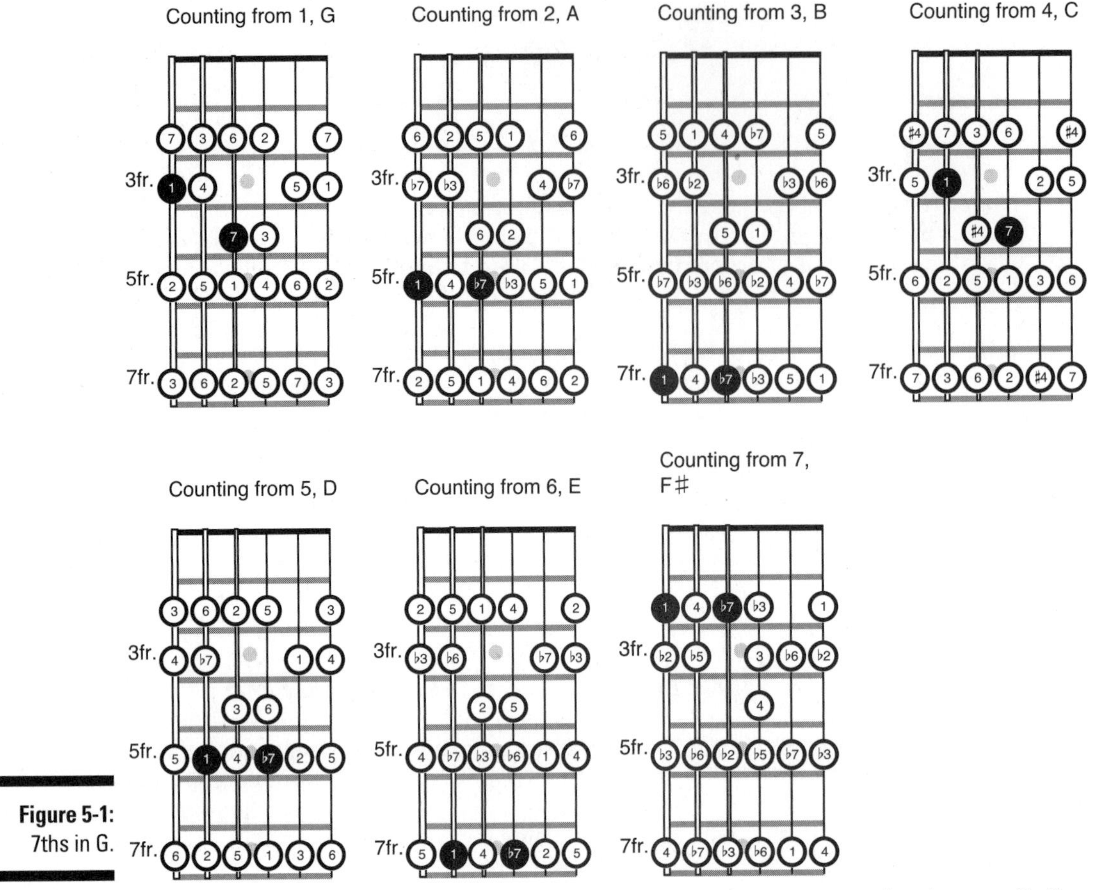

Figure 5-1: 7ths in G.

Illustration courtesy of Desi Serna

- **G:** 1-3-5-7, G-B-D-F♯, G major 7 (Gmaj7, GM7, GΔ)
- **A:** 1-♭3-5-♭7, A-C-E-G, A minor 7 (Amin7, Am7, A-7)
- **B:** 1-♭3-5-♭7, B-D-F♯-A, B minor 7 (Bmin7, Bm7, B-7)
- **C:** 1-3-5-7, C-E-G-B, C major 7 (Cmaj7, CM7, CΔ)
- **D:** 1-3-5-♭7, D-F♯-A-C, D dominant 7 (D7)
- **E:** 1-♭3-5-♭7, E-B-G-D, E minor 7 (Emin7, Em7, E-7)
- **F♯:** 1-♭3-♭5-♭7, F♯-A-C-E, F♯ minor 7♭5, half diminished 7th (F♯min7♭5, F♯m7♭5, F♯-7♭5, F♯ø)

When you add the 7ths in the preceding list to standard major and minor barre chords (E form and A form; see Chapter 4), you get the new chord shapes shown in Figure 5-2. In this example and all the rest in this chapter, the numbers represent intervals, which are important to look at so that you see how each chord shape is constructed. You're on your own to work out fingerings, but your fingers will easily fall into place with these chord shapes. Try playing forward and backward through the scale with 7th chords.

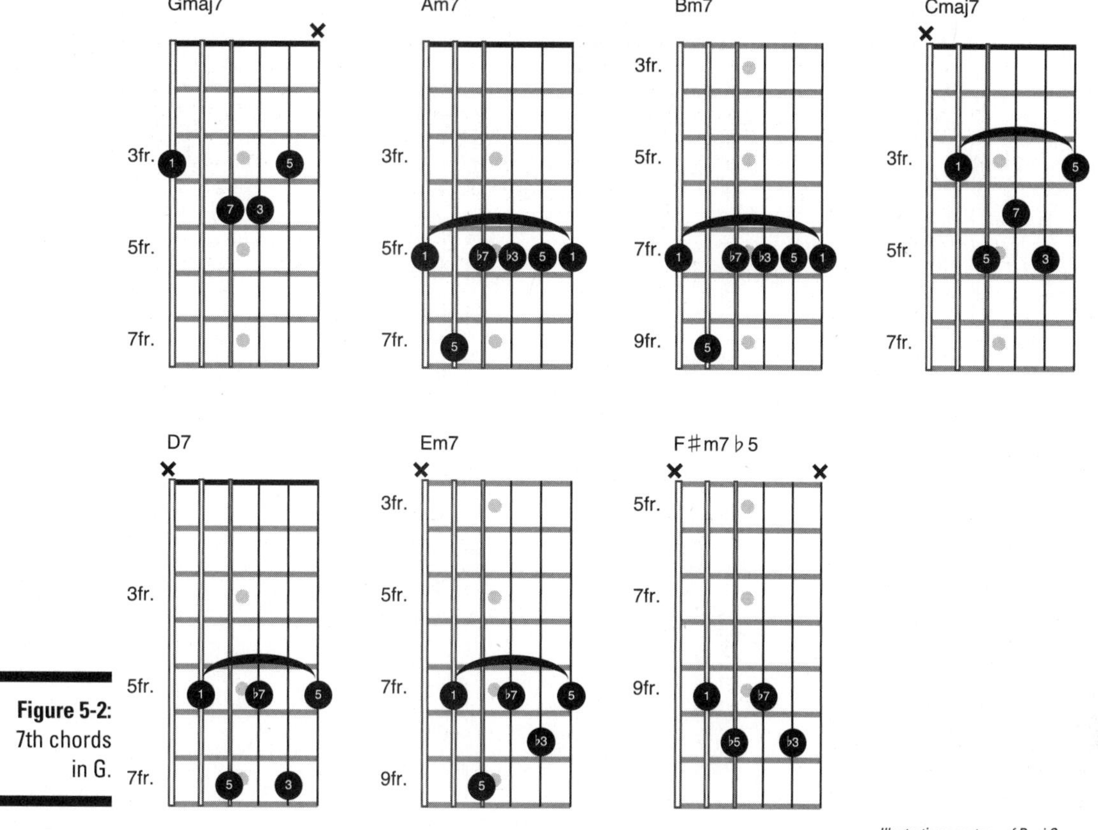

Figure 5-2: 7th chords in G.

Illustration courtesy of Desi Serna

PLAY THIS!

Watch Video Clip 8 to hear and see 7th chords in G.

You can also play through 7th chords in the open position, as shown in Figure 5-3. Again, the numbers represent intervals. Work out your own fingerings.

The 7th chord sequence in the G major scale is the same in all major scales. All major scales naturally produce maj7 chords on their 1st degrees, m7 chords on their 2nd degrees, and so on.

Figures 5-4 through 5-6 include tab with 7th chords in the keys of A, C, and D. With each key, you get to know some new 7th chord shapes. In most cases, you can figure out where the 7th is in each shape by playing the regular major or minor form first, then switching to the 7th chord. The new note that's added to make the chord shape a 7th is the 7th! You can move these shapes away from the open position and use them as full or partial barre chords to play 7th chords for other notes around the fretboard.

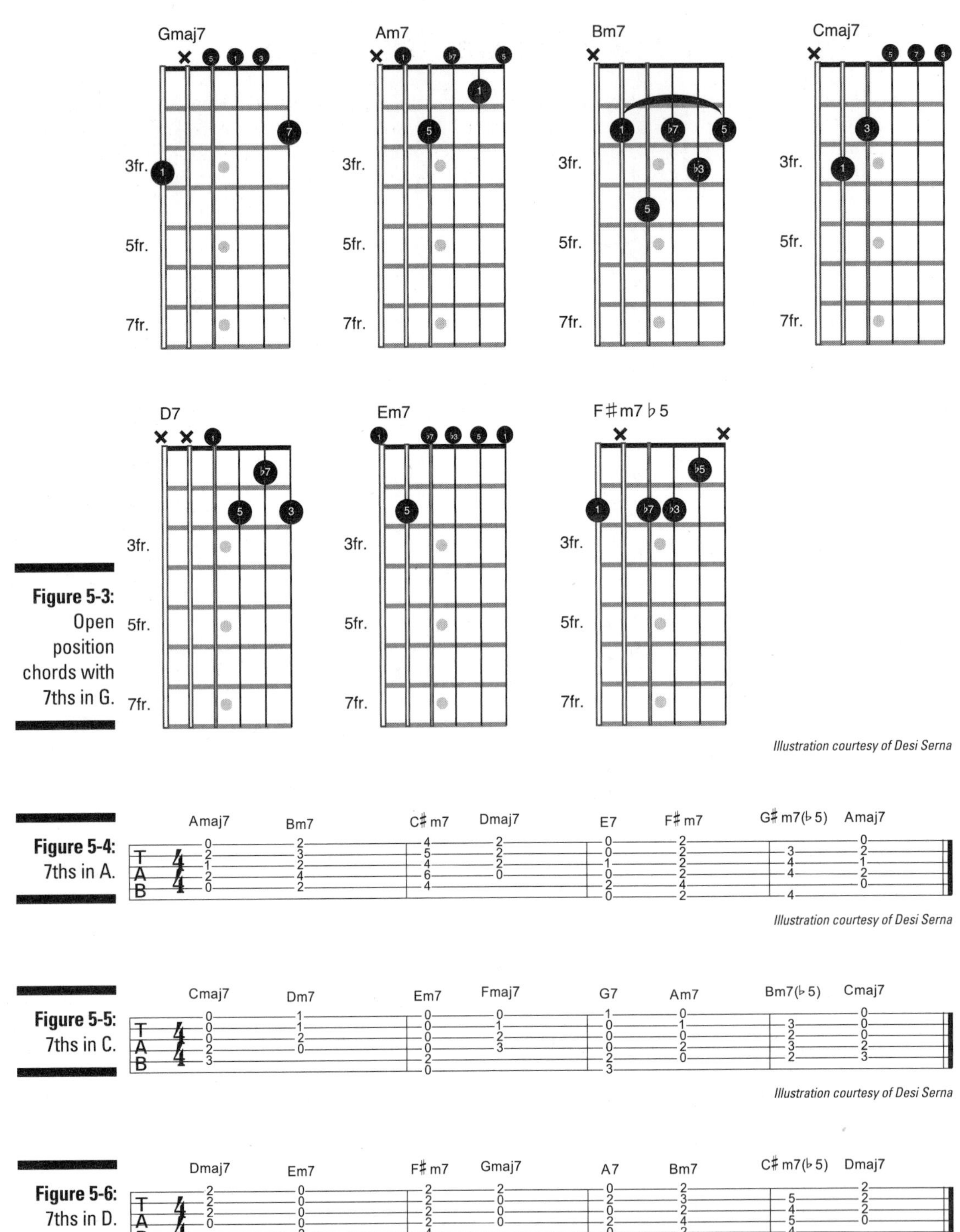

Figure 5-3: Open position chords with 7ths in G.

Illustration courtesy of Desi Serna

Figure 5-4: 7ths in A.

Illustration courtesy of Desi Serna

Figure 5-5: 7ths in C.

Illustration courtesy of Desi Serna

Figure 5-6: 7ths in D.

Illustration courtesy of Desi Serna

Playing major and minor 7th chords

As you can see in all the previous figures, there's more than one way to put together a 7th chord shape. Figure 5-7 shows a few more m7 examples, namely variations on the open Em7 and Am7 forms. Expect to see these shapes used elsewhere on the fretboard as full or partial barre chords. To understand why these variations work, look at the intervals to see how they appear in multiple locations.

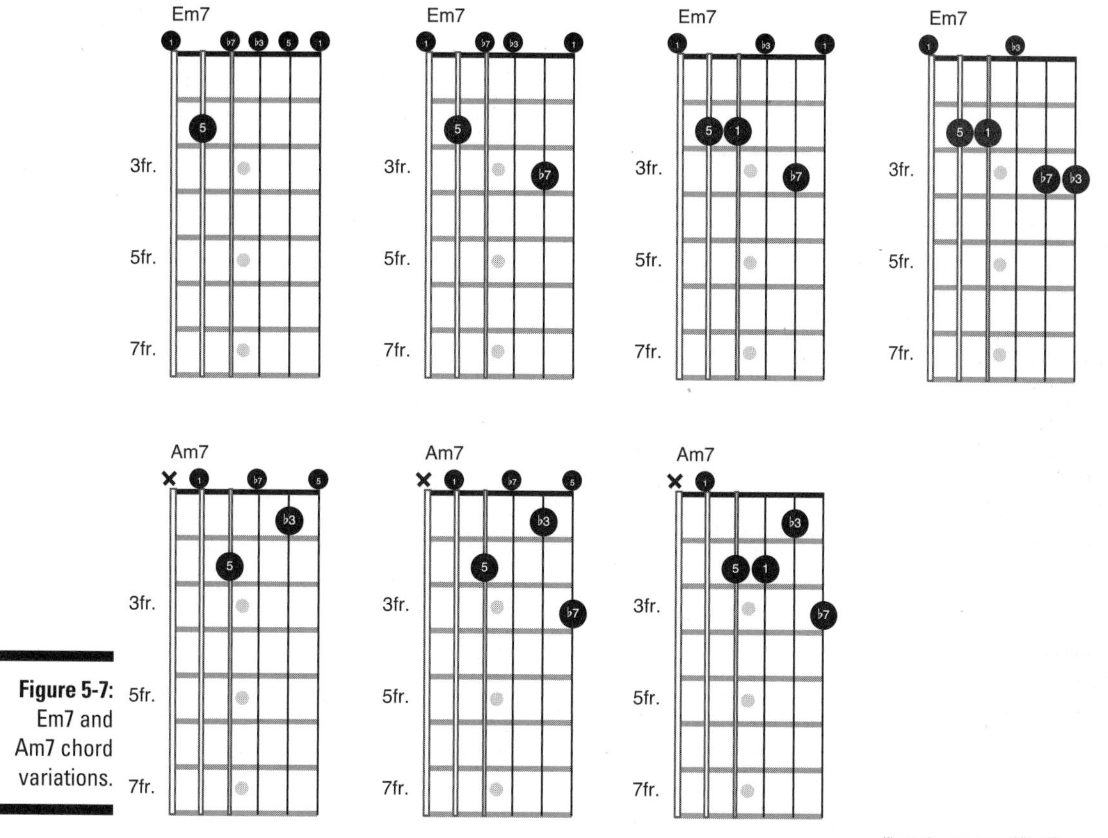

Figure 5-7: Em7 and Am7 chord variations.

Illustration courtesy of Desi Serna

The following songs all feature some type of maj7 chord.

"Across the Universe" by The Beatles

"Band on the Run" by Wings

"Best of My Love" by the Eagles

"Californication" by Red Hot Chili Peppers

"Don't Know Why" Norah Jones

"Dreams" by Fleetwood Mac

"Dust in the Wind" by Kansas

"Everyday" by Dave Matthews Band

"Fire and Rain" by James Taylor

"Hold Your Head Up" by Argent

"I Can't Tell You Why" by the Eagles

"Just Remember I Love You" by Firefall

"One" by U2

"Ooh Baby Baby" by Linda Ronstadt

"Plush" by Stone Temple Pilots

"Riviera Paradise" by Stevie Ray Vaughan

"Serenade" by Steve Miller Band

"Show Me the Way" by Peter Frampton

"Solsbury Hill" by Peter Gabriel

"Space Oddity" by David Bowie

"Stairway to Heaven" by Led Zeppelin

"Ten Years Gone" by Led Zeppelin

"These Eyes" by The Guess Who

"This Guy's in Love with You" by Herb Alpert

"Typical Situation" by Dave Matthews Band

"Tighten Up, Pt. 1" by Archie Bell and the Drells

"Under the Bridge" by Red Hot Chili Peppers

"Ventura Highway" by America

"What It's Like" by Everlast

"You've Got a Friend" by James Taylor

As you work through the song lists in this chapter, keep in mind that some examples may include other types of chords in addition to the chords that pertain to the particular list. You get introduced to more chord types as you progress through the chapter. You may want to revisit the songs in each list after you finish this chapter.

The following songs all feature some type of m7 chord:

"Black Water" by The Doobie Brothers

"Cold Shot" by Stevie Ray Vaughan

"Daughters" by John Mayer

"Fly Like an Eagle" by Steve Miller Band

"The Hook" by Blues Traveler

"It's Too Late" by Carole King

"Jump, Jive an' Wail" by Brian Setzer Orchestra

"Let It Ride" by Bachman-Turner Overdrive

"Let's Stay Together" by Al Green

"Long Train Running" by The Doobie Brothers

"Oye Como Va" by Santana

"Say It Ain't So" by Weezer

"Tears in Heaven" by Eric Clapton

"Wish You Were Here" by Pink Floyd

"Wonderwall" by Oasis

"You Ain't Seen Nothin' Yet" by Bachman-Turner Overdrive

Playing dominant 7th chords

The three major chords in the major scale occur on the 1st, 4th, and 5th scale degrees. You know these chords by number as I, IV, and V. In the key of G, these chords are G, C, and D. You may expect them all to make similar major 7th chords, but they don't. G and C have a major 7th, but D has a flat or minor 7th.

A major triad with a minor 7th is technically called a *dominant 7th,* but, and this is where things get confusing, it's simply referred to as a *7th.* You always have to specify major 7th chords as maj7, but you can simply use "7" to label dominant 7ths. In other words, if a 7 by itself follows a letter name, then that chord is dominant (a major triad with a minor 7th). So in the G major scale, the three major chords with 7ths become Gmaj7, Cmaj7, and D7.

The dominant 7th chord naturally occurs on chord V in the major scale.

Dominant 7th chords are extremely common in music. You see some of the most popular forms along with their intervals in Figure 5-8. Keep in mind that you can move these shapes around to produce dominant 7th chords for other notes.

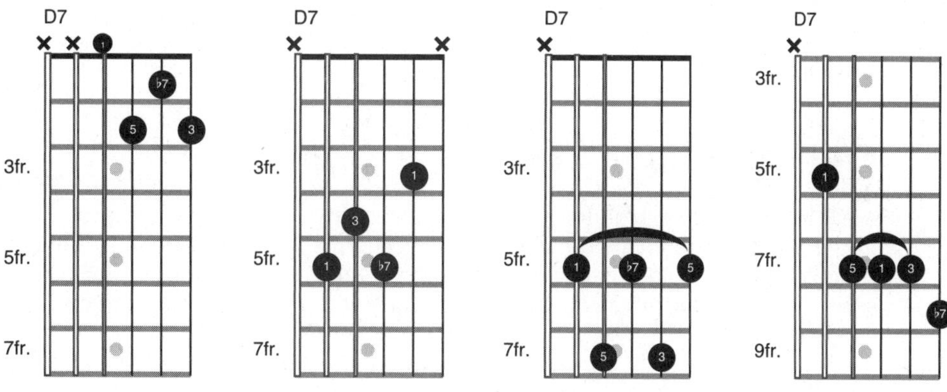

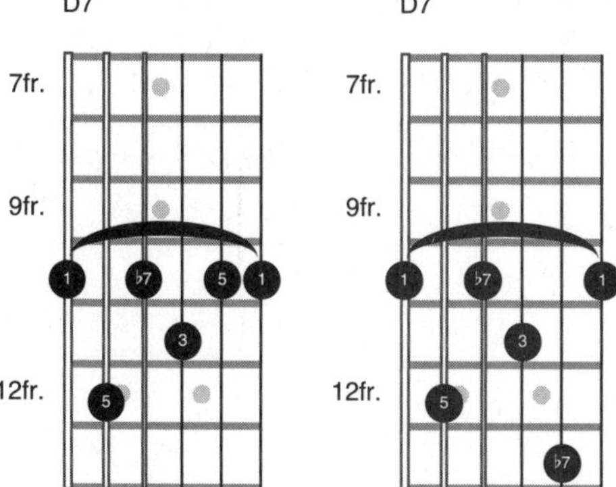

Figure 5-8: D dominant 7ths.

Illustration courtesy of Desi Serna

The following songs all feature some form of dominant 7th chord:

"Alive" by Pearl Jam

"Black" by Pearl Jam

"Black Horse & the Cherry Tree" by KT Tunstall

"Born On the Bayou" by Creedence Clearwater Revival

"Brown Eyed Girl" by Van Morrison

"Couldn't Stand the Weather" by Stevie Ray Vaughan

"Cowboy" by Kid Rock

"Crossroads (Live at Winterland)" by Cream

"Get Down Tonight" by K.C. and the Sunshine Band

"Margaritaville" by Jimmy Buffet

"No More Mr. Nice Guy" by Alice Cooper

"Nothing Else Matters" by Metallica

"Papa's Got a Brand New Bag" by James Brown

"Pride and Joy" by Stevie Ray Vaughan

"Roadhouse Blues" by The Doors

"Taking Care of Business" by Bachman-Turner Overdrive

"Tears in Heaven" by Eric Clapton

"The Way" by Fastball

"Wild Honey Pie" by The Beatles

Playing minor 7th flat 5 chords

The 7th scale degree produces a chord that requires a little extra explanation. As a triad, it has a root, 3rd, and ♭5th; it's called a *minor ♭5*. Add a 7th and it becomes a *minor 7♭5*. For example, the F♯ in the G major scale becomes F♯m7♭5. You see how to form a m7♭5 chord with the root on the 5th string in Figure 5-2 and with the root on the 6th string in Figure 5-3.

You can also call the minor ♭5 a *diminished triad,* because a ♭5th is also called a *diminished* 5th. Add a 7th and it becomes a *half-diminished* chord. So F♯m7♭5 can also be called F♯ half diminished (F♯ø). Why is it only *half* diminished? Because a fully diminished chord, also called a *diminished 7th*, actually has a double flat 7th (♭♭7). You see and play fully diminished chords in Chapter 10. For now, keep in mind that a diminished triad and a full diminished chord are not completely the same thing. In fact, I prefer to call the 7th triad in the major scale m♭5 to avoid confusing it with a full diminished chord.

The following songs feature a m7♭5 chord (that is, half diminished). Some of them have other types of 7 chords mixed in, too.

"Change the World" by Eric Clapton

"I Will Survive" by Gloria Gaynor

"Smooth" by Santana

"Still Got the Blues" by Gary Moore

Working with 2nds and 9ths

There are many types of chords that include 2nds and 9ths, but the three that you're most likely to encounter are sus2, add9, and 9 chords. You start with the sus2 chord, a chord that has its 3rd replaced or suspended by a 2nd.

Sus2 chords

Sus2 chords are stacked 1-2-5 or some combination thereof. The two most common sus2 chord shapes are based on A and D in the open position, as shown in Figure 5-9, with numbers representing intervals. Notice that neither chord has a 3rd. For this reason, the chords are called sus and the 2nds are still called 2nds even though they extend more than an octave away from the chord roots. You can move these shapes up and play them as full or partial barre chords to produce sus2 chords for other notes.

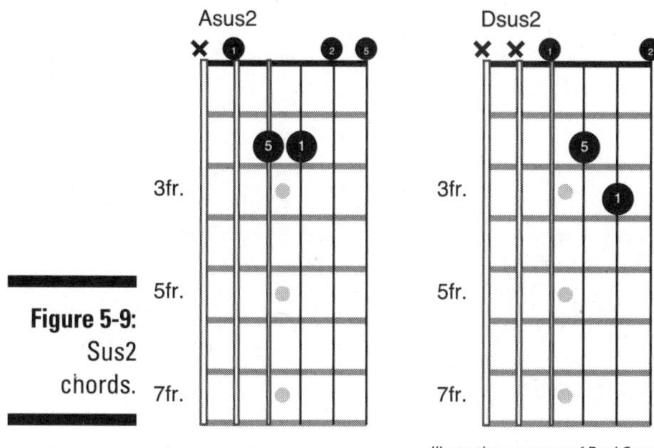

Figure 5-9: Sus2 chords.

Illustration courtesy of Desi Serna

Add9 chords

Technically, an add9 is a 2nd that's extended in the next register and added to a chord that still retains its 3rd. It's supposed to be stacked 1-3-5-9, with the 9th above the 3rd, but you occasionally see it stacked differently on guitar. You may also hear and see this chord identified as an add2. You see common add9 examples in Figure 5-10.

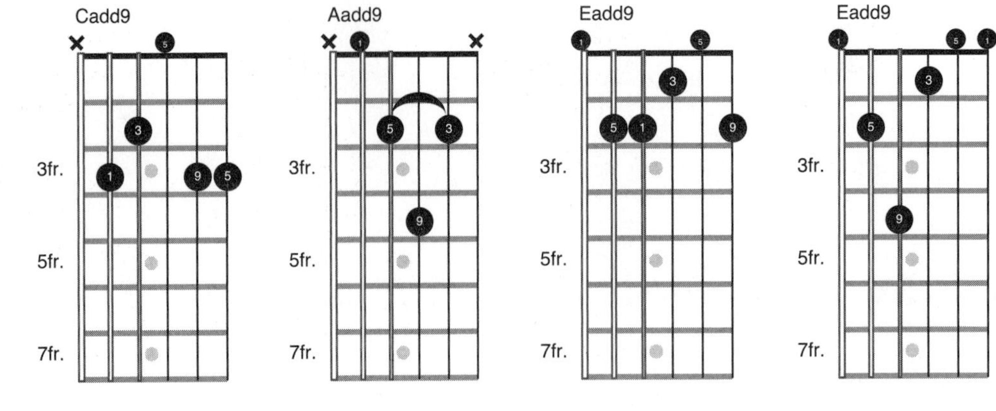

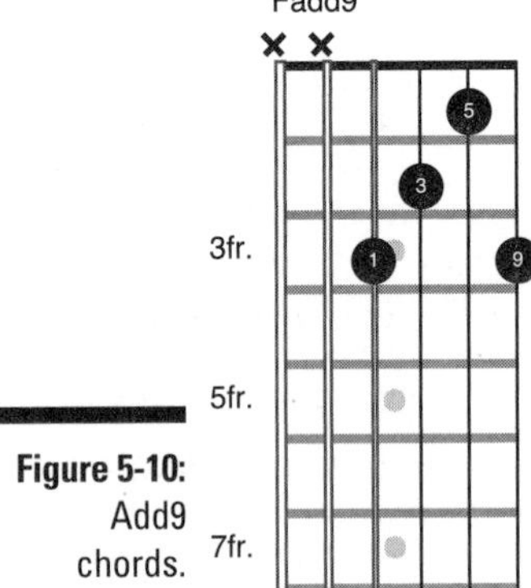

Figure 5-10: Add9 chords.

Illustration courtesy of Desi Serna

Note: Major chords with major 7ths are called *maj7*. When a chord name includes *maj* along with a number other than 7, it's implied that a 7th is also present. For example, a Gmaj9 chord is a Gmaj7 with an added 9th. It's formula is 1-3-5-7-9. (This is different from a Gadd9, 1-3-5-9, which is a plain major triad with an added 9th, no 7th.)

Minor chords with 2nds and 9ths

2nds and 9ths are more likely to be added to major chords, but you occasionally see them in minor chords, too. When a minor 3rd is replaced with a 2nd, the chord is still called a sus2. After all, its formula is still 1-2-5. For example, Am, 1-♭3-5, becomes Asus2, 1-2-5. If you add a 2nd or 9th but retain the minor 3rd, the chord is called minor add9 and is usually written as m(add9). Chords written as m(add9) are some combination of 1-♭3-5-9. Figure 5-11 shows a few examples.

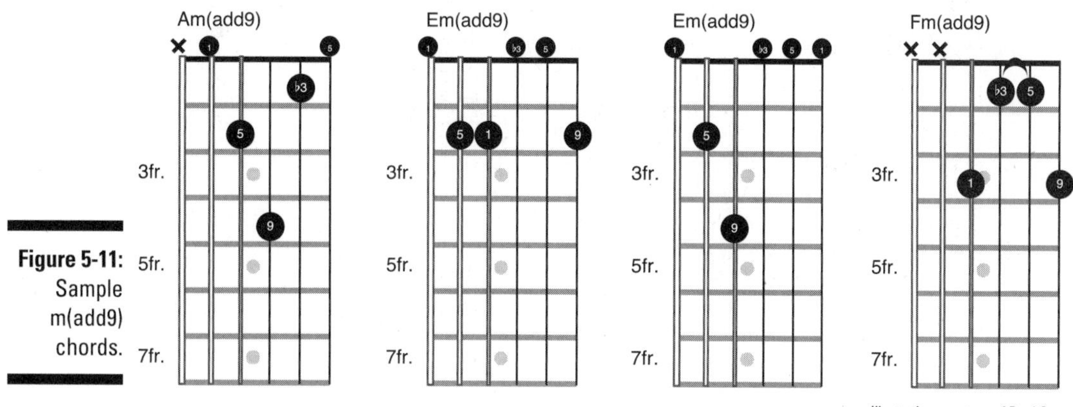

Figure 5-11: Sample m(add9) chords.

Illustration courtesy of Desi Serna

Note: Minor chords with minor 7ths are called *m7*. When a chord name includes *m* along with a number other than 7, it's implied that a 7th is also present. For example, an Em9 chord is an Em7 with an added 9th. Its formula is 1-♭3-5-♭7-9. (This is different from an Em(add9), 1-♭3-5-9, which is a plain minor triad with an added 9th, no 7th.)

Here is a list of songs that each feature at least one major or minor chord as either a sus2 or add9:

"Black Diamond" by Kiss

"Breathe" by Faith Hill

"Castles Made of Sand" by Jimi Hendrix

"Every Breath You Take" by The Police

"Everyday" by Dave Matthews Band

"Fire and Rain" by James Taylor

"Good Riddance (Time of Your Life)" by Green Day

"If I Had $1,000,000" by Barenaked Ladies

"Message in a Bottle" by The Police

"Old Apartment" by Barenaked Ladies

"So Much to Say" by Dave Matthews Band

"Sweet Home Alabama" by Lynyrd Skynyrd

"Talkin' 'Bout a Revolution" by Tracy Chapman

"There She Goes" by Sixpence None the Richer

"What I Am" by Edie Brickell and the New Bohemians

"Wonderwall" by Oasis

Sus2 and add9 chords naturally occur on all but chords iii and vii in the major scale.

9th chords

In addition to add9 and m(add9) chords, you see chords like G9, C9, and D9 in music. When a chord name includes a 9 that isn't preceded by *add, m*, or anything else, then the implied chord is a *dominant* 9th, which is a dominant 7th chord with a 9th (see the earlier section "Playing dominant 7th chords" for details). The formula for 9th chords is 1-3-5-♭7-9. It naturally occurs on chord V in the major scale and is the only type of chord with both a 7th and 9th that regularly occurs in popular music.

Just as dominant 7th chords are represented by only a 7, dominant 9th chords are marked only with a 9. Guitar players frequently use 9th chords, especially in blues music. Figure 5-12 shows a few of the most common shapes. With the G9 shapes, the root notes used for tracking are on the 6th string (shown in the white dots) and not usually played.

As you play complex chords, it's not always possible or practical to include all chord tones. As a result, you often leave some chord members out as seen with the G9/B and G9/F in Figure 5-12, both of which omit the root.

The following songs all feature 9th chords:

"Come On (Part II)" by Jimi Hendrix

"Cult of Personality" by Living Colour

"Jeff's Boogie" by Jeff Beck

"Jump, Jive an' Wail" by Brian Setzer Orchestra

"Oye Como Va" by Santana

"Play that Funky Music" by Wild Cherry

"(They Call It) Stormy Monday" by The Allman Brothers Band

"Tore Down" by Eric Clapton

"Wall of Denial" by Stevie Ray Vaughan

Note: Extended dominant chords are dominant 7th chords with extensions added. They include the 7th and all extensions leading up to the number in the chord name. So D11 is 1-3-5-♭7-9-11 and D13 is 1-3-5-♭7-9-11-13. Because guitar players can't stack chords like this, if these chords occur at all, they're played as fragments with some chord members left out.

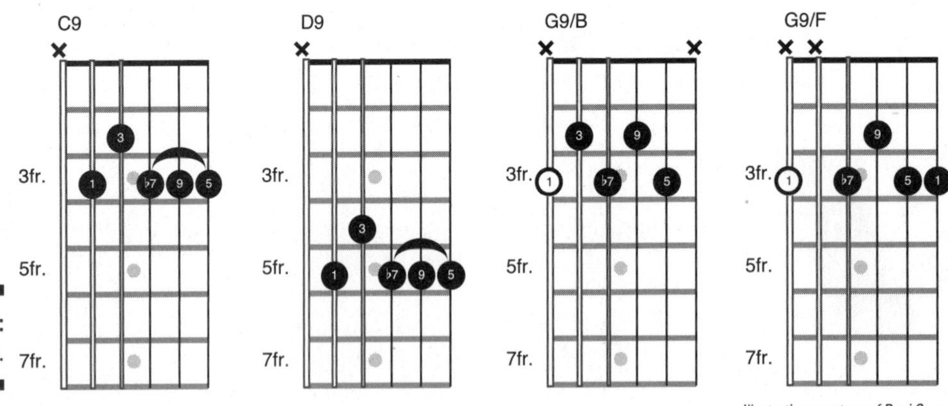

Figure 5-12: 9th chords.

Illustration courtesy of Desi Serna

Working with 4ths and 11ths

By far the most common type of 4th chord that you encounter is a sus4, where a 4th replaces the 3rd and a chord is stacked 1-4-5. On occasion, a 4th is added and the 3rd is retained, in which case you view the formula as either 1-3-4-5 or 1-3-5-11 and call it either add4 or add11.

Sus4 chords

Figure 5-13 includes a handful of sus4 chords in various keys. Sus4 chords naturally occur on chords I and V. You can also move these shapes up the neck and use them as full or partial barre chords. The F shape is one example of a barre chord; it's actually a partial E form.

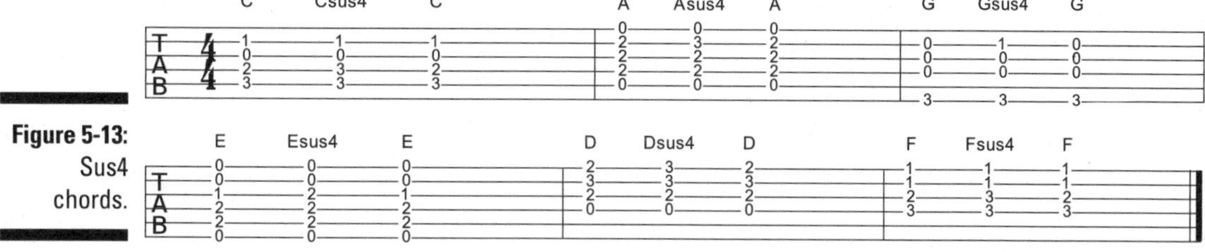

Figure 5-13: Sus4 chords.

Illustration courtesy of Desi Serna

In a major scale, sus4 chords occur on the 1st and 5th degrees. For example, the G major scale produces both a Gsus4 and a Dsus4. You may expect the other major chord in the key, C, to also produce a sus4 chord, but it doesn't. When you count from C in the G major scale, its 4th is F♯, a half step higher than a perfect 4th interval. The 4th degree in the major scale always has a ♯4th. You often hear this naturally raised interval in a song's melody, but you don't usually hear it in the guitar chords. In fact, even though the 4th chord in a key technically has a ♯4th, guitarists are far more likely to use a regular (perfect) 4th on it instead, probably not knowing the difference.

Add4 chords

Figure 5-14 offers a few examples of add4 chords, which can also be called add11 depending on how the chords are stacked and your preference. Notice that the Cadd4, stacked 1-4-5-1-3, keeps its 3rd, E (the 1st string open). Likewise, the Gadd11, stacked 1-3-5-1-11-1, keeps its 3rd, B (2nd fret of the 5th string). The Dadd4, stacked 1-3-4-1-5, is a type of C form moved up two frets without barring.

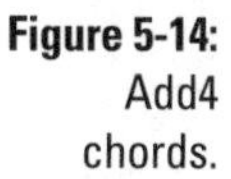

Figure 5-14: Add4 chords.

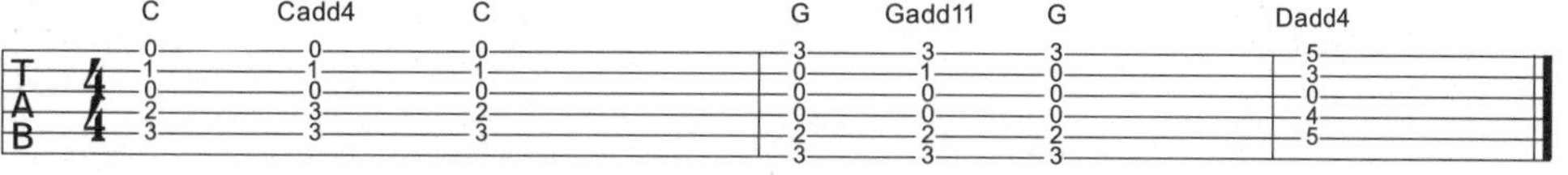

Illustration courtesy of Desi Serna

Play the Dadd4 in Figure 5-14 with the 1st string open and it becomes Dadd4(add9). The 1st string, E, is a 9th to D.

The following songs feature some form of sus4 or add4:

“All Shook Up” by Elvis Presley

“Brass in Pocket” by The Pretenders

“Can’t You See” by Marshall Tucker Band

“Closer to Fine” by Indigo Girls

“Eye of the Tiger” by Survivor

“Heaven” by Los Lonely Boys

“Jack and Diane” by John Mellencamp

“Little Wing” by Jimi Hendrix

“Margaritaville” by Jimmy Buffet

“Signs” by Tesla

“Stairway to Heaven” by Led Zeppelin

“Summer of ’69” by Bryan Adams

“Tears in Heaven” by Eric Clapton

“Under the Bridge” by Red Hot Chili Peppers

“What I Like About You” by The Romantics

“Yellow Ledbetter” by Pearl Jam

Playing 6th Chords and Blues Shuffles

A 6th chord is some combination of 1-3-5-6 (see Figure 5-15). If a 6th extends beyond the 7th, it’s still called a 6th unless a 7th is also present in the chord, in which case it’s called a major 13th.

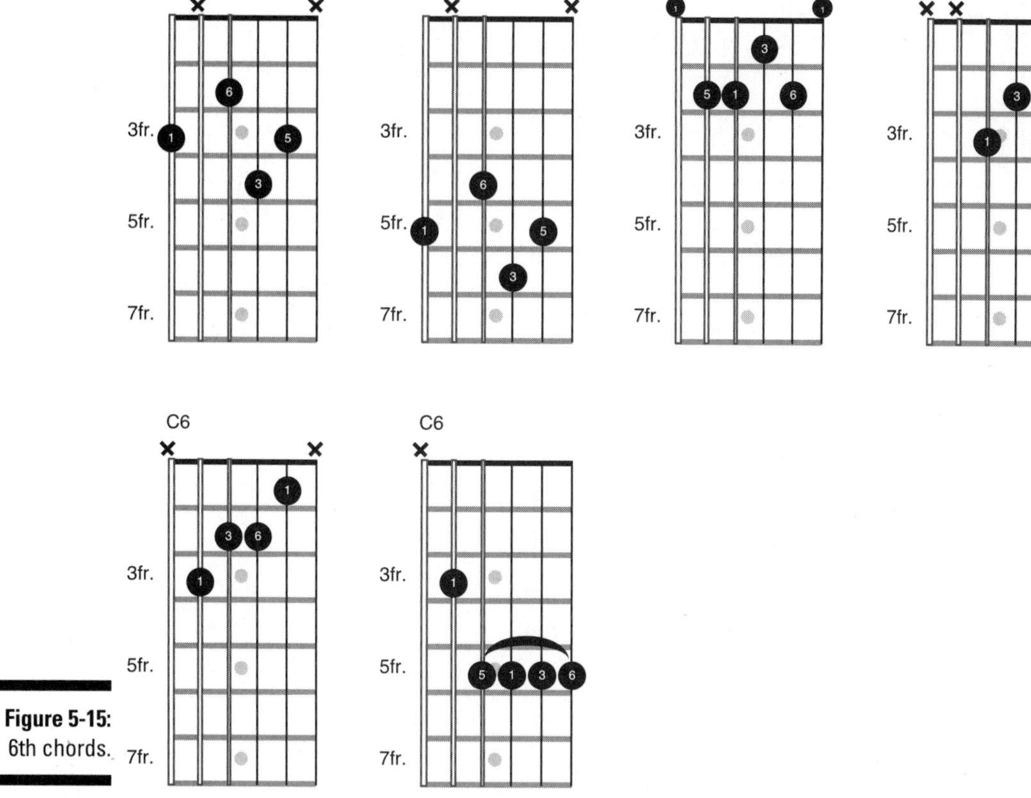

Figure 5-15: 6th chords.

Illustration courtesy of Desi Serna

The following songs feature 6th chords:

"Bad Moon Rising" by Creedence Clearwater Revival

"Brass in Pocket" by The Pretenders

"Laughing" by The Guess Who

"Lenny" by Stevie Ray Vaughan

"Lie in Our Graves" by Dave Matthews Band

By far the most common use of 6ths on guitar is when guitarists play the so-called "blues shuffle" or "boogie-woogie" that accompanies many rock 'n' roll, rockabilly, and blues songs. In a blues shuffle, a root and 5th are alternated with a root and 6th, as shown in Figure 5-16. Here, the progression is A-D-E-A, I-IV-V-I in A major. On these major scale degrees, 6ths occur naturally.

Figure 5-16: Blues shuffle with 6ths.

Illustration courtesy of Desi Serna

Watch Video Clip 9 to see and hear the 6ths example from Figure 5-16.

The following songs are all good examples of using a blues shuffle with 6ths:

"Glory Days" by Bruce Springsteen

"Jet Airliner" by Steve Miller Band

"Johnny B. Goode" by Chuck Berry

"Keep Your Hands to Yourself" by Georgia Satellites

"Love Struck Baby" by Stevie Ray Vaughan

"Life By the Drop" by Stevie Ray Vaughan

"Red House" by Jimi Hendrix (bass)

"Rocky Mountain Way" by Joe Walsh

"Taking Care of Business" by Bachman-Turner Overdrive

"Truckin'" by Grateful Dead

Adding Harmony with Pedal Point

A *pedal point* (also known as a *pedal tone* or just a *pedal*) in music is a sustained or repeated note that's sounded against chord progressions and melodies. The term originates from organ music where the player sustains a low tonic or dominant pitch with the foot pedals, allowing him to easily play chords and melodies above this note on the keyboard.

The use of pedal point often creates harmony that includes added chord tones and extensions, especially when you place the pedal in an upper register. This particular technique is sometimes called an *inverted pedal tone*. In Figure 5-17, you see a simple I-vi-IV-V progression in G: G-Em-C-D, with the note G, 3rd fret of the 1st string, held on top of each chord.

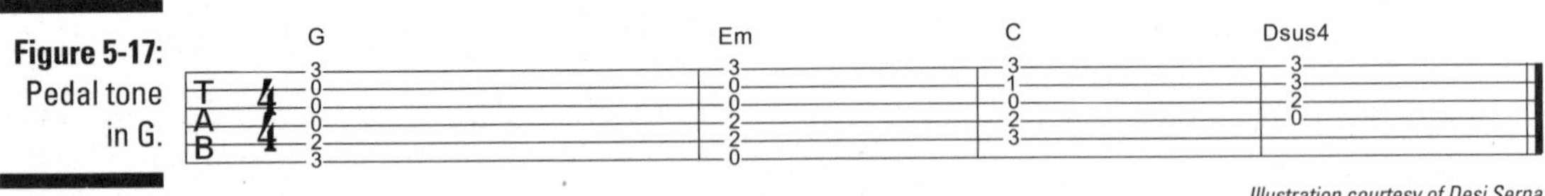

Figure 5-17: Pedal tone in G.

Illustration courtesy of Desi Serna

Because G, Em, and C already have the G note in them, their names don't have to change here. The D chord, however, becomes Dsus4 with the added G on the 1st string.

Figure 5-18 presents another example based on the same chords, this time sustaining both a G and a D above the chords. This technique is sometimes called a *double pedal tone*. Notice how Em and C are renamed to reflect the added chord tones. Adding D to Em makes Em7 and adding D to C makes Cadd9.

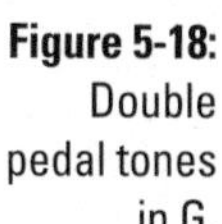

Figure 5-18: Double pedal tones in G.

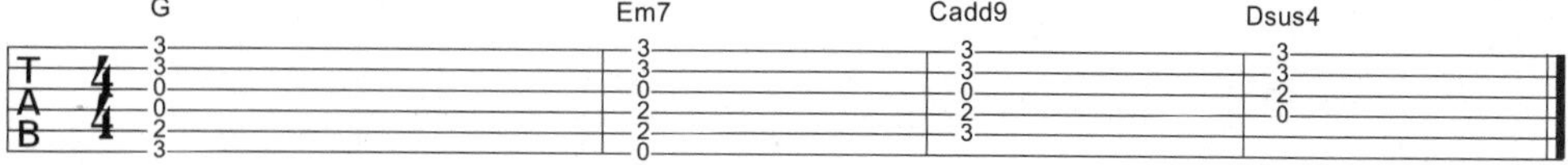

Illustration courtesy of Desi Serna

Two good examples of songs that use pedal tones like this are "Wonderwall" by Oasis and "Wish You Were Here" by Pink Floyd.

Take note that chords with added chord tones and complicated names are often the result of the pedal tone technique. The chords to "Wonderwall" are written as Em7-G-Dsus4-A7sus4. Fortunately, though, these chords are much easier to play than they look. In fact, many composers don't even have these chord names in mind when they put the simple chord fingerings together.

Playing Pedal Tones with Two Guitars

Although a single instrument can play a pedal and a chord at the same time (as you see in the examples in the previous section), in many cases, one instrument plays the pedal tone while other instruments play the standard chords. For example, one guitar may hold or repeat notes on upper strings, while another guitar plays through chord changes on the lower strings (see Figure 5-19). To hear the musical effect shown in Figure 5-19, record yourself playing one of the parts and then play the other part along with the recording.

Figure 5-19: Pedal tone with two guitars.

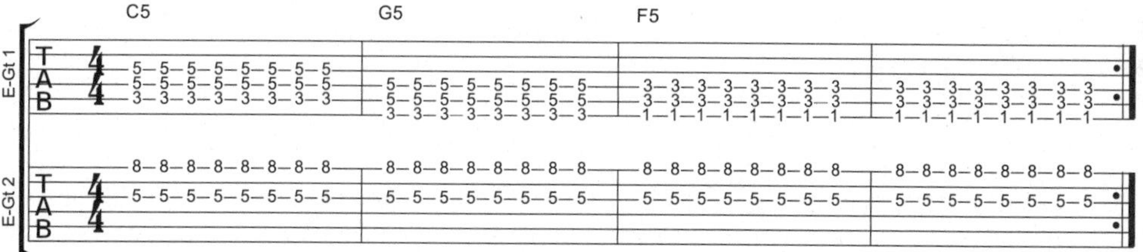

Illustration courtesy of Desi Serna

See how to record and play the example from Figure 5-19 by watching Video Clip 10.

You hear a pedal like this during the chorus to "All the Small Things" by Blink 182. One guitar plays the chords C5-G5-F5 while another pedals on C octaves in an upper register. All together the harmony you hear is C5-Gsus4-F5. In "I Love Rock 'n' Roll" by Joan Jett and the Blackhearts, two guitars play through the chord progression E5-A5-B5, while a third guitar pedals on E octaves creating the sound of E5-A5-Bsus4. "Cinnamon Girl" by Neil Young features a one-note guitar solo that's essentially a D note pedaled over the chord changes D-Am7-C-G, creating the sound of D-A7sus4-Cadd9-G.

To see an example of a two-guitar, double pedal tone, take a look at Figure 5-20. Here, the second guitar pedals on two different pitches over a I-V-vi-IV chord progression in D. The two pitches, D and A, are the root and 5th of the tonic chord, D. The combined harmony of the two guitars becomes more complex than the individual parts. The first guitar may be playing only D5-A5-B5-G5, but the addition of the pedal tones by the second guitar creates the harmonies D5-Asus4-Bm7-Gsus2. This is the same kind of sound that you hear in Figure 5-18, only split between two guitars.

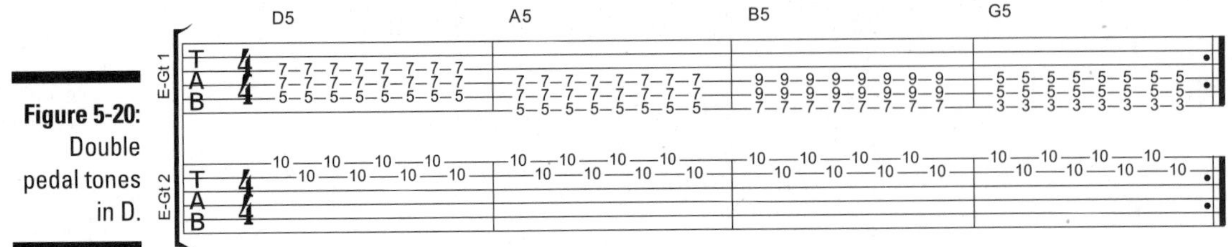

Figure 5-20: Double pedal tones in D.

Illustration courtesy of Desi Serna

Part III

Getting to Know Keys, Modes, and Chord Progressions

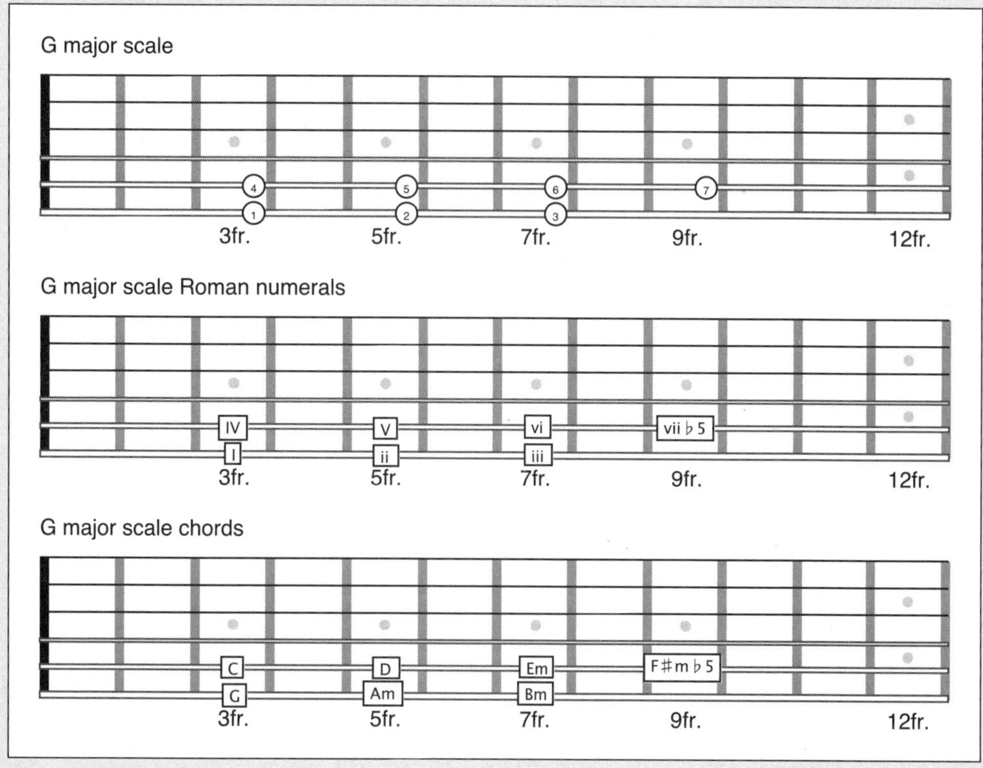

Go to www.dummies.com/extras/guitartheory for a free article that shows how the chord progression used in "Like a Rolling Stone" by Bob Dylan breaks down and fits into the major scale.

In this part . . .

- Group chords together by drawing them from the major scale. Use Roman numerals and barre chord patterns to map out keys on the fretboard. Play popular chord progressions and transpose them to new keys.
- Analyze a piece of music to identify the tonic, the key, and the parent major scale. Identify when a song is in a mode. Play relative major and relative minor and explore different types of number systems.
- Follow key changes and recognize the role of dominant function. Appreciate chord progressions that don't fit into one scale and make good use of borrowed chords, modal interchange, secondary dominants, and the circle of fifths.
- Fill in the gaps with passing chords and voice leading and practice playing diminished and augmented chords.

Chapter 6

Playing Chord Progressions by Numbers

In This Chapter

- Progressing to chord progressions, using the major scale
- Numbering chords in a key with Roman numerals
- Visualizing chord patterns on the fretboard
- Playing through popular chord progressions

Have you ever wondered what it means to play a "one, four, five"? Why do some guitarists seem to pick up on new chord changes so easily, almost knowing what's coming next in a song the first time through? What's the trick to transposing a song to a new key quickly and easily without having to fuss with key signatures and notes and rebuilding chords?

In music, different songs often use the same types of chord changes. On the fretboard, these chord changes make patterns that guitarists visualize and follow by number. The chords and numbers are based on the triads and degrees of the major scale that you get to know in Chapter 3.

The neat thing about using patterns is that all keys look and feel the same. Numbers stay the same from key to key, too. You can pick up a chord progression (or series) from one key and move it to another as easily as moving a chord shape or scale pattern.

In this chapter, you play by numbers, using some of the most recognizable chord progressions in popular music. You find out how to identify the chords of any key instantly and reproduce chord progressions in new positions in the snap of a finger.

Listen to Audio Track 6 to hear sample chord progressions and get an overview of this chapter.

Drawing Chord Progressions from the Major Scale

A *chord progression* is any series of chords used in a piece of music. For example, the chord progression to "Wild Thing" by The Troggs is A-D-E-D. Chords can go together in all sorts of ways, but they're usually drawn from a scale, specifically, the major scale.

You use the major scale to stack groups of three intervals called *triads* (see Chapter 3 for everything you need to know about triads). These triads harmonize the scale and form chords. Each scale degree produces a different chord and number. The sequence of major and minor chords found in the major scale looks like this:

1-2-3-4-5-6-7

Major-minor-minor-major-major-minor-minor♭5 (also called a *diminished triad;* see Chapter 3)

Using the key of G as an example, the major scale chords are

G-A-B-C-D-E-F♯

1-2-3-4-5-6-7

G-Am-Bm-C-D-Em-F♯m♭5

Play through this key by using the standard barre chords shown in Figure 6-1.

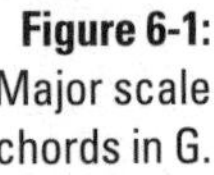

Figure 6-1: Major scale chords in G.

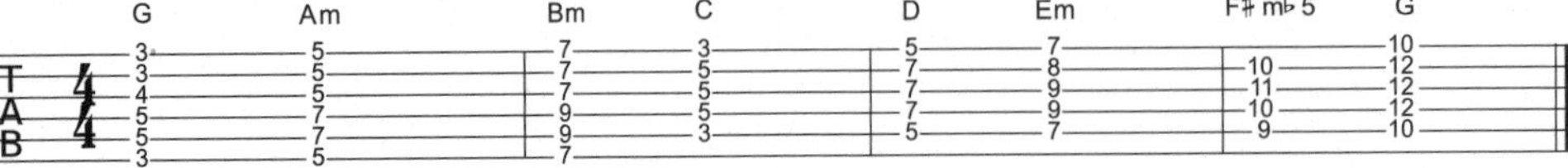

Illustration courtesy of Desi Serna

Using Roman Numerals to Represent Chords

In traditional music theory, Roman numerals (I, II, III, IV, and so on) represent both the degrees of the major scale and the chord quality of each chord. Uppercase Roman numerals represent major chords, while lowercase numerals represent minor chords. Table 6-1 lists the Roman numerals that represent chords, along with the major/minor sequence of the major scale and a sample key of G major.

Table 6-1 Roman Numerals Used to Represent Chords

Chord Number	*Uppercase Roman Numeral*	*Lowercase Roman Numeral*	*Major/Minor Sequence of the Major Scale*	*G Major Scale*
1	I	i	I	G
2	II	ii	ii	Am
3	III	iii	iii	Bm
4	IV	iv	IV	C
5	V	v	V	D
6	VI	vi	vi	Em
7	VII	vii	vii♭5	F♯m♭5

Visualizing Numbers on the Fretboard

Figure 6-2 shows the number pattern made by the G scale on the fretboard. Notice that the chords in this pattern are the same chords shown in Figure 6-1. Guitarists come to know this pattern very well because songs regularly use chord progressions that move through it in predictable ways.

G major scale

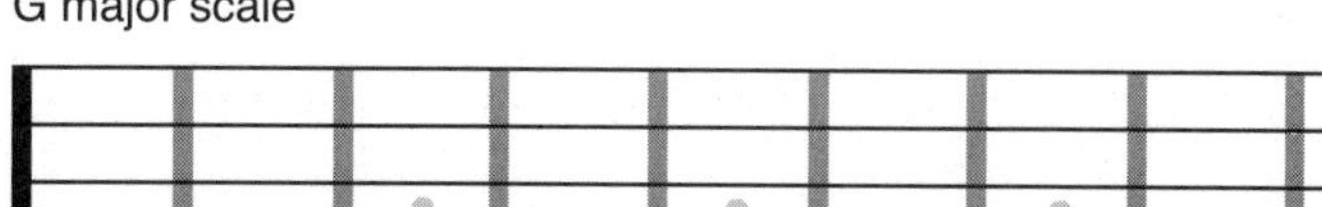
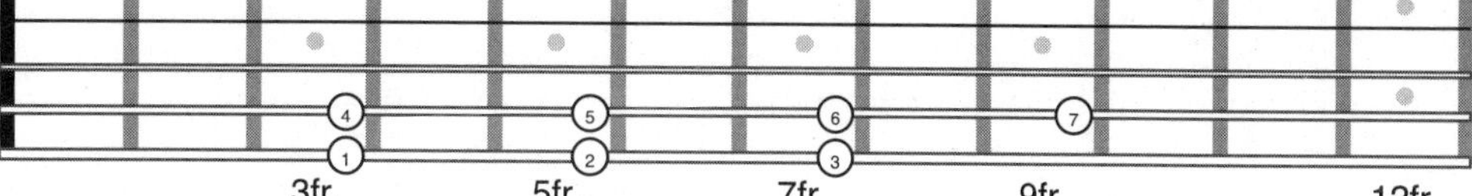

G major scale Roman numerals

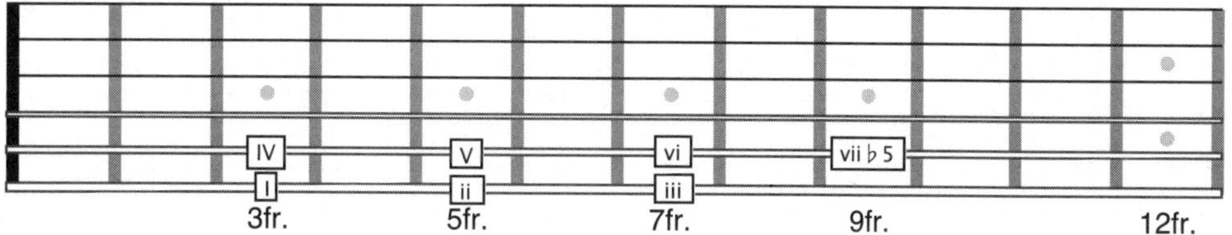

G major scale chords

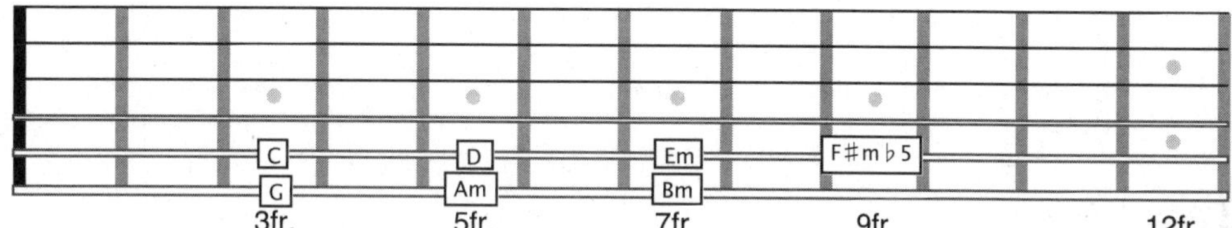

Figure 6-2: Major scale chord pattern in G.

Illustration courtesy of Desi Serna

Hear and see me play through the chord pattern from Figure 6-2 by watching Video Clip 11.

This chord pattern is the basis for the first half of this chapter and needs to be memorized now. While you play through it, call out each chord number as you play it. As you rehearse, try the following different combinations:

1. **Play chords I through vi forward and backward.**
2. **Play just the majors (I, IV, and V) forward and backward.**
3. **Play just the minors (ii, iii, and vi) forward and backward.**
4. **Alternate between the 6th and 5th strings by playing I-IV, ii-V, and iii-vi.**

Most progressions are based on the first six chords of the major scale, so you can disregard the seventh chord, vii♭5, and leave it out of the patterns. The minor triad with a flattened 5th is also called a *diminished triad.* The diminished triad is not to be confused with or used in the same way as full diminished and diminished 7th chords, which you play in Chapter 10.

Transposing to New Keys

After you memorize the G major chord pattern that I explain in the preceding section, you can instantly play the chords in any new key simply by moving to a different position. For example, move the whole chord pattern up two frets and play in the A major scale. Or move up four frets and play in the B major scale. Wherever you begin this pattern, the 1st scale degree is your key. No matter which note you start on, you always produce the correct chords for that scale. The best part is that you don't have to concern yourself with the actual notes and chords you use; just pick a starting point and play the numbered pattern as shown in Figure 6-3. That's all there is to it!

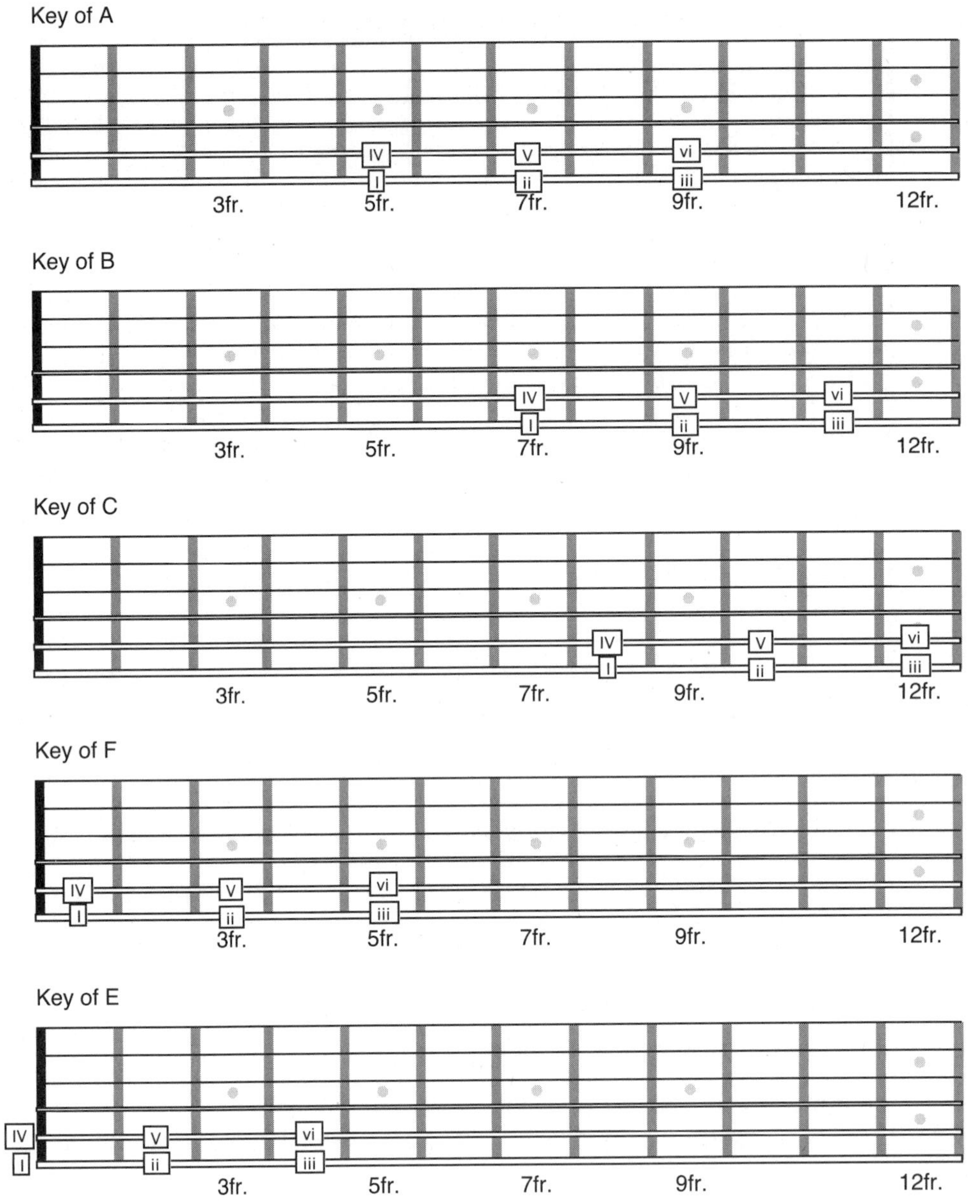

Key of A

IV V vi
I ii iii
3fr. 5fr. 7fr. 9fr. 12fr.

Key of B

IV V vi
I ii iii
3fr. 5fr. 7fr. 9fr. 12fr.

Key of C

IV V vi
I ii iii
3fr. 5fr. 7fr. 9fr. 12fr.

Key of F

IV V vi
I ii iii
3fr. 5fr. 7fr. 9fr. 12fr.

Key of E

IV V vi
I ii iii
3fr. 5fr. 7fr. 9fr. 12fr.

Figure 6-3: Playing by number in new keys.

Illustration courtesy of Desi Serna

With this chord pattern, all keys look and feel the same. I don't even include the notes and chord names in Figure 6-3 because I want you to think in terms of numbers. Just keep track of the note on your starting point, chord I. Notice that this pattern also works with I and IV as open chords in the key of E.

Playing Common Chord Progressions

You use the numbered chord pattern to put together chord progressions. This is where you get into playing by numbers. Songs can center on any number (chord) and combine numbers (chords) in any order and any amount. The most basic type of progression uses just the major chords, numbers I, IV, and V.

Playing I-IV-V chord progressions

By far the most common type of chord progression is the I-IV-V (that's *one, four, five,* in case the Roman numerals are throwing you off). A *I-IV-V chord progression* is any combination of the three major chords in a key. You find an example of this chord progression in the song "Wild Thing" by The Troggs. Its chords, A, D, and E, are I, IV, and V in the A major scale. Start the chord pattern at the 5th fret of the 6th string and play through the three major chords. That's it! If anyone asks you how to play the song, you can say, "Oh, it's just an ordinary I-IV-V in A. No big deal." You'll sound like a real pro!

The following list provides some other common songs based on I-IV-V. To play through these, find the scale note on the 6th string, start the chord pattern, and then follow the numbers I list. You can also play along with the recordings of these songs, if you have them. In some of the examples, the recorded guitar parts may not use plain barre chords, but you can still practice strumming along using the barre chords in the pattern. These songs may have other chords and progressions in them too, but the main sections are as follows:

I-IV-V in A

"Stir it Up" by Bob Marley

"When the Sun Goes Down" by Kenny Chesney

V-I-IV-I in A

"What I Like about You" by The Romantics

I-IV-I-V in G

"Brown Eyed Girl" by Van Morrison

I-IV-V-IV in G

"Hang on Sloopy" by The McCoys

V-IV-I in G

"Magic Carpet Ride" by Steppenwolf

"Seven Bridges Road" by the Eagles

"Sweet Home Alabama" by Lynyrd Skynyrd

I-IV-I-V in F

"The Lion Sleeps Tonight" by The Tokens

I-IV-V in F

"Twist and Shout" by The Isley Brothers

I-IV-V-IV in F

"The Joker" by Steve Miller Band

I-IV-V-IV in B♭

"Walking on Sunshine" by Katrina and The Waves

Mix of I-IV-V in E

"I Love Rock 'n' Roll" by Joan Jett and the Blackhearts

"I Wanna Be Sedated" by the Ramones

"Walk of Life" by Dire Straits

You can form major and minor chords in other ways besides the standard barre chords I use in this chapter. (Skip to Chapter 4 for details.) But using a different type of chord shape doesn't change a chord progression. For example, G-C-D is always I-IV-V, whether you use standard barre chords, open chords, or something else.

Playing major chord progressions

When a song centers on a major chord, it's called a *major chord progression.* Notice that in the previous song list the actual order of the chords varies. Also, some examples, like "What I Like about You" by The Romantics, don't even start on chord I. With the chord pattern that you're using, progressions can center on any chord. Major chord progressions typically center on chord I or V, but IV is also an option. You work with centering music on different scale degrees more in Chapters 7 and 8.

Adding minor chords ii, iii, and vi

In the next group of lists, you see chord progressions that incorporate the minor chords in the pattern ii, iii, and vi. These examples are in different scales, so be sure to position the chord pattern with chord I on the right starting note. As you play through these progressions, remember to call out the numbers while you're at it.

ii chord

"Heaven" by Los Lonely Boys (I-ii G with guitars tuned down one half-step to E♭)

"One Night at a Time" by George Strait (I-ii-IV A)

"Upside Down" by Jack Johnson (I-ii and I-ii-IV-V E)

"What's Up?" by 4 Non Blondes (I-ii-IV A)

iii chord

"All She Wants to Do Is Dance" by Don Henley (V-I-iii-IV G)

"Do You Believe in Love" by Huey Lewis and the News (I-iii-IV-V B)

"The Weight" by The Band (I-iii-IV A)

vi chord

"Earth Angel (Will You Be Mine)" by The Penguins (I-vi-IV-V B♭)

"Every Breath You Take" by The Police (I-vi-IV-V A♭)

"Hit Me with Your Best Shot" by Pat Benatar (Mix of I-IV-V-vi E)

"Hurts So Good" by John Mellencamp (I-V-vi-IV A)

"I'm Yours" by Jason Mraz (I-V-vi-IV B)

"Stand by Me" by Ben E. King (I-vi-IV-V A)

"When I Come Around" by Green Day (I-V-vi-IV G)

Playing minor chord progressions

When a song centers on a minor chord, it's called a *minor chord progression.* It can be any progression that centers on chord ii, iii, or vi in the major scale. The following song examples all start and center on a minor chord. The major scales that these progressions are based in are indicated in parentheses. For example, "Black Magic Woman" is vi-ii-iii in the F major scale, so position the chord pattern to start on F. Find out more about minor chord progressions in Chapter 7.

"All Along the Watchtower" by Jimi Hendrix (vi-V-IV-V E with guitars tuned down one half-step to E♭)

"Black Magic Woman" by Santana (mix of vi-ii-iii F)

"Evil Ways" by Santana (ii-V F)

"Layla (Unplugged)" by Eric Clapton (vi-IV-V F)

"Livin' on a Prayer" by Bon Jovi (vi-IV-V G)

"Moondance" by Van Morrison (ii-iii G)

"Oye Como Va" by Santana (ii-V G)

"Paranoid" by Black Sabbath (vi-V-I-IV G)

"Rockin' in the Free World" by Neil Young (vi-V-IV G)

"Who Will Save Your Soul" by Jewel (ii-IV-I-V G)

Starting Numbers on the 5th String

In this section, you build a new chord pattern that starts on the 5th string. The chords and scale degrees are still drawn from the major scale. The numbers stay the same, too. But the pattern looks and feels different because chords I, ii, and iii are placed on the 5th string, while the others — IV, V, and vi — get moved over to the 6th string. This pattern doesn't line up as nicely as the last one, but it's used just as much and needs to be played. Starting on the 5th string gives you better access to some keys by allowing you to play them in more comfortable positions. You start in the key of C with chord I at the 3rd fret of the 5th string, as shown in Figure 6-4. This example also includes the vii♭5 chord so you can complete the scale, but it won't be used once you begin playing chord progressions.

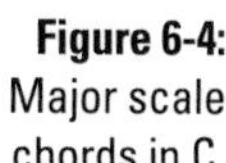

Figure 6-4: Major scale chords in C.

Illustration courtesy of Desi Serna

Figure 6-5 shows what the chords from the preceding figure look like as a fretboard pattern. You focus on using only the first six chords on the fretboard because vii♭5 is rarely, if ever, used.

The chords shown in Figure 6-5 are exactly the same as the C chords in the pattern that begins at the 8th fret of the 6th string from the previous section. The only difference is that you play in a different position. Take a moment to play through this pattern forward and backward while calling out the numbers as you go.

Generally speaking, you use this new chord pattern in keys that would reach too high on the fretboard when based on the 6th string. For example, in the keys of B, C, and D, it's difficult to reach up to the iii and vi chords. Plus, barre chords near the 12th fret are voiced too high — that is, they sound too high-pitched for most rhythm playing. In Figure 6-6, you move this pattern around and play in some different keys. Notice that the same pattern also works in the key of B, using an open E chord on IV. You always need to think about using open strings!

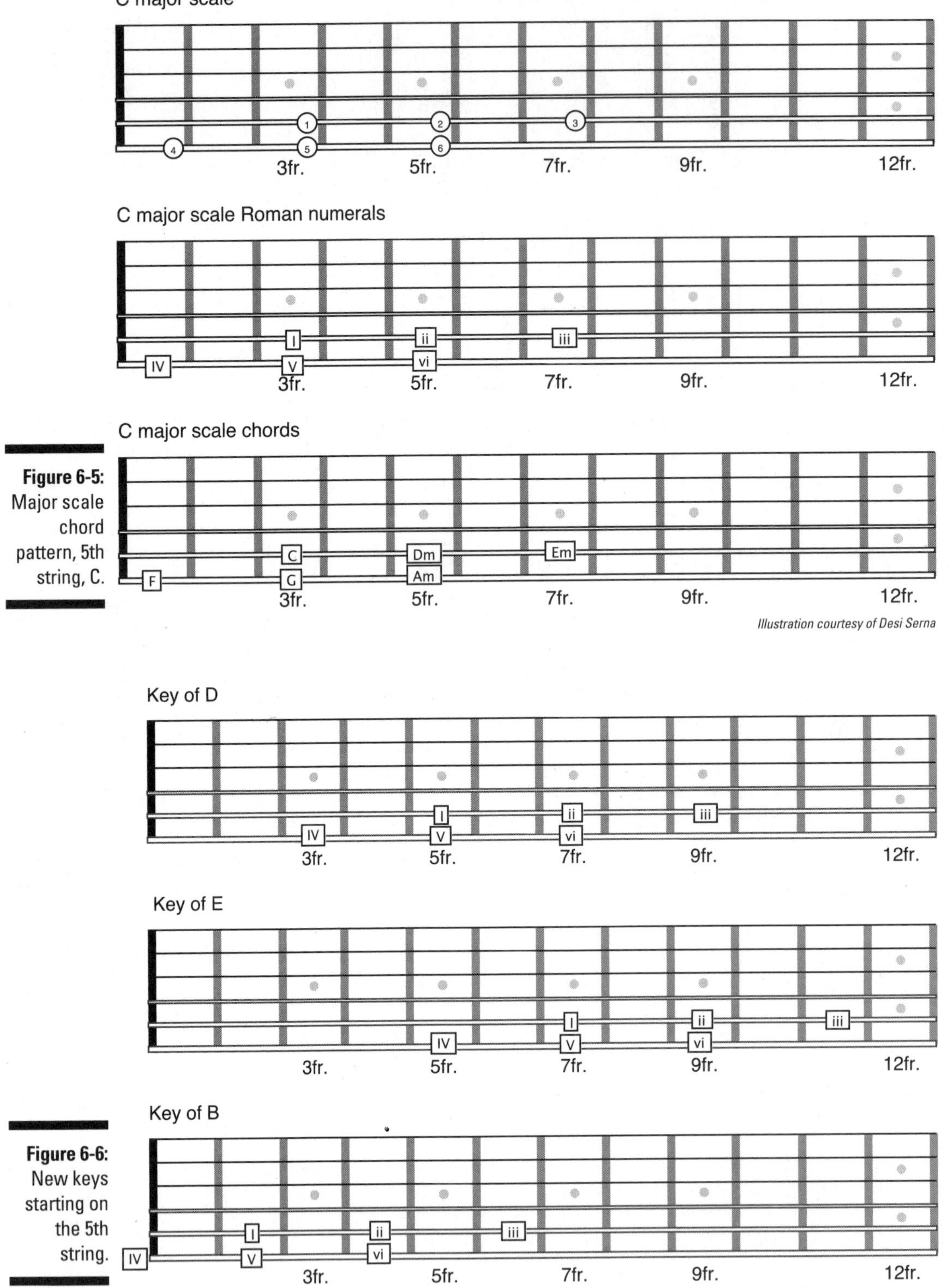

Figure 6-5: Major scale chord pattern, 5th string, C.

Illustration courtesy of Desi Serna

Figure 6-6: New keys starting on the 5th string.

Illustration courtesy of Desi Serna

The following songs are all variations of I-IV-V that work well in the 5th string chord pattern:

"Angel Of Harlem" by U2 (I-IV-V C)

"Authority Song" by John Mellencamp (I-IV-V D)

"Baba O'Riley" by The Who (I-V-IV F)

"Bad Moon Rising" by Creedence Clearwater Revival (I-V-IV D)

"Crimson and Clover" by Tommy James and the Shondells (I-V-IV B)

"Do Ya" by Electric Light Orchestra (I-V-IV D)

"Feliz Navidad" by Jose Feliciano (IV-V-I D)

"The First Cut Is the Deepest" by Sheryl Crow (I-V-IV D)

"Good Lovin'" by The Rascals (I-IV-V-IV D)

"Hold My Hand" by Hootie and the Blowfish (I-IV-V B)

"I Could Never Take the Place of Your Man" by Prince (I-V-IV C)

"I Still Haven't Found What I'm Looking For" by U2 (I-IV-V D♭)

"A Life of Illusion" by Joe Walsh (I-IV-V D)

"Nothing but a Good Time" by Poison (V-IV-I D)

"Twist and Shout" by The Beatles (I-IV-V D)

"She's So Cold" by The Rolling Stones (V-I-IV-V C)

"Southern Cross" by Crosby, Stills & Nash (V-IV-I D)

"Yellow Ledbetter" by Pearl Jam (I-V-IV E)

The next list of songs includes examples with minor chords that work well in the 5th string chord pattern:

"Beast of Burden" by The Rolling Stones (I-V-vi-IV E)

"Blessed Be Your Name" by Matt Redman (I-V-vi-IV B)

"Dy'er Mak'er" by Led Zeppelin (I-vi-IV-V C)

"Friend of God" by Israel Houghton (I-vi-ii-I D)

"Jessie's Girl" by Rick Springfield (I-V-vi-IV-V-I D)

"Heard It in a Love Song" by Marshall Tucker Band (I-iii-IV-V D)

"How Great Is Our God" by Chris Tomlin (I-vi-IV-V D♭)

"Lean on Me" by Bill Withers (I-ii-iii-IV, IV-iii-ii-I C)

"Let It Be" by The Beatles (I-V-vi-IV, I-V-IV-I C)

"Louie, Louie" by The Kingsmen (V-I-ii-I D)

"Runaround Sue" by Dion (I-vi-IV-V D)

"Two Princes" by Spin Doctors (I-vi-V-IV D)

"Unchained Melody" by The Righteous Brothers (I-vi-IV-V C)

"Under the Bridge" by Red Hot Chili Peppers (I-V-vi-iii-IV E)

"With or Without You" by U2 (I-V-vi-IV D)

"You Are the Woman" by Firefall (I-iii-ii-V D)

This next list has songs that not only use minor chords but center on one, mostly chord vi, creating minor keys.

"Californication" by Red Hot Chili Peppers (vi-IV C)

"Don't Fear the Reaper" by Blue Oyster Cult (vi-V-IV-V C)

"Horse with No Name" by America (ii-iii D)

"Maria, Maria" by Santana (vi-ii-iii C)

"Otherside" by Red Hot Chili Peppers (vi-IV-I-V C)

"The Thrill Is Gone" by B.B. King (vi-ii-vi-IV-iii-vi D)

Playing Chord Progressions with Open Chords

You can use the two chord patterns I cover in this chapter to track chord progressions in the open position too, although doing so takes some extra work and requires that you identify the actual note name of each chord.

To play in the key of G using common open chords, visualize the 6th string chord pattern starting on G at the 3rd fret (Figure 6-2) and replace each barre chord with an open chord. Here's how:

1. **Visualize the 1st barre chord, the I chord (G), but play an open G chord instead.**
2. **Visualize the 2nd chord, the ii chord (Am), but play an open Am instead.**
3. **Because there's no open chord iii (Bm), play Bm at the 2nd fret of the 5th string close to the open position instead.**
4. **Use common open chords to play chords IV, V, and vi (C, D, and Em).**
5. **Play through all the chords forward and backward, calling out the numbers as you go.**

   Follow along with your eye using the 6th string chord pattern even though you're not using its barre chords.

Watch Video Clip 12 for a demonstration on how to play by number in the open position.

After you get the hang of playing like this in G, you can move the chord pattern and use open chords in other keys like F and A. When you do this, play open chords when you can and use the barre chords to fill in the rest, staying as close to the open position as possible. For example, in the key of F, you can play the Am, C, and Dm as open chords, but you have to use the barre chords to play the rest. In the key of A, you can play A, D, and E as open chords, Bm and C♯m at the 2nd and 4th frets of the 5th string, and F♯m at the 2nd fret of the 6th string.

Do the same thing with the 5th string chord pattern starting in the key of C. In C, you can play all the chords as open chords except for F, which guitarists usually play as a partial barre chord when it's paired with open chords. Move the chord pattern and use open chords in other keys; just remember to stay as close to the open position as possible when you need to fill in with barre chords.

After you get the hang of playing in the open position, you can revisit any of the song lists in this chapter and try working out the progressions using open chords. When you do, call out the numbers as you go so that in time you know your way around the open position by number as well as you do the barre chord patterns.

Chapter 7

Knowing Music Inside Out: Identifying Tonics, Keys, and Modes

In This Chapter

- Getting familiar with tonics
- Defining relative major and relative minor
- Identifying modes and parent major scales
- Renumbering chords and progressions
- Comparing scale formulas and structures

When musicians say that a song is in the "key of" this or that, they can mean a few different things. They may be referring to the primary pitch or chord that the music centers on, the major scale that the notes and chords are drawn from, or the mode that everything is based on. In this chapter, you get to know the different types of keys associated with music, and you find out how to renumber chords and progressions to reflect the modes of the major scale. You also gain a little insight into key signatures, an element of standard written notation.

Although this chapter gets a bit technical, don't be discouraged. Analyzing keys, modes, and songs helps you discover new things about the inner workings of music. This, in turn, makes you a better player, composer, and improviser. The information in this chapter also helps you as you work with other topics throughout the book.

Note: This chapter focuses primarily on helping you understand modes as key centers; you play modal scale patterns and work on modal improvisations in Chapter 13.

Listen to Audio Track 7 to get an idea of what this chapter is all about.

Understanding the Relationship between Major and Minor Scales

Every piece of music has a tonal center called a *tonic.* The tonic is the primary pitch or chord that everything else revolves around. It's where a piece of music sounds resolved or complete and usually where the music begins and ends.

Generally speaking, the tonic also determines a song's *key.* There are two basic types of music tonalities and keys: major and minor. If a piece of music centers on a major chord, then it's considered to be in a major key. If music centers on a minor chord, it's a minor key. For instance, if a song centers on a G chord, you say it's in the *key of G.* Similarly, when an Em chord is the center, you call it the *key of E minor.*

Traditionally, music has been taught as being in either the major or minor scale. I use the major scale in previous chapters to measure intervals, build chords, and chart chord progressions. I also use it in Chapter 12 to cover the whole neck with major scale patterns and to work on improvisation. The good news is if you know the major scale, then you also know the minor scale. The minor scale is drawn from the 6th degree of the major scale. Start any major scale on its 6th degree and you have a minor scale. For example, the 6th degree in the G major scale is E. The E minor scale is simply the notes of G major starting on E, as you see here:

G major scale

1-2-3-4-5-6-7

G-A-B-C-D-E-F♯

E minor scale

1-2-3-4-5-6-7

E-F♯-G-A-B-C-D

The relationship between the major and minor scales (and between the 1st and 6th chords) is often described as being *relative.* For example, in the key of G, I and vi are G and Em. G major is the *relative major* of E minor, and E minor is the *relative minor* of G major. This relative relationship holds true in all keys. In the key of C, for example, the I chord is C major and the vi chord is A minor. They, too, are relative major and minor chords and scales. In written music, relative major and minor keys actually share the same key signature.

Just as you use G major scale notes to play the E minor scale by starting on the 6th degree, you use G major scale chords to play in the key of E minor. The following list shows the chords for both the G major scale and its relative minor, E minor. Notice how the E minor scale features the very same chords, starting on the 6th degree:

G major

1-2-3-4-5-6-7

G-Am-Bm-C-D-Em-F♯m♭5

E minor

1-2-3-4-5-6-7

Em-F♯m♭5-G-Am-Bm-C-D

As you discover in Chapter 6, the major scale chords are represented with Roman numerals that look like this:

I-ii-iii-IV-V-vi-vii♭5

Rearrange the major scale with the 6th degree in the first position and you get this sequence:

vi-vii♭5-I-ii-iii-IV-V

Numbering the Relative Minor

The major scale has seven degrees with a triad built on each one. In music, uppercase Roman numerals represent major chords, and lowercase Roman numerals represent minor chords, as you can see in this example:

1-2-3-4-5-6-7

I-ii-iii-IV-V-vi-vii♭5

You may recognize this example as the major scale. After all, in music, you use the major scale as your starting place for naming chords, scale degrees, and intervals. From this perspective, the pattern of whole steps and half steps between the scale degrees of the major scale are what you think of as the naturally occurring ones.

If the distance between any two scale degrees changes for some reason, you can reflect this change with an *accidental* — typically a sharp or a flat. For example, a flattened 3rd scale degree is written ♭3 and is a half step lower than the one found in a regular major scale. A sharpened 4th, ♯4, raises the 4th scale degree by a half step, and a flattened 7th, ♭7, lowers the 7th by a semitone . . . you get the idea.

When numbering scale degrees, you always regard the tonic as 1. Because the tonic in the E minor scale is E, you count the E as 1 and renumber everything else from there, as you see here:

E minor

1-2-♭3-4-5-♭6-♭7

E-F♯-G-A-B-C-D

i-ii♭5-♭III-iv-v-♭VI-♭VII

Em-F♯m♭5-G-Am-Bm-C-D

Keep in mind that the notes and chords of E minor are still the same as G major. The only difference is that you've rearranged the chords to begin with E. Don't forget to adjust the Roman numerals to match the new order. Because the major/minor sequence changes if you count the E as 1, you adjust the case of the Roman numerals to reflect the correct chord quality for each scale degree. For example, the 1st chord is now minor, so you have to write it with a lowercase Roman numeral: i. The 3rd chord changes from minor (iii) to major (III), and so on.

Accounting for any interval changes

When you renumber chords from the tonic, you also need to indicate any changes to the intervals between the chords. To see what I mean, compare the original G major scale with the new E minor scale:

G major

1-2-3-4-5-6-7

G-A-B-C-D-E-F♯

I-ii-iii-IV-V-vi-vii♭5

G-Am-Bm-C-D-Em-F♯m♭5

E minor

1-2-♭3-4-5-♭6-♭7

E-F♯-G-A-B-C-D

i-ii♭5-♭III-iv-v-♭VI-♭VII

Em-F♯m♭5-G-Am-Bm-C-D

Major scale intervals are what you think of as the naturally occurring ones. In the major scale, the distance from the 1st to 3rd degrees is two whole steps, better known as a major 3rd. But when you start counting from E, the distance from 1 to 3 is only one and a half steps, better known as a minor or flattened 3rd. As a result, the 3rd degree is preceded by a flat sign (♭3), as is its chord (♭III). For the same reason, the 6th and 7th degrees and chords are also flattened (♭6 and ♭7, ♭VI and ♭VII).

In Figure 7-1, you see what G major looks like on the fretboard as both scale degrees and Roman numeral chords, followed by the same notes and chords numbered to reflect E minor. Notice in the last diagram that you end up playing the same chords either way.

G major scale

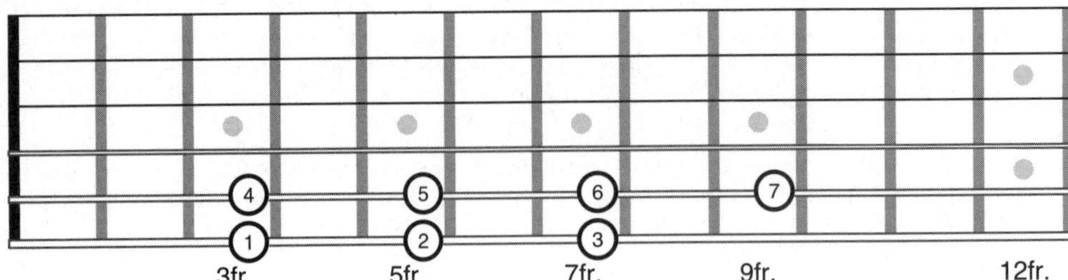

G major scale Roman numerals

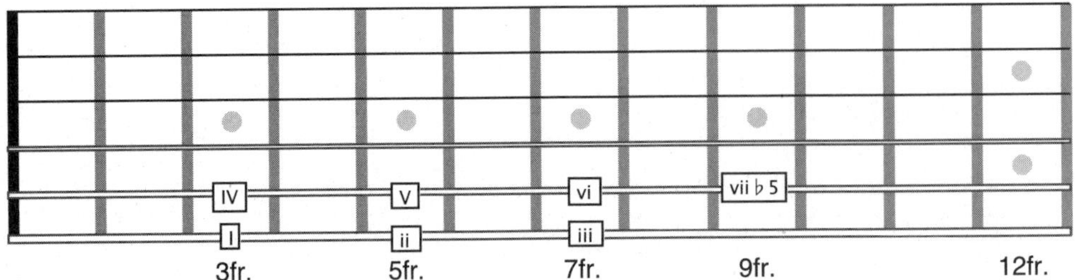

E minor scale

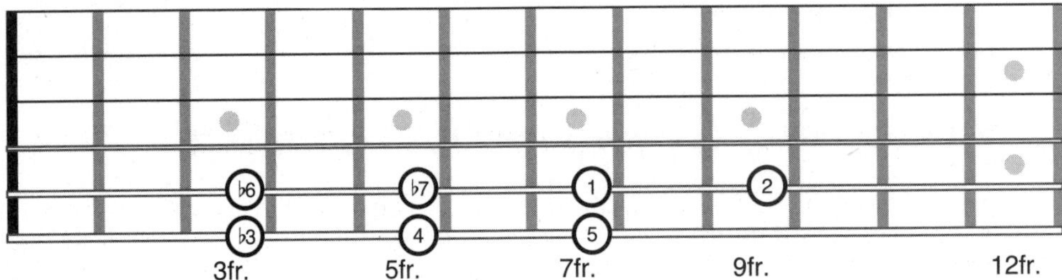

E minor scale Roman numerals

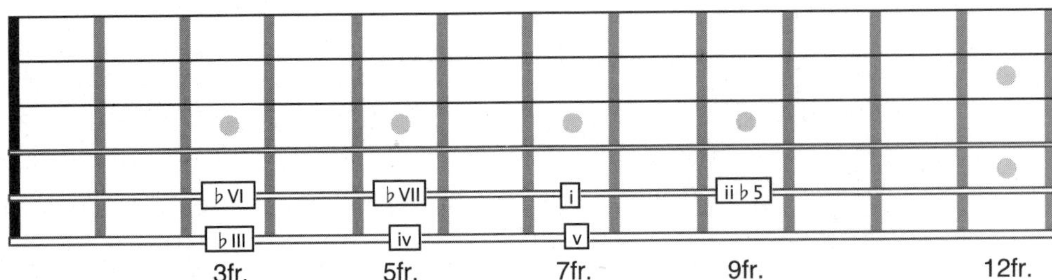

Same chords either way

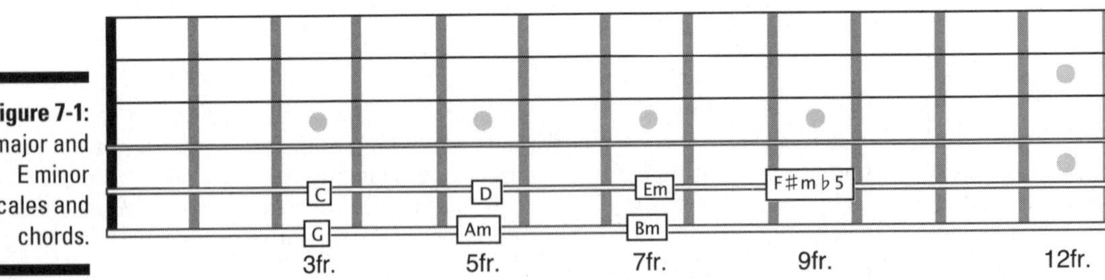

Figure 7-1: G major and E minor scales and chords.

Illustration courtesy of Desi Serna

PLAY THIS!

You can see a brief demonstration on playing in G major and E minor by watching Video Clip 13.

Looking at a few minor key song examples

Now that you know how to renumber the relative minor scale to reflect its starting point, consider a minor key song example, "Livin' on a Prayer" by Bon Jovi. It features the chord progression Em-C-D. In the G major scale, this progression is vi-IV-V. Of course, you could number this progression by the chord positions in G major; after all, G is the *parent major scale,* the scale that E minor is drawn from. However, musicians are more likely to use a number system that puts the tonic chord, Em, in the first position. If you go by the chord positions in the E minor scale, the progression becomes i-♭VI-♭VII. That's *one, flat six,* and *flat seven,* in case the Roman numerals are throwing you off.

For another example, consider the key of C. A minor is relative to C major where C and A are I and vi. To play the A minor scale, simply use the notes of C major, but start on the 6th degree, A. Likewise, use the C major chords, but start on Am. Use Figure 7-2 to play this relative major and minor scale on the fretboard. Notice that this new key starts the relative major on the 5th string, a pattern I introduce in Chapter 6.

Take the song "Maria Maria" by Santana, which uses the chords Am, Dm, and Em. In C major, these chords are vi, ii, and iii, but because the Am chord is the tonic, the chords are better known as i, iv, and v. That's *one, four,* and *five,* all as minor chords. In major keys, the most popular types of chord progressions are based on the three major chords I, IV, and V. Similar progressions are also popular in minor keys, where the three chords all appear as minor: i, iv, and v; this type of progression is called a *minor one-four-five.* Santana's "Black Magic Woman" is also a minor i-iv-v, only in a different key. It uses the chords Dm, Gm, and Am, which are vi, ii, and iii from the F major scale. When you renumber everything counting from the relative minor, Dm, the chords become i, iv, and v.

You can identify relative major and minor keys by using the two types of chord patterns shown in Figures 7-1 and 7-2 (which you also find in Chapter 6). Wherever you move these patterns on the fretboard, chords I and vi are always the relative major and minor. Want to know the relative minor for B? Play a major scale chord pattern starting on B and then move to chord vi. That's the relative minor — always! Want to know the parent major scale for C♯m? Play C♯m on the fretboard, count it as vi, and then move to chord I. That's the relative major — always!

Here are a few more songs based in the relative minor. For your reference, I include numbering for both the relative minor and relative major. You may find it easier to work out the chord progression by number in a familiar major scale pattern first (shown in parentheses) and then renumber it according to its relative minor tonic.

"All Along the Watchtower" by Jimi Hendrix (guitars tuned down one half step to E♭)

C♯m-B-A-B

i-♭VII-♭VI-♭VII in C♯ minor (vi-V-IV-V in E major)

"Layla" by Eric Clapton

Dm-B♭-C-Dm

i-♭VI-♭VII-i in D minor (vi-IV-V-vi in F major)

"Smells like Teen Spirit" by Nirvana

F5-B♭5-A♭5-D♭5

i-iv-♭III-♭VI in F minor (vi-ii-I-IV in A♭ major)

"The Thrill Is Gone" by B.B. King

Bm-Em-Bm-G-F♯m-Bm

i-iv-i-♭VI-v-i in B minor (vi-ii-vi-IV-iii-vi in D major)

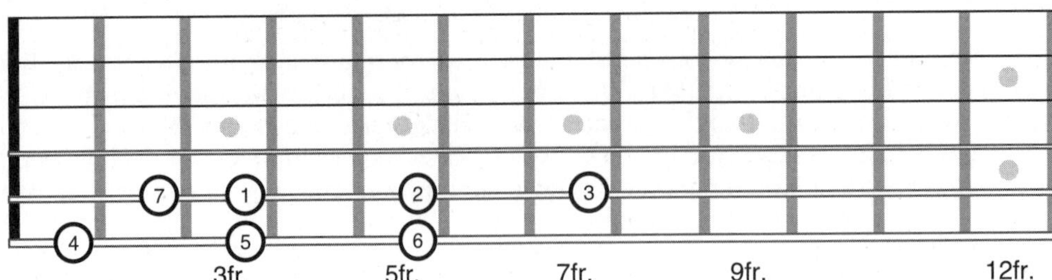

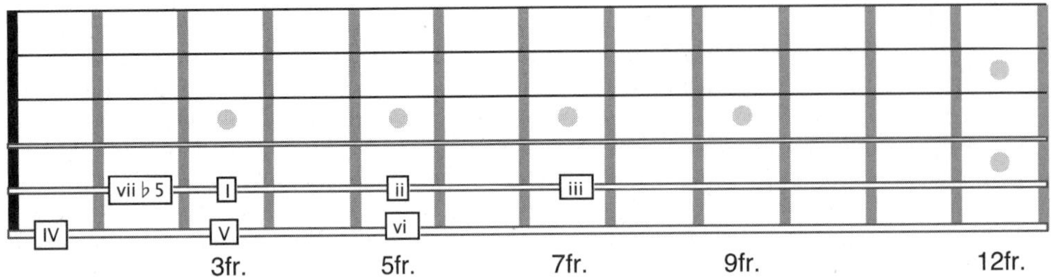

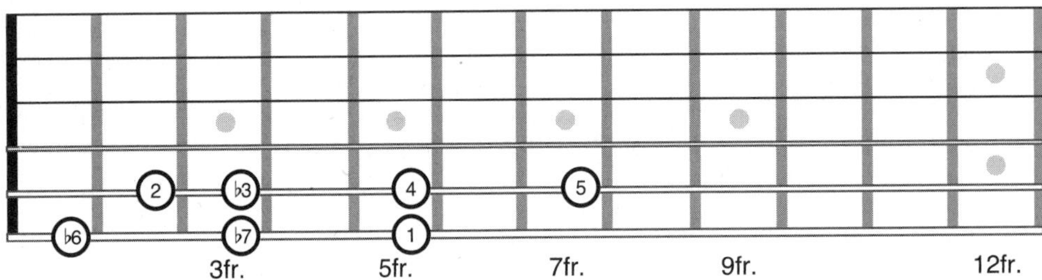

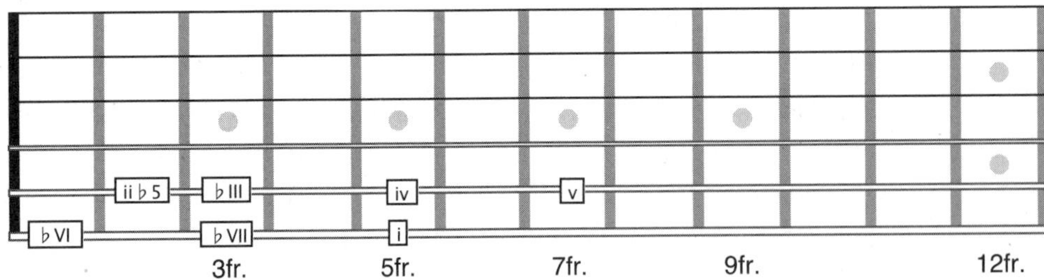

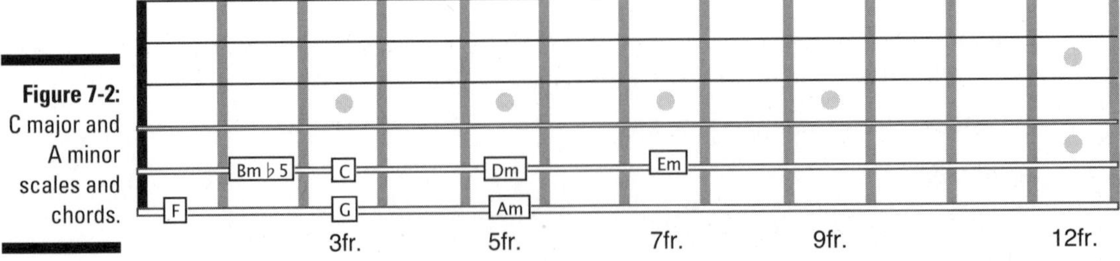

Figure 7-2: C major and A minor scales and chords.

Illustration courtesy of Desi Serna

Implied flats in minor keys

In minor keys, the flattened scale degrees, such as the 3rd and 6th, are often assumed rather than specifically mentioned or written. For example, in the key of E minor, a musician may refer to the G as the 3rd of the key without specifying that it's the flattened 3rd. Likewise, the three chord may be written simply as III with the minor key itself implying that it's ♭III. The same is true for ♭VI and ♭VII, so you may hear and see them simply referred to as VI and VII.

Identifying the Modes of the Major Scale

Relative major and relative minor aren't the only types of keys you can have in music. In fact, any degree in the major scale can function as the tonic (or key) and serve as the starting place in the scale, so because the major scale has seven degrees, it also has seven possible starting points, or *modes.*

In a major scale, three degrees produce major triads and chords — I, IV, and V — so any one of these can be the mode of a piece of music. The major scale also has three degrees that produce minor chords — ii, iii, and vi — and each one of these can also be the mode of a piece of music.

Notice that I don't mention the 7th scale degree as a modal option. The 7th chord in the major scale has a minor-flat-five quality (diminished triad), which has a dissonant and unresolved sound. The instability of its sound makes it impractical to base a piece of music on it. I can't remember hearing any song centering on vii♭5.

Each mode of the major scale is identified by a Greek name:

- Ionian (I)
- Dorian (ii)
- Phrygian (iii)
- Lydian (IV)
- Mixolydian (V)
- Aeolian (vi)
- Locrian (vii♭5)

Ionian (I)

Ionian is the first mode of the major scale — when the 1st scale degree functions as the tonic. Because it centers on a major chord (I), it's considered a major key. It's better known as the *plain* or *relative major scale,* and it's one of the most commonly used modes. Refer to Figure 7-1 to see how to view the fretboard in Ionian mode. Just think *major scale.*

Any type of chord progression that's based in a major scale and centers on chord I is Ionian mode. Some chord progression and song examples include

"Twist and Shout" by The Beatles

D-G-A

I-IV-V in the D major scale.

D Ionian (better known as simply D major)

"Stir It Up" by Bob Marley

A-D-E

I-IV-V in the A major scale

A Ionian (better known as simply A major)

"The Lion Sleeps Tonight" by The Tokens

F-B♭-F-C

I-IV-I-V in the F major scale

F Ionian (better known as simply F major)

"Wonderful Tonight" by Eric Clapton

G-D-C-D

I-V-IV-V in the G major scale

G Ionian (better known as simply G major)

"I'm Yours" by Jason Mraz

B-F♯-G♯m-E

I-V-vi-IV in the B major scale

B Ionian (better known as simply B major)

"What's Up?" by 4 Non Blondes

A-Bm-D-A

I-ii-IV-I in the A major scale

A Ionian (better known as simply A major)

Dorian (ii)

Dorian is the second mode of the major scale — when the 2nd scale degree functions as the tonic. Because it centers on a minor chord (ii), it's considered a minor key. Although this type of minor scale isn't as common as Aeolian mode (the natural or relative minor; see the later section) it does come up from time to time, so you need to look out for it.

In the same way that you renumber the relative minor, you can renumber all the modes of the major scale, starting from their tonics to reflect their unique interval structures and chord qualities. Here's what happens to the G major scale when you reorganize its notes and chords, beginning with the 2nd degree, A, to produce A Dorian mode:

G major

1-2-3-4-5-6-7

G-A-B-C-D-E-F♯

I-ii-iii-IV-V-vi-vii♭5

G-Am-Bm-C-D-Em-F♯m♭5

A Dorian

1-2-♭3-4-5-6-♭7

A-B-C-D-E-F♯-G

i-ii-♭III-IV-v-vi♭5-♭VII

Am-Bm-C-D-Em-F♯m♭5-G

Notice how the interval structure changes from G major to A Dorian. When you start the scale from the 2nd degree, it has a flattened 3rd and 7th. Also, the Roman numerals change to reflect the new chord qualities of each degree.

In Figure 7-3 you see how A Dorian looks on the fretboard, using the G major scale chord pattern that begins on the 6th string. In this example, you see G major first and then the same notes and chords reorganized starting on A. You can move this pattern around the fretboard and produce Dorian mode in other keys.

You can see a brief demonstration on playing in A Dorian by watching Video Clip 14.

The example in Figure 7-3 is just a starting point. You can play in A Dorian mode anywhere on the fretboard by using G major scale notes and chords and centering on the 2nd degree, A.

Modes are thought of as their own scales too. You can think of the Dorian scale either as a major scale with a flattened 3rd and 7th or as a minor scale with a major 6th. Its most defining characteristic is the major 6th because minor scales usually have a flattened 6th. Having the major 6th changes how the Dorian scale sounds melodically. It also changes the chord structure. The major 6th makes Dorian's 4th chord major, something that doesn't occur in a natural minor scale. The major 6th also makes the 2nd chord in Dorian mode minor with a perfect 5th, allowing for i-ii chord progressions.

Here are a few sample chord progressions and songs based on the 2nd degree of the major scale. For your reference, I include numbering for both the mode and the parent major scale (the common major scale that the mode is drawn from). You may find it easier to work out the chord progression by number in a familiar major scale pattern first (shown in parentheses) and then renumber it according to its modal tonic.

"Oye Como Va" by Santana

Am7-D9

i-IV in A Dorian (ii-V in the G major scale)

"Moondance" by Van Morrison

Am7-Bm7

i-ii in A Dorian (ii-iii in the G major scale)

"Who Will Save Your Soul" by Jewel

Am-C-G-D

i-♭III-♭VII-IV in A Dorian (ii-IV-I-V in the G major scale)

"Evil Ways" by Santana

Gm-C

i-IV in G Dorian (ii-V in the F major scale)

"Horse with No Name" by America

Em-F♯m11

i-ii in E Dorian (ii-iii in the D major scale)

In addition to using the patterns shown in Figure 7-3, you may also find yourself playing Dorian mode while in the chord pattern that begins on the 5th string. Figure 7-4 shows you how to reorganize the C major scale to fit with its 2nd mode, D Dorian. "Another Brick in the Wall (Part II)" by Pink Floyd has chord changes based in D Dorian in this position. You can also move this pattern around the fretboard to produce Dorian mode in other keys.

G major scale

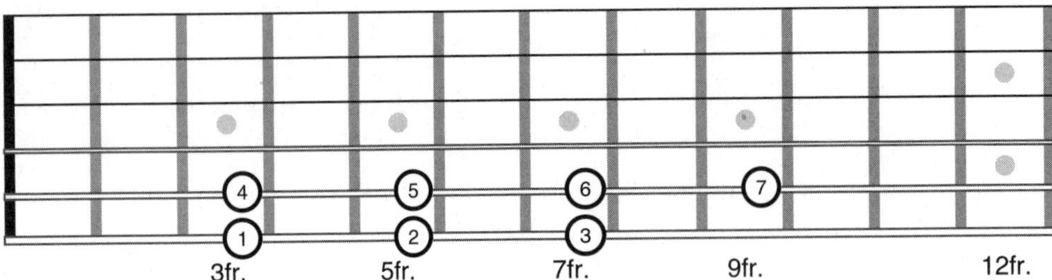

G major scale Roman numerals

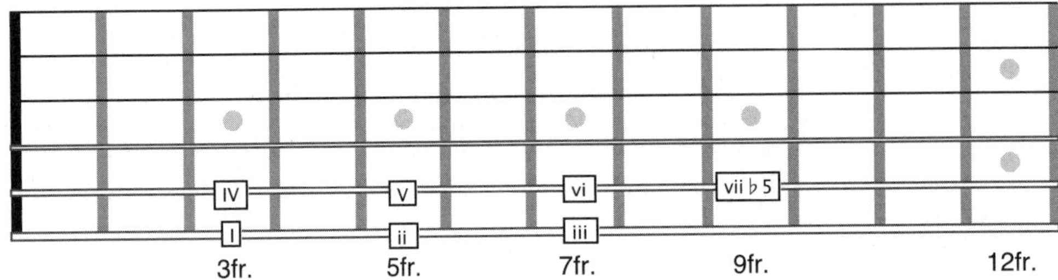

A Dorian mode

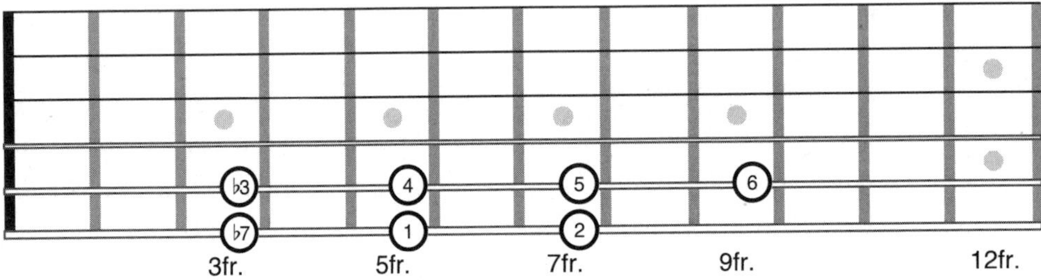

A Dorian mode Roman numerals

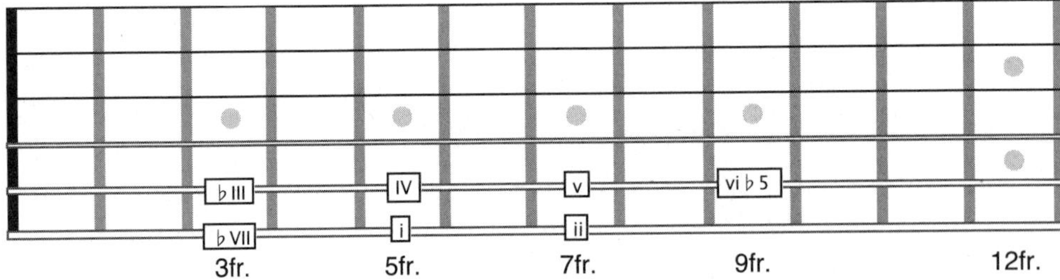

Same chords either way

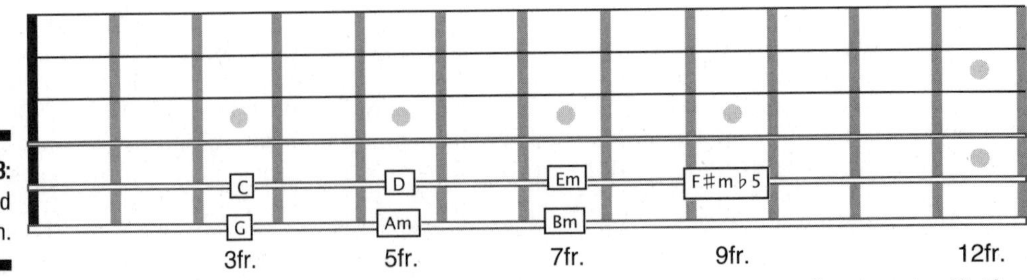

Figure 7-3: G major and A Dorian.

Illustration courtesy of Desi Serna

C major scale

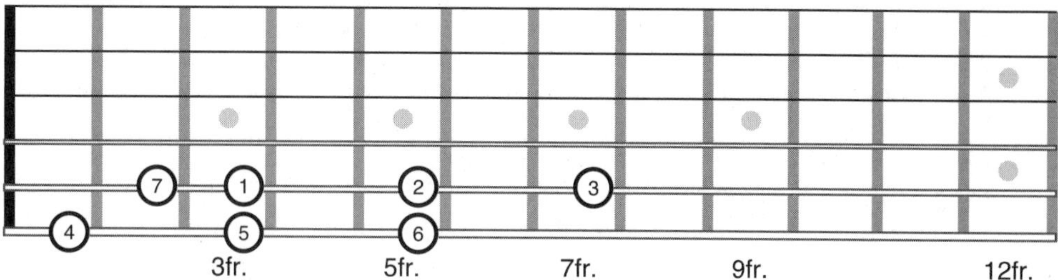

C major scale Roman numerals

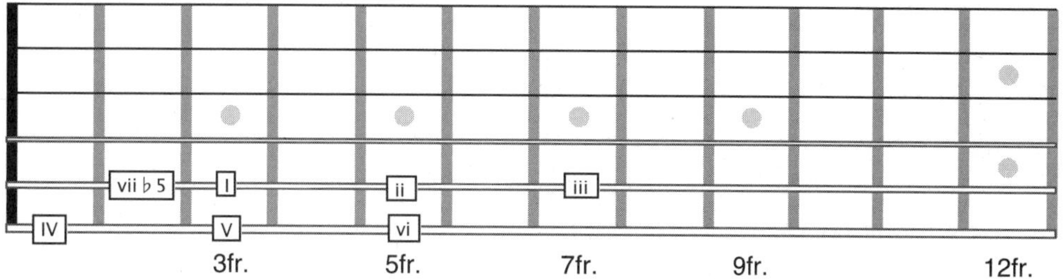

D Dorian mode

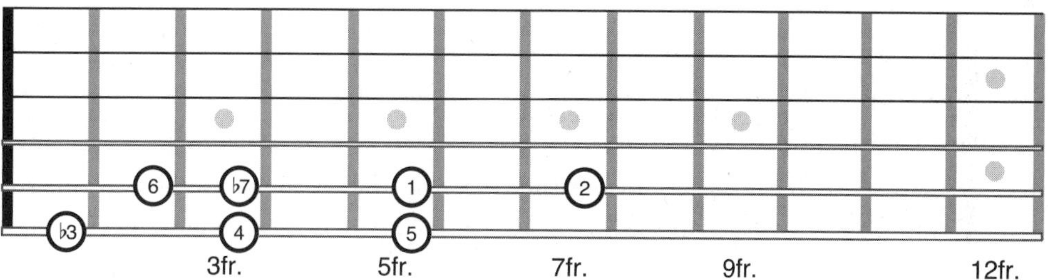

D Dorian mode Roman numerals

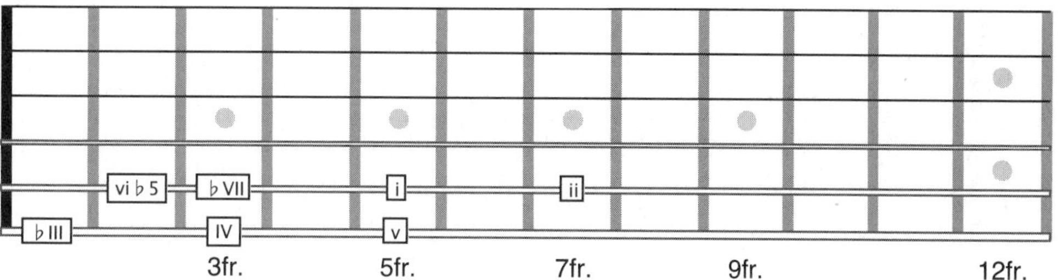

Same chords either way

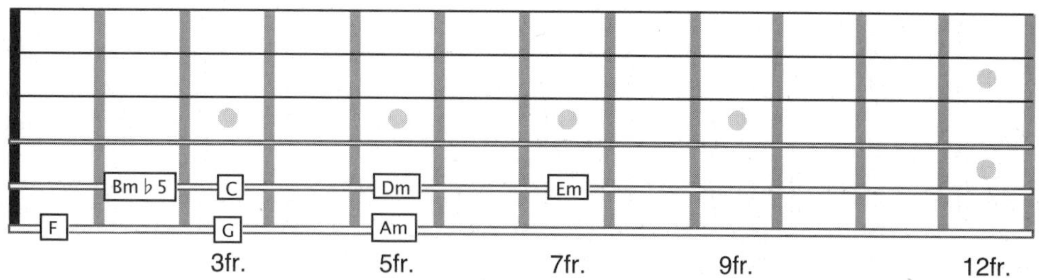

Figure 7-4: C major and D Dorian.

Illustration courtesy of Desi Serna

You refer to modes by their tonic pitch and Greek name. So *A Dorian* means the tonic pitch is A and it's the 2nd scale degree in the major scale. If A is 2, then G must be 1 and the parent major scale. *G Dorian* means the tonic pitch is G and it's the 2nd degree in the major scale. If G is 2, then F is 1 and the parent major scale. Because mode names don't indicate the parent major scale, you have to figure them out on your own.

Phrygian (iii)

Phrygian is the third mode of the major scale — when the 3rd scale degree functions as the tonic. It's considered a minor key because it centers on a minor chord. This type of minor scale is pretty uncommon, but some heavy metal artists use it for its dark, unusual sound. Here's what happens to the G major scale when you reorganize its notes and chords, beginning with the 3rd degree, B, to produce B Phrygian mode:

G major

1-2-3-4-5-6-7

G-A-B-C-D-E-F♯

I-ii-iii-IV-V-vi-vii♭5

G-Am-Bm-C-D-Em-F♯m♭5

B Phrygian

1-♭2-♭3-4-5-♭6-♭7

B-C-D-E-F♯-G-A

i-♭II-♭III-iv-v♭5-♭VI-♭vii

Bm-C-D-Em-F♯m♭5-G-Am

Phrygian is a type of minor scale with a flattened 2nd as its most defining characteristic. Figure 7-5 shows how B Phrygian comes from its parent major scale, G.

Remember that the example in Figure 7-5 is just a starting point. You can play B Phrygian anywhere on the fretboard as long as you use notes and chords from the G major scale and center on B. When playing in B Phrygian, most guitarists opt to put the chords Bm and C right next to each other on the same string.

You can also move the pattern in Figure 7-5 around the fretboard to play Phrygian mode in other keys. Figure 7-6 shows how E Phrygian is taken from its parent major scale, C. This example puts you into a chord pattern that begins on the 5th string. You can move this pattern around to play in other Phrygian keys, too. In E Phrygian, guitarists seem to prefer playing off of the open 6th string, putting an E5 and F5 right next to each other.

G major scale

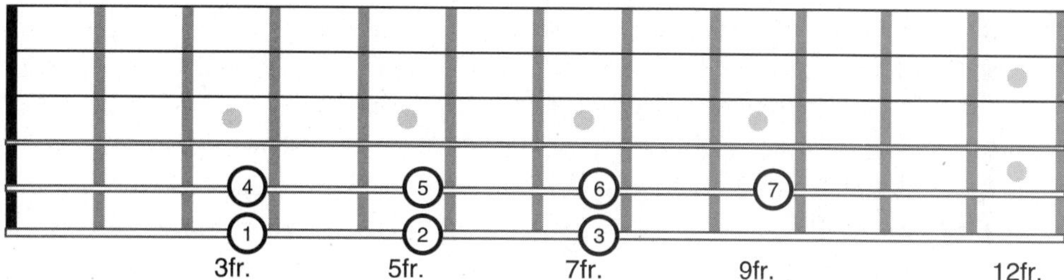

G major scale roman numerals

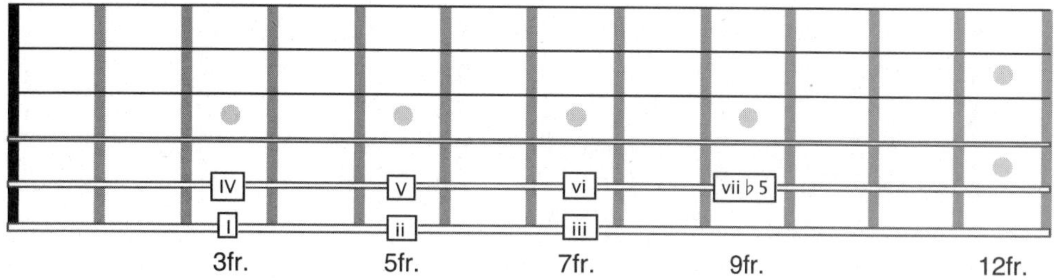

B Phrygian mode

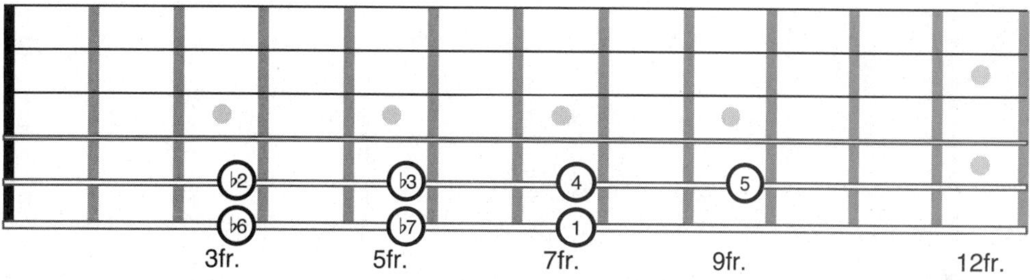

B Phrygian mode Roman numerals

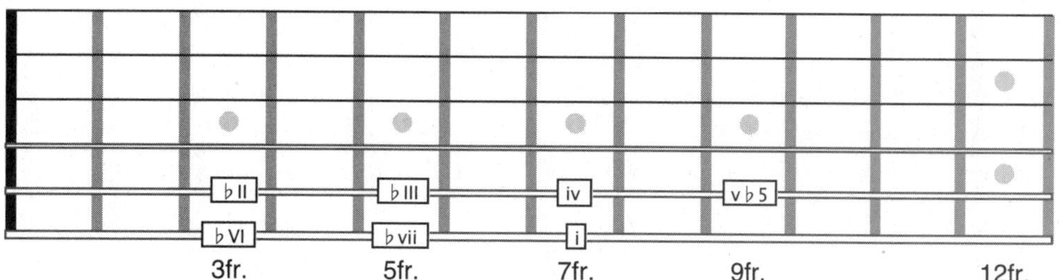

Same chords either way

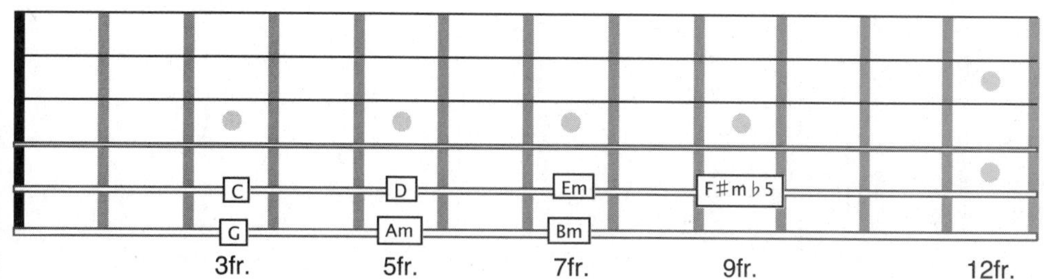

Figure 7-5: G major and B Phrygian.

Illustration courtesy of Desi Serna

C major scale

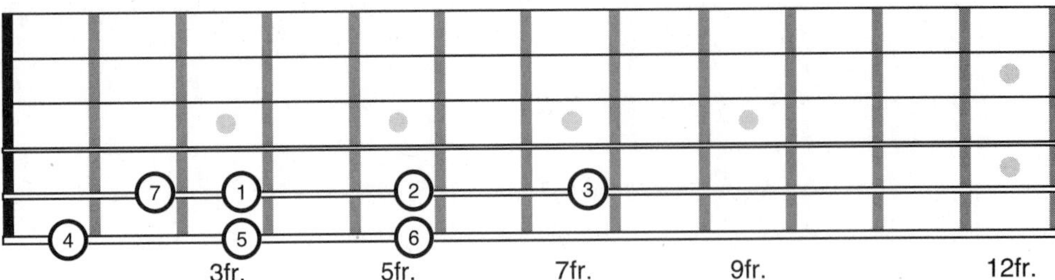

C major scale Roman numerals

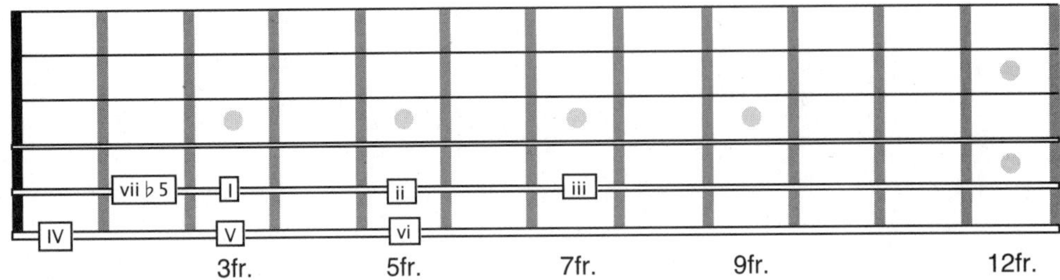

E Phrygian mode

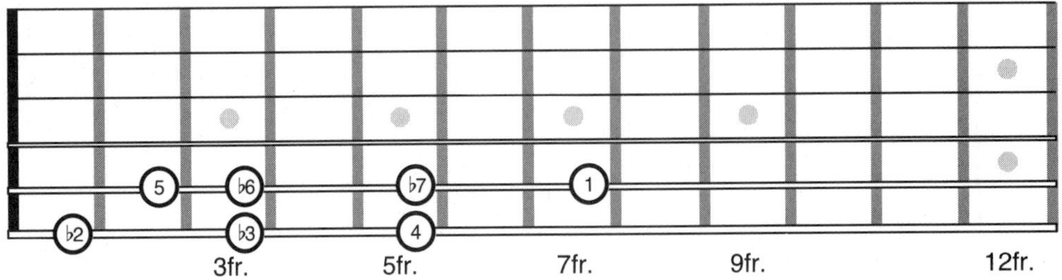

E Phrygian mode Roman numerals

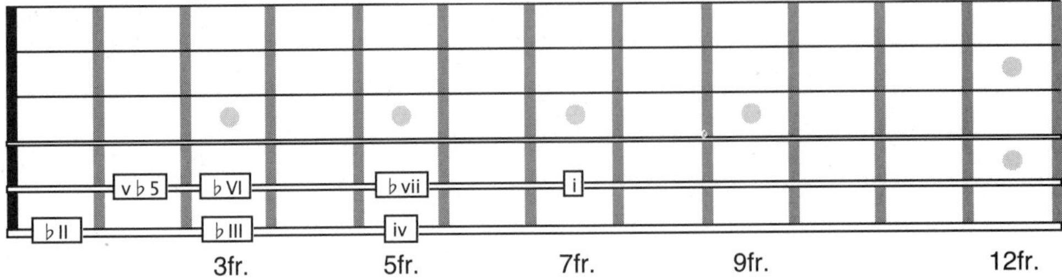

Same chords either way

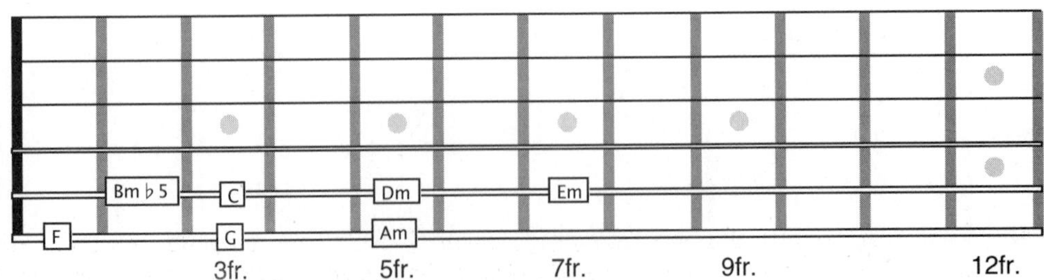

Figure 7-6: C major and E Phrygian.

Illustration courtesy of Desi Serna

Here are some sample chord progressions and songs based on the 3rd degree of the major scale. You may find it easier to work out the chord progression by number in a familiar major scale pattern first (shown in parentheses) and then renumber it according to its Phrygian tonic.

"The Sails of Charon" by Scorpions

B5-C5

i-♭II in B Phrygian (iii-IV in the G major scale)

"Remember Tomorrow" by Iron Maiden

Em-F

i-♭II in E Phrygian (iii-IV in the C major scale)

"War" by Joe Satriani (guitars tuned down one half step to E♭)

E5-F5

i-♭II in E Phrygian (iii-IV in the C major scale)

"Symphony of Destruction" by Megadeth

F5-E5

♭II-i in E Phrygian (IV-i in the C major scale)

Though this progression starts on the ♭II chord, F5, the i chord, E5, is functioning as the tonic in the song example.

Songs don't always stay in one key. Some of the songs listed in this chapter have certain modal sections but then move on to other keys. For example, "War" by Joe Satriani starts in E Phrygian but then cycles through other types of keys from there. Similarly, "Moondance" by Van Morrison starts in A Dorian but then changes to other modes. For now, you can just focus on the song sections that pertain to the mode discussions in this chapter. You get to know key changes in Chapter 8.

Lydian (IV)

Lydian is the fourth mode of the major scale — when the 4th scale degree functions as the tonic. Because it centers on a major chord, it's considered a major key. Rarely do you hear a song that's completely in Lydian mode. Instead, this mode usually occurs only temporarily in a song, until the music moves to a more stable tonic like I. Here you see what happens to the G major scale when you reorganize its notes and chords, beginning with the 4th degree, C, to produce C Lydian mode:

G major

1-2-3-4-5-6-7

G-A-B-C-D-E-F♯

I-ii-iii-IV-V-vi-vii♭5

G-Am-Bm-C-D-Em-F♯m♭5

C Lydian

1-2-3-♯4-5-6-7

C-D-E-F♯-G-A-B

I-II-iii-♯iv♭5-V-vi-vii

C-D-Em-F♯m♭5-G-Am-Bm

The most defining characteristic of Lydian mode is its sharpened 4th, which is why many musicians think of it as a major scale with a sharpened 4th. In Figure 7-7, you see C Lydian taken from its parent major scale, G.

G major scale

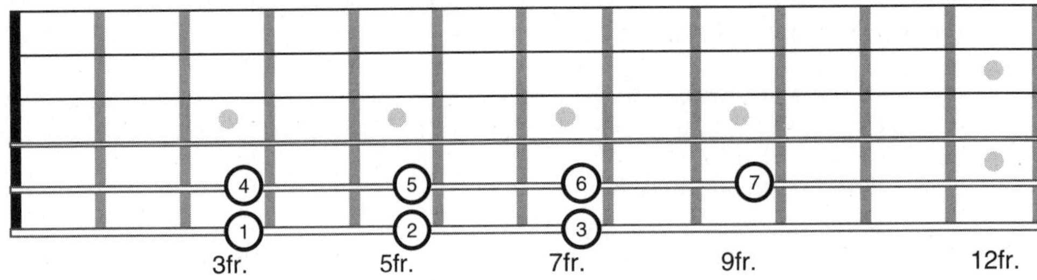

G major scale Roman numerals

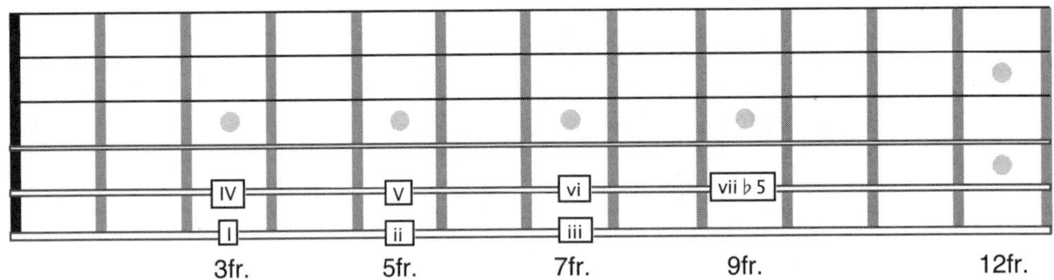

C Lydian mode

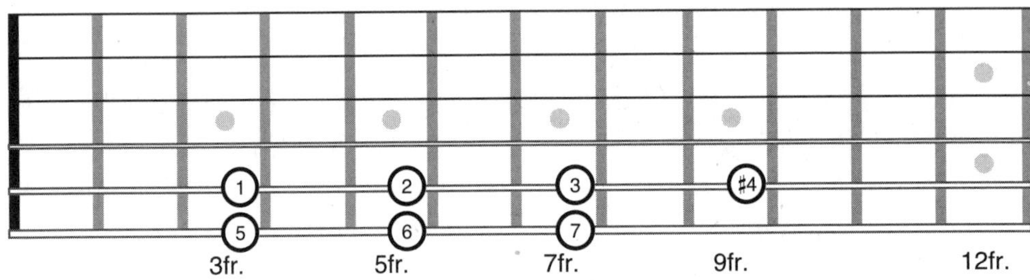

C Lydian mode Roman numerals

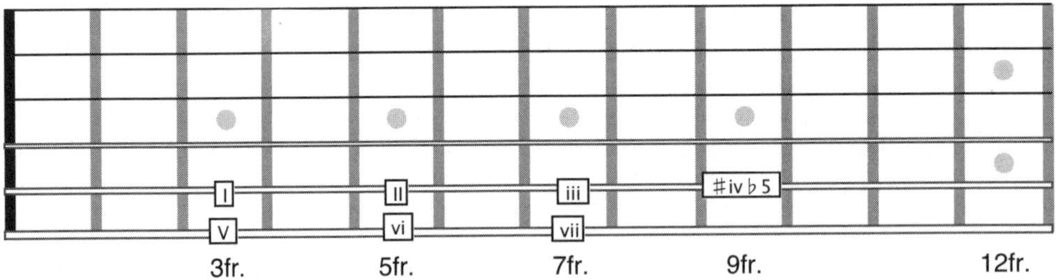

Same chords either way

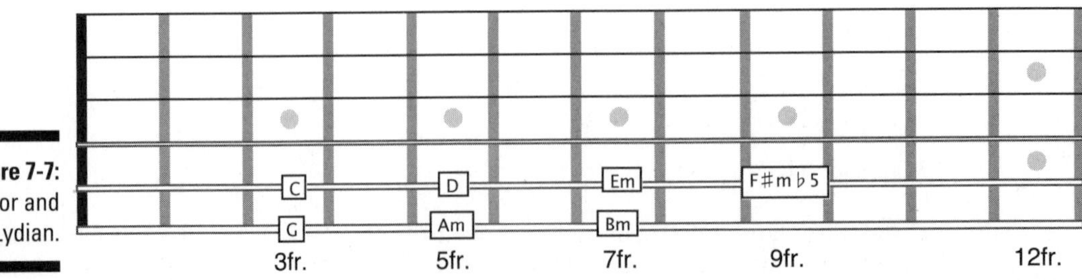

Figure 7-7: G major and C Lydian.

Illustration courtesy of Desi Serna

You can play C Lydian anywhere on the fretboard as long as you use notes and chords from the G major scale and center on C. You can also move the pattern in Figure 7-7 around the fretboard to play Lydian mode in other keys.

Figure 7-8 puts you in a new major scale pattern that begins on the 5th string. Here, the parent major scale is C and the mode is F Lydian. Again, this is just a starting point. You find the same notes and chords elsewhere on the fretboard, and you can move this pattern around to play in other keys.

Here are a few sample chord progressions and songs based on the 4th degree of the major scale:

"Dreams" by Fleetwood Mac

Fmaj7-G6

I-II in F Lydian (IV-V in the C major scale)

"Just Remember I Love You" by Firefall

Fmaj7-G6

I-II in F Lydian (IV-V in the C major scale)

"Jane Says" by Jane's Addiction

G-A

I-II in G Lydian (IV-V in the D major scale)

"Here Comes My Girl" by Tom Petty

A-B

I-II in A Lydian (IV-V in the E major scale)

"Man on the Moon" by R.E.M.

C-D

I-II in C Lydian (IV-V in the G major scale)

"Hey Jealousy" by Gin Blossoms

D-E-F♯m-E

I-II-iii-II in D Lydian (IV-V-vi-V in the A major scale)

"Space Oddity" by David Bowie

Fmaj7-Em

I-vii in F Lydian (IV-iii in the C major scale)

C major scale

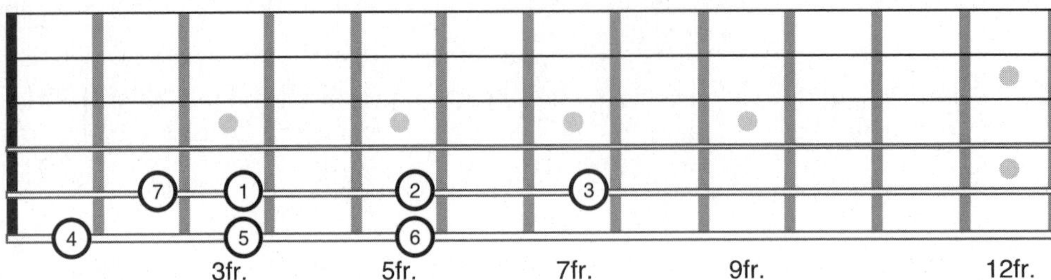

C major scale Roman numerals

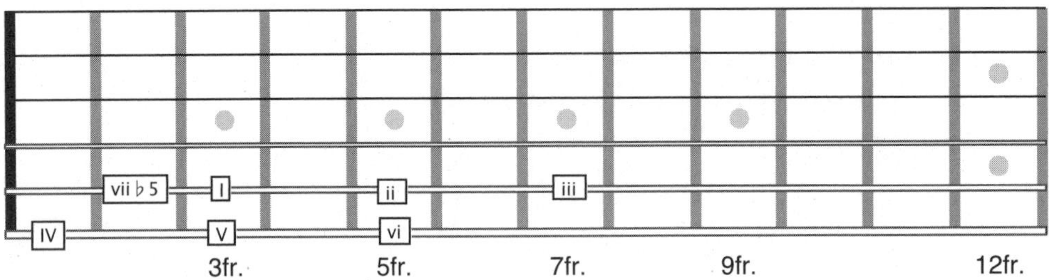

F Lydian mode

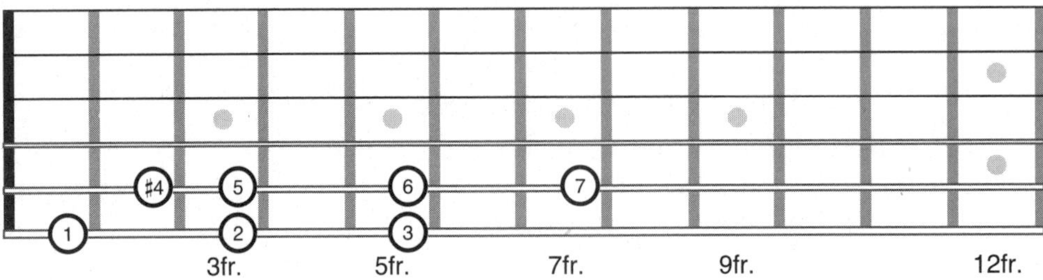

F Lydian mode Roman numerals

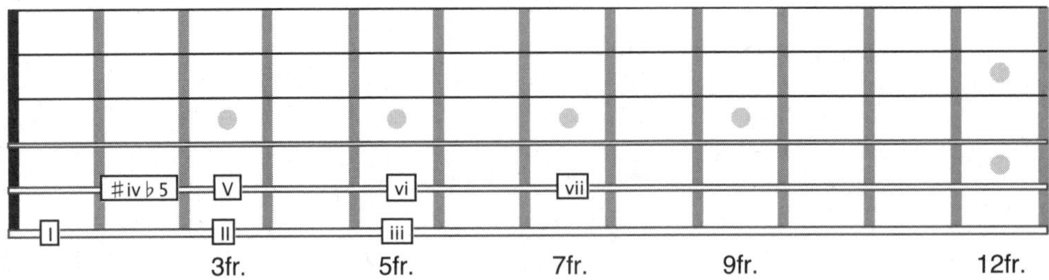

Same chords either way

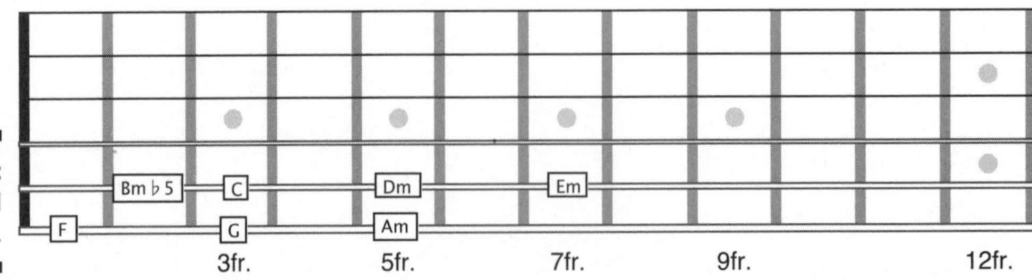

Figure 7-8: C major and F Lydian.

Illustration courtesy of Desi Serna

Mixolydian (V)

Mixolydian is the fifth mode of the major scale — when the 5th scale degree functions as the tonic. It centers on a major chord, so it's considered a major key. It's also called the *dominant scale* because the 5th degree of the major scale is named the *dominant pitch* (see Chapter 9) and forms a dominant 7th chord. This mode is fairly common, almost as much as the relative major and minor. Here you see what happens to the G major scale when you reorganize its notes and chords, beginning with the 5th degree, D, to produce D Mixolydian mode:

G major

1-2-3-4-5-6-7

G-A-B-C-D-E-F♯

I-ii-iii-IV-V-vi-vii♭5

G-Am-Bm-C-D-Em-F♯m♭5

D Mixolydian

1-2-3-4-5-6-♭7

D-E-F♯-G-A-B-C

I-ii-iii♭5-IV-v-vi-♭VII

D-Em-F♯m♭5-G-Am-Bm-C

Mixolydian mode is often thought of as a major scale with a flattened 7th, its most defining characteristic. Mixolydian also features a ♭VII chord, a major chord one whole step below the tonic. Figure 7-9 shows D Mixolydian taken from its parent major scale, G.

You can play D Mixolydian anywhere on the fretboard as long as you use notes and chords from the G major scale and center on D. You can also move the pattern in Figure 7-9 around the fretboard to play Mixolydian mode in other keys.

Figure 7-10 puts you in a new major scale pattern that begins on the 5th string. Here the parent major scale is C and the mode is G Mixolydian. Of course, you find the same notes and chords elsewhere on the fretboard, so you can move this pattern around to play in other keys, too.

G major scale

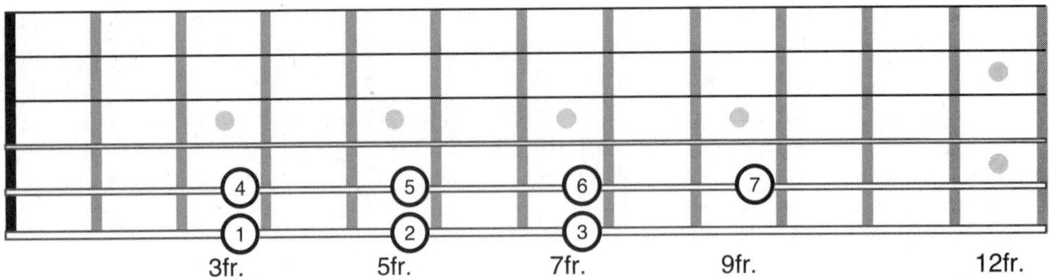

G major scale roman numerals

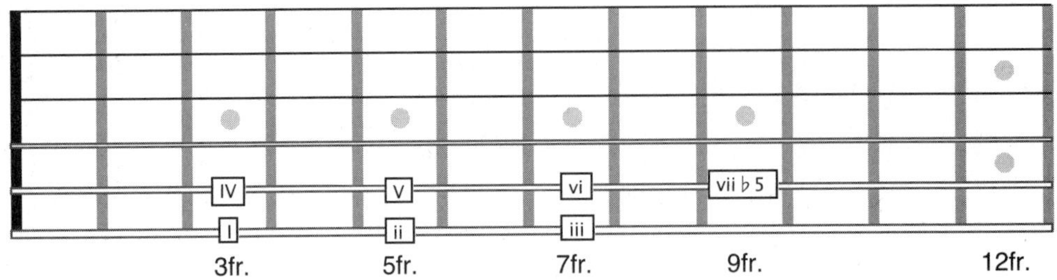

D Mixolydian mode

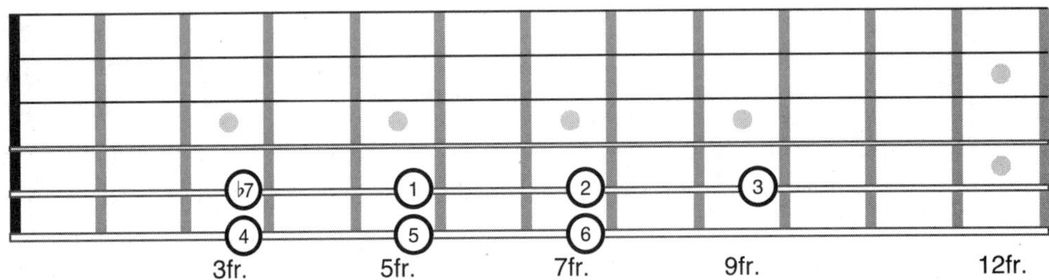

D Mixolydian mode Roman numerals

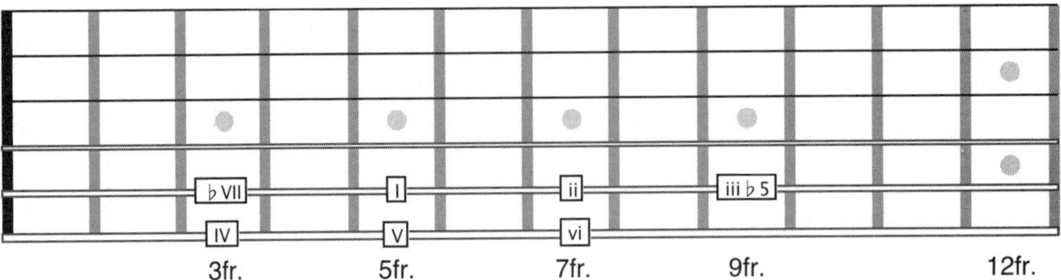

Same chords either way

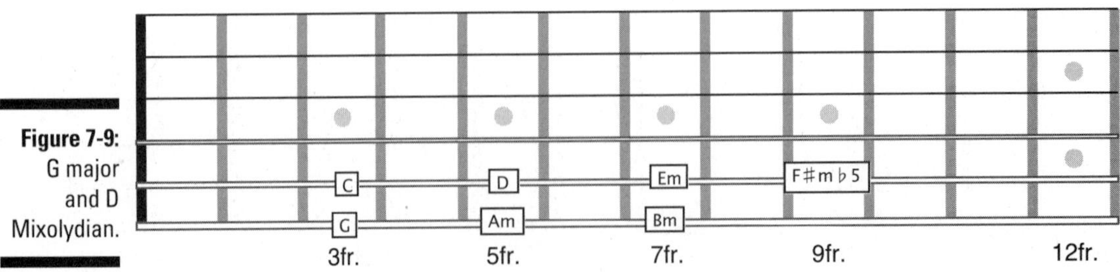

Figure 7-9: G major and D Mixolydian.

Illustration courtesy of Desi Serna

C major scale

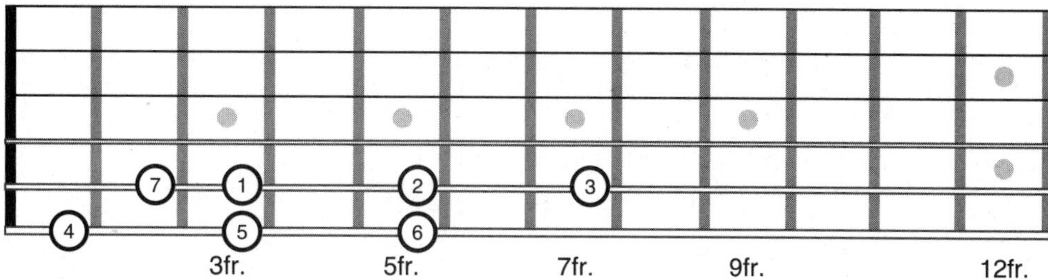

C major scale Roman numerals

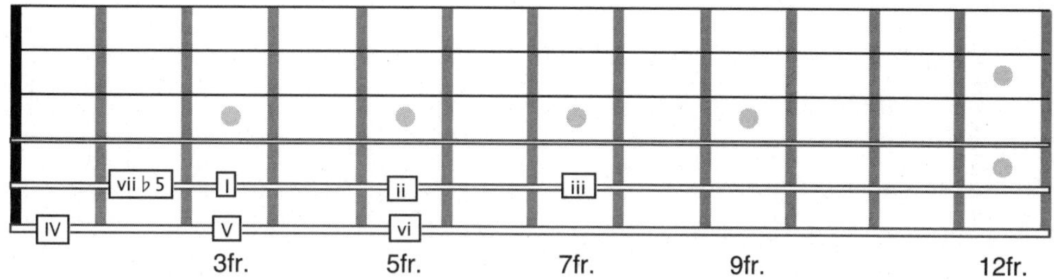

G Mixolydian mode

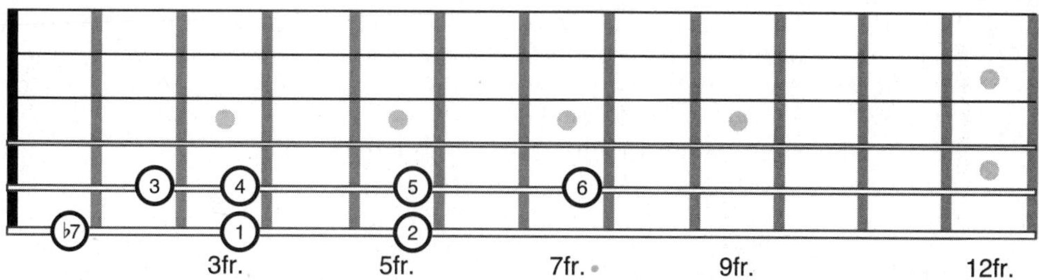

G Mixolydian mode Roman numerals

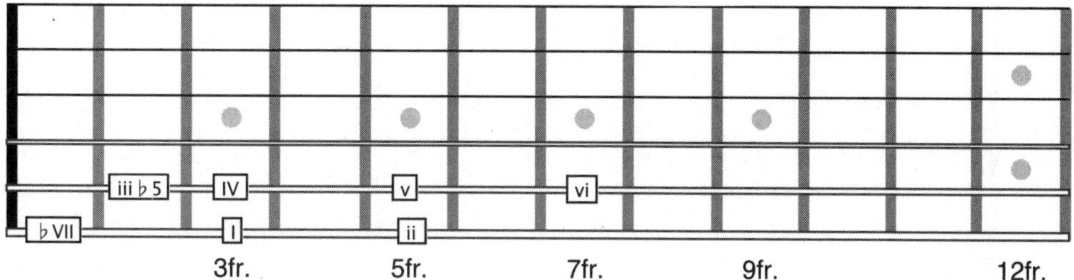

Same chords either way

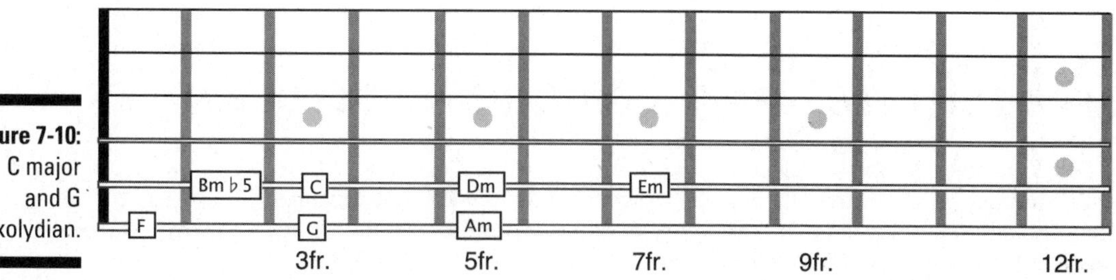

Figure 7-10: C major and G Mixolydian.

Illustration courtesy of Desi Serna

Here are some sample chord progressions and songs based on the 5th degree of the major scale:

"Seven Bridges Road" by the Eagles

D-C-G-D

I-♭VII-IV-I in D Mixolydian (V-IV-I-V in the G major scale)

"Southern Cross" by Crosby, Stills & Nash

A-G-D-A

I-♭VII-IV-I in A Mixolydian (V-IV-I-V in the D major scale)

"Louie Louie" by The Kingsmen

A-D-Em-D

I-IV-v-IV in A Mixolydian (V-I-ii-I in the D major scale)

"What I Like about You" by the Romantics

E-A-D-A

I-IV-♭VII-IV in E Mixolydian (V-I-IV-I in the A major scale)

"Cinnamon Girl" by Neil Young

D-Am7-C-G

I-v-♭VII-IV in D Mixolydian (V-ii-IV-I in the G major scale)

Another important feature of the Mixolydian mode is the minor chord on the 5th degree. You hear it used in the song "Louie Louie" by The Kingsmen. Many musicians mistake this song for being a common I-IV-V chord progression in A major. If you listen carefully to the recording, however, you can clearly hear the chords A, D, and *Em,* not E major. This progression is actually I-IV-v with a minor v chord. That's Mixolydian mode!

Aeolian (vi)

Aeolian is the sixth mode of the major scale — when the 6th scale degree functions as the tonic. Because it centers on a minor chord, it's considered a minor key. In fact, it's better known as the *natural* or *relative minor scale.* You work with this mode in the earlier section "Numbering the Relative Minor."

Locrian (vii♭5)

Locrian is the seventh mode of the major scale — when the 7th scale degree functions as the tonic. As I mention earlier, the 7th chord in the major scale has a minor-flat-five quality (diminished triad), which produces a dissonant and unresolved sound. I've never come across a song that uses it, so I don't spend much time on it here. Nevertheless, it's still considered a type of minor key.

Key Signatures and Common Discrepancies

Generally, major keyed songs center on the 1st degree of the major scale, while minor keyed songs center on the 6th degree. However, you can also center music on one of the other major scale degrees. As a result, you can't assume that a major key is always Ionian or that a minor key is always Aeolian.

Looking past the key signature to figure out a song's mode

Here's where things get tricky. Although the major scale has multiple modes, musicians generally think of and notate music as being in only the relative major and relative minor, even when another mode is being used. So songs in the major modes (Ionian, Lydian, and Mixolydian) are all treated as if they were plain major, or in Ionian mode, while songs in the minor modes (Dorian, Phrygian, and Aeolian) are all treated as if they were natural minor, or in Aeolian mode.

Music publishers generally disregard the mode and write everything as if it were in a plain major or natural minor key, going off of the tonic chord. For example, if a piece of music centers on a G chord, it's notated with a key signature reflecting the G major scale even if it's really G Lydian or G Mixolydian. Likewise, if a piece of music centers on an Em chord, it's notated with a key signature reflecting E natural minor even if it's really E Dorian or E Phrygian. Then any necessary *accidentals* (sharps, flats, or natural signs) are used for notes that fall outside of the key signature. As a result, you receive no initial instruction that the music you're reading is based in a scale other than the scale reflected in the key signature. This isn't a problem for sight-readers; they're used to playing everything off the page anyway, accidentals and all. But if you want to know how a piece of music was composed or if you plan to improvise a guitar solo, you need to understand the real parent major scale being used.

Take the song "Seven Bridges Road" by the Eagles, for example. The primary chord progression is in D Mixolydian mode. The notes and chords are from the G major scale (G-A-B-C-D-E-F♯), and the 5th scale degree, D, functions as the tonic. Because the tonic chord is D, music publishers notate the song as if it were in a plain D major key signature, which includes two sharps, F♯ and C♯. Then every time a C-natural note occurs in the music, both in the melody and in the chords, they specially mark it with a natural sign (♮) to cue you not to use the C♯ note reflected in the key signature (see Figure 7-11).

Figure 7-11: D Mixolydian with D major key signature.

Illustration courtesy of Desi Serna

If Figure 7-11 were written with a key signature for G major, you wouldn't need any accidentals. But, alas, things are never that easy.

Publishers often use the same technique when a piece of music is in Lydian; they write it as if it were plain major and then rely on accidentals to make any necessary changes. For example, C Lydian, which is drawn from the G major scale, is written with a key signature of C, implying the plain C major scale. Then a sharp sign appears each time an F♯ occurs throughout the music.

The same thing happens in minor keys, too. Take, for example, "Oye Como Va" by Santana. This song centers on an Am chord and is said to be in the key of A minor. However, saying *A minor* implies *A natural minor,* the relative minor of C major. That's incorrect. A natural minor features an F-natural and produces a Dm chord. But this song features F♯s and D major chords. The parent major scale is really G major. Nevertheless, you usually see this song marked with a key signature of A minor with sharp signs next to all the F notes used in the score (see Figure 7-12). ***Note:*** If Figure 7-12 were written with a key signature for G major, you wouldn't need any accidentals. You can expect to see the same technique used with Phrygian; it's notated as natural minor and then corrected with accidentals.

Figure 7-12: A Dorian with A minor key signature.

Illustration courtesy of Desi Serna

One reason that using the relative major and minor keys is standard procedure among musicians is that music often draws from more than one scale. *Modal interchange,* which I discuss in Chapter 8, is a common composition technique that mixes different *parallel scales* (scales that each draw from a different parent major scale yet center on the same pitch). For example, G major, G Lydian (D major scale), and G Mixolydian (C major scale) are parallel scales. When a song mixes all three of these modes, changing the key signature every time the notes and chords from a parallel scale appear is hardly practical. Instead, you can give the song one key signature and just use the corresponding accidentals for notes that fall outside of it.

Considering some common discrepancies in music notation

Although the practice of notating music as if it were plain major or natural minor is standard procedure for music publishers, you occasionally come across a score that truly reflects the mode. For example, if a song is in A Dorian mode, the score may actually use the key signature for G major, its true parent major scale. The score may also include a performance note, such as "A minor tonality" or "A Dorian mode," to clue you into the fact that the G scale is being used although the G note isn't the tonic. Likewise, if a song is in A Mixolydian mode, you may see the key signature for D major and a note such as "A major tonality" or "A Mixolydian mode."

I occasionally come across these kinds of scores that actually tell it like it is, but they're definitely not the norm. So don't count on them! Instead, get used to examining the elements of every piece of music to determine whether it's really using the scale reflected in the key signature.

Here are a few other important issues to keep in mind as you work through different pieces of music to determine their modes and scales:

- Modes aren't always properly identified in music circles. If you ask musicians what key "Oye Como Va" by Santana is in, most of them will say A minor. Although Dorian mode is a type of minor key, you know there's more to it than that. Unfortunately, musicians usually refer to only the initial tonic of a song and leave all the other details, including modes, up to you to figure out.
- Some musicians always name the key after the first chord, even if it isn't the true tonic. For example, "Sweet Home Alabama" by Lynyrd Skynyrd is tonally centered around a G chord, and most of the guitar solos are based on G major pentatonic. Nevertheless, many guitar players say that the song is in the key of D simply because the chord progression starts on a D chord.

- Some musicians identify a key without considering its major or minor quality. For example, many musicians would say that "Black Magic Woman" by Santana and "Twist and Shout" by The Beatles are both in the key of D. You just have to know that one is minor and the other is major because the songs have two completely different parent major scales.
- Some musicians think about the key based on the notes in the melody rather than on the chords. For example, the vocal melody in "Give Me One Reason" by Tracy Chapman outlines notes from F♯ minor played over an F♯ major chord. For this reason, a musician, particularly a singer, may think that the song is in the key of F♯ minor when it's really in F♯ major.
- Some guitar players confuse the key of a song with the type of pentatonic scale they're playing. "Pride and Joy" by Stevie Ray Vaughan is tonally centered around an open E major chord (guitars tuned down a half step to E♭). Nevertheless, much of the guitar solos are based on an E minor pentatonic scale, leading some guitar players to say that the song is in the key of E minor.
- Some pieces of music don't even have a complete parent major scale. They simply focus on a tonic by means of some basic intervals, though not enough to piece together full chords, a chord progression, or an entire major scale. You see this technique in the songs "Boom Boom" by John Lee Hooker, "Voodoo Child (Slight Return)" by Jimi Hendrix, and "Whole Lotta Love" by Led Zeppelin. All three songs use mostly minor pentatonic scales. Likewise, in some hard rock and heavy metal songs, you see power chords and chromatic steps without any parent major scale represented in the chords, the chord progression, or even the melody itself.

Comparing Scale Formulas and Structures

A *scale* or *chord formula* is its pattern of steps and intervals. For example, a major triad is 1-3-5. A major scale is 1-2-3-4-5-6-7. The following charts compare the different scale formulas of the major scale modes that are used for keys and chord progressions. Don't worry about memorizing all the charts; just use them as a tool to help you better understand the relationship between the modes and their structures and the major scale.

Table 7-1 compares the interval structure for the six main modes of the major scale. (I don't include the Locrian mode because it's more of a theoretical mode.) I point out the relative major and relative minor here because they're used the most and are considered to be plain, natural scales. I also include the Roman numerals so you can see how the major and minor chord sequences relate to the major scale.

Table 7-1 Modes and Interval Structures

Degree/Chord	*Mode Name*	*Interval Structure*	*Roman Numeral Sequence*
I	Ionian (plain major)	1-2-3-4-5-6-7	I-ii-iii-IV-V-vi-vii♭5
ii	Dorian	1-2-♭3-4-5-6-♭7	i-ii-♭III-IV-v-vi♭5-♭VII
iii	Phrygian	1-♭2-♭3-4-5-♭6-♭7	i-♭II-♭III-iv-v♭5-♭VI-♭vii
IV	Lydian	1-2-3-♯4-5-6-7	I-II-iii-♯iv♭5-V-vi-vii
V	Mixolydian	1-2-3-4-5-6-♭7	I-ii-iii♭5-IV-v-vi-♭VII
vi	Aeolian (natural minor)	1-2-♭3-4-5-♭6-♭7	i-ii♭5-♭III-iv-v-♭VI-♭VII

Table 7-2 shows you what all these chords look like when you build out each mode in the sample scale of A major.

Table 7-2 Building Each Mode in the Scale of A Major

Mode Name	*Chords*
A Ionian (plain major)	A-Bm-C♯m-D-E-F♯m-G♯m♭5
B Dorian	Bm-C♯m-D-E-F♯m-G♯m♭5-A
C♯ Phrygian	C♯m-D-E-F♯m-G♯m♭5-A-Bm
D Lydian	D-E-F♯m-G♯m♭5-A-Bm-C♯m
E Mixolydian	E-F♯m-G♯m♭5-A-Bm-C♯m-D
F♯ Aeolian (natural minor)	F♯m-G♯m♭5-A-Bm-C♯m-D-E

Finally, Table 7-3 provides a chart of parallel modes. Here, the term *parallel* means different scales that all center on the same primary pitch. In the comparison in this table, the tonic pitch remains A for each mode. You compare A major to A Dorian to A Phrygian and so on. The parent major scale is different in each example here.

Table 7-3 Parallel Modes with A as the Tonic

Mode Name	*Chords*	*Parent Scale*
A Ionian (plain major)	A-Bm-C♯m-D-E-F♯m-G♯m♭5	1st mode of A major scale
A Dorian	Am-Bm-C-D-Em-F♯m♭5-G	2nd mode of G major scale
A Phrygian	Am-B♭-C-Dm-Em♭5-F-Gm	3rd mode of F major scale
A Lydian	A-B-C♯m-D♯m♭5-E-F♯m-G♯m	4th mode of E major scale
A Mixolydian	A-Bm-C♯m♭5-D-Em-F♯m-G	5th mode of D major scale
A Aeolian (natural minor)	Am-Bm♭5-C-Dm-Em-F-G	6th mode of C major scale

Seeing the chords of parallel modes like this gives you an idea of how many options you have when approaching a composition in the key of A. What key of A are you going to use? A major or A minor? Plain A major, Mixolydian, or Lydian? Natural A minor, Dorian, or Phrygian? Perhaps you want to try a mixture of modes, a technique you find out about in Chapter 8.

Chapter 8

Following Key Changes

In This Chapter

- Changing keys and chord progressions
- Mixing modes and borrowing chords
- Playing the circle of 5ths

When you're playing songs, sometimes seeing how a chord progression fits into a key (specifically, one of the major scale chord patterns you play in Chapter 6) is really easy. Other times the chords used in a piece of music seem to be completely unrelated. The main reason for this variation is that a song doesn't have to stay in one key or one type of scale. In fact, composers often switch from one key to another within the same song or combine chords from different scales to form one chord progression.

In this chapter, you employ some common techniques to play more complicated and more interesting chord progressions. These techniques include changing keys, mixing modes, borrowing chords, and using the circle of fifths.

Properly identifying key changes and similar modulations can help you better understand the music you listen to and play, so don't be tempted to skip this chapter! If you're a composer or songwriter, you'll like the variety that key changes offer. If you're a lead guitarist, you'll be able to tell when to change scale patterns for solos.

Listen to Audio Track 8 to hear some key change examples and get an idea of what this chapter is all about.

Getting to Know Key Changes by Switching Tonics within a Scale

You may think of music as having a main chord or pitch called the *tonic,* as well as a *parent scale* that the tonic and the rest of the chord progression are drawn from. In many songs, the tonic changes at some point, and sometimes the parent scale changes, too.

Technically, a *key change* is a change from one tonic or tonal center to another. This may or may not also include a change in key signature on a written score. So when you come across a chord that doesn't fit into the same key as the other chords it's played with, you need to look elsewhere to figure out where it comes from. (***Note:*** The use of modal interchange and borrowed chords usually revolves around a consistent tonic, so these types of techniques aren't considered key changes in the classic sense, though they do employ the use of other scales. Skip to the later section "Using Modal Interchange and Borrowed Chords" for details.)

The first type of key change that you play is one where the tonic changes but the parent major scale stays the same. A perfect example of this is when a song switches between being centered on the relative major and being centered on the relative minor, though songs can switch between other scale degrees, too.

Switching between relative major and minor

In Figure 8-1, you play a series of changes that first center on an Am chord and then switch to the relative major, C. Here, the Am is chord vi from the C major scale and the C chord is I.

Figure 8-1: Relative major and minor modulation.

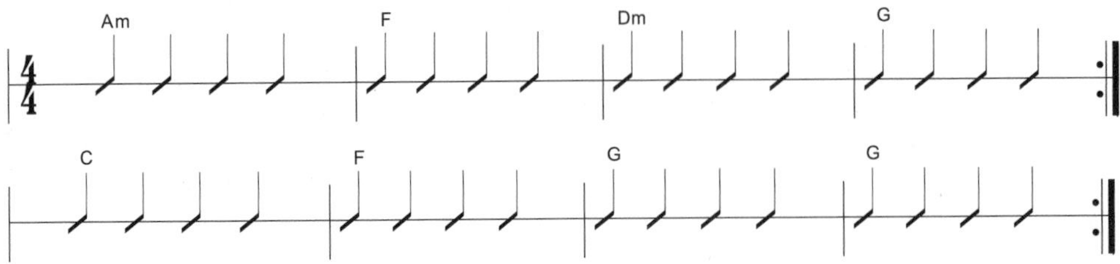

Illustration courtesy of Desi Serna

"Mr. Jones" by Counting Crows switches in a manner similar to the example in Figure 8-1. It starts out being centered on the vi chord, Am, in the C major scale but then switches to the I chord, C, at the chorus. U2's "Staring at the Sun" also switches from Am to C from verse to chorus. "D'yer Mak'er" by Led Zeppelin does the opposite, starting out on C and then switching to Am during the chorus. "Girl" by The Beatles has a chord progression that first centers on Cm but then changes to E♭ major, the vi and I chords from the E♭ major scale. "Runaway" by Del Shannon centers on B♭m during the verse and D♭ during the chorus, which are vi and I in D♭ major.

Switching between other scale degrees

Sometimes a song switches between scale degrees other than the relative major and minor. For example, "Tangerine" by Led Zeppelin starts out on Am. But it's not vi from the C major scale; it's actually ii from the G major scale. The song then moves to the I chord, G, during the chorus. "Landslide" by Fleetwood Mac, which is played with a capo at the 3rd fret, using G major chord shapes, first focuses on the IV chord (an open C chord shape) before later settling on the I chord (an open G chord shape).

The modulation in "Landslide" is a change from Lydian to Ionian (see Chapter 7 for details on these and other modes). You hear the same type of change from IV to I in various scales in "Just Remember I Love You" by Firefall, "Here Comes My Girl" by Tom Petty, "Man on the Moon" by R.E.M., "Hey Jealousy" by Gin Blossoms, and "Space Oddity" by David Bowie.

Transposing a Progression

Sometimes a song's chord progression is moved, or *transposed,* up or down by a particular interval for a section; the song's tonic changes by the same interval. Figure 8-2 shows an example of a transposed chord progression that starts out in the key of C before transposing and reproducing the same chord progression a whole step higher in the key of D.

Watch Video Clip 15 to see and hear the transposed chord progression from Figure 8-2.

"My Girl" by The Temptations changes keys in the same way as the example in Figure 8-2. This type of key change is sometimes called the *truck driver modulation* because it feels like the song has shifted into a higher gear. It often occurs at the end of a song to make the final repeated chorus sound different and climactic.

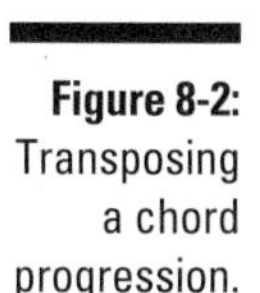

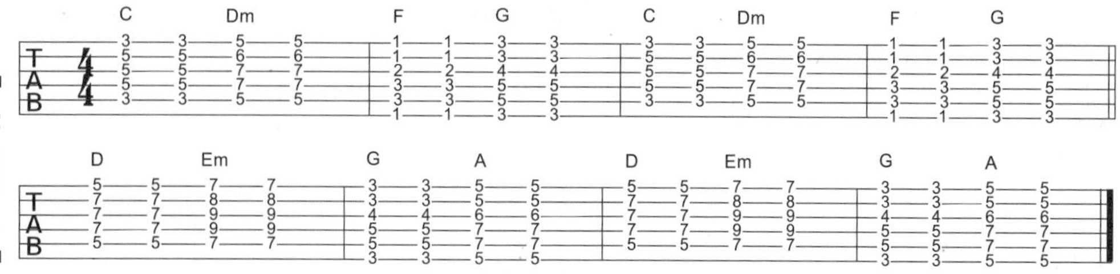

Figure 8-2: Transposing a chord progression.

Illustration courtesy of Desi Serna

Chord transpositions aren't always a whole step. In fact, transpositions can take many shapes and sizes:

- A transposition may be only a half step, as is the case in "Crazy" by Patsy Cline, which modulates from B♭ to B; "Crimson and Clover" by Tommy James and the Shondells, which modulates from B to C; and "Surrender" by Cheap Trick, which modulates from B to C.
- A transposition may be a step and a half, as you see in "To Be with You" by Mr. Big, "Livin' on a Prayer" by Bon Jovi, and "Play That Funky Music" by Wild Cherry, which all modulate from E to G.
- A transposition may be short-lived. "Are You Gonna Go My Way" by Lenny Kravitz briefly modulates from E to G at 00:46 by moving the riff up three frets and then moves back down to E at 00:54. "Funk #49" by the James Gang has an A minor pentatonic riff that starts at 0:37, moves up a whole step to B minor at 0:38, and returns to A at 0:48.
- More than one transposition may occur in the same song. "Play That Funky Music" by Wild Cherry, "You Really Got Me" by The Kinks, "Pinball Wizard" by The Who, and "California Girls" by The Beach Boys all touch on three or more keys.

When a song modulates up or down a half step, whole step, or more, it's easy to follow on guitar. Usually, you simply need to move the barre chords and/or scale patterns up or down.

How you describe a key change is a matter of preference. One way to describe chord transpositions is by their intervals. For instance, in some of the previous examples, the progression modulates by three half steps, or three frets on the guitar, so you can say that each song modulates up a minor 3rd. Similarly, "You Really Got Me" modulates up a 4th from A to D at one point. For another example, you can say that "My Girl" modulates up two semitones, one whole step, a 2nd, or two frets.

Take a look at a few more examples of transposing a chord progression:

- The verses to "I Walk the Line" by Johnny Cash all use a I-IV-V chord progression. You first hear it in F, and then the song modulates to B♭ and then E♭. Each key repeats the same progression, and each modulation is up a perfect 4th. The music then modulates back down to the key of B♭ and eventually returns to the original key of F.
- "My Generation" by The Who moves through three key changes from G, up a tone to A, up a semitone to B♭, and up another tone to finish in C. "Wrong Way" by Sublime moves through E, A, F♯, and B. Both of these songs use I-♭VII chord changes in each key.
- John Mellencamp's "I Need a Lover" is built from a I-V-IV-V chord progression in the keys of B♭, F♯, B, and E, all before the verse even starts! The song finally settles in the key of F♯ for most of the verses and choruses, but it modulates up to the key of A at the 4:35 mark before ending.

Changing Key and Progression

Sometimes when a song moves to a new key, that change introduces a completely different chord progression. In Figure 8-3, you start with a chord progression in A, followed by a new chord progression in a different key, C. The last chord in the example, E, leads back to A, the tonic of the first chord progression.

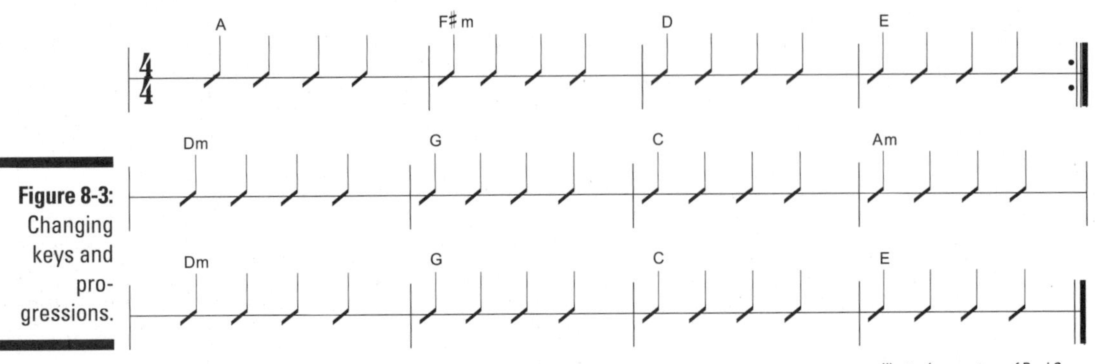

Figure 8-3: Changing keys and progressions.

"Oh, Pretty Woman" by Roy Orbison uses a key change similar to the one in Figure 8-3. In it, you hear a verse with a chord progression based in A major and a bridge with a new chord progression based in a different key, C. Both the key and the chord progression change. There's also a bit of borrowing back and forth before everything finally settles back to the original key of A (more on borrowed chords in a moment). Technically, you could also say that the opening and verse switch tonics within the key of A. The riff (called the Intro and Interlude in some scores) starts on an E chord, giving you the impression that E is the key, before surprising you with a verse centered on A.

You hear something similar in "Summer of '69" by Bryan Adams, where the bridge presents both a new key and a new chord progression. The main part of the song centers on D and the D major scale, while the bridge centers on F and the F major scale with a new chord progression. Another example, "Tears in Heaven" by Eric Clapton, mainly centers on A and the A major scale, but the bridge changes to C and uses a somewhat different chord progression.

Coincidentally, all three of these songs modulate up a ♭3rd at the bridge.

Get your record collection out or open up your favorite media player, because I have more examples for you! "What I Like about You" by the Romantics has a bridge that is completely different from the rest of the song. So does "Every Breath You Take" by The Police. "Stuck with You" by Huey Lewis and the News changes from C in the verse to D in the chorus with a slightly different progression. "Layla" by Derek and the Dominos starts out centered on Dm with F major chords and then changes to a completely different progression centering on C♯m and E, using chords mostly from E major. "School's Out" by Alice Cooper starts in E Dorian but eventually settles into the chorus key of G minor with a completely different progression. "Sweet Child O' Mine" by Guns N' Roses is centered in D Mixolydian mode through the first half of the song but switches to E minor and a new progression just past the halfway mark (guitars tuned down one half step to E♭).

When tracking a song with chords that don't all fit into one key, break the song into individual parts that can each fit into a key. All the song examples in this section have parts that are almost like mini, separate songs in themselves, put together to form a larger whole.

Using Modal Interchange and Borrowed Chords

Modal interchange, sometimes called *modal mixture,* is a technique through which you combine chords from parallel scales. A *parallel scale* is any scale that starts on the same pitch. For example, the A major scale and the A minor scale are parallel. Because the tonic pitch remains the same with modal interchange, it isn't considered a key change. However, you do play, or borrow, chords from other keys (which is where the term *borrowed chord* comes from).

In Table 8-1, you see seven different scales and sets of chords that start on A. The first six are modes from the major scales Ionian through Aeolian. The last scale is the A harmonic minor. Because harmonic minor occurs only on the V chord, as I explain in Chapter 14, I've written the chords for A harmonic minor by using A natural minor (Aeolian) for everything except V7, the most defining characteristic of harmonic minor.

Table 8-1 Parallel Scales in A

Scale/Mode	*Numbers/Chords*
A Ionian (major scale)	A-B♯m-C♯m-D-E-F♯m-G♯m♭5 I-ii-iii-IV-V-vi-vii♭5
A Dorian	Am-Bm-C-D-Em-F♯m♭5-G i-ii-♭III-IV-v-vi♭5-♭VII
A Phrygian	Am-B♭-C-Dm-Em♭5-F-Gm i-♭II-♭III-iv-v♭5-♭VI-♭vii
A Lydian	A-B-C♯m-D♯m♭5-E-F♯m-G♯m I-II-iii-♯iv♭5-V-vi-vii
A Mixolydian	A-Bm-C♯m♭5-D-Em-F♯m-G I-ii-iii♭5-IV-v-vi-♭VII
A Aeolian (natural minor)	Am-Bm♭5-C-Dm-Em-F-G i-ii♭5-♭III-iv-v-♭VI-♭VII
A harmonic minor	Am-Bm♭5-C-Dm-E7-F-G i-ii♭5-♭III-iv-V7-♭VI-♭VII

With all these chords to choose from, you have the potential to compose a great variety of chord progressions. Pretty cool, right?

Playing modal interchanges

In the following sections you take a look at some common modal interchanges. These include mixing up major modes, mixing minor modes, and even going back and fourth between major and minor.

Mixing major with Mixolydian

One of the most common and simplest modal interchanges mixes the plain major scale (Ionian mode) with the Mixolydian mode. Here, you take I-IV-V from A major and add the ♭VII chord from Mixolydian. This gives you a total of four major chords: A, D, E, and G (see Figure 8-4).

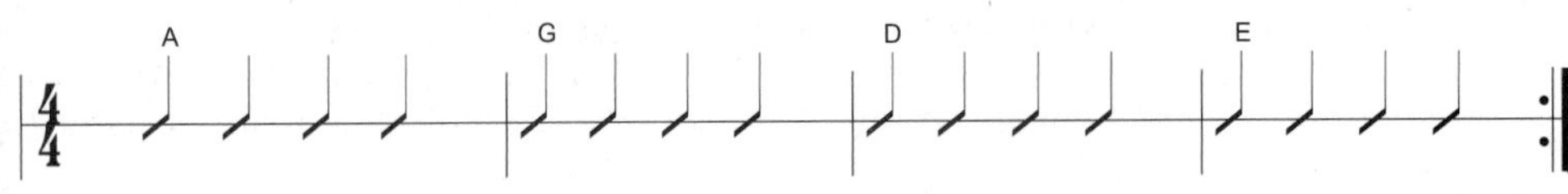

Figure 8-4: Mixing A major and A Mixolydian.

Illustration courtesy of Desi Serna

Watch Video Clip 16 to see and hear the example of mixing major and Mixolydian from Figure 8-4.

In Figure 8-4, the G chord is borrowed from the A Mixolydian mode, with the parent scale of D major. Remember that when you borrow a chord, you also borrow its parent major scale. With a progression like A-G-D-E, lead guitarists need to change their scale patterns on the G chord from A major to D major in order for the notes to pair up properly with the chord.

A perfect example of mixing two major modes like this is "Wild Thing" by The Troggs, which uses A-D-E during the chorus and G-A during the verse. Other songs that mix modes in a similar way using the very same chords include "Tangled Up in Blue" by Bob Dylan, "Shooting Star" by Bad Company, and "Bold as Love" by Jimi Hendrix (guitars tuned down a half step to E♭).

Table 8-2 lists some more popular songs that use this type of modal interchange, this time in various keys. Each key centers on a major chord and mixes the major scale and the parallel Mixolydian mode (for example, B major scale and B Mixolydian mode, G major scale and G Mixolydian scale, and so on). The focus here is on the use of I-IV-V along with ♭VII, but some of these examples mix in other chords, such as minor ones, as well.

Table 8-2 Popular Songs That Mix Major with Mixolydian

Key	*Chords*	*Numbers*	*Song Examples*
B	B-E-F♯-A	I-IV-V-♭VII	"Crimson and Clover" by Tommy James and the Shondells "California Girls" by The Beach Boys "Touch of Grey" by Grateful Dead "Scarlet Begonias" by Grateful Dead
G	G-C-D-F	I-IV-V-♭VII	"Pink Houses" by John Mellencamp "Sweet Home Alabama" by Lynyrd Skynyrd "Ramblin' Man" by The Allman Brothers Band (guitars tuned up a half step to F) "Heaven" by Los Lonely Boys (guitars tuned down a half step, or just play in G♭) "Don't Do Me Like That" by Tom Petty "Free Bird" by Lynyrd Skynyrd "Like A Rock" by Bob Seger (played with a capo at first fret creating the key of G♯) "Little Wing" by Jimi Hendrix
E	E-A-B-D	I-IV-V-♭VII	"R.O.C.K. in the U.S.A." by John Mellencamp "Sympathy for the Devil" by The Rolling Stones "With a Little Help from My Friends" by The Beatles "Hold On Loosely" by 38 Special "Living After Midnight" by Judas Priest "Sundown" by Gordon Lightfoot (capo 2)
D	D-G-A-C	I-IV-V-♭VII	"Comfortably Numb" by Pink Floyd "Bouncing Around the Room" by Phish

If you're a lead guitarist, you need to remember to change scales with each mode. Specifically, play Mixolydian mode over the ♭VII chord. For instance, in the key of G examples, play G major scale patterns over chords G, C, and D, but play C major scale patterns over chord F. G Mixolydian is the 5th mode of C and where the F chord comes from.

Mixing major with Lydian

Another type of modal interchange mixes the major scale with Lydian. The key of A Lydian includes a B major chord which can be added to A major's A, D, and E. In this case, the B chord is II, a major two chord, so the chord numbers look like this: I-II-IV-V.

You can use this type of chord progression in any key. Figure 8-5 shows an example in D. Here, I-II-IV-V is D-E-G-A.

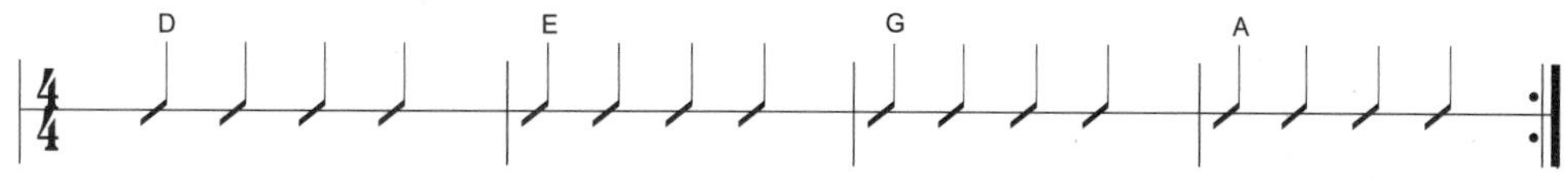

Figure 8-5: Mixing D major and D Lydian.

Illustration courtesy of Desi Serna

Both of the songs "American Girl" by Tom Petty and "Eight Days a Week" by The Beatles mix D major and D Lydian in a manner similar to the example in Figure 8-5. Lead guitars need to be sure to switch scale patterns over the II chord, E. In the key of D, switching to Lydian means playing A major scale patterns because D Lydian is the second mode of A.

Mixing major with minor

To try out another type of modal interchange, mix the major scale with the minor scale, or Aeolian mode. In the key of A, the A minor scale has three major chords to use — C, F, and G. By number, they are ♭III, ♭VI, and ♭VII.

One common combination uses the ♭VI and ♭VII chords and puts three major chords — F, G, and A — right in a row and a whole step apart. In Figure 8-6, the A-D part is I-IV from A major, and the F-G part is ♭VI-♭VII from A minor.

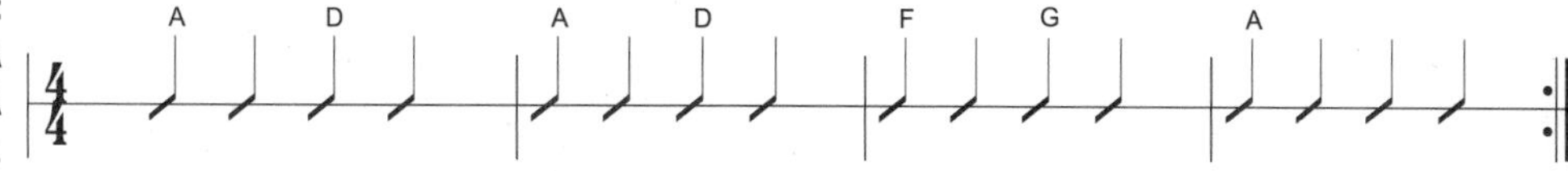

Figure 8-6: Mixing A major and A minor.

Illustration courtesy of Desi Serna

The Beatles use a similar chord progression in their song "Lady Madonna." "Suffragette City" by David Bowie also uses ♭VI and ♭VII, plus a ♭III from A minor and a II from A Lydian. "Under the Bridge" by Red Hot Chili Peppers has a bridge section that interchanges A major and A minor with the chords A-C-G-F (you can also think of them as A-Am-G-F) around the 2:52 mark and Fmaj7-E7-G near 3:08.

Other popular songs that use three major chords each a whole step apart and that finish on a tonic like this include "Crazy Little Thing Called Love" by Queen (B♭-C-D), "Running Down a Dream" by Tom Petty (C-D-E), "With a Little Help from My Friends" by The Beatles (C-D-E), and "Home Sweet Home" by Mötley Crüe (A♭-B♭-C). In each case, the last chord is the major tonic, and the two chords before it are borrowed from the parallel minor.

Another well-known example of a ♭VI-♭VII-I progression appears in the video game Super Mario Bros. Sometimes known as the "Mario cadence," this progression shows up in the fanfare that sounds at the end of each level with the chords A♭-B♭-C, as well as in the main theme.

In all these major/minor interchanges, your leads need to switch to minor scale patterns over the chords from the relative minor. Switching from A major to A minor scale patterns means using C major patterns, because A minor is the sixth mode of C.

Playing minor modal interchanges

Modal interchanges also take place in songs that have a minor tonic chord. The following sections highlight some of the most common minor chord modulations.

Mixing Aeolian with Dorian

Aeolian and Dorian are the two most commonly mixed minor modes. The main difference between them is that Aeolian has a minor iv chord, while Dorian has a major IV chord. One way to mix these modes is to use both types of IV/iv chords in a song (see Figure 8-7).

Figure 8-7: Mixing A minor and A Dorian.

Illustration courtesy of Desi Serna

"Fly Like an Eagle" by Steve Miller Band uses an interchange similar to the one shown in Figure 8-7. The song is in the key of A minor, but you hear both a D major and a D minor chord. "All My Love" by Led Zeppelin makes the same change in the same key: Am with both a Dm and D chord. "Tangerine" by Led Zeppelin starts in A Dorian, switches to G major for the chorus, and later changes again to A natural minor for the guitar solo. "Staring at the Sun" by U2 uses chords drawn from A natural minor during the verse and C major with a borrowed D chord during the chorus. "Ecstasy" by Rusted Root mixes D Dorian, D natural minor, and D major.

Mixing minor with harmonic minor

Minor key songs often mix natural minor and Dorian chords with a V7 from harmonic minor (see Figure 8-8).

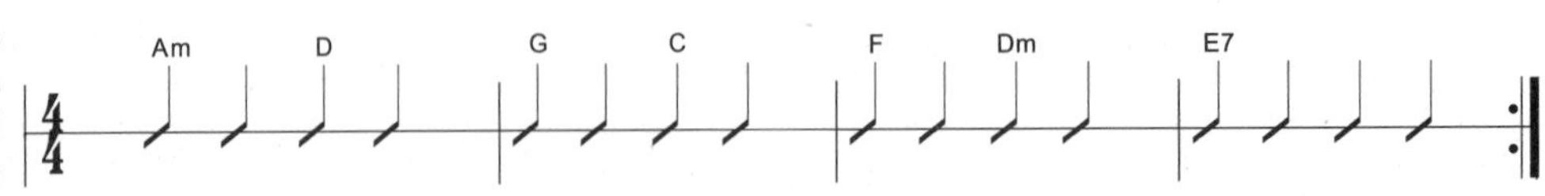

Figure 8-8: Mixing A minor, A Dorian, and A harmonic minor.

Illustration courtesy of Desi Serna

A perfect example of a song that mixes A minor modes and harmonic minor like Figure 8-8 is "Wild World" by Cat Stevens. The traditional folk song "House of the Rising Sun" uses another variation of the same interchange (see Figure 8-9).

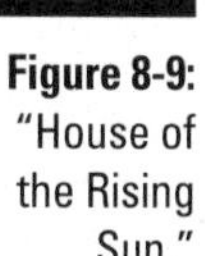

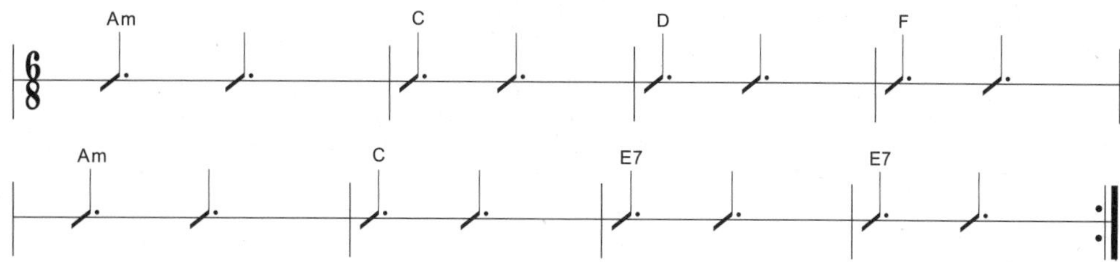

Figure 8-9: "House of the Rising Sun."

Illustration courtesy of Desi Serna

Watch Video Clip 17 to see and hear the "House of the Rising Sun" example from Figure 8-9.

Other songs that mix A minor modes and harmonic minor include "Moondance" by Van Morrison, and "Stairway to Heaven" and "Babe I'm Gonna Leave You" by Led Zeppelin. "Straight On" by Heart mixes B natural minor, Dorian, and harmonic minor.

"Crazy on You" by Heart and "While My Guitar Gently Weeps" by The Beatles both mix A natural minor, Dorian, and the harmonic minor, plus A Ionian, the relative major.

Two songs — "Smoke on the Water" by Deep Purple and "Grease" from the musical motion picture *Grease* — have chord changes that mix all three minor modes (Aeolian, Dorian, and Phrygian). "Smoke on the Water" has the chords Gm and F from G Aeolian, C from G Dorian, and A♭ from G Phrygian. "Grease" has the chords Bm, E, and F♯m7 from B Dorian; Em7, D, C, and Bm from B Phrygian; Em7, and F♯m7 from B Aeolian; and even E7 from B harmonic minor.

With modal interchange, the parent major scale changes, but the tonic pitch remains the same. For example, "Crazy on You" uses A Aeolian, A Dorian, and A Ionian, each of which is built from a different parent major scale, but the tonic pitch remains A throughout the song.

Some of the examples in this section, like "All My Love," "Staring at the Sun," and "Wild World" are minor keyed songs that use modal interchange in the verses but modulate to the relative major for the chorus. "Tangerine" begins in A Dorian and modulates to G Ionian.

Using a minor iv chord in a major key

Another type of chord change is when a minor iv chord is used in a major key. Normally, IV is major in a major key, as in a I-IV-V chord progression. However, many songs put a iv chord in between IV and I to create some kind of chromatic voice leading, as shown in Figure 8-10. In the progression F-Fm-C in C major, the 3rd of the F chord, A, leads to the 3rd of Fm, A♭, which in turn moves to the 5th of the C chord, G. You can see the minor iv chord as borrowed from C minor, the parallel minor key.

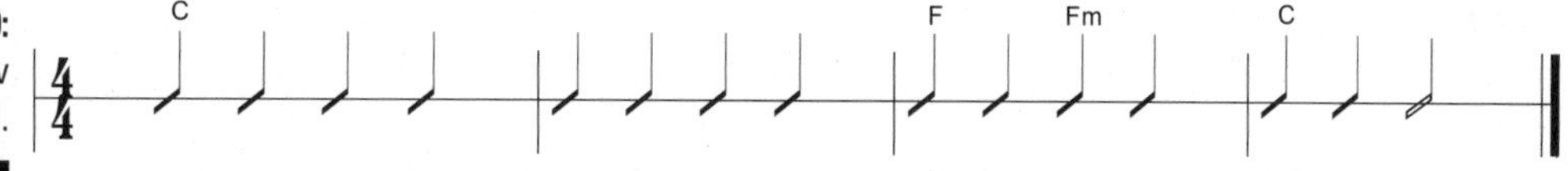

Figure 8-10: Minor iv chord.

Illustration courtesy of Desi Serna

The Beatles use this minor iv chord change quite a bit. For example, you hear it in "Nowhere Man" with a iv chord, Am, leading to the I chord of E, and in "Across the Universe" where iv-I is Gm leading to D (guitars tuned down one half step to E♭).

Here are a few more songs that feature iv chords:

"The Air That I Breathe" by The Hollies (Fm in the key of C)

"Don't Do Me Like That" by Tom Petty (Cm in the key of G)

"Don't Look Back in Anger" by Oasis (Fm in the key of C)

"More Than Words" by Extreme (Cm in the key of G with the guitars tuned down a half step to E♭)

"Sleepwalk" by Santo & Johnny (Fm in the key of C)

"Space Oddity" by David Bowie (Fm in the key of C)

"That Thing You Do" from the film *That Thing You Do!* (Am in the key of E)

"You're My Best Friend" and "Play The Game" by Queen (Fm in the key of C)

Using the Circle of Fifths for Circle Progressions

No discussion on keys would be complete without mentioning the *circle of fifths,* sometimes called the *cycle of fifths.* In music theory, the circle of fifths represents relationships between the different key signatures. Key signatures used in standard notation may not be relevant to how guitar players approach music on the fretboard, but knowing how to move in fifths and recognizing songs that use chord progressions that follow this pattern certainly is useful.

The circle of fifths can work two ways: moving up by 5ths or moving down by 5ths. Look at the ascending version first. If you start on an F major chord and play its V chord, C, you move up a 5th: F-G-A-B♭-C, 1-2-3-4-5. In a similar way, a 5th above C is G, and so on. If you continue in this manner, you can cycle through all 12 possible roots and return to where you started — F major. Figure 8-11 presents the complete circle of ascending fifths starting on F.

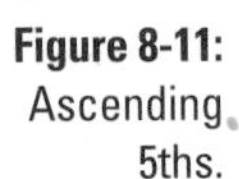
Figure 8-11: Ascending 5ths.

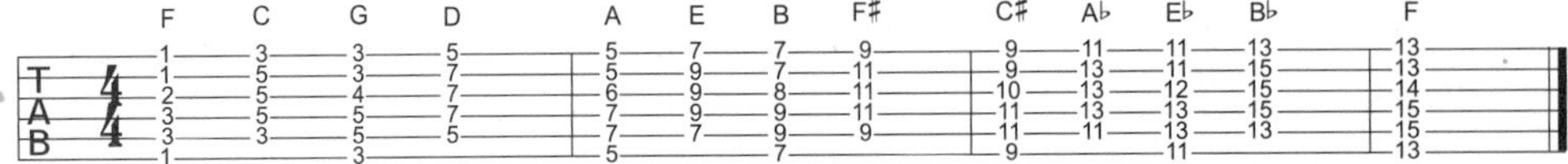

Illustration courtesy of Desi Serna

Watch Video Clip 18 to see and hear the ascending 5ths from Figure 8-11.

You can also play through the circle of descending 5ths. Start on F and count down five to get to B♭. In other words, just play through Figure 8-11 backward.

The circle of fifths is useful for playing chord progressions. Start on any chord, play its dominant, or V chord, and cycle through all 12 chromatic chords. Use either the ascending 5ths version or the descending one. Starting on different roots in the cycle can help you practice different ways of patterning and routing chord progressions on the guitar.

Figure 8-12 shows you one way to build a circle progression based on 5ths. Here, the tonic is E, the goal of the progression. A sequence of ascending 5ths precedes it, starting with C.

Figure 8-12: A circle of fifths progression.

Many songs feature circle chord progressions. Here are just a few examples:

- "Hey Joe" by Jimi Hendrix is based on the progression in Figure 8-12.
- "Hush" by Deep Purple has the 5ths progression: A♭-E♭-B♭-F-C during the "Nah, nah-nah-nah, nah-nah-nah, nah-nah-nah" section.
- "Time Warp" from the film *The Rocky Horror Picture Show* has the progression F-C-G-D-A during the chorus "Let's Do the Time Warp again."
- The chorus to "Jumpin' Jack Flash" by The Rolling Stones has the progression D-A-E-B.
- The bridge of "Here Comes the Sun" by The Beatles moves in 5ths with C-G-D-A-E.

Applying the same circle to fourths

You may notice something about the circle of fifths: It's also a circle of fourths! In C major, C to F is a descending 5th (C-B-A-G-F, 1-2-3-4-5), but you can also count up to F (C-D-E-F, 1-2-3-4). Both are correct. A musician's particular view is the result of training, preference, and use. Classical musicians usually talk about the circle of fifths, while jazz and popular musicians often talk about the circle of fourths.

Here are some songs that use sections of this 4th pattern:

- The chords in "Spinning Wheel" by Blood, Sweat & Tears moves in 4ths with A7-D7-G7-C.
- "Country Boy" by Ricky Skaggs has a solo section that moves in 4ths: E7-A7-D7-G7.
- The opening to "Light My Fire" by The Doors is built from the progression G-D-F-B♭-E♭-A♭-A. Starting with the F chord through to A♭, you have an ascending cycle of fourths progression.

The potential of the circle of fifths/fourths is to cycle through all 12 possible chromatic pitches. However, you can also move up by 4ths through the chords of a particular key while keeping to diatonic (major scale) chords. Take, for example, the C major scale. You cycle through its seven possible diatonic chords by ascending 4ths, as shown in Figure 8-13.

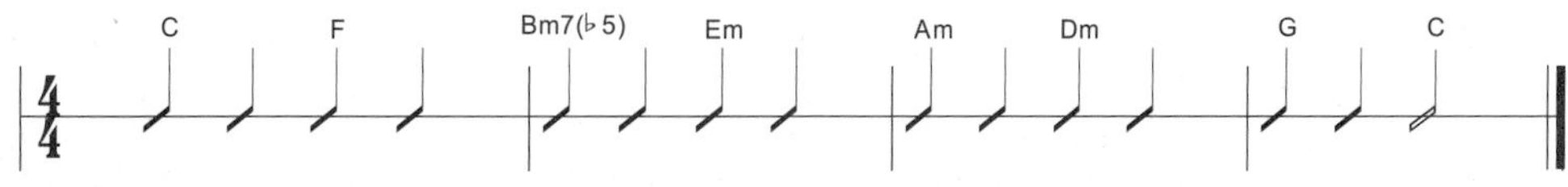

Figure 8-13: Diatonic ascending 4ths.

Here are some songs that use the circle of fourths to cycle through a particular key while keeping to diatonic chords:

- "Still Got the Blues" by Gary Moore and "I Will Survive" by Gloria Gaynor are built on the circle of fourths in A minor: Am-Dm-G-C-F-Bm7♭5-E7. The final E7 chord is from A harmonic minor and leads back to Am to start the progression again.
- "El Farol" by Santana uses the progression Am-Dm-G-C-F-Dm-E7.
- "Wild World" by Cat Stevens uses Am-D-G-C F-Dm-E7, almost all 4ths.
- "Yesterday, When I Was Young" by Roy Clark is built from the chord progression Gm-C-F-B♭-Gm-A7-Dm. Gm-C-F-B♭ moves in 4ths.

Sometimes songs move through the circle of fourths by using a combination of diatonic chords and secondary dominants. For example, "Still the Same" by Bob Seger has the changes Em-Am-Dm-G during the verse and E-A-Dm-G in the chorus. In the chorus, you see the secondary dominants E and A. Both sets of chord changes move in ascending 4ths. Turn to Chapter 9 to get to know secondary dominants.

Here are two more examples of circle of fourths progressions, which include secondary dominants:

- "Rocky Raccoon" by The Beatles uses the progression Am7-D7-G7-C. A C/B chord (C with B in the bass) leads back to Am to begin the cycle again.
- "No Matter What" by Badfinger moves in 4ths, starting on F♯m7: F♯m7-B7-E7-A7-D7. This section of the song finishes off with Bm and A and features some chromatic voice leading.

Seeing circle progressions in action

So far, you've covered various chord progressions built out of root movements of 5ths and 4ths, but how is a lead guitarist supposed to play over these types of progressions? As you discover in Chapter 9, secondary dominants borrow not only their chord function but also their notes from another scale. As a result, you treat them as V chords and use the dominant scale, Mixolydian mode, for your solos.

Figure 8-14 presents a tab of a simple sequential bass line that works with the progression E-A-D-G.

E7 A7 D7 G7

Figure 8-14: Circle progression bass line.

Illustration courtesy of Desi Serna

Notice that a root, 3rd, 5th, 6th, and ♭7th are played over each chord. These scale degrees belong to a Mixolydian mode; the ♭7th should give it away. As a lead guitarist, you can play complete Mixolydian scales over each chord, as many jazz and country players often do when dealing with dominant chords. However, if you consider yourself a blues or rock player, you may want to take a different approach.

Generally speaking, blues and rock guitar players like to keep things simple, both technically and musically. They don't try to chase a series of dominant chords by changing scales for each one. Instead, they may choose to use one scale that works over the complete progression, often a minor pentatonic.

Take a look at "Hey Joe" by Jimi Hendrix, which uses an ascending 5ths progression C-G-D-A-E. The roots of these chords are all found in the E minor scale. In fact, the chords themselves belong to either E minor or E Dorian, the two most popular minor modes. For this reason, the E minor pentatonic scale can work over the complete progression. It even works over the E major chord, creating a minor-over-major blues sound (see Chapter 15). Jimi Hendrix built the "Hey Joe" guitar solo out of mostly E minor pentatonic in the 12th position.

Chapter 9

Dominant Function and Voice Leading

In This Chapter

- Getting to know the functions of dominant 7th chords
- Playing sample chord progressions
- Leading from one chord voicing to another

The *dominant chord* (or the chord built on the 5th degree of a scale) is a fairly important chord in music because its structure and tendency toward the tonic chord really help define the tonal center of a progression. In this chapter, you get to know dominant chords and find out how to use them in your music. You also take a look at secondary dominants, which allow you to use the dominant sound to strengthen a progression toward chords other than the tonic. In addition, you discover the ins and outs of voice leading.

Listen to Audio Track 9 to hear examples of dominant function and voice leading plus get an idea of what this chapter is all about.

Chord Function and the Dominant Chord

The word *dominant* refers to two things in guitar theory:

- The first is the 5th degree of the major scale, named the *dominant.*
- The second is a major triad with a minor 7th, called the *dominant 7th chord,* which naturally occurs on the 5th scale degree.

The chord function on V is the most important example of this. Because it's built on the 5th scale degree, or the dominant note, the V chord has what's sometimes called a *dominant function.* In a chord progression like I-V, the dominant chord has a sense of movement, or instability, that makes the progression want to continue leading back to the tonic, chord I. You can intensify this leading quality of V by adding a 7th to the chord, making V7, or a *dominant 7th chord.* Every major scale has a naturally occurring V7 chord: G7 in C major, D7 in G major, A7 in D major, and so on. Figure 9-1 gives you a sample I-V7 chord progression in C.

Figure 9-1: I-V7 chord progression.

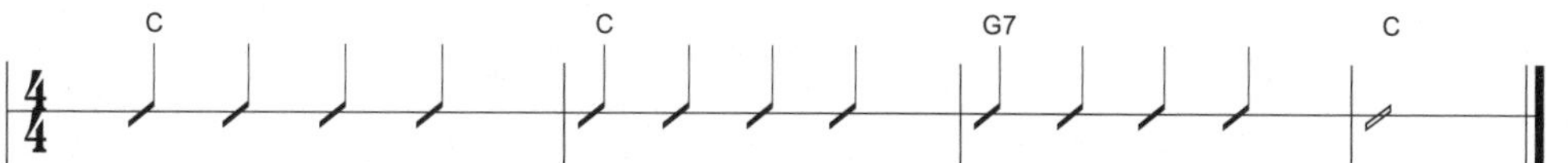

Illustration courtesy of Desi Serna

Musicians also use the dominant 7th chord for its sound quality, or color. You hear this use in blues-based music, where the dominant 7th sound is a huge part of its style. These *static dominant 7th chords,* as they're called, don't necessarily need to resolve to a tonic chord.

Naming notes, scale degrees, and chords

The notes of a scale are usually numbered 1st, 2nd, 3rd, and so on. You use Arabic numbers when you're talking about the notes themselves and Roman numerals when you're talking about the chords built on those notes. So in C major, *3* or *the 3rd* is the note E, and *iii* is the chord E-G-B.

The different scale degrees also have names. *Dominant* refers to the 5th scale degree. For example, G is the dominant of C major, and B is the dominant of E major. Here's a complete list of the names for the different scale degrees:

1 Tonic

2 Supertonic

3 Mediant

4 Subdominant

5 Dominant

6 Submediant

7 Leading note or leading tone

You can also call the V chord a dominant chord. For example, the dominant chord of C major is G-B-D.

There are a couple reasons why V resolves so well on I. Understanding these reasons requires you to examine the intervals within a V chord to see how they relate to chord I. This involves taking a look at the leading tone and the tritone.

Leading with the leading tone

As a listening experiment, play up a major scale, starting from the tonic note, but instead of playing a full octave, stop on the 7th scale degree. Using C major as an example, play up the scale from C to B and hold on the B. The scale sounds incomplete: The B wants to lead back to the C to sound complete. This is why the 7th scale degree is also called the *leading tone* or *leading note* of a scale.

If you turn to the pitches of the V chord, you find that it contains the leading tone of its parent scale, which is one of the reasons why it has such a strong tendency toward I. For example, the V chord of C major is G. The G chord is made up of the pitches G, B, and D — its root, 3rd, and 5th. The 3rd of the chord is a B, the leading tone of C major.

Tension rises with a tritone

To intensify the tendency for V to lead to I, simply add a 7th to the chord, making V7. This added pitch comes from the 4th degree of a major scale. The interval from the 4th to the 7th of a major scale is an *augmented 4th,* while the interval from the 7th back up to the 4th is a *diminished 5th.* Both of these intervals are made up of three whole tones and can be called *tritones,* which, not surprisingly, means *three tones.* Examples of tritones are B-F in C major and G♯-D in A major.

When you play these examples of tritones, you can hear that a tritone is a fairly unstable, or dissonant-sounding, interval. As a matter of fact, it sounds so unstable that when it appears in a chord like V7, the chord itself has a strong tendency to move to a more stable one. For example, the B and F of G7 want to move to the C and E of C, and the G♯ and D of E7 want to move to the A and C♯ of A.

Figure 9-2 shows two versions of a G7 chord, with the tritones shaded in black. Follow each one of these chord shapes with a C chord and you hear resolution.

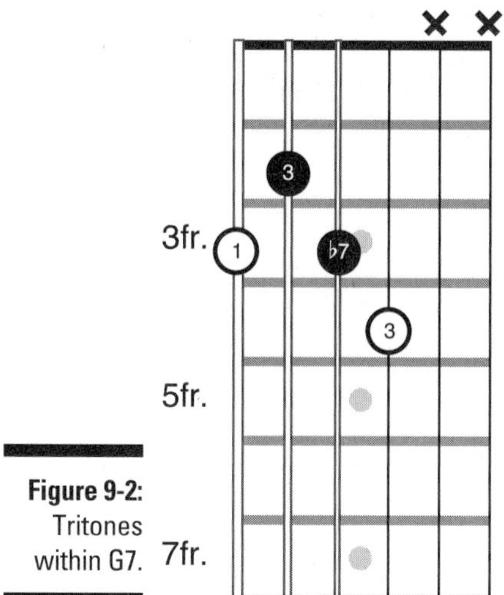

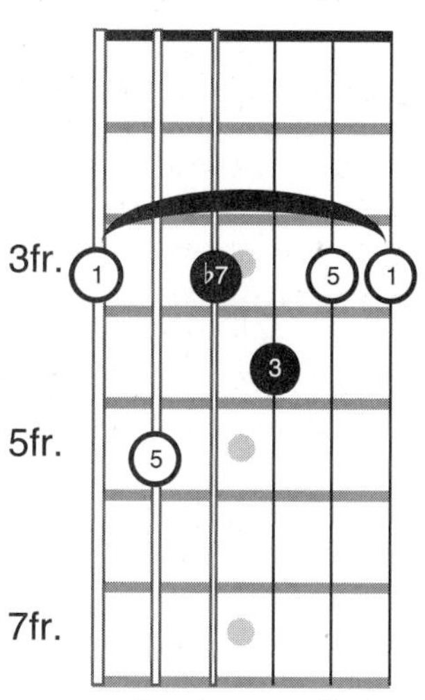

Figure 9-2: Tritones within G7.

Illustration courtesy of Desi Serna

Playing songs with dominant function

Some songs are based on simple progressions that contain only the I and V chords (also known as the tonic and dominant chords). Songs like "You Never Can Tell" by Chuck Berry, "Jambalaya" by Hank Williams, and "Achy Breaky Heart" by Billy Ray Cyrus are all good examples of this basic chord progression. Play any one of these songs and stop on the V chord. Notice that the music doesn't sound complete or resolved, but as though it wants to continue back to chord I. That's an example of dominant function.

In traditional uses, the V7-I progression appears to close a section or phrase of music (see Figure 9-3).

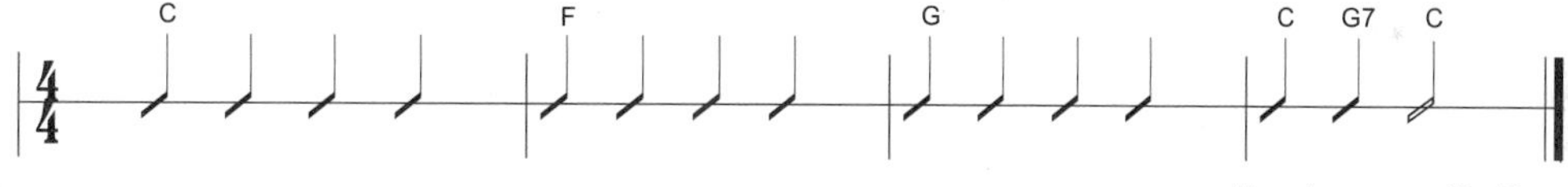

Figure 9-3: Closing progression.

Illustration courtesy of Desi Serna

Watch Video Clip 19 to see a demonstration of a closing progression.

You hear many examples of functioning dominant 7th chord progressions in traditional folk songs. Think of songs like "Skip to My Lou," "Shortnin' Bread," "Go Tell Aunt Rhody," "Down in the Valley," "Clementine," and "Buffalo Gals." Figure 9-4 shows a folk song example in the style of "He's Got the Whole World in His Hands." If you know the words, sing along.

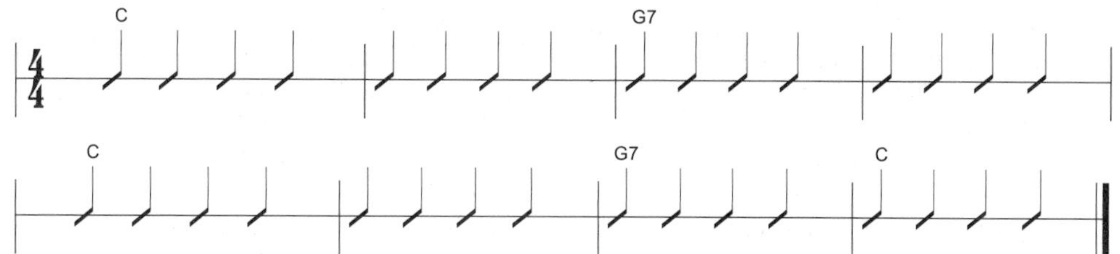

Figure 9-4: "He's Got the Whole World in His Hands."

Illustration courtesy of Desi Serna

You can figure out the chords to most two-chord folk songs simply by singing or humming the melody while playing along with I and V7 in any key. Just pick a key, any key, and try it. For example, in the key of C, I and V7 are C and G7; in the key of G, I and V7 are G and D7. You can also try D and A7, E and B7, or F and C7.

"Twist and Shout" by The Beatles is a great example of a V7 chord that has a dominant function. After the guitar solo, you hear six measures of the dominant 7th chord sung one note at a time by each of the band's members. The root of the chord, A, appears in the first measure, followed by the 3rd, C♯, in measure 2, the 5th of the chord, E, in measure 3, and finally the 7th, G, in measure 4. After two more measures of climactic, rock 'n' roll screaming, this musical tension resolves to the I chord, D, and the music continues on.

Secondary Dominants

The relationship between the tonic and dominant chords in music is so strong that composers sometimes use a dominant function on chords other than the tonic, like on the ii chord or perhaps even the V chord itself. These non-tonic-but-still-dominant chords are called *secondary dominants.* You recognize them in chord progressions as major chords where you're expecting minor ones and especially as dominant 7th chords where you're expecting simple triads.

For an example, look at the C major progression: C-Am-Dm-G7. A common variation on this progression is C-Am-D7-G7, as shown in Figure 9-5. You would normally expect a D minor chord rather than a D7 chord in C major, but if you think about this progression, you can see that the D7 chord is the dominant 7th of G.

Figure 9-5: Secondary dominant C-Am-D7-G7.

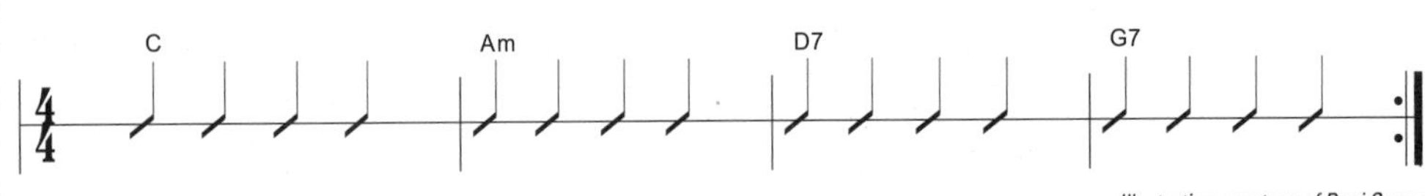

Illustration courtesy of Desi Serna

Drawing attention to some common secondary dominants

Musicians use secondary dominants on almost any chord in a key to provide some variety to a progression and to give some temporary focus to another chord. For example, the D7 chord in Figure 9-5 has a different sound quality than a simple D minor chord, which is what you normally find in the key of C. Because the chord has a dominant function, it draws attention to the following G7 chord. It's as if the chord progression temporarily changes keys to G.

You can lead to almost any chord with its own dominant. A chord's dominant is a major chord or dominant 7th chord that's a 5th away from the chord itself. Building on the example in Figure 9-5, you could lead to D with A7, which is five steps away from D, the interval of a 5th, as shown in Figure 9-6.

Figure 9-6: Secondary dominants C-A7-D7-G7.

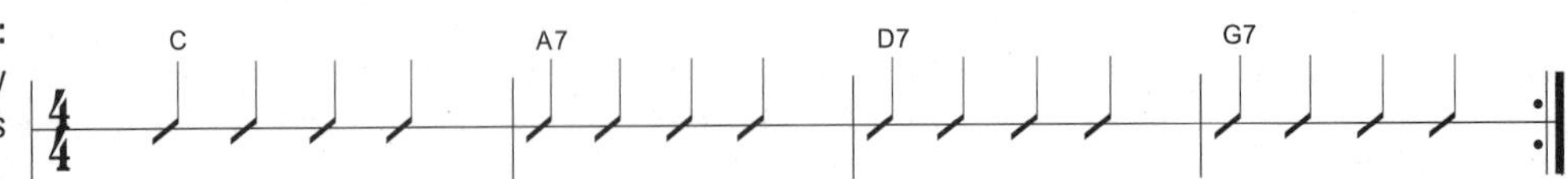

Illustration courtesy of Desi Serna

To see and hear the secondary dominant from Figure 9-6, watch Video Clip 20.

Keep going! The 5th of A is E, and an E7 chord can lead to any type of A chord. Figure 9-7 shows an example of E7 leading to A7 in a series of dominant 7th chords that begins on E7 and moves to C.

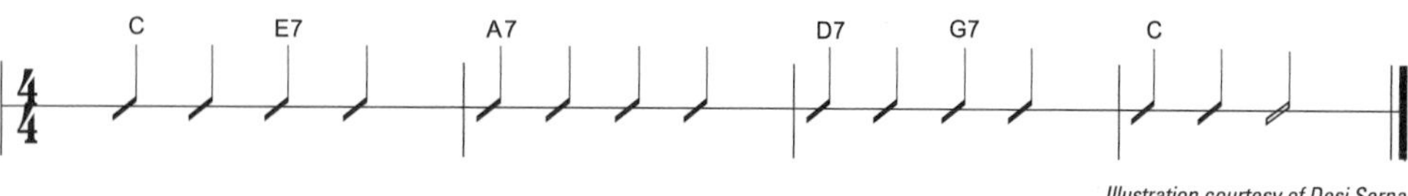

Figure 9-7: Secondary dominants C-E7-A7-D7-G7.

Illustration courtesy of Desi Serna

Another common secondary dominant progression is I7-IV. In C major, this progression is C7 moving to F. An example of this secondary dominant's use is in the larger progression F-G-C-C7-F-G-C that you see in Figure 9-8. The progression is in C major, but the C7 chord is functioning as a dominant 7th of the F chord.

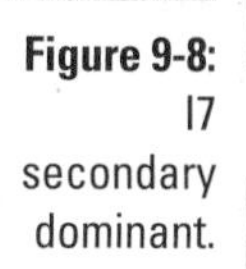

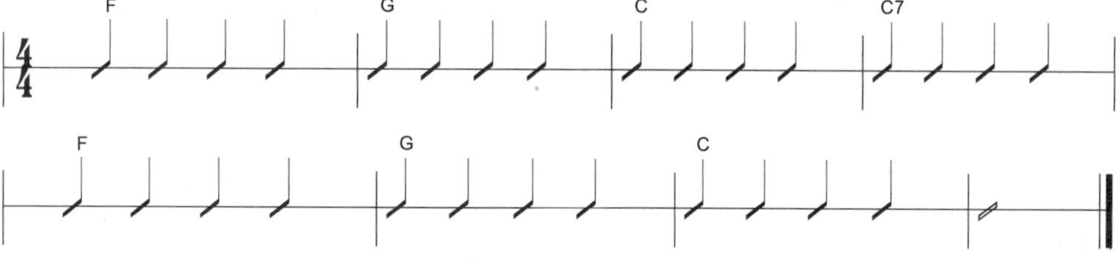

Figure 9-8: I7 secondary dominant.

Illustration courtesy of Desi Serna

The most common secondary dominants are the ones you see here — those that lead to I, ii, IV, V, and vi. Musicians generally don't use secondary dominants that lead to vii♭5, and although V7 of iii is possible, it isn't very common.

Thinking of secondary dominants as mini key changes

A secondary dominant is really just an altered version of an existing chord. This change to the chord is to create a dominant 7th. What gives it its secondary dominant function is that it leads to another chord a 5th below. So the I chord is altered to I7 to create movement toward IV, the ii chord is altered to II7 to highlight V, and so on.

In this way, secondary dominants are like mini key changes. Think of the chord progression in C major where G7 leads to C. This is a common V7-I progression in C major. But what if these two chords appeared in F major, as in the progression F-Dm-G7-C? Although the progression as a whole is in F major (I-vi-II7-V), the G7 chord has notes in it that don't belong to this key but instead belong to C major. For your solos to work in this chord progression, you have to start out in F major and then switch patterns to C major when you reach the G7 chord. Finally, when the C chord sounds, you have to switch back to F major patterns.

G7 is the dominant 7th chord of C major. When G7 appears in any key other than C and leads to a C chord, it's a secondary dominant. The same is true for any other functioning dominant 7th chord.

When playing over a secondary dominant, you need to switch to its parent major scale. Take another look at the secondary dominants progressions shown in Figures 9-5 through 9-7 to see what I mean:

- Figure 9-5 is I-vi-II7-V7 in C. The D7 chord belongs to the key of G. Use G major patterns over D7 and then return to C major on the G7 chord. When you play G major patterns over the D7 chord, you're actually playing in D Mixolydian, the dominant scale.

  Switching scales like this is no easy task! For the most part, you hear solos played over progressions like this only in jazz and country styles.
- Figure 9-6 is I-VI7-II7-V7 in C. The A7 chord belongs to the key of D, and D7 belongs to the key of G. Use D major patterns over A7 and G major patterns for D7. Return to C major on the G7 chord. A D major scale over A7 results in A Mixolydian mode, or an A dominant scale. Here, you have to switch scales twice.
- Figure 9-7 is I-III7-VI7-II7-V7-I in C. E7 belongs to A major, A7 belongs to D, and D7 belongs to the key of G. Think *dominant scale* over each dominant 7th chord. That is, for each dominant 7th chord, play its parent major scale.

Switching scales over secondary dominants can be quite a challenge, but fortunately, making the switch isn't always necessary. With the right note selection, you can stay in one scale and avoid any troublesome notes. To see what I mean, refer to the "Aura Lee" example in Figure 9-9. Notice that the melody remains in the key of C even though secondary dominants appear in the progression. Notice that the song uses an F note over an A7 chord even though the F isn't part of the A dominant scale.

"Aura Lee" is an old American Civil War song that Elvis Presley adapted for his hit single "Love Me Tender." The traditional version has several secondary dominants.

Figure 9-9: Aura Lee.

Illustration courtesy of Desi Serna

A note on reading music

To be honest, books like *Mel Bay's Modern Guitar Method,* the granddaddy of all guitar methods, are more about learning how to read standard musical notation than learning how to play guitar. Nevertheless, these books are worth the time and effort it takes to work through them because reading music is a useful skill to have. Learning how to read notes and rhythms can influence how you think about music and play the guitar even when you don't have any sheet music in front of you. You don't have to be able to read like a concert violinist; just focus on the basics. I recommend that you learn up to at least the point where you can count and play sixteenth notes.

Most traditional guitar methods include songs and exercises that are based on very simple V7-I chord progressions, where the dominant 7th chord is a functioning dominant 7th. For example, every song that has written-in chord progressions in *Mel Bay's Modern Guitar Method Grade 1* (the blue book) includes dominant 7th chords.

Although secondary dominants work best when they're dominant 7th chords, in some cases, they can be simple major chords. This approach works when you're altering a chord that's originally minor. For example, if you adjust a ii chord to II, it becomes a secondary dominant of V. If you change iii to III, it becomes a secondary dominant of vi. For I to work as a secondary dominant of IV, however, you have to adjust the chord to I7.

When you see II-V or VI-ii, the first chord in the progression is a secondary dominant. Another possible secondary dominant is III-vi. Sometimes, however, it's useful to think of this particular progression as V-i in the relative minor key with the major V chord a result of the harmonic minor scale. (We explore this concept in Chapter 15.)

Although approaching the progressions in this section as a lead guitarist may be challenging, playing the chord progressions themselves isn't hard at all. Plus, after you get a handle on what secondary dominants are, you begin to recognize how common they are in popular music. With some careful listening, you can hear that players often don't even attempt to solo over them. What a relief!

Songs that use secondary dominants

The following songs all feature chord progressions that make use of a secondary dominant either as a dominant 7th chord or, in some cases, a major chord on a minor scale degree. I point out the secondary dominants in parentheses.

"Act Naturally" by The Beatles (Chorus: II chord leads to V)

"Every Breath You Take" by The Police (Chorus: II chord leads to V)

"Faith" by George Michael (Chorus: II chord leads to V)

"Heart of Glass" by Blondie (Chorus: II chord leads to V)

"Hello Mary Lou" by Ricky Nelson (Chorus: III chord leads to vi and II chord leads to V)

"Hey Good Lookin'" by Hank Williams (Verse: II chord leads to V)

"Hey Jude" by The Beatles (Verse: I7 chord leads to IV)

"Honky Tonk Women" by The Rolling Stones (Verse: II chord leads to V)

"Margaritaville" by Jimmy Buffett (Verse: I7 chord leads to IV)

"Out of My Head" by Fastball (Chorus: I7 chord leads to IV; Verse and chorus: II chord leads to V)

"Patience" by Guns N' Roses (Verse: II chord leads to V)

"Running on Faith" by Eric Clapton (Verse: I7 chord leads to IV)

"The Star-Spangled Banner" (U.S. national anthem) (Verse: II chord leads to V)

"That'll Be the Day" by Buddy Holly (Verse: II chord leads to V)

"The Way" by Fastball (Verse: VI chord leads to ii)

Note: Because the progression in "The Way" is in a minor key, you can renumber it to a I chord leading to iv.

Voice Leading

In music composition, *voice leading* is the technique of writing smooth transitions from one chord to another, using common tones between chords and stepwise motion between their different pitches. Voice leading allows composers to take advantage of relationships between chords when connecting them in order to create more melodic lines.

You can see an example of voice leading in the chord progression C-E7-F-G-C. With the pitches of these chords, you have a stepwise musical line G-G♯-A-B-C. The 5th of the C chord, G, moves to the G♯ of E7, then to the A of the F chord, then to the B of G, and finally to the C of the C chord. This voice leading explains why an E7 chord can lead well into an F chord, even though these chords don't have a V-I relationship. In Figure 9-10, I voice this line in the higher part of the chords to clearly show it. In practice, you may not actually play the chords with these specific chord shapes.

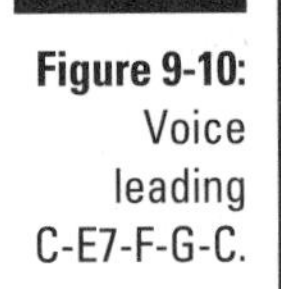

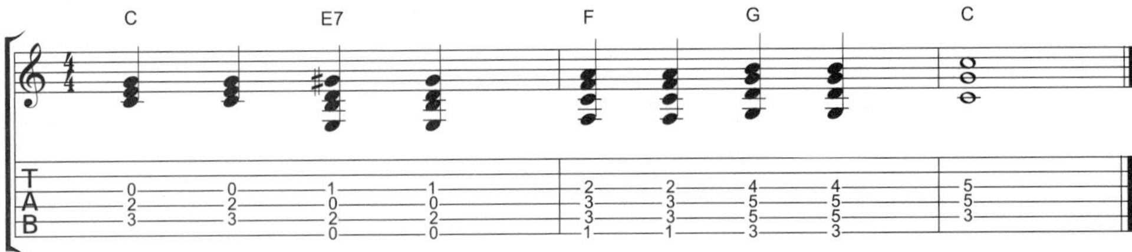

Figure 9-10: Voice leading C-E7-F-G-C.

Illustration courtesy of Desi Serna.

To see and hear the voice leading example from Figure 9-10, watch Video Clip 21.

Again, there's no V-I relationship between E7 and F. The chords are actually III7-IV in C major. But the voice leading makes it work anyway.

The defining musical features of many songs owe their greatness, at least in part, to similar III7-IV voice-leading techniques. For example, "Imagine" by John Lennon, "Don't Look Back in Anger" by Oasis, "Space Oddity" by David Bowie, and "The Air That I Breathe" by The Hollies all feature an E7 chord leading to F in the key of C. "The Way" by Fastball has C♯7 leading to D in the key of A, and "Interstate Love Song" by Stone Temple Pilots has G♯ leading to A in the key of E.

While I'm on the subject of voice leading, I should point out a few more examples, ones that don't necessarily involve a dominant 7th chord. Look for similar lines, both *chromatic* (moving up or down in half steps) and *diatonic* (moving through the major scale), in the music you're playing. Voice-leading techniques are easy to recognize when they happen in the bass part. A good example is a progression like the one shown in Figure 9-11. You can hear this progression in the opening to "Stairway to Heaven" by Led Zeppelin. If you've ever wondered why these chords fit together so well, take a look at the chromatic bass line that moves down the 4th string.

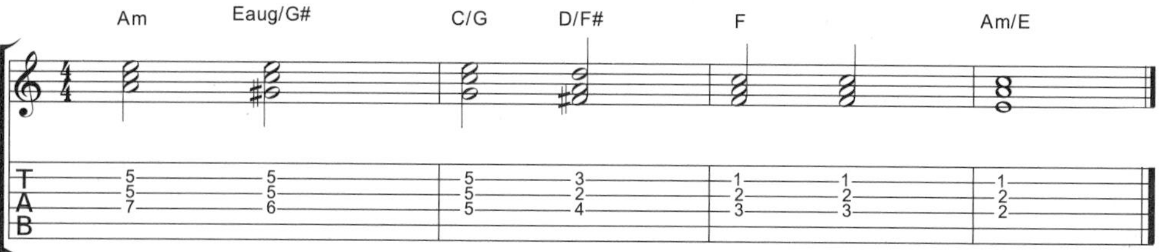

Figure 9-11: Bass voice leading — Round 1.

Illustration courtesy of Desi Serna.

Another clear example of voice leading in the bass part is shown in Figure 9-12. Here, the bass line descends from A to E. Notice the half step movement from G to E. Led Zeppelin uses this kind of progression in the song "Babe I'm Gonna Leave You," and The Beatles use something similar in their song "While My Guitar Gently Weeps."

Figure 9-12: Bass voice leading — Round 2.

Illustration courtesy of Desi Serna

You see a similar descending chromatic bass line over the changes G-D/F♯-F-C/E-E♭maj7 in the verse of "Plush" by Stone Temple Pilots.

Hearing voice leading with the progression I-Imaj7-I7-IV is also fairly common. In C major, the chords are C-Cmaj7-C7-F, and they're often connected with the descending chromatic line C-B-B♭-A — C from the C chord, B from Cmaj7, B♭ from C7, and A from the F chord. Here the voice leading is internal, placed within the chords, not in the bass. In Figure 9-13, I voice the chords with this line by moving along the 3rd string. You hear a similar chord progression in "Something" by The Beatles.

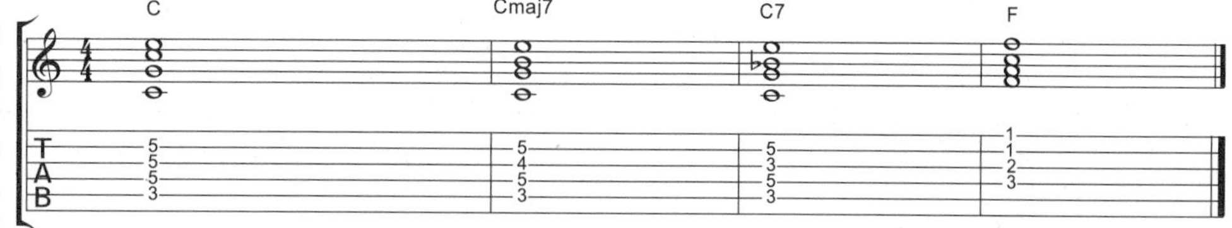

Figure 9-13: I-Imaj7-I7-IV voice leading.

Illustration courtesy of Desi Serna

One final example is the progression I-Imaj7-I6-I, or C-Cmaj7-C6-C, in C major. Here, the voice leading is purely diatonic, that is, sticking with the major scale. These chords are linked together with the descending line C-B-A-G. "Jingle Bell Rock" by Bobby Helms connects its chords with a similar progression. See Figure 9-14.

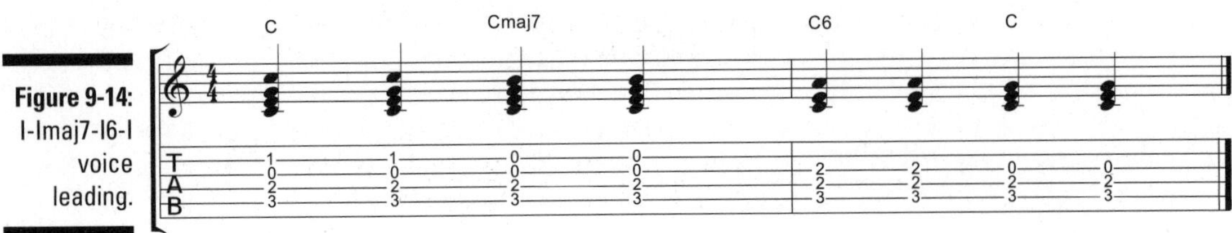

Figure 9-14: I-Imaj7-I6-I voice leading.

Illustration courtesy of Desi Serna

Chapter 10

Filling the Gaps with Passing Chords

In This Chapter

- Playing chromatic passing chords
- Getting to know diminished chords
- Using augmented chords

To connect chords that are a whole step apart, composers often use *passing chords,* which use some of the pitches in between a key's chords. Typically, passing chords have an unusual sound when you play them by themselves; however, when you place them between the right chords, they act like a sonic bridge that leads from one set of pitches to another. In the right sequence, a passing chord makes complete musical sense to your ear as it smoothly transitions from one chord to another.

Passing chords add variety and movement to chord progressions and are fairly common in popular music. If you've ever wondered why some chords in a song seem completely out of place yet sound so perfect, then you've experienced passing chords before. In this chapter, you get to know them even better by exploring the use of chromatic, diminished, and augmented chords.

Listen to Audio Track 10 to hear examples of passing chords and get an idea of what this chapter is all about.

Getting to Know Chromatic Passing Chords

When you move a chord shape up or down by one half step as you move to another chord, you're using a *chromatic passing chord.* For example, when a progression moves from V to IV, which are a whole step apart, you can add a chromatic passing chord between them to smooth out the transition. Figure 10-1 shows an example in the key of F. In measure 3, B is a chromatic passing chord connecting the C and B♭ chords, V and IV.

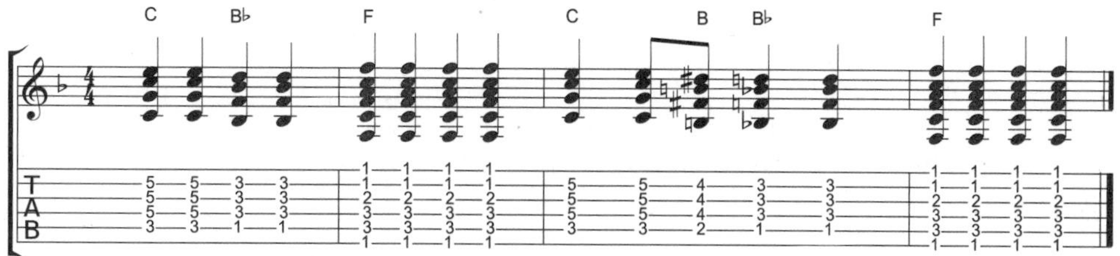

Figure 10-1: Chromatic passing chord in F.

Illustration courtesy of Desi Serna

You can hear and see this chromatic passing chord example by watching Video Clip 22.

"The Wind Cries Mary" by Jimi Hendrix uses a chromatic passing chord like the one shown in Figure 10-1. The verse features the chord changes C-B-B♭-F. The song also features a chromatic movement in the introduction with the chords E♭-E-F.

Hendrix uses chromatic passing chords in other songs, too. For instance, "Bold as Love" places a G♯ chord between G and A, ♭VII and I, at the end of measure 8 just before the beginning of the chorus. (This particular song is in A major with borrowing from the Mixolydian mode and guitars tuned down a half step to E♭.) If you're craving another Hendrix song with this type of passing chord, check out "Little Wing," which features a chromatic passing chord between Bm and Am in measure 5.

Figure 10-2 presents another example that uses chromatic passing chords. Here, the key is E minor. The progression starts with a G major chord and moves downward by semitones to Em through F♯ and F. While the G chord belongs to E minor, F♯ and F are simply serving as passing chords as the progression moves to Em. To hear this type of progression in a song, listen to "I'm a Man" by the Spencer Davis Group.

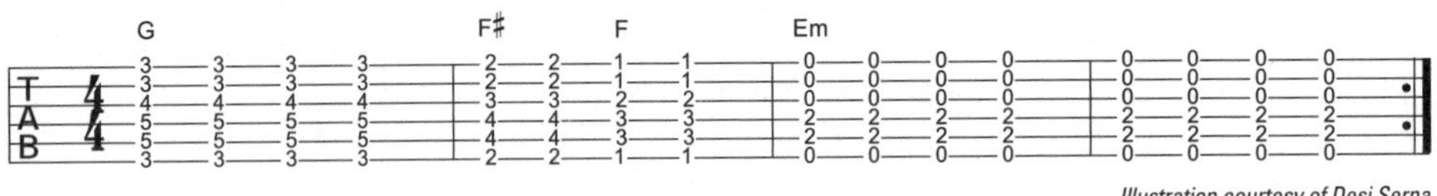

Figure 10-2: Chromatic passing chords in E minor.

Illustration courtesy of Desi Serna

"Life Without You" by Stevie Ray Vaughan connects the relative major and minor chords in a similar way, except that it does so in the key of A (guitars tuned down a half step to E♭) with the chords A-G♯-G-F♯m. Throughout the song, these chords also appear in an ascending fashion as F♯m-G-G♯-A. In other parts of the verse, you hear chromatic chord movement from I up to a major III chord and from IV down to a major II chord.

Figure 10-3 presents an example of chromatic passing chords in the key of G. This progression uses all major chords with chromatic passing chords between G-A and A-B.

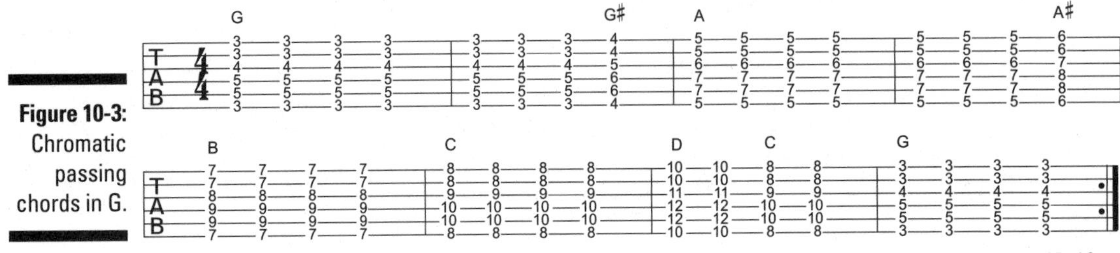

Figure 10-3: Chromatic passing chords in G.

Illustration courtesy of Desi Serna

"Bad, Bad Leroy Brown" by Jim Croce features the same type of progression shown in Figure 10-3. It uses the progression I-II-III-IV-V in the key of G, all major chords with chromatic passing chords between I-II and II-III.

Passing chords in blues

Blues players often use chromatic half step motion to move into the main chords of a 12-bar blues chord progression. For example, many blues players approach a I chord or IV chord from either a half step above or below. Take a look at Figure 10-4, which is written in the key of G. In the first line, you see the IV chord, C9, approached by the D♭9 chord that's one half step above it. In the second line, the I chord, G7, is approached by G♭7, which is one half step below it. A passing chord can connect the V chord to the IV chord, as well, as you see at the beginning of the third line with the progression from D9 (the V chord) to C9 (the IV chord) via D♭9, the passing chord. A common ending to a blues song is to play the I chord, move up a fret, and then move back down again. You see an example of this at the end of the third line with the progression from the I chord, G7, to A♭7 and back down again. Sometimes blues players reverse this ending, moving from I down a fret and back up again.

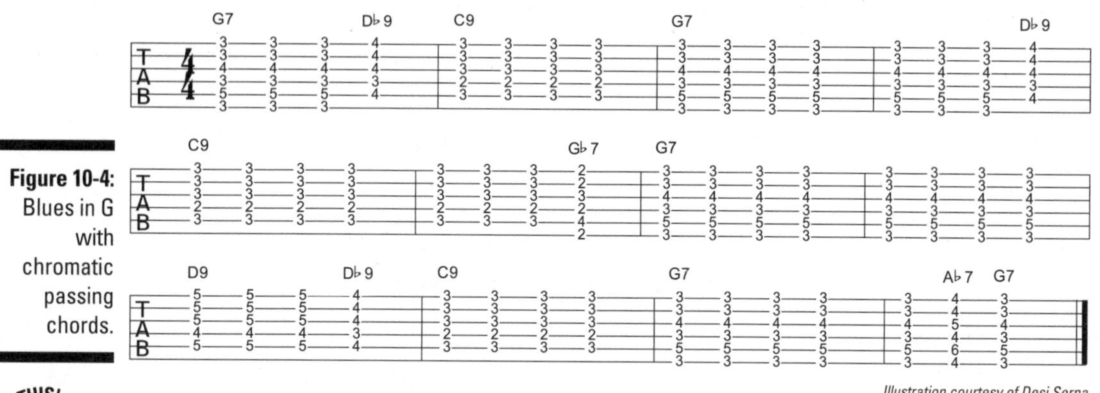

Figure 10-4: Blues in G with chromatic passing chords.

Illustration courtesy of Desi Serna

You can hear and see this blues in G progression by watching Video Clip 23.

The chromatic passing chord technique appears in rock 'n' roll, too. Both "Jailhouse Rock" by Elvis Presley and "Heartache Tonight" by the Eagles have progressions in which the main chords are approached by a half step.

Figure 10-5 presents another example of a 12-bar blues in G with a more complex and jazzy progression that touches on chords ii (Am7) and iii (Bm7) from the major scale plus a ♭VI chord (E♭9). The chromatic movement is seen on all the flattened chords.

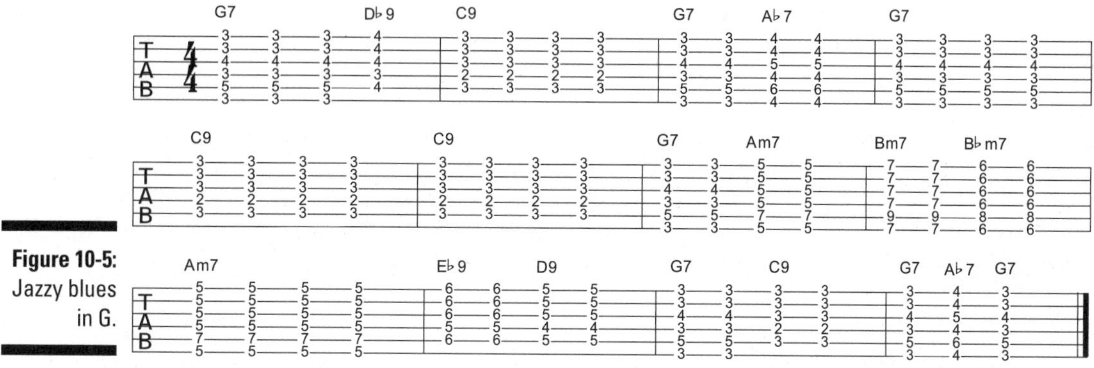

Figure 10-5: Jazzy blues in G.

Illustration courtesy of Desi Serna

"Stormy Monday" by the Allman Brothers Band, a blues in G song, uses chromatic passing chords in a similar manner to the example in Figure 10-5. Both a ♯I chord and a ♯II chord appear in this song. Several versions of this song exist, but the IV and V chords are often approached chromatically from above by one fret.

We gonna get funky

Funk is another style of music that uses a lot of chromatic passing chords in its chord changes. For example, it's very common for composers to move a tonic chord up or down a fret, as shown in Figure 10-6.

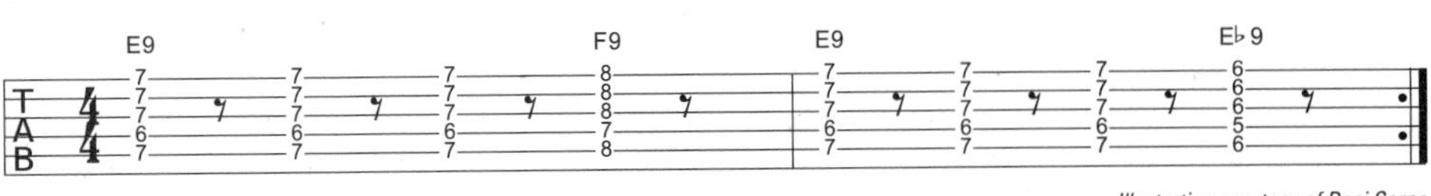

Figure 10-6: Funk in E with chromatic chords.

Illustration courtesy of Desi Serna

Sometimes guitar players move tonic chords up or down more than one fret with a couple of chromatic steps. For example, "Play That Funky Music" by Wild Cherry has an E9 chord played with F♯9 and F9. Similarly, Stevie Ray Vaughan plays an E9 together with an E♭9 and F9 in "Wall of Denial."

Chromatic ch-ch-ch-ch-changes

Figure 10-7 presents a chromatic example in C that features a passing chord in between the Em7 and Dm7 chords. "Changes" by David Bowie does something similar with the changes (no pun intended) C-Dm7-Em7-E♭m7-Dm7-G7 in C major when he sings, "So I turned myself to face me." The E♭m7chord is a nice chromatic passing chord between iii (Em7) and ii (Dm7). The song's introduction also features half step movement.

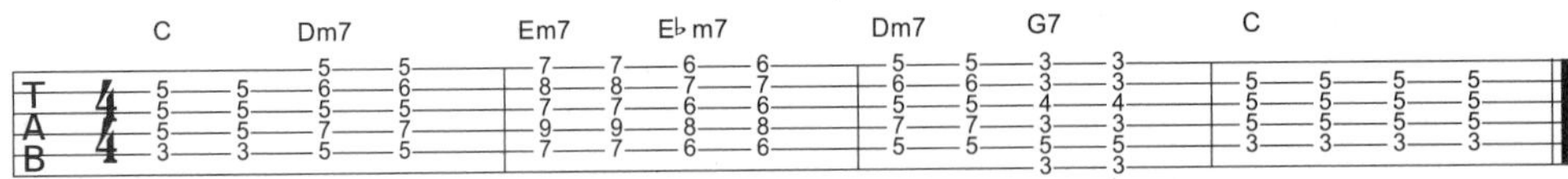

Figure 10-7: Chromatic changes in C.

Illustration courtesy of Desi Serna

For a well-known, more traditional song that uses chromatic passing chords moving through the C major scale, consider the popular Christmas song "White Christmas." The beginning of each verse contains the progression Cmaj7-Dm7-Cmaj7-Bmaj7-Cmaj7-Dm7-D♯m7-Em7. This progression includes a half step into the I chord (from Bmaj7 to Cmaj7) and another one in between the ii (Dm7) and iii (Em7) chords.

Getting to Know Diminished Chords

Diminished chords are chords that you never use as anything other than a passing chord. They sound very dissonant and unstable by themselves, almost unusable. But when placed between the right chords, they make great transitions. Generally speaking, diminished chords have a jazzy flavor to them, and they appear in styles that emphasize voice leading and dominant functions (see Chapter 9).

There are three types of diminished chords: Diminished triads, half diminished, and diminished 7th, which is also called a fully diminished chord.

The diminished triad is what naturally occurs on the 7th degree of the major scale. It's built 1-♭3-♭5. That's a root, minor 3rd, and flat (or diminished) 5th, three minor 3rds in a row. You can also call this minor♭5. In the key of G, the 7th triad is F♯-A-C. That's F♯dim (F♯°) or F♯m♭5. In traditional theory, diminished triads are one of the four types of basic triads: major, minor, diminished, and augmented.

If you add a 7th to the diminished triad in the major scale, then you get 1-♭3-♭5-♭7. In the key of G, this is F♯-A-C-E. That's three minor 3rds from 1-♭3-♭5 and then a major 3rd from ♭5-♭7. This is called a *half* diminished chord for reasons you see in a moment. You can also call this a minor7♭5.

A *diminished 7th* chord is a diminished triad with a *double flat* 7th (♭♭7), which is also considered a diminished 7th interval. It's built 1-♭3-♭5-♭♭7. An F♯dim7 or F♯°7 is built using the notes F♯-A-C-E♭. That's all minor 3rds! This is considered to be a *fully diminished* chord because of its consecutive minor 3rd intervals. This type of chord does not occur naturally in the major scale.

When it comes to using diminished chords as passing chords, usually full or diminished 7ths are used, and they're not usually placed on the 7th scale degree. So diminished chords and their usage are not really associated with the diminished triad that occurs in the major scale on the 7th degree. Instead, you think of them as something different. This is the reason why I prefer to call the 7th major scale triad minor♭5 and it's 7th chord minor7♭5. It helps me to avoid confusing it with fully diminished 7th chords and their usage.

Musicians often use the term *diminished* on its own to refer to fully diminished 7th chords.

Fingering diminished chord shapes

One of the interesting features of fully diminished chords is that you can think of them as being built out of a series of minor 3rds. For example, a Bdim7 chord is built from the notes B-D-F-A♭. Each chord tone is a minor 3rd, or three frets, above the previous one. If you were to continue another minor 3rd above the A♭, you'd return to B.

To combine the notes of a Bdim7 to make chord shapes on the guitar you need to transpose some pitches up an octave. Figure 10-8 shows the most common diminished chord fingerings.

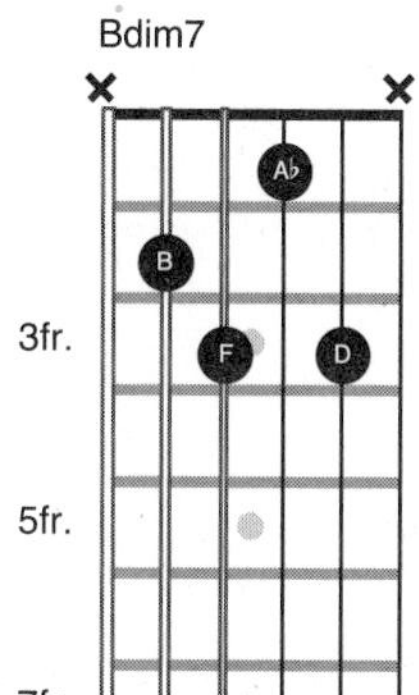

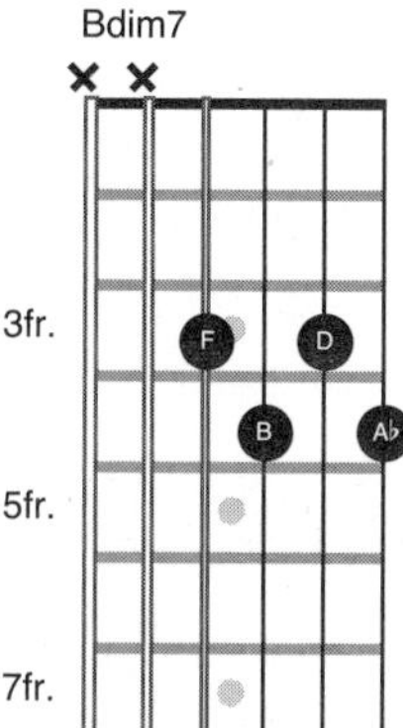

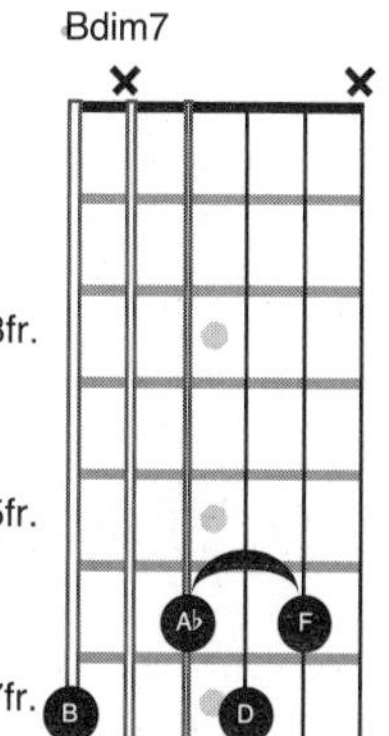

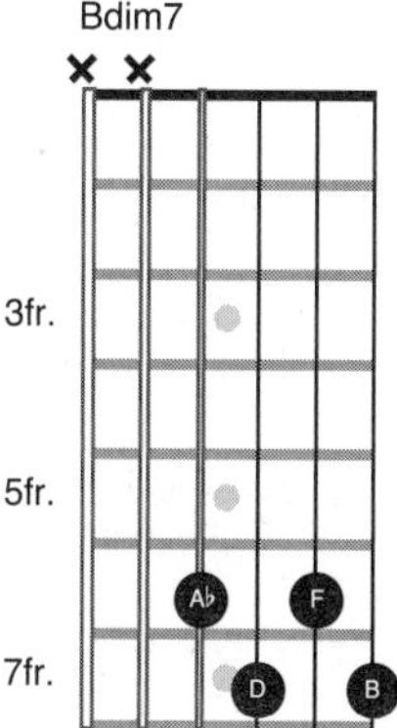

Figure 10-8: B diminished 7th chords.

Illustration courtesy of Desi Serna

You can hear and see these Bdim7 chords by watching Video Clip 24.

Playing diminished 7th chord inversions

Another interesting feature of diminished 7th chords is the way you play their inversions on the fretboard. Because diminished 7th chords are built out of all minor 3rds, you can simply move any fully diminished 7th chord fingering up or down three frets for an *inversion* (a reordering of the notes creating a new chord voicing). Move the same chord fingering three frets again, and you have the next inversion. Continue in this way until you cycle back to your starting point an octave higher or lower (see Figure 10-9).

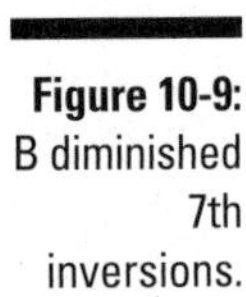

Figure 10-9: B diminished 7th inversions.

Using diminished 7ths as passing chords

Guitarists always use diminished 7th chords as passing chords. One common usage is to connect chords I and ii in the major scale. In Figure 10-10, you see an example in A major, where you add a diminished chord between the A and Bm chords in two different positions using two different diminished 7th chord shapes.

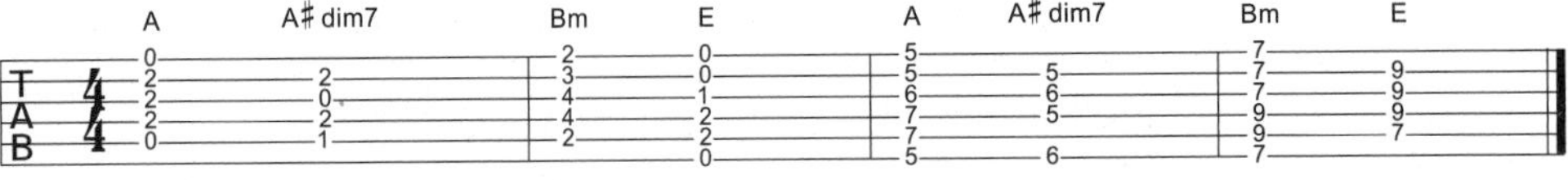

Figure 10-10: Diminished 7th passing chord in A.

You can hear and see this diminished passing chord example by watching Video Clip 25.

"Friends in Low Places" by Garth Brooks uses the same type of diminished 7th chord as Figure 10-10. The guitar introduction is based on the verse's chord progression I-ii-V in G, and you add a diminished 7th chord between I and ii to create the progression A-A♯dim7-Bm7-E, played with a capo at the 2nd fret with the chord shapes G-G♯dim7-Am7-D.

Similarly, "Shower the People" by James Taylor uses the chords C-C♯dim7-Dm, played with a capo at the 3rd fret as A-A♯dim7-Bm. Here, the diminished 7th chord connects a V and vi chord.

In Figure 10-11, a diminished 7th chord (C♯dim7) connects the ii chord (Cm7) and a first inversion I7 chord (B♭7/D) in the key of B♭. The figure shows the chord changes in two positions.

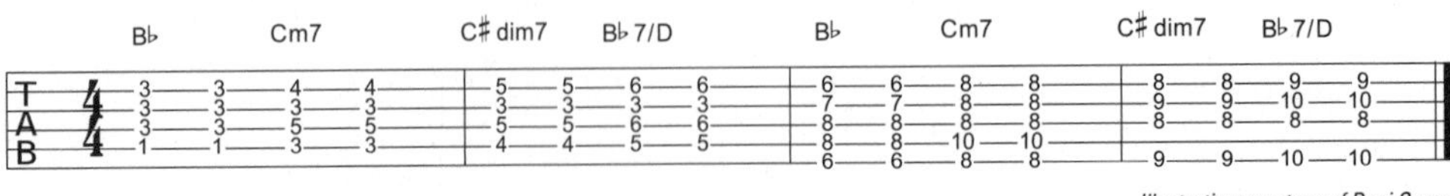

Figure 10-11: Diminished 7th passing chord between ii and I7.

Diminished chords like the ones shown in Figures 10-10 and 10-11 appear in "Crazy" by Patsy Cline. At the end of the first verse, you hear a I-ii-V turnaround in the key of B♭. There's a diminished 7th chord connecting the I and ii chords, creating the progression B♭-Bdim7-Cm7-F7. This song also features a diminished 7th chord between ii and an inversion of the I7 chord at the end of the second verse, creating the progression B♭-Cm7-C♯dim7-B♭7/D.

Another example is the bridge to "Ain't Gone 'n' Give Up on Love" by Stevie Ray Vaughan, which features a keyboardist playing the chords D-Em7-Fdim7-D7/F♯, followed by A7-Bm7-Cdim7-A7/C♯ (guitars tuned down one half step to E♭). Try working these chord changes out on your guitar.

In Figure 10-12, a diminished 7th chord connects IV and I in the key of C. Here, the voice leading moves from the root of the IV chord to the root of the diminished 7th chord and finally to the 5th of the I chord: F-F♯-G. The diagram shows this progression in two different positions. You clearly see this line on the 6th string in the second version with the way I put C's 5th, G, in the bass (though you don't need to always voice these chord changes this way). Patsy Cline's "Crazy" also connects IV and I like this in the key of B♭.

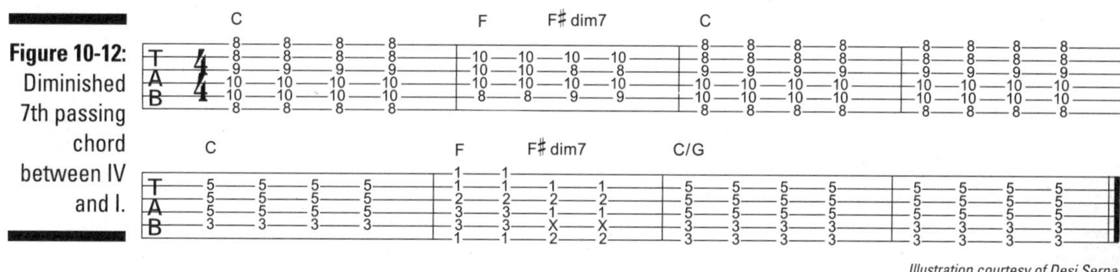

Figure 10-12: Diminished 7th passing chord between IV and I.

Illustration courtesy of Desi Serna

Listen carefully to the following songs and you'll hear diminished 7th chords:

"Dance with Me" by Orleans

"Don't Look Back in Anger" by Oasis

"Every Time You Go Away" by Paul Young

"Michelle" by The Beatles

"My Sweet Lord" by George Harrison

"Private Investigation" by Dire Straits

"Ten Years Gone" by Led Zeppelin

Diminished 7th chords are especially prevalent in jazz standards. I usually don't reference jazz songs because most guitar players who listen to popular music aren't familiar with the old standards from the jazz era. Nevertheless, if you have a jazz songbook like *The Real Book,* you'll find diminished 7th chords in many of its selections. Two good examples that you may have heard are "Stormy Weather" and "The Way You Look Tonight," both of which are performed by many different artists.

The popular guitar-driven Christmas song "Jingle Bell Rock" by Bobby Helms is a great song to learn for guitar players who want an introduction to jazzy elements like dominant function, voice leading, and diminished 7th chords.

Inaccuracies in Internet tabs

As you probably know, many of the free guitar tabs you find on the Internet are inaccurate. This is especially true for songs that include advanced musical concepts like diminished chords. As I was doing research for this chapter, I was disappointed to see that many of the songs I reference are written incorrectly on free guitar tab sites. Apparently, many of the people posting free tabs don't really understand diminished chords. With this in mind, when you look up the songs I mention in this chapter, you may need to consult professionally transcribed tabs rather than the free versions online.

Substituting diminished 7th chords for dominant 7th chords

Guitarists often use diminished 7th chords as substitutes for dominant 7th chords. For example, you can play the typical jazz progression Cmaj7-A7-Dm7-G7 as Cmaj7-C♯dim7-Dm7-G7. In this case, the C♯dim7 chord replaces A7. You actually see this kind of progression that connects I and ii in Figure 10-10 as well as in both "Friends in Low Places" and "Crazy."

This substitution works for a couple of reasons:

- C♯dim7 has many of the same notes as A7. C♯dim7 has C♯, E, G, and B♭, and A7 has A, C♯, E, and G. Notice the three notes they have in common: C♯, E, and G. Basically, the C♯dim7 chord is like an A7 chord, except that it's missing the root note A.
- C♯dim7 contains the leading note of the chord of resolution; the C♯ is the leading note (see Chapter 9) of D.

The main thing you need to remember when substituting diminished 7th chords for dominant 7ths is this: The root of the diminished chord is the 3rd of the dominant 7th chord. Here are a few examples:

- The 3rd of A7 is C♯, so you can substitute C♯dim7 for A7.
- The 3rd of G7 is B, so you can use Bdim7 in place of G7.
- The 3rd of C7 is E, so you can use Edim7 in place of C7.

Playing Augmented Chords

Augmented chords are another type of chord that you can use as passing chords, though they can also function as dominant chords. Basically, *augmented chords* are major chords with raised (or augmented) 5ths. They're popular in styles of music that use dominant function and voice leading, like jazz.

An *augmented triad* is one of the four basic types of triads (the other three are major, minor, and diminished; see Chapter 3 for details). An augmented triad is like a major triad with a raised 5th; it has a root, a major 3rd, and an augmented 5th: 1, 3, ♯5. Augmented triads don't naturally occur in the major scale, so think of it as an altered chord — a major triad with a sharpened 5th.

Figure 10-13 compares four different D major chords with Daug (also written D+) chords in different positions on the neck. In each example, the 5th of D, A, is raised to form the augmented chord.

Figure 10-13: Augmented chord shapes.

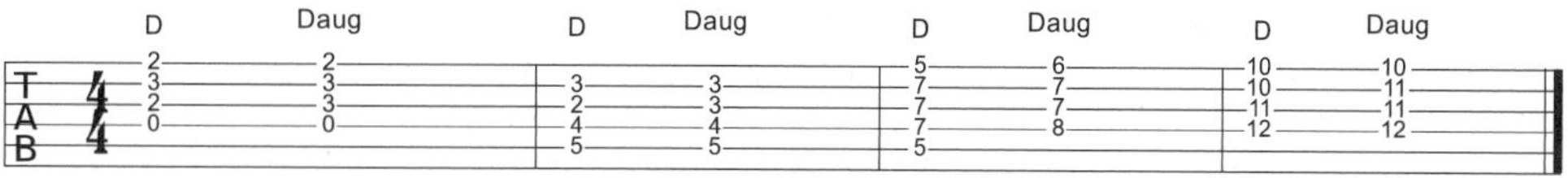

Illustration courtesy of Desi Serna

Playing augmented chord inversions

An augmented chord really just consists of a series of stacked major 3rds. For example, Caug is C, E, G♯; C to E is a major 3rd, as is E to G♯. If you add another major 3rd above G♯, you get B♯, which is the same as C. Because of this property, to invert an augmented triad on the guitar, all you have to do is move the chord's shape up a major 3rd two whole steps. Similarly, by moving the shape down a major 3rd on the neck, you also get an inversion of the chord.

Figure 10-14 presents the inversions of two common augmented chord shapes on Daug. Try playing through them forward and backward to help you understand how these inversions work.

Figure 10-14: Augmented chord inversions.

Illustration courtesy of Desi Serna

Using augmented chords for dominant function

Having a strong sense of harmonic movement, augmented chords can produce an effect similar to dominant function with a Vaug leading to I. For instance, like V7, an augmented chord built on V has a leading tone in it that moves to the tonic pitch. The raised 5th also creates harmonic tension that resolves upward — in this case, to the 3rd of the tonic chord.

Figure 10-15 shows an example of an augmented chord in the key of G. The Daug chord moves to the tonic chord G. The pitches in Daug are D, F♯, and A♯. The F♯ leads to G, the root of the tonic chord. The raised 5th, A♯, leads to the 3rd of the G chord, the pitch B.

Figure 10-15: Augmented dominant function.

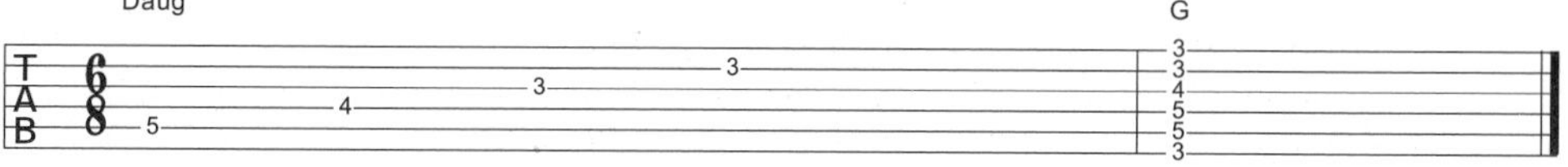

Illustration courtesy of Desi Serna

You hear a Daug chord and its resolution at the very beginning of Stevie Ray Vaughan's version of "The Things That I Used to Do" (guitars tuned down one half step to E♭). This same chord appears in the famous live version of "Stormy Monday" by the Allman Brothers Band. The same chord an octave higher begins "School Days" by Chuck Berry, and a first inversion Gaug chord leads to C in "No One Needs to Know" by Shania Twain.

In "Crying" by Roy Orbison, you see the chord progression D-Daug-G-Gm-D-A7-D. Here, the Daug chord grows out of the D chord, functioning as a secondary dominant of G in a way that's similar to that of a D7 chord (see Chapter 9 for details on secondary dominants). Orbison's choice of chords allows for an interesting chromatic line starting on the 5th of the D chord through to the 3rd of the Gm chord: A-A♯-B-B♭.

Other songs that feature augmented chords include "The Warmth of the Sun" by The Beach Boys and "From Me to You" by The Beatles.

Using augmented chords in voice leading

Voice leading is a technique where a set of chord changes includes notes that step or lead from one chord to the next. Another common use of augmented chords is to connect a major triad to a 6th chord, as in the progression I-Iaug-I6. Here, the augmented chord connects I and I6 with a chromatic line. The 5th of the I chord moves to the 6th of the I6 chord through a sharpened 5th.

Figure 10-16 shows this progression in C major with the addition of a I7 chord at the end: C-Caug-C6-C7. You see the chromatic line G-G♯-A-B♭ on the 3rd string of the first three measures. Take a close look at the pitches in these chords. C is built out of the pitches C-E-G; Caug is built out of C-E-G♯; C6 is built out of C-E-A; and C7 is built out of C-E-G-B♭. See how this progression naturally gives rise to the chromatic line G-G♯-A-B♭? In measures 1 through 4, this line appears on the 3rd string. In 5 through 8, this line appears on the 2nd string.

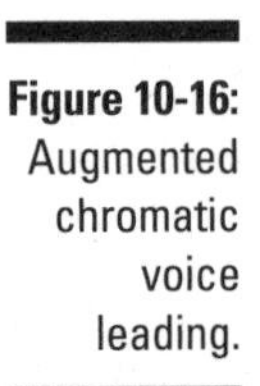

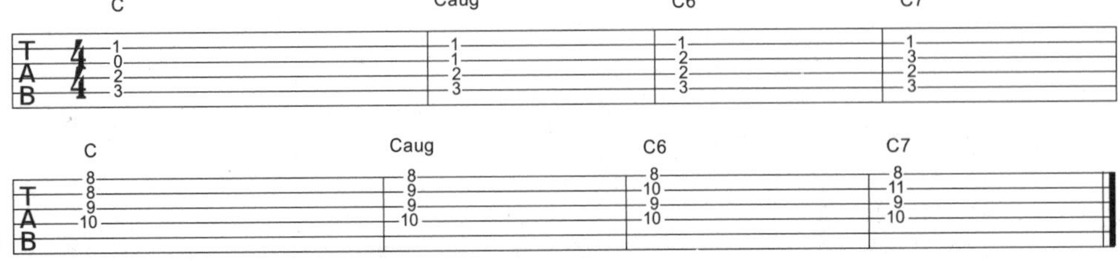

Figure 10-16: Augmented chromatic voice leading.

Illustration courtesy of Desi Serna

You can hear and see this example of augmented chromatic voice leading by watching Video Clip 26.

Many songs use augmented chords in voice leading. Here are just a few popular examples:

"Baby Hold On" by Eddie Money uses an augmented chord in the verse. Built out of the chords D and Daug, the augmented chord here comes in on the second half of each line of the verse, creating a sense of harmonic tension that resolves back into the D major chord at the beginning of each new line. You experience the real goal of the augmented chord in the last line of the verse, where D6 and finally D7 prepare the next section of the song.

"Because" by The Dave Clark Five has the chords G-Gaug-G6-G7 at one point and augmented chords as dominants with G-Gaug-C-Cm-G and D-Daug-G at another.

"It's All Been Done" by Barenaked Ladies has the following chord progression in the bridge: D-Daug-D6-D7-G.

"(Just Like) Starting Over" by John Lennon opens with A-Aaug-A6-Aaug.

"Laughing" by The Guess Who has the progression A-Aaug-A6-A7-Dmaj7-Dm7-C♯m7-E.

In the famous opening to "Stairway to Heaven" by Led Zeppelin, you see two lines moving in opposite directions in the outer voices in the first three chords: A-B-C played on the 1st string and A-G♯-G on the 4th string functioning as a bass line. The pitches C and E on strings 3 and 2 are held throughout. The 1st chord is clearly A minor, while the chord on G♯ can be considered a G♯ augmented (called Eaug/G♯ in some scores) with a B note on top.

Part IV
Playing Guitar Scales

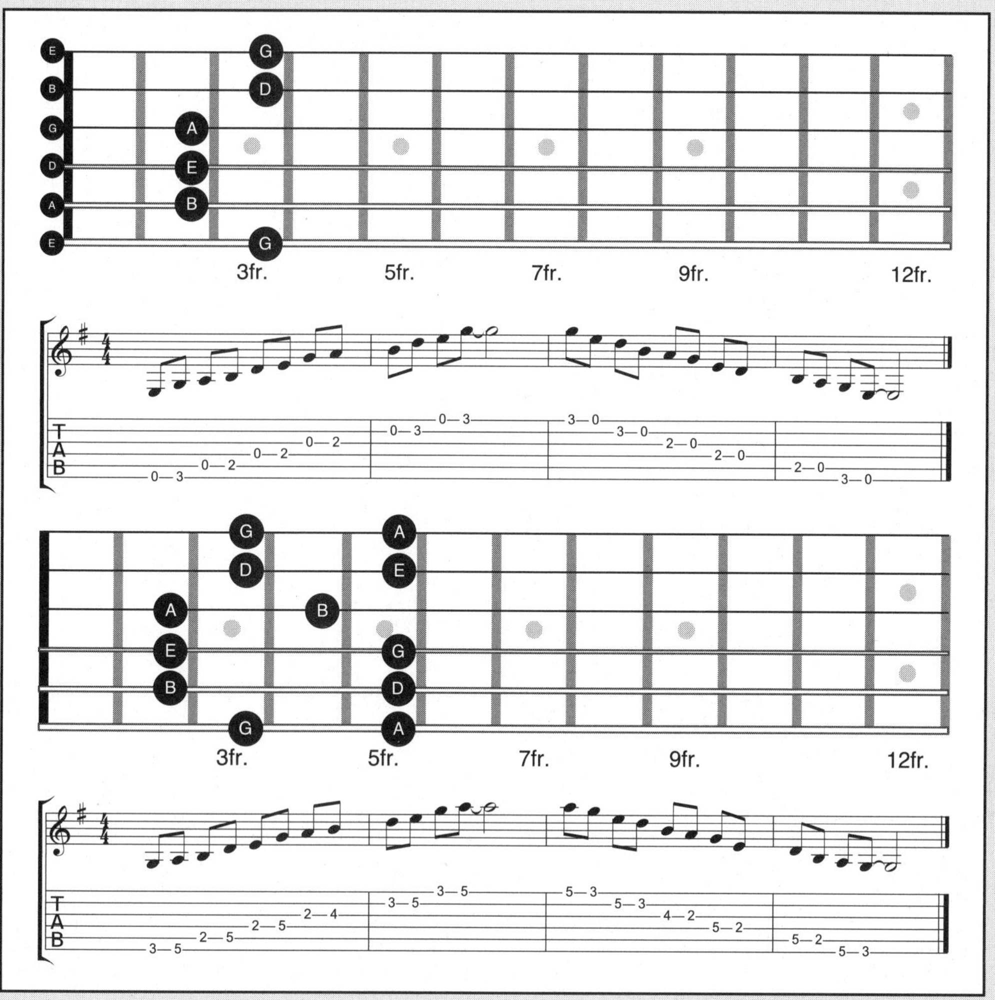

Head to www.dummies.com/extras/guitartheory for an article that shows you how to play through four basic lead patterns that can be applied to most music.

In this part . . .

- Identify the types of scales that guitarists use to play melodies, riffs, solos, and bass lines.
- Finger, play, connect, and apply pentatonic scale patterns, major scale patterns, and modes. See which scales are used in popular guitar songs.
- Find out how to play harmonic minor chord progressions and use the harmonic minor scale.
- Apply scales to blues-based music and discover how to play over a 12-bar blues chord progression.

Chapter 11

Preparing for Riffs and Solos with the Pentatonic Scale

In This Chapter

- Getting to know the pentatonic scale
- Covering the neck with the five pentatonic patterns
- Applying the pentatonic scale over chords
- Connecting fretboard positions and changing keys
- Looking at which popular songs use the pentatonic

Guitar players use the box-shaped patterns of the pentatonic scale to play riffs, solos, melodies, and bass lines. In fact, many guitar greats, such as Jimi Hendrix and Eric Clapton, made names for themselves using the very pentatonic scale patterns I present in this chapter. Master these patterns, and you'll be on your way to similar fame (well, maybe).

In this chapter, I give you a little background on the pentatonic scale and show you how to use it to form patterns on the guitar fretboard. You play through these patterns, connect them to cover the whole guitar neck, and transpose them to different keys. After you play the pentatonic scale across the fretboard, you're set to go learn songs. I reference some popular songs that use these pentatonic scale patterns so you can go get some hands-on experience with them.

Note: The information in this chapter is geared toward guitarists who want to play riffs, solos, and bass lines. If you're primarily interested in rhythm guitar and songwriting, you may want to spend less time in this chapter or possibly skip it altogether for now. But before you make up your mind, keep in mind that even rhythm guitar players and songwriters use scales now and then. After all, rhythm guitar parts sometimes include pentatonic riffs, and songwriters can use the pentatonic scale to compose melodies and harmonies.

Getting to Know the Pentatonic Scale

A musical *scale* is a series of pitches (or notes) played one pitch at a time in an ascending or descending order. Together, notes from scales build chords, create melodies, and produce harmonies. When people sing, the sound they make goes up and down in a scale. When you hear a guitar riff or solo, you're hearing a scale.

Listen to Audio Clip 11 to hear what the pentatonic scale sounds like and how it's used.

The *pentatonic scale* is a five-tone scale with — you guessed it — five notes in it (which makes sense considering *penta* means "five" and *tonic* means "tone"). The pentatonic scale may have only five notes, but these notes are scattered all over the place. Melodies, riffs, and solos often play through the scale until the series is complete and then continue up or down, playing higher and lower occurrences of the same notes in other registers. To accomplish this type of pattern on guitar, you need to be able to move both vertically and horizontally across the fretboard.

When guitar players learn scales, they work on covering one small area of the neck at a time and then connect these individual positions to cover the whole guitar neck. Each position creates a unique pattern. In the next section, I show you how to play the pentatonic scale across the whole neck by covering five different positions with five different patterns.

Guitarists and songwriters can choose from many different music scales, ranging from the simple to the complex, the familiar to the exotic. But popular music — the songs you hear played on Top 40 and classic rock radio stations — primarily uses pentatonic and major scales.

Covering the Fretboard with the Pentatonic Scale

The easiest way to get to know the pentatonic scale is to begin working in the key of E minor because it uses all the open strings on the guitar and is very common in popular music. The E minor pentatonic scale consists of the notes E-G-A-B-D. Figure 11-1 shows all the occurrences of these notes on the fretboard.

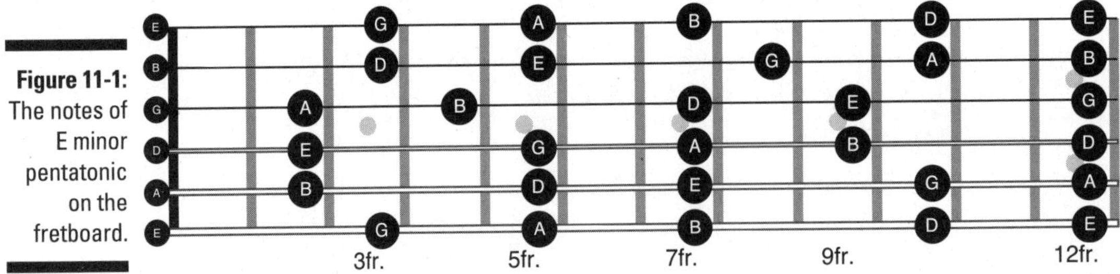

Figure 11-1: The notes of E minor pentatonic on the fretboard.

Illustration courtesy of Desi Serna

Yikes! Looks confusing, doesn't it? Don't worry. To make the pentatonic scale more accessible, I break it into five small patterns, each of which is covered in the following sections.

Starting with pattern 1

Pentatonic pattern 1 consists of all the scale notes on all the strings that fit between the open strings and the 3rd fret (see Figure 11-2). The circles to the far left represent open strings, which you play without the left hand. The notes in the 2nd and 3rd frets have to be fingered.

For your reference I indicate the notes in each pentatonic pattern in this chapter, but you don't need to memorize them. Instead, just focus on the patterns themselves.

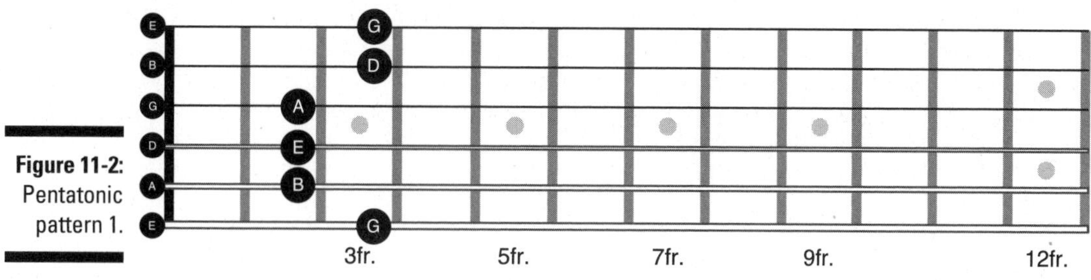

Figure 11-2: Pentatonic pattern 1.

Illustration courtesy of Desi Serna

Practicing pattern 1 up and down the scale

Follow the tab in Figure 11-3 to play through this pentatonic scale pattern in an ascending and descending fashion. When you play up the scale (ascending), you start with the lowest-pitched note and then move to the note that's next highest in pitch. When you play down the scale (descending), you start with the highest-pitched note and then move to the note that is next lowest in pitch.

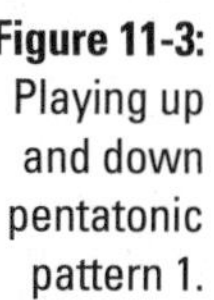

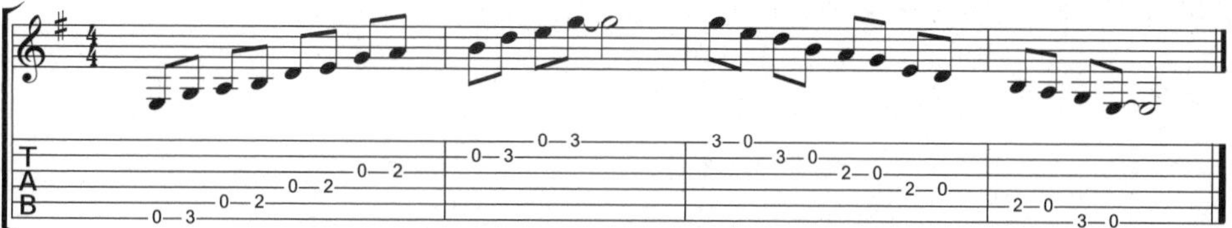

Figure 11-3: Playing up and down pentatonic pattern 1.

Illustration courtesy of Desi Serna

Notice that when you play up the scale, you start with an open string and follow it with a fretted note. In contrast, when you play down the scale, you start with a fretted note and follow it with an open string. Use Video Clip 27 to hear and see how to play up and down pentatonic scale patterns. The video also demonstrates how to finger and connect pentatonic patterns, topics you get to in the upcoming sections.

Fingering and picking the scale

What fingering you use for any scale pattern is a matter of preference. However, with pentatonic pattern 1 in the open position, I recommend that you use your 2nd finger to fret all the notes in the 3rd fret and your 1st finger to fret all the notes in the 2nd fret. You don't have to follow this rule all the time, but it's a good way to get started.

As far as your right hand goes, most guitar players play scales using a pick, although some do use their fingers (this action is called *fingerpicking* or *fingerstyle*). I recommend that you use a pick unless you're completely committed to being a fingerstyle-type player like Chet Atkins or Mark Knopfler. Using a pick is easier to do than developing the fingerpicking skill necessary to play scales well. Throughout this chapter, I assume that you're using a pick.

As you use your guitar pick, try to alternate strokes on each note. In other words, play the first note with a downstroke, the second note with an upstroke, the third note with a downstroke, and so on. (If you prefer not to use a pick, then alternate either your 1st and 2nd fingers or your 1st finger and thumb on your right hand.) Alternating your pick or fingers isn't necessary at this point, but it's a skill that you eventually need to develop to play efficiently and keep up with the pace of most songs.

Songs that feature the notes of pattern 1 in E minor pentatonic in the 1st position include

"Back in Black" by AC/DC

"Susie Q" by Creedence Clearwater Revival

"Sweet Home Alabama" by Lynyrd Skynyrd

"Wish You Were Here" by Pink Floyd

Playing pentatonic pattern 2

In Figure 11-4, you see all the notes of E minor pentatonic that fit between frets 2 and 5. Notice that half of the notes in this new pattern 2 position you use in pattern 1. Visualizing how shapes and patterns connect is the key to navigating the fretboard.

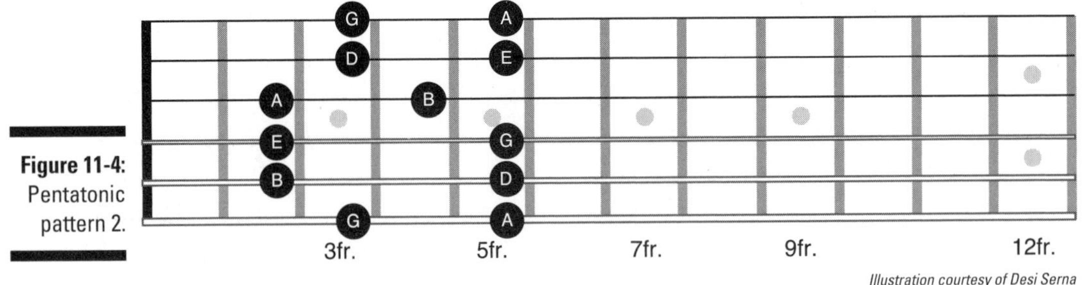

Figure 11-4: Pentatonic pattern 2.

Illustration courtesy of Desi Serna

Figure 11-5 shows pattern 2 ascending and descending in tab.

Figure 11-5: Playing up and down pentatonic pattern 2.

Illustration courtesy of Desi Serna

Fingering pattern two

Because pattern 2 doesn't include any open strings, you have to finger every note. As I mention in the preceding section, fingerings are a matter of preference. That being said, Figures 11-6 and 11-7 show the two fingerings I recommend you at least try.

In Figure 11-6, you see the *one-finger-per-fret approach.* Because this scale pattern spans across four frets, you can assign one finger per fret. With this approach, your 1st finger plays all the notes in the 2nd fret, your 2nd finger plays all the notes in the 3rd fret, your 3rd finger plays all the notes in the 4th fret, and your 4th finger plays all the notes in the 5th fret. Notice that the first note of this pattern is at fret 3, not fret 2. So you start this pattern with your 2nd finger.

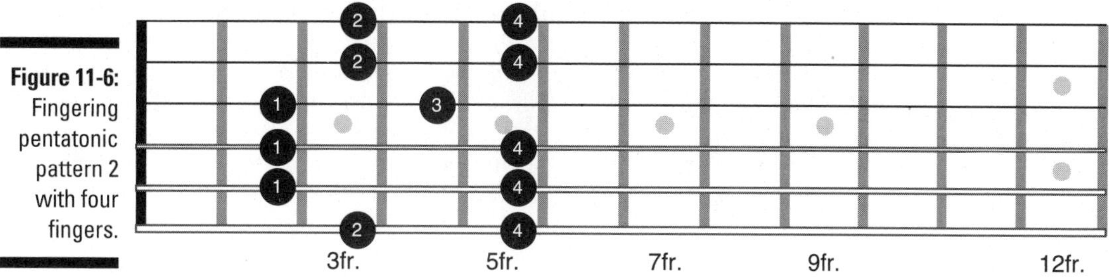

Figure 11-6: Fingering pentatonic pattern 2 with four fingers.

Illustration courtesy of Desi Serna

Figure 11-7 shows another way to play pattern 2 — by using the *three-finger approach.* Many guitar players, including some of the most skilled guitar soloists like Eddie Van Halen and Stevie Ray Vaughan, have done the bulk of their lead playing with the first three fingers. For most players, these fingers tend to be stronger and more coordinated than the 4th finger. Others find using three fingers too much of a stretch, especially in a position where the frets are far apart.

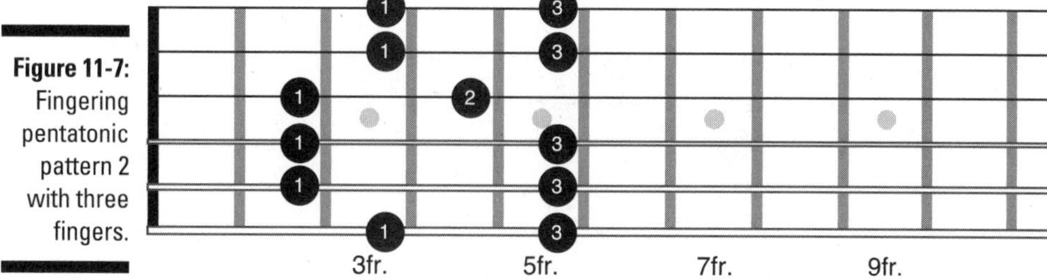

Figure 11-7: Fingering pentatonic pattern 2 with three fingers.

Illustration courtesy of Desi Serna

Note: In the video clips, I primarily use the one-finger-per-fret approach to make it easier for you to see where I'm placing my fingers. But normally I favor the three-finger approach.

No matter what fingering you decide to use, don't try to play pentatonic pattern 2 with only one finger or with only your first two fingers. The goal is to keep your left hand in one stationary position and still reach every note with your fingers. Some players can do this by using only fingers 1 and 3. Experiment with the options I describe here and pick whichever one is most comfortable for you.

Practicing and reviewing

After you decide on a fingering, play up and down pentatonic pattern 2 by starting on the lowest-pitched note and ascending from there. When you reach the top — the top being the highest-pitched note in this position — reverse the order of the notes and play descending. If you need help doing this, just follow the guitar tab shown in Figure 11-5.

If making it through the whole pattern is too much to grasp right now, just work on playing half of it first. For example, you can play just the notes on strings 6, 5, and 4. After you memorize them, add the 3rd string. Continue to add one string at a time until you've memorized the whole thing. Also, practice alternate picking with your right hand as you go.

After you have pattern 2 under your belt, review pentatonic pattern 1 to make sure you haven't forgotten it. Remember, a portion of pattern 1 is reused in pattern 2, and it's important to visualize how the patterns connect. When you're ready to continue, proceed to pattern 3.

The way I number the five pentatonic patterns here is just for reference so that I have a way to refer to each piece of the whole pentatonic puzzle. Although the patterns themselves are universally the same among all guitar players, different players learn the patterns in different orders. For example, some guitar players practice pattern 2 first and so call it pattern 1. Generally speaking, my numbering system is the most common, but you may come across the same patterns numbered differently by another guitar player or teacher. Don't let this confuse you. The numbers don't mean anything. Focus on the patterns themselves.

Playing pentatonic pattern 3

Figure 11-8 shows all the notes of E minor pentatonic pattern 3, which fit between frets 4 and 8.

Note: I don't include a tab for pattern 3. If you don't feel comfortable following the diagram in Figure 11-8 and playing through the pattern without a tab, skip to Figures 11-3 and 11-5 to practice patterns 1 and 2 until you get more comfortable.

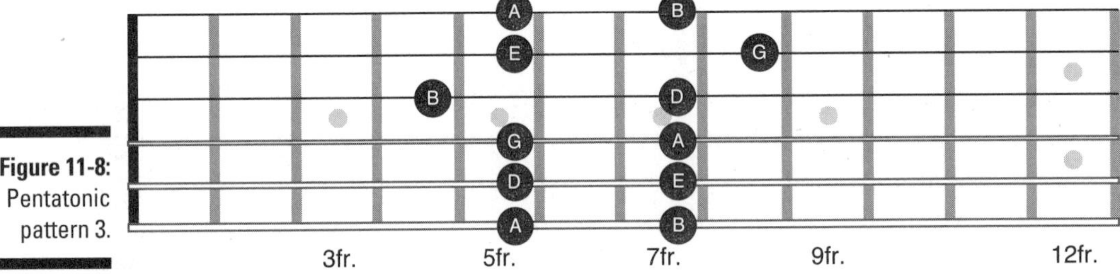

Figure 11-8: Pentatonic pattern 3.

Illustration courtesy of Desi Serna

Pentatonic pattern 3 is unique because it spans across five frets. All the other pentatonic scale patterns span across four frets. Therefore, you can't use the one-finger-per-fret fingering approach with pattern 3 (unless, of course, you're lucky enough to have an extra finger growing out of your left hand). Most guitar players play all the notes in frets 4 and 5 with the 1st finger and all the notes in frets 7 and 8 with the 3rd finger. You can also try using your 4th finger at the 8th fret of string 2.

Play up and down pentatonic pattern 3 until you've memorized it completely, taking it in pieces as I suggest with pattern 2 if you need to (see the preceding section). Alternate your pick as you go. When you're finished, review patterns 1 and 2 to make sure that you haven't forgotten them. As you review them, note how a portion of each pattern gets reused in the next pattern.

When you visualize and feel how different patterns connect, you can better navigate the fretboard and understand how things go together.

Playing pentatonic pattern 4

Like all pentatonic scale patterns, pattern 4 (shown in Figure 11-9) reuses part of pattern 3, which comes before it. It also fits neatly into four frets, so you can try the one-finger-per-fret fingering approach here. After you memorize pattern 4, take some time to review patterns 1 through 3, noticing the parts of the patterns that get repeated.

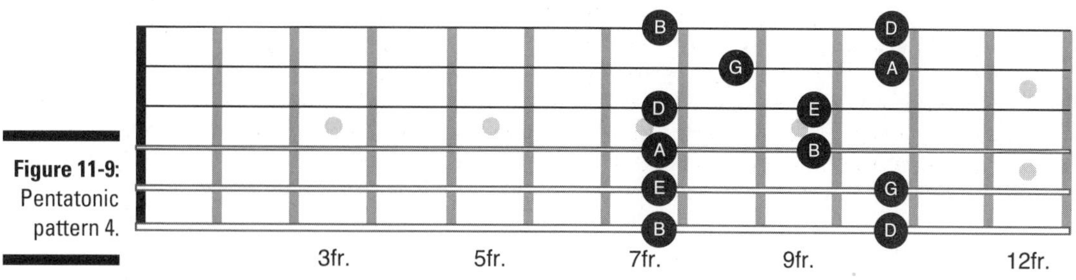

Figure 11-9: Pentatonic pattern 4.

Illustration courtesy of Desi Serna

Finishing up with pentatonic pattern 5

Pentatonic pattern 5 is unique in that it's completely symmetrical (see Figure 11-10). You can try beginning this pattern with your 2nd finger and using the one-finger-per-fret approach, though there's nothing in the 11th fret for your 3rd finger to play. You can also try using just your 1st and 3rd fingers, which seems to work well in this position because of the narrow fret spacing. Take note of how a portion of pattern 4 is reused in pattern 5.

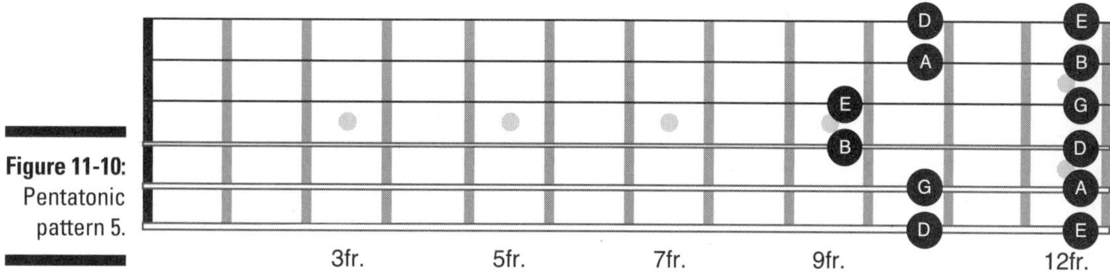

Figure 11-10: Pentatonic pattern 5.

Illustration courtesy of Desi Serna

After you memorize pattern 5, review and practice all the patterns by following these steps:

1. **Start with pattern 1 and play through it in both directions, ascending and decending.**
2. **Lift your hand and reset it in the next position for pattern 2. Play up and down the scale.**
3. **Repeat steps 1 and 2 for the remaining patterns, 3 through 5.**
4. **Play through all the patterns again, but this time, start with pattern 5 and move backward from pattern to pattern until you finish with pattern 1.**
5. **Continue your practice by changing the scale direction you start with.**

   In other words, instead of always starting each pattern with the lowest note on the 6th string and then ascending from there, start on the other end with each pattern's highest note on the 1st string and descend the scale first.

You can practice pentatonic scale patterns not only to prepare you to play popular music but also to develop your finger strength, coordination, and technique.

Connecting all the patterns

When you feel comfortable playing through all five pentatonic scale patterns, the next step is to connect them to cover the rest of the fretboard. To do so, simply connect pattern 5 to another pattern 1, as shown in Figure 11-11. This new pattern 1 is identical to the original except that it's located an octave higher on the fretboard. You no longer use open strings — instead you must fret every note between frets 12 and 15. Notice that the new pattern 1 reuses a portion of pattern 5.

Because pattern 1 spans across four frets, you can try the one-finger-per-fret fingering. However, using just two or three fingers also works well in this position, where the fret spacing is narrow.

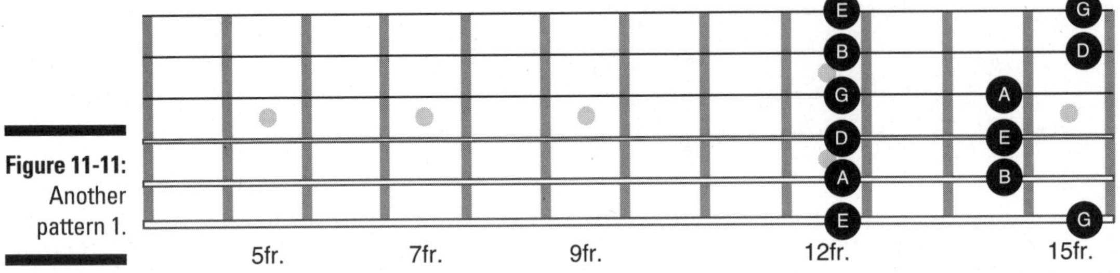

Figure 11-11: Another pattern 1.

Illustration courtesy of Desi Serna

When I say *connect* the patterns, all I mean is to play up and down each pattern and then move to the next position and play up and down that pattern. When you finish a pattern in one direction, stop and restart the same pattern in the opposite direction. Then stop again, lift your fingers, move to the next position, and begin playing up and down the next pattern. Beware that I *don't* mean you should be able to play through all the patterns without stopping. And I certainly *don't* mean that you should be able to play the pentatonic notes in order from one end of the neck to the other without repeating notes. You're going to stop and start, and you're going to repeat notes because the same notes make up all the pentatonic patterns.

Connecting in ascending order

From the new pattern 1, you can connect to another pattern 2, also an octave higher from the original. Continue to connect patterns until you either run out of fretboard or, as is the case on acoustic guitar, you can't reach any higher. Figure 11-12 includes a fretboard diagram with 24 frets showing what the pentatonic scale notes look like between frets 12 and 24. Can you make out the five patterns?

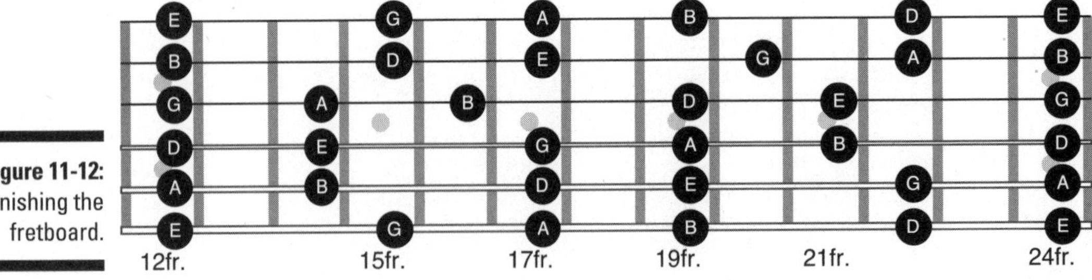

Figure 11-12: Finishing the fretboard.

Illustration courtesy of Desi Serna

The narrower the fret spacing gets, the more difficult it becomes to use a one-finger-per-fret fingering. You may not even be able to fit three fingers in the highest positions. No need to fret (pun intended)! When you're reaching to the very end of the neck, just go with whichever fingers you can squeeze into the frets. You may also try reeling your head back and making a face like you're writhing in pain — that's what Hendrix did and the crowd loved it!

Connecting in descending order

After you finish connecting the patterns in a forward fashion, restart where you left off and move backward. For example, say that you left off with pentatonic pattern 4 between frets 19 and 22. Pattern 4 connects backward to pattern 3, 3 connects back to 2, 2 connects back to 1, and 1 connects back to 5. From there, you can play patterns 5, 4, 3, 2, and 1, ending in the open position where you first practiced pattern 1 (see the earlier section "Starting with pattern 1" for details).

Changing directions and mixing things up

As you connect the patterns, you don't have to start every pattern on string 6. You can start on string 1 and play down the pattern (descending) first and then up the pattern (ascending) second. Whatever you do to connect the patterns, just be sure to practice playing each pattern in both directions.

After you master how to play up and down each pattern, you can try alternating the direction in which you start for each pattern as you connect. For example, play pattern 1 ascending only, then play pattern 2 descending only, then play pattern 3 ascending only, and so on.

Using the Pentatonic Scale as Major and Minor

The pentatonic scale can function as both major and minor. In the previous section, you start with E minor pentatonic, but the same notes and patterns can also produce G major pentatonic. To understand how this works, look at Figure 11-13. Notice how both an E minor (Em) chord and a G major chord fit into pentatonic pattern 1 in the open position. The gray dots indicate the notes of the chords.

The first note in pentatonic pattern 1 is always your minor tonic (pitch center). In the case of Figure 11-13, it's E. You can fit an Em chord in the scale, too — that is, all the notes of an Em chord are found within the scale. The second note in pattern 1 is always your major tonic. In this case, it's G. You can also fit a G major chord in the scale.

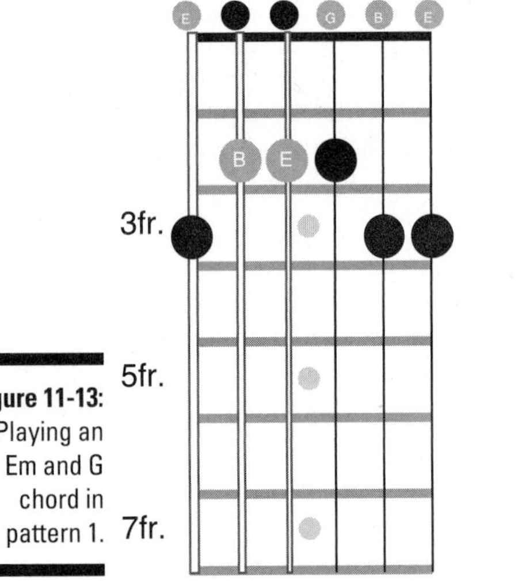

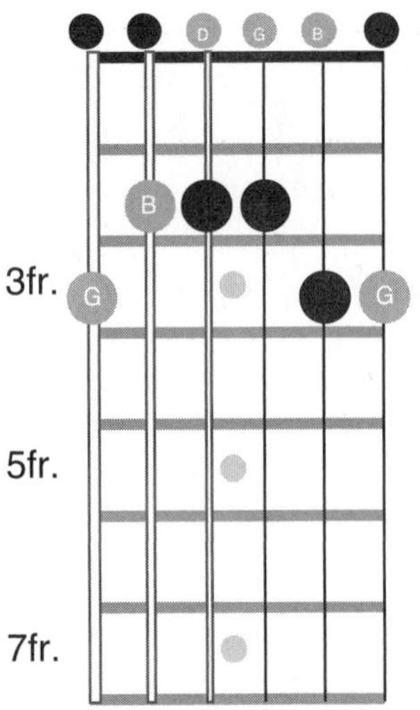

Figure 11-13: Playing an Em and G chord in pattern 1.

Illustration courtesy of Desi Serna

You can play E minor pentatonic over an Em chord or a progression that revolves around Em. For example, "Rockin' in the Free World" by Neil Young centers on an Em chord, and the notes of E minor pentatonic work over it. You can play G major pentatonic over a G chord or a progression that revolves around G. For example, "Wonderful Tonight" by Eric Clapton centers on a G chord, and the notes of G major pentatonic work over it.

Watch Video Clip 28 to hear and see the use of E minor and G major pentatonic.

All five pentatonic patterns consist of the same notes and are simply pieces of the same scale. So if you're using E minor pentatonic over an Em chord, you're not confined to any one position. You can move freely through any of the patterns as long as you connect them properly and stay in key. The same goes for when you're using the scale as G major pentatonic.

The only difference between E minor and G major pentatonic is which note functions as the *tonic* (or tonal center) of the scale. When you use E minor pentatonic, the E note is the tonal center and your point of resolution. Likewise, when you use G major pentatonic, the G note is the tonal center and your point of resolution.

Figure 11-14 shows all the E notes that are located in the pentatonic patterns, plus some commonly used Em chord shapes in gray. Various forms of Em show up in every position and pattern, but for simplicity's sake, I illustrate only those chord forms that guitar players typically use. When a song features E minor pentatonic, more often than not it's using the portion of the patterns that centers on these chord shapes.

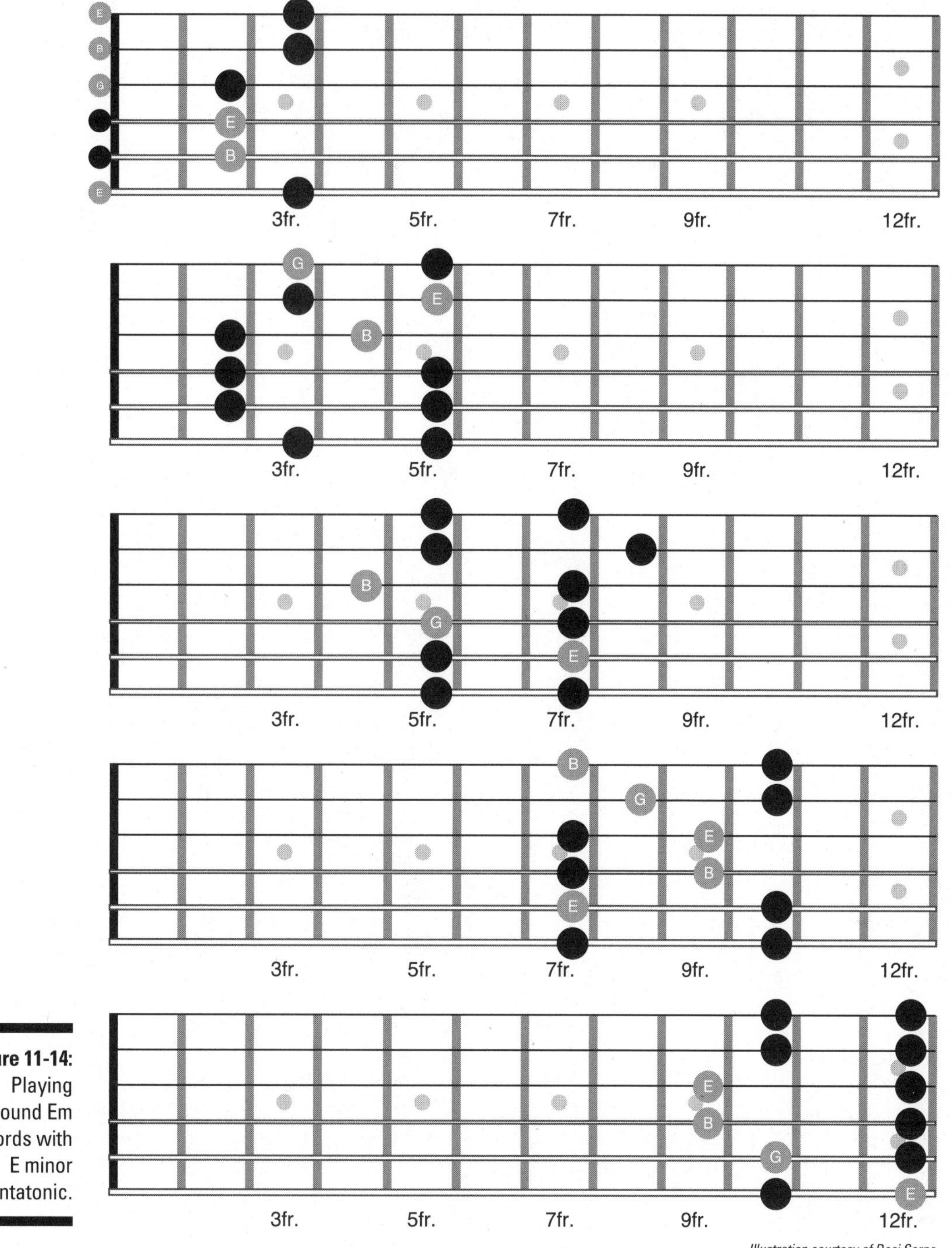

Figure 11-14: Playing around Em chords with E minor pentatonic.

Illustration courtesy of Desi Serna

In Figure 11-15, you can see where all the G notes as well as some G chords are located in the pentatonic patterns. You may recognize these chords as the CAGED forms from Chapter 4. In this figure, you start with the G form in pentatonic pattern 1 and then continue with the CAGED sequence E-D, C-A.

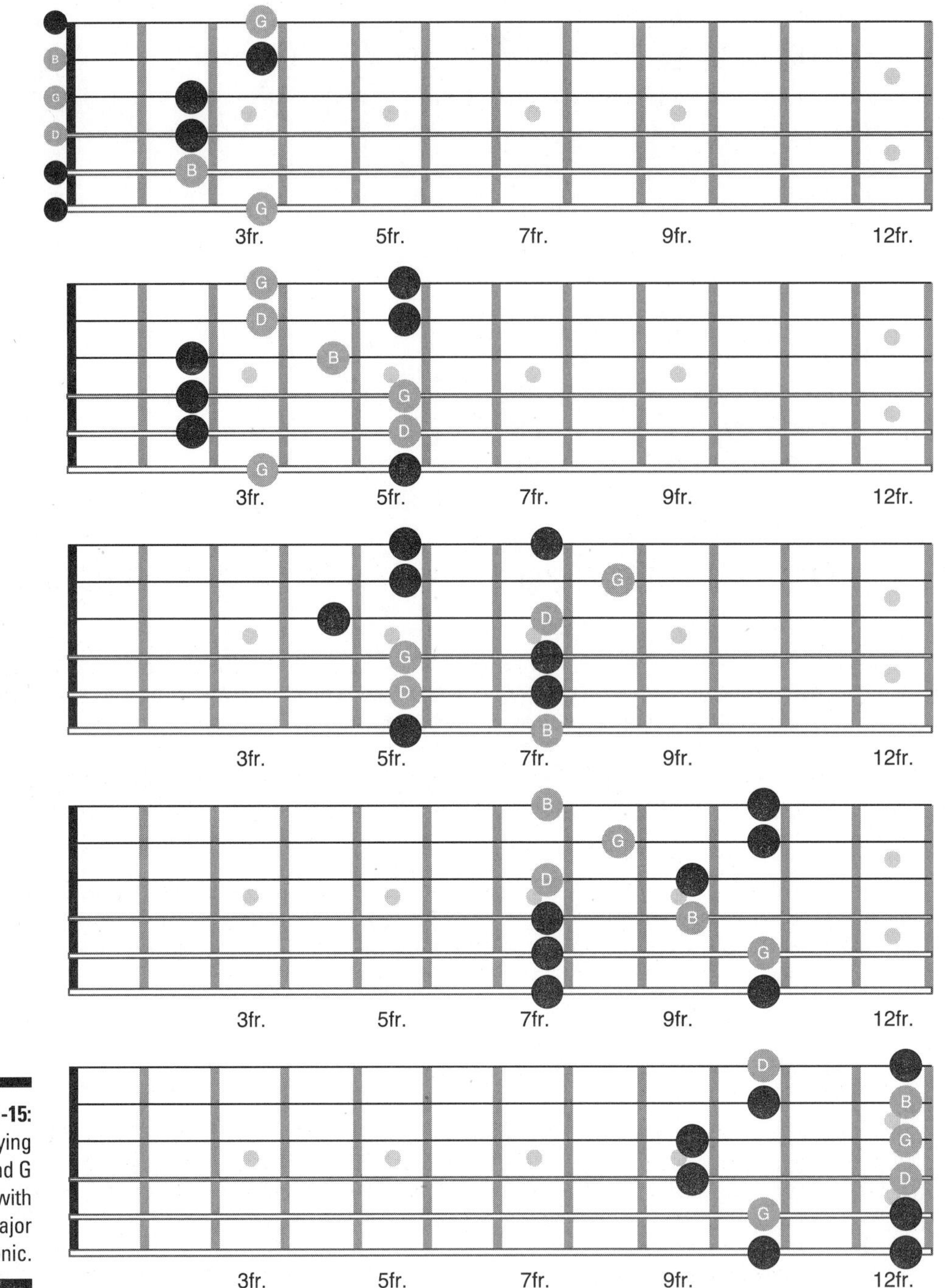

Figure 11-15: Playing around G chords with G major pentatonic.

Illustration courtesy of Desi Serna

You can play the pentatonic scale patterns I cover in this section over any piece of music that centers on an Em or G chord. Some songs centering on Em chords include

"Cocaine" by Eric Clapton

"Horse with No Name" by America

"Nothing Else Matters" by Metallica

"Paranoid" by Black Sabbath

"Rockin' in the Free World" and "Heart of Gold" by Neil Young

"Susie Q" by Creedence Clearwater Revival

Some songs centering on G chords include

"Cliffs of Dover" by Eric Johnson

"Knockin' On Heaven's Door" by Bob Dylan

"Last Kiss" by Pearl Jam

"Love the Lord" by Lincoln Brewster

"Ring of Fire" by Johnny Cash

"Sweet Home Alabama" by Lynyrd Skynyrd

"Wonderful Tonight" by Eric Clapton

Playing the Pentatonic Scale in Other Keys

At this point, you may be feeling pretty good about playing pentatonic scale patterns. But guess what? You've only learned one key! There are many more keys to cover. Don't worry though, because transposing the pentatonic scale and playing in other keys is easier than you may think. With scale patterns on guitar, the patterns remain the same regardless of which key you're playing in — you just change the position you play them in. Just as you can move a barre chord around the neck and play the same type of chord only on a different root note, you can shift the pentatonic patterns and play the same kind of scale only on a different tonic note.

As you rehearse new pentatonic keys, play along with music while you're at it. Doing so makes your practicing sound a lot more interesting. Also, experiment with playing acoustic and electric guitar. If you're playing plugged in, experiment with different sound effects like overdrive, distortion, reverb, and delay.

Playing in F minor and A♭

The next key to play in after you get plenty of practice with the combined keys of E minor and G (see the previous section) is the key of F minor and A♭ major. You can start this key by following the diagrams in Figure 11-16. In this new key, everything has been moved up one fret from the previous key of E minor and G.

Instead of putting the note names in the circles, I list the intervals, with "1" representing the 1st scale degree or tonic. The first diagram shows you what the interval structure looks like with F as the tonic, which produces F minor pentatonic. The second diagram shows you what the interval structure looks like with A♭ functioning as the tonic, which produces A♭ major pentatonic. Don't worry about memorizing all these intervals; I just put them in to give you additional perspective.

This is a complete view of the pentatonic scale across the whole neck, but you should break the notes down into five different patterns and play them one at a time.

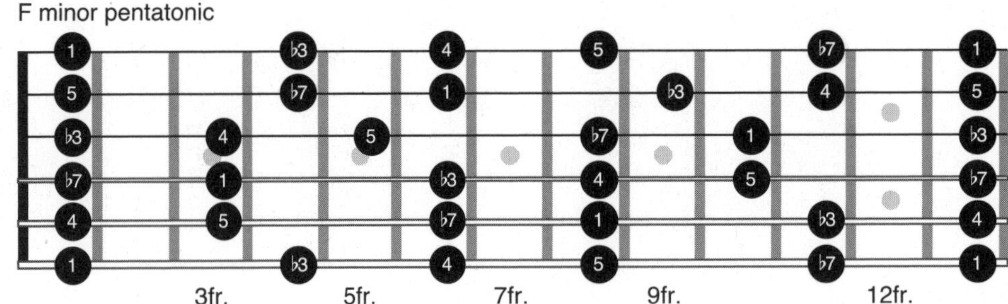

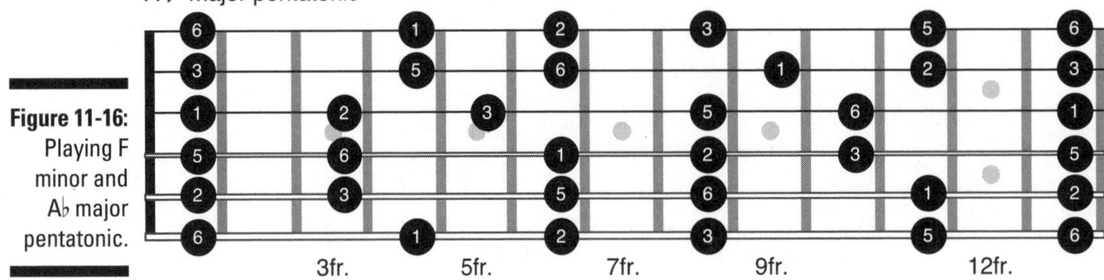

Figure 11-16: Playing F minor and A♭ major pentatonic.

Illustration courtesy of Desi Serna

Watch Video Clip 29 to see the pentatonic scale transposed to new keys.

Practice playing in the key of F minor and A♭ major by ascending and descending through each pattern 1 through 5. As you go, connect one pattern to the next until you can't go any higher. After you finish, restart in the position you left off with and connect backward until you return to your original starting position.

Although the fret numbers change from key to key, the pattern shapes always stay the same. Initially, you may get thrown off in the F minor and A♭ major key because you're used to the patterns starting at certain frets and fitting between the inlaid markers on your fretboard in a particular way (as they did in E minor and G). Just keep practicing, and you'll soon be able to feel that the patterns are still the same.

In addition to the patterns, the location of the two tonics and their common chord shapes remain the same, too. The first note in pattern 1 is still your minor tonic, and the second note in pattern 1 is still your major tonic. In this case, the minor tonic is F, and the major is A♭. The same chord shapes that are common in the E minor and G major key are common in this key and all others.

You can play these pentatonic scale patterns over any piece of music that centers on either an Fm or A♭ chord. A good song to play over in F minor is "Another One Bites the Dust" by Queen, and a good one for A♭ is "Every Breath You Take" by The Police.

Playing in F♯ minor and A major

As you move up to transpose again, the next key that you can play the pentatonic scale patterns in is F♯ minor and A major. Use the diagrams in Figure 11-17 as you practice patterns 1 through 5 in this new key (see the preceding section for details on the practice process).

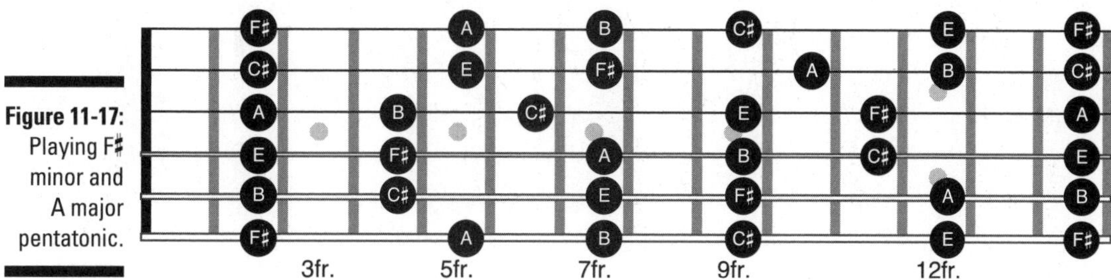

Figure 11-17: Playing F♯ minor and A major pentatonic.

Illustration courtesy of Desi Serna

You can play these pentatonic scale patterns over any piece of music that centers on either an F♯m or A chord. Some songs that center on F♯m include

"Time" by Pink Floyd

"The Way" by Fastball

Some songs that center on A include

"Achy Breaky Heart" by Billy Ray Cyrus

"Amie" by Pure Prairie League

"Blessed Be Your Name" by Matt Redman

"Franklin's Tower" by Grateful Dead

"Southern Cross" by Crosby, Stills & Nash

"Stand By Me" by Ben E. King

"Take Me Home, Country Roads" by John Denver

"When the Sun Goes Down" by Kenny Chesney

Playing in G minor and B♭ major

When playing in the next key, G minor and B♭ major, you begin pattern 1 at the 3rd fret, as shown in Figure 11-18. Starting in this position leaves you room to fit a pattern 5 before it. When you play pattern 5 in this position, you use two open strings — the 4th and 3rd. In this example, I put pattern 1 in gray just to make it easier for you to see your starting point.

The higher pattern 1 is positioned on the fretboard, the more space you have to fill behind it leading back to the open position. As you continue to move up to new keys, you increasingly play more patterns behind pattern 1. You can still start a new key in pattern 1 and connect forward until you can't play any higher on the neck, but as you move backward, don't stop when you reach pattern 1. Instead, keep moving backward until you can't play any lower. Don't forget to use the open strings when they apply.

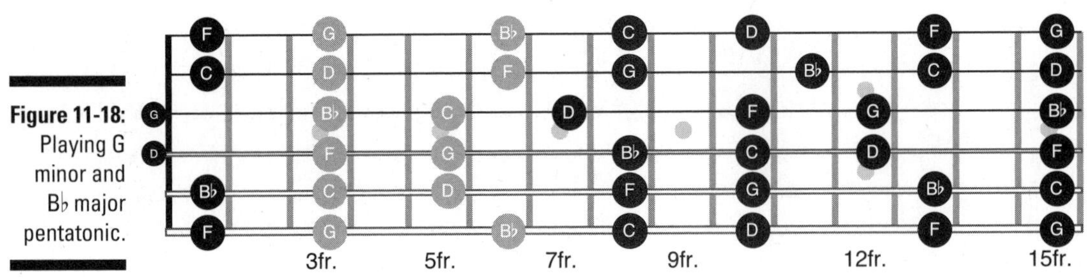

Figure 11-18: Playing G minor and B♭ major pentatonic.

Illustration courtesy of Desi Serna

You can play these pentatonic scale patterns over any piece of music that centers on either a Gm or B♭ chord. Some songs that center on Gm include

- "Born Under a Bad Sign" by Cream
- "I Can't Make You Love Me" by Bonnie Raitt
- "I Shot the Sheriff" by both Bob Marley and Eric Clapton
- "Lady Marmalade" by Patti Labelle
- "Money for Nothing" by Dire Straits

Some songs that center on B♭ include

- "Earth Angel" by The Penguins
- "One Love" by Bob Marley

Playing in G♯ minor and B major and other keys

I recommend that you continue to move up the fretboard to get used to playing the pentatonic scale patterns in other keys. The more you practice, the more skill you'll develop. As you practice transposing, you can start keys at each and every fret. I don't need to diagram every key because the patterns stay the same. But if you feel a little lost, turn to the previous sections for help on how to move from patterns 1 to 5 and back again in the different keys. The next key to practice after G minor and B♭ major is G♯ minor and B major, followed by A minor and C major, and so on.

Playing in A minor and C major

The key of A minor and C major is one of the most popular guitar keys, so I ought to get you started with it. Figure 11-19 illustrates the pentatonic patterns in the key of A minor and C major. When you start pattern 1 at fret 5, as shown in gray in the figure, you can fit a pattern 5 and a pattern 4 before it. Pattern 5 starts at the 3rd fret of the 6th string. Pattern 4 starts on the 6th string open.

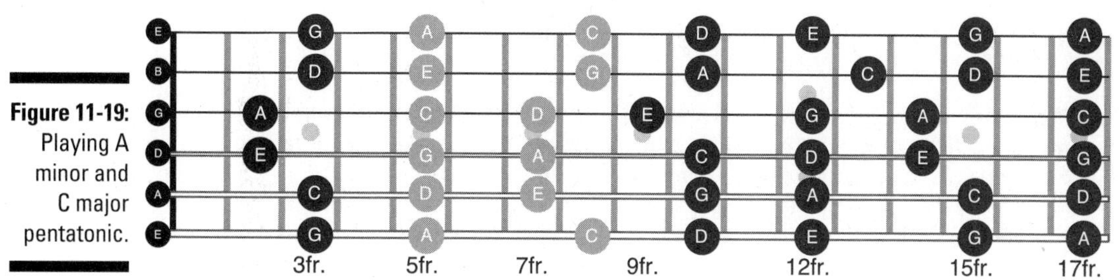

Figure 11-19: Playing A minor and C major pentatonic.

Illustration courtesy of Desi Serna

You can play these pentatonic scale patterns over any piece of music that centers on either an Am or C chord. Some songs that center on Am include

- "Brick House" by The Commodores
- "Californication" by Red Hot Chili Peppers
- "Fly Like an Eagle" by Steve Miller Band
- "Fred Bear" by Ted Nugent
- "It's Too Late" by Carole King
- "Maria, Maria" by Santana
- "Moondance" by Van Morrison
- "Mr. Jones" by The Counting Crows
- "One" by U2
- "Oye Como Va" by Santana
- "Rhiannon" by Fleetwood Mac
- "Stairway to Heaven" by Led Zeppelin
- "Who Will Save Your Soul" by Jewel

Some songs that center on C include

- "Down on the Corner" by Creedence Clearwater Revival
- "I Melt with You" by Modern English
- "Jambalaya (On the Bayou)" by Hank Williams
- "La Bamba" by Los Lobos
- "Let It Be" by The Beatles
- "My Girl" by The Temptations
- "No Woman No Cry" by Bob Marley
- "Unchained Melody" by The Righteous Brothers
- "You Never Can Tell" by Chuck Berry

Applying the Pentatonic Scale

When you apply the pentatonic scale to music, the general rule is to match the scale to the tonic. If the tonic is a major chord, then play the same corresponding major pentatonic scale. For example, use A major pentatonic over a song that centers on an A major chord (as in "Amie" by Pure Prairie League). If the tonic is a minor chord, then play the same corresponding minor pentatonic scale. For example, use A minor pentatonic over a song that centers on an Am chord (as in "Stairway to Heaven" by Led Zeppelin).

What if you're not sure what the tonic chord is in a piece of music? Here's one way to figure it out:

1. **Put on a piece of music and let it play.**
2. **Play notes on your guitar along the 6th string.**

   Begin with the open string and then climb chromatically from the 1st fret to the 2nd fret and so on until you reach a pitch that sounds like the tonal center of the music.
3. **After you find the right tonic, put your first finger on it and play pentatonic pattern 1.**

   This will produce the minor pentatonic.
4. **Now put your 4th finger on the same tonic and play the major pentatonic.**

   This means that you begin pattern 1 three frets below the tonic with your 1st finger.
5. **Determine whether the minor or major pentatonic is the better fit for the music.**
6. **After you get oriented in the right key, you're free to move about the fretboard and use any positions and patterns in that key.**
7. **Melt some faces.**

Generally, minor pentatonic is played over minor chords and major pentatonic over major chords. Keep in mind, however, that rules are meant to be broken. Many popular styles of music, such as blues, country, and rock 'n' roll, use the minor pentatonic over a major chord. Perfect examples of this include "Hey Joe" by Jimi Hendrix, "When Love Comes to Town" by U2, and "Sundown" by Gordon Lightfoot. The tonic chord in all three of these songs is major, yet the guitar solos use mainly the minor pentatonic. In these cases, using a minor pentatonic over a major chord works and fits the bluesy style of the music. (For more on playing over blues chords, see Chapter 15.)

Playing Pentatonic Scale Songs

I know what you're thinking — I really don't want to spend my time memorizing and practicing scale patterns; I wanna rock! Lucky for you, you can! In this sidebar, I provide some great examples of pentatonic riffs, solos, and bass lines that you can use to expand your pentatonic prowess. Each song part listed here shows you something about making real music so you don't feel like you're just playing up and down patterns. The more songs you play, the more familiar you'll become with pentatonic scale patterns and the more your sense of phrasing will develop. Eventually, you'll be able to compose and improvise in your own unique style.

"All Right Now" by Free, guitar solos (A minor and A major)

"American Woman" by Lenny Kravitz, guitar solo (B & C minor)

"Amie" by Pure Prairie League, guitar intro (A major)

"Are You Gonna Go My Way" by Lenny Kravitz, guitar riff (E minor)

"Back In Black" by AC/DC, guitar riff (E minor)

"Better Together" by Jack Johnson, guitar intro (F major)

"Beverly Hills" by Weezer, guitar solo (F minor)

"Blue Sky" by The Allman Brothers Band, guitar intro and solo (E major)

"Born Under a Bad Sign" by Cream, bass (G minor)

"Breakdown" by Tom Petty, guitar 2 intro (A minor)

"Couldn't Stand the Weather" by SRV, guitar intro, E♭ tuning (B, A, G minor)

"Gasoline Alley" by Rod Stewart, guitar/vocal melody (E major)

"Good Times Bad Times" by Led Zeppelin, guitar solo (E minor)

"Green River" by Creedence Clearwater Revival, guitar riff (E minor)

"Hey" by Red Hot Chili Peppers, guitar interlude (C minor)

"Hey Joe" by Jimi Hendrix, guitar solo (E minor)

"I Can't Make You Love Me" by Bonnie Raitt, vocal melody (G minor)

"I Love Rock 'N' Roll" by Joan Jett, guitar and bass verse (E minor), guitar solo (E major)

"I Shot the Sheriff" by Bob Marley/Eric Clapton, guitar riff at chorus end (G minor)

"I Wanna Rock" by Twister Sister, guitar solo (A minor)

"I Will Possess Your Heart" by Death Cab For Cutie, bass line (D minor)

"Jealous Again" by The Black Crowes, guitar solo (G major)

"Jessica" by The Allman Brothers Band, bass intro and chorus (A major)

"La Grange" by ZZ Top, guitar intro (A minor)

"Lady Marmalade" by Patti Labelle, bass and guitar (G minor)

"Let Her Cry" by Hootie and the Blowfish, guitar solo (G major)

"Let It Be" by The Beatles, guitar 1 verse 2 (C major)

"Lowrider" by War, bass (G minor)

"Maggie May" by Rod Stewart, guitar solo (D major)

"Man in the Box" by Alice In Chains, guitar riff/vocal melody, solo, E♭ tuning (E minor)

"Meet Virginia" by Train, guitar solo (E minor)

"Money" by Pink Floyd, guitar and bass intro and verse (B minor)

"Money for Nothing" by Dire Straits, guitar riff (G minor)

"My Generation" by The Who, bass solo (G minor)

"My Girl" by The Temptations, guitar riff (C & F major)

"Paranoid" by Black Sabbath, guitar solo (E minor)

"Pawn Shop" by Sublime, guitar solo (E minor)

"Purple Haze" by Jimi Hendrix, guitar riff (E minor)

"Runnin' Down a Dream" by Tom Petty, guitar solo (E minor)

"Susie Q" by Creedence Clearwater Revival, guitar solo (E minor)

"Stayin' Alive" by The Bee Gees, guitar riff (F minor)

"Turn Off the Light" by Nelly Furtado, guitar solo (E minor)

"Tweezer" by Phish, guitar intro (A minor)

"Upside Down" by Jack Johnson, guitar riff (E major)

"Voodoo Child (Slight Return)" by Jimi Hendrix, guitar riff, solo, E♭ tuning (E minor)

"Yellow Ledbetter" by Pearl Jam, guitar solo (E major)

Chapter 12

Playing Music's Primary Melody Maker: The Major Scale

In This Chapter

- Getting to know the major scale
- Breaking the major scale into five patterns
- Keeping things interesting as you practice the major scale
- Determining what scale a song is drawn from
- Trying out three-note-per-string patterns

The major scale is perhaps the most important tonal element in all of music. You use it for building chords, measuring intervals, charting chord progressions, and playing melodies and harmony. I touch on the major scale in one way or another in every chapter of this book. Here, I explain the basics of the scale and focus on major scale patterns — the kind used for playing melodies, riffs, lead guitar solos, and bass lines.

Listen to Audio Track 12 to hear examples of the major scale and get an idea of what this chapter is all about.

Getting Familiar with the Major Scale

The major scale is a seven-step scale that's built using a formula of whole and half steps. You can play a major scale by starting on any pitch and moving up in the following specified steps (W = whole step; H = half step):

W-W-H-W-W-W-H

For example, if you start on the open 6th string, the 2nd note is a whole step (two frets) higher at the 2nd fret. From there, the next note is a whole step higher at the 4th fret. Figure 12-1 shows how to play a complete major scale by starting on the open 6th string and following the preceding pattern of whole and half steps. In case you're wondering, this is the E major scale because the first note is E.

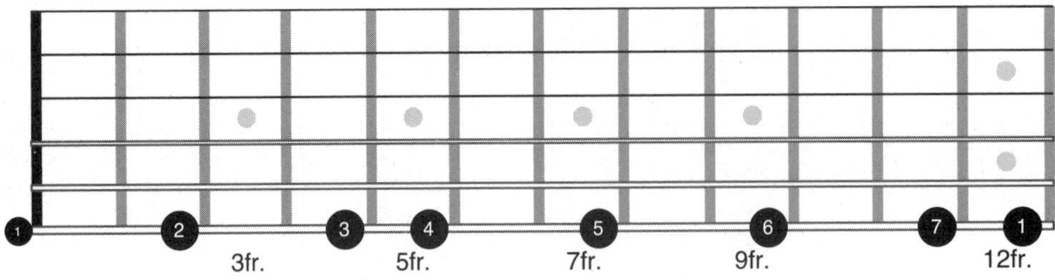

Figure 12-1: Major scale starting on the open 6th string.

Illustration courtesy of Desi Serna

You can follow this same formula to build major scales from other starting positions, too. In Figure 12-2, for example, I start you first on F at the 1st fret of the 6th string and then on G at the 3rd fret, creating F and G major scales, respectively.

F major scale

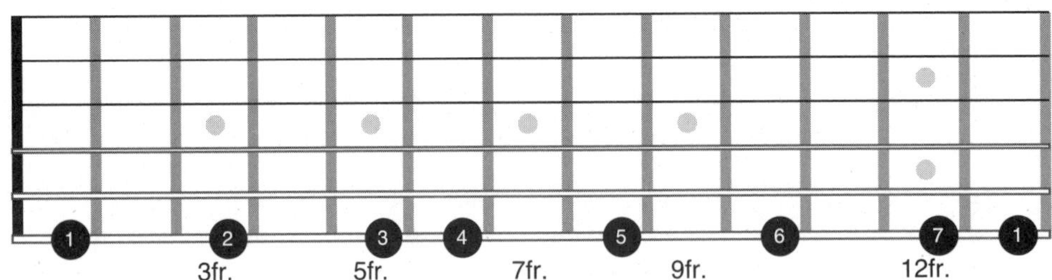

G major scale

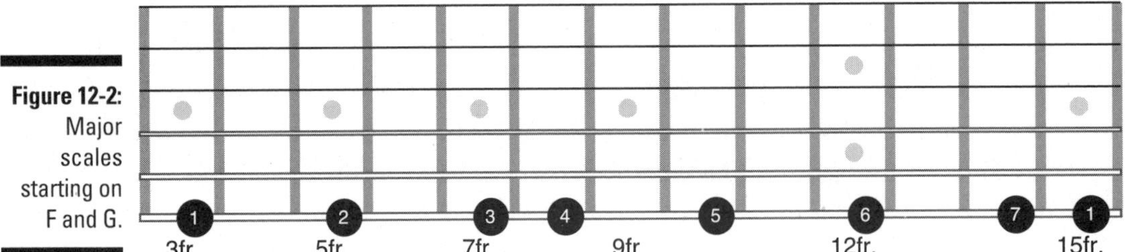

Figure 12-2: Major scales starting on F and G.

Illustration courtesy of Desi Serna

You don't have to play scales straight up one string as the previous examples do. On the guitar, you can play up a scale by shifting over to a higher pitched string at any point. Figure 12-3 shows you a handful of different ways to play through the G major scale. Each way involves playing the notes in slightly different positions, but they're the same notes in the same scale. The step formula is the same, too, although you may have a hard time seeing this when you shift strings. (You don't need to memorize these patterns just yet. Right now, I'm just illustrating a point.)

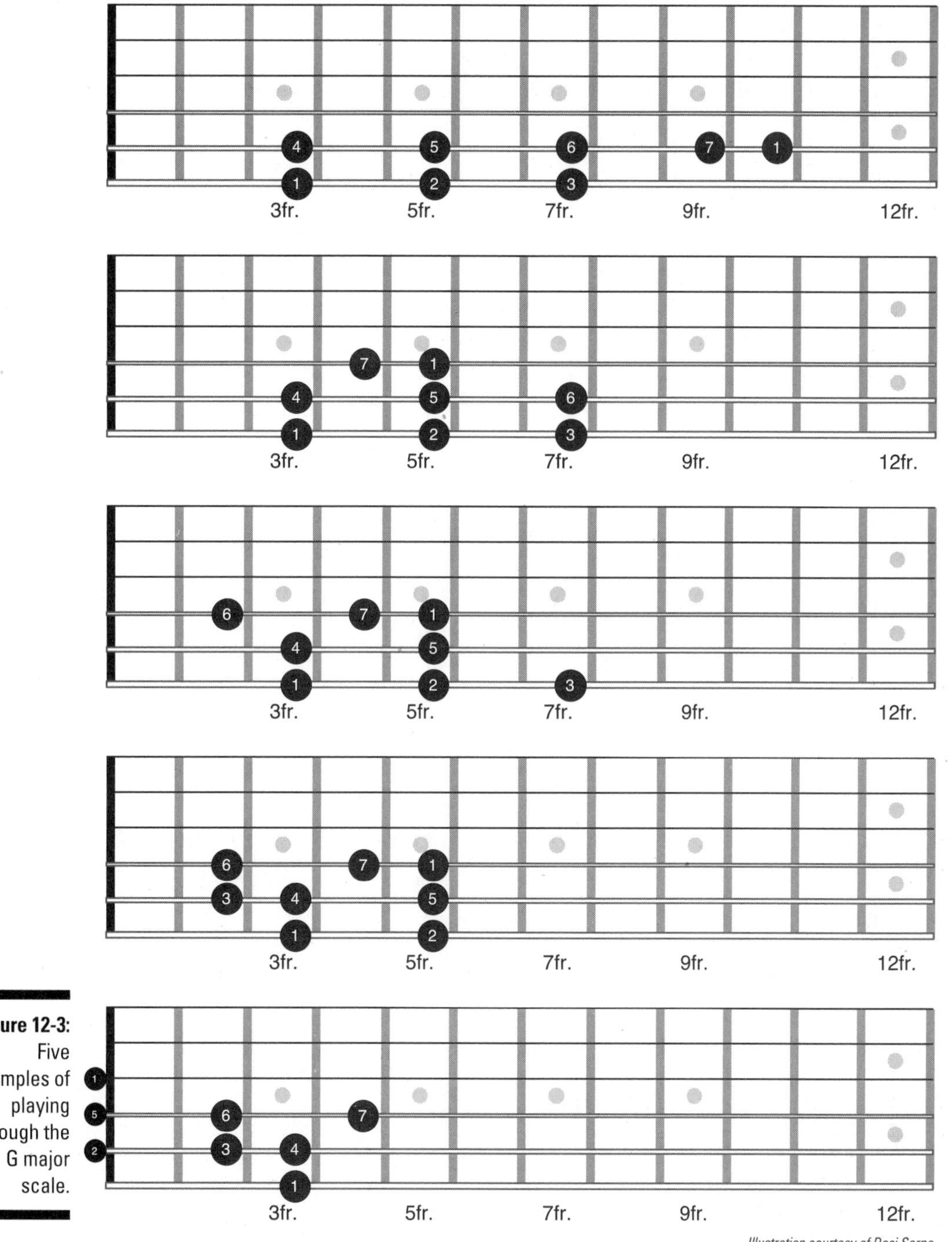

Figure 12-3: Five examples of playing through the G major scale.

Illustration courtesy of Desi Serna

In addition to playing major scale notes in different positions, you can play up into higher registers. I give you a few examples in Figure 12-4. These patterns all start on the same pitch that the preceding Figure 12-3 ended on. (Again, don't worry about memorizing these at the moment.)

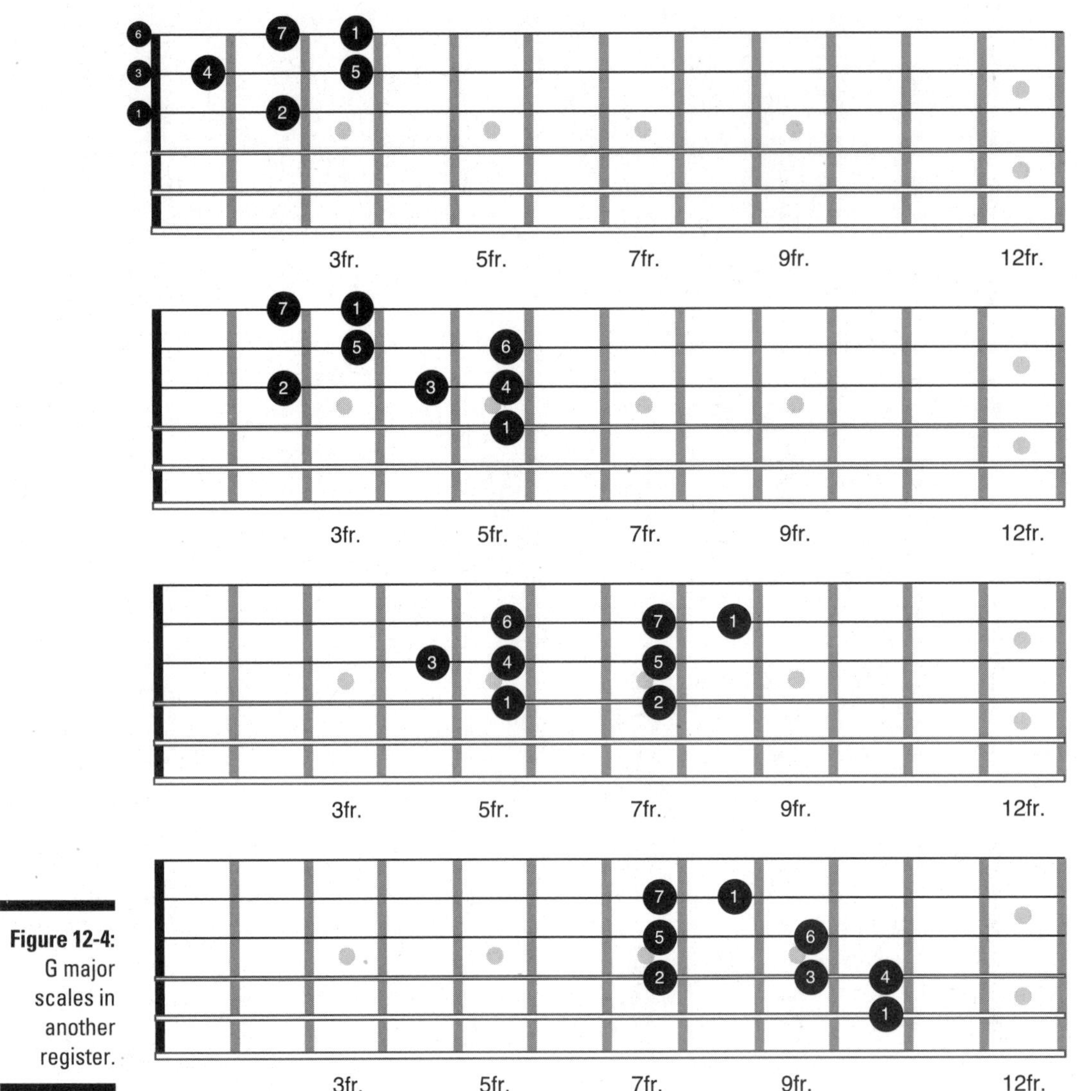

Figure 12-4: G major scales in another register.

Illustration courtesy of Desi Serna

Playing the Major Scale as Five Smaller Patterns

The notes of the major scale are located all over the guitar neck. For instance, Figure 12-5 shows you all the locations of G major scale notes between frets 0 and 15.

To make the major scale more useful, you break it into smaller positions, or *patterns,* that are easier to finger and memorize. You then cover the whole guitar neck by connecting these individual patterns.

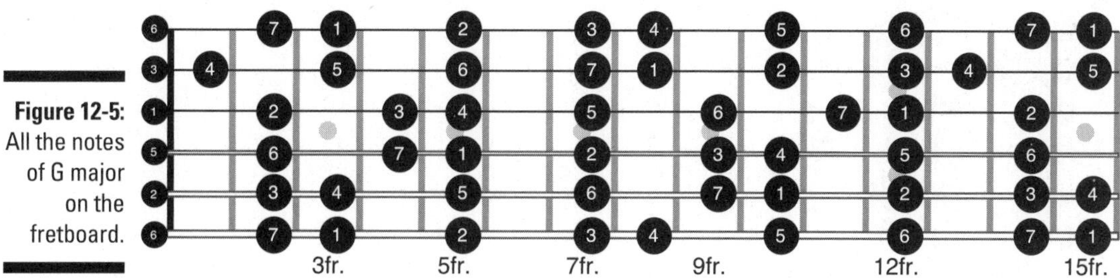

Figure 12-5: All the notes of G major on the fretboard.

Illustration courtesy of Desi Serna

Guitar players break up the fretboard several ways — for example, as five major scale patterns, as seven major scale patterns, as two notes per string, or as three notes per string. The truth is there's no one correct way to learn the major scale. As long as you play a bit of the scale in each position and can connect them to cover the whole neck, you're good to go. That being said, the most common way to start playing the major scale is by breaking it into five patterns.

Breaking down the G major scale

Figure 12-6 breaks the G major scale notes from Figure 12-5 into five smaller patterns. The numbers indicate the scale degrees. Each of the five patterns allows you to play in the G scale in a particular position. When you combine all five patterns, they cover the whole fretboard.

Watch Video Clip 30 for a demonstration on how to play the five major scale patterns in G.

The five major scale patterns use a combination of two and three notes per string. As a result, each pattern covers a span of four to five frets, which most guitarists find very manageable to finger and play.

Play each pattern ascending and descending — that is, low-pitched notes to high-pitched notes and then high to low when you play in reverse — until you have it completely memorized. Take one pattern at a time and work with it for a while. You may need only five minutes to memorize it, or you may need a whole day or more. Either way, after you master a pattern, move on to the next one. With each new pattern you learn, go back and review the ones that come before it. As you practice, notice the following:

- **A portion of each pattern is reused in the pattern that follows it.** Recognizing this simple fact can help you connect the patterns and remember that all five patterns are made up of the same notes in the same scale.
- **You don't start a pattern on the tonic, G; instead, you start on whichever note from the scale is available on the 6th string in each position.** When you're first trying to cover a whole position with a certain type of scale, play all the notes that are within reach in the span of frets that you're covering. Don't worry about which scale degree you actually start and end on. But do try to keep track of the scale tonic in each pattern, specifically, the tonics on the 6th and 5th strings. The tonics are marked with the number 1.

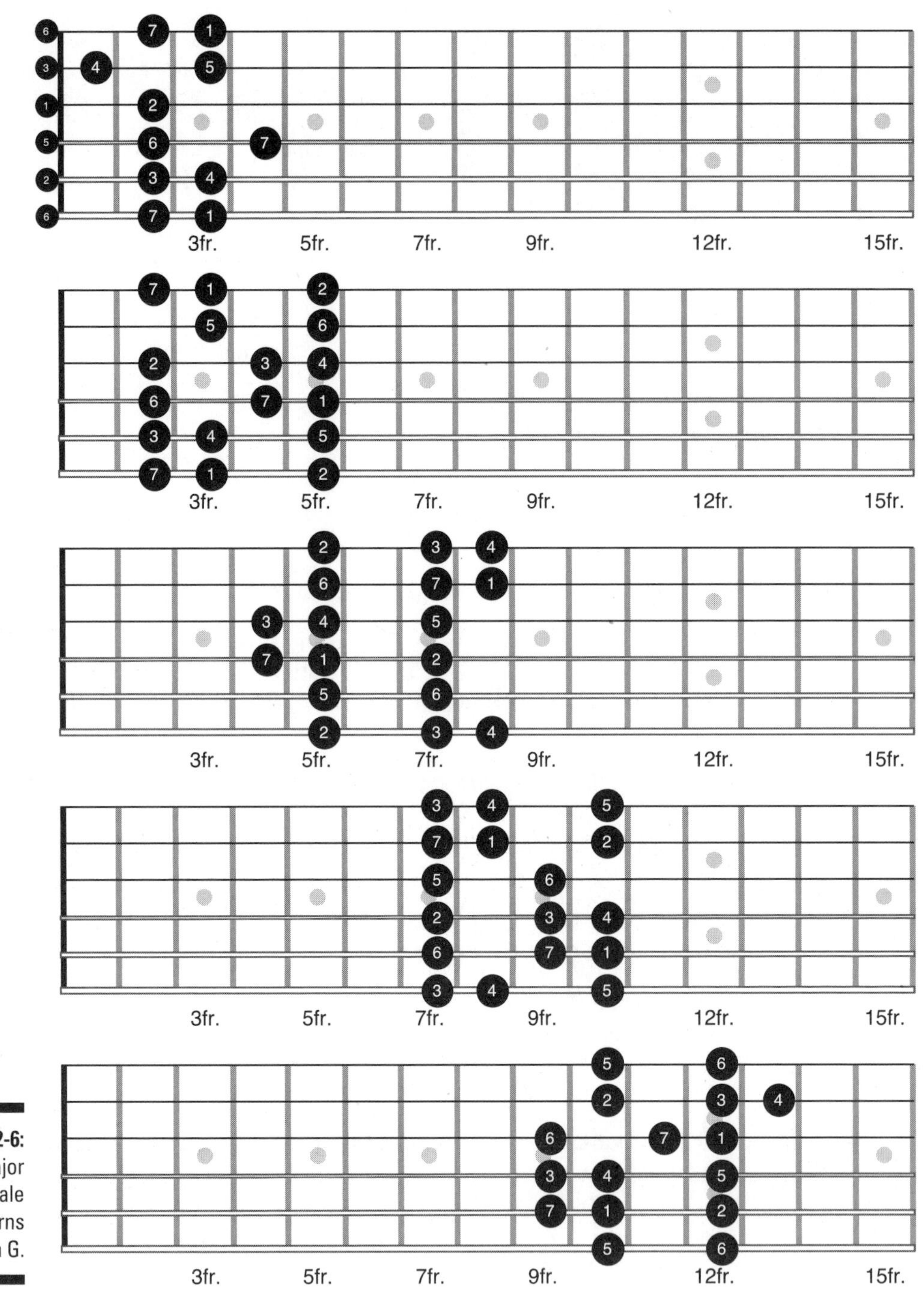

Figure 12-6: Five major scale patterns in G.

Illustration courtesy of Desi Serna

Focusing on fingering

In Figure 12-7, you see suggested fingerings for playing through the five major scale patterns in G, with the numbers representing the four fingers on your fretting hand. You primarily use a one-finger-per-fret approach. In patterns that span more than four frets, you must make adjustments.

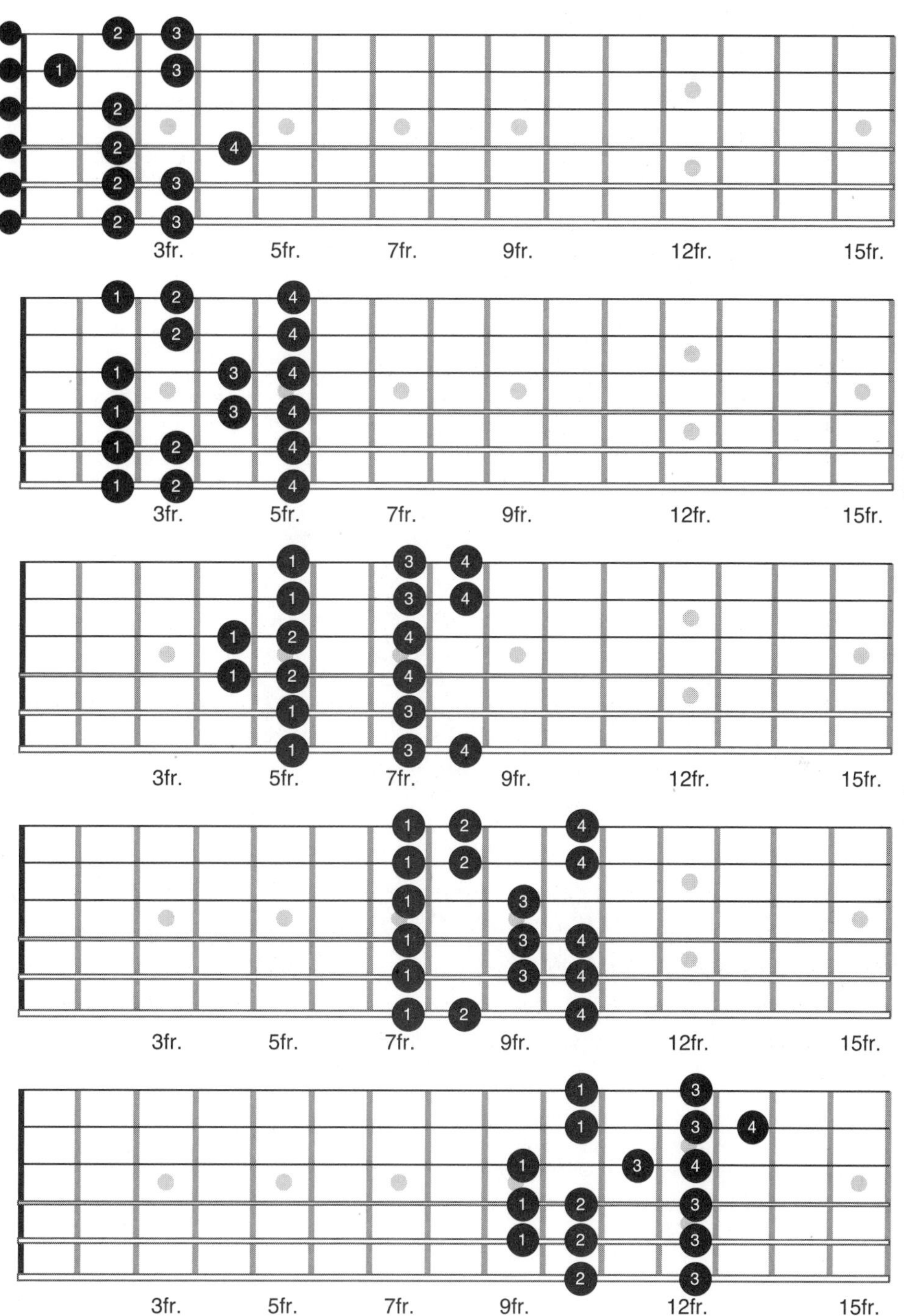

Figure 12-7: Major scale fingerings.

Illustration courtesy of Desi Serna

There's no perfect or correct way to finger the major scale patterns. Your choice of fingering depends on your personal preference and any articulations or stylistic ideas, such as slides, bends, hammer-ons, or pull-offs, that you may be applying to a given piece. Ultimately, the fingering that makes you play and sound the best is the right fingering for you to use. So be sure to experiment as you work your way through the major scale patterns.

Personally, I don't like the finger grouping 1-3-4 because my 3rd and 4th fingers don't always play well together. As a result, I often change 1-3-4 to 1-2-3. Others may find this fingering awkward and a bit of a stretch, but it feels far more natural and comfortable to me.

While you're fingering the major scale patterns, you may as well get your right-hand skills in order, too. I recommend that you alternate your guitar pick. If you're completely committed to fingerstyle playing, you can alternate fingers, finger and thumb, or some other combination. Whatever you do, work toward picking cleanly and at a steady pace.

Connecting the five patterns to cover the whole fretboard

After you work through all five patterns, you can connect the last one to the beginning and continue up past the 12th fret, as shown in Figure 12-8. Play until you either run out of frets or can't reach any higher (notice that you run out of frets and can't complete the final pattern — it's missing a 4 in what would be the 25th fret). At that point, start where you left off and connect the same patterns backward until you return to the open position. Remember that each pattern uses portions of the patterns around it. Visualizing how the patterns overlap and fit together helps you connect them to cover the whole fretboard.

You often see major scale patterns numbered in scale books and lessons. For example, the first pattern that you play in Figure 12-6 may be called pattern 1, followed by pattern 2, and so on. Depending on which key you learn first and which position you start in, you may see another pattern called pattern 1. The reality is that the major scale patterns don't have any official names or numbers. Any numbers you see are arbitrary and used for reference only. The numbers don't correspond to anything else, either, so a major scale pattern 1 isn't related to another scale's pattern 1 or the first CAGED form, for example.

Practicing the Major Scale without Getting Bored

Playing up and down scale patterns isn't exactly the most enjoyable way to spend your time. Frankly, it can be tedious, and it may even feel pointless to you. Sure, eventually, you'll be able to use the scale to play things that you enjoy, like melodies, riffs, lead guitar solos, and bass lines, but what can you do now while you're still getting the patterns down? Lucky for you, I offer a few ideas in the following sections for how to add a little fun to your practice sessions. Enjoy!

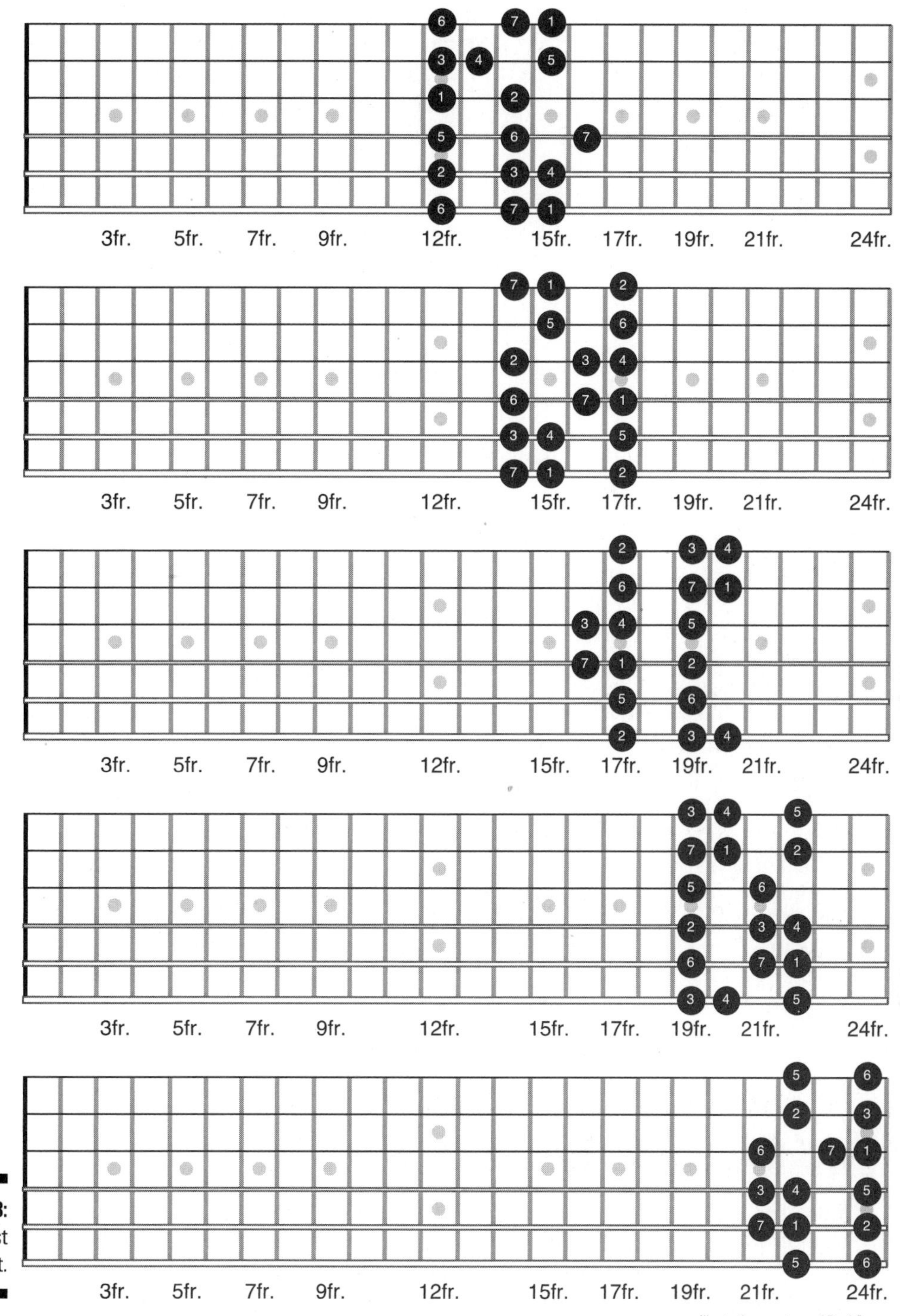

Figure 12-8: Playing past the 12th fret.

Illustration courtesy of Desi Serna

Playing along with accompaniment

The five major scale patterns will absolutely come alive if you play them along to some accompaniment. Just put on some music that's in the same key as the scale and let the music play as you run up and down the patterns.

So if you're in the G major scale, pick music that's also drawn from that scale. This can be any piece of music based on the following chords:

1-2-3-4-5-6-7

G-A-B-C-D-E-F♯

I-ii-iii-IV-V-vi-vii♭5

G-Am-Bm-C-D-Em-F♯m♭5

If you're having a hard time choosing a song that's drawn from the G major scale, why not try one of the following classics?

"Cliffs of Dover" by Eric Johnson

"Friend of the Devil" by Grateful Dead

"Knockin' on Heaven's Door" by Bob Dylan

"Redemption Song" by Bob Marley

"Ring of Fire" by Johnny Cash

"Sweet Home Alabama" by Lynyrd Skynyrd

"Wonderful Tonight" by Eric Clapton

You don't need to learn how to play the guitar parts in these songs. Just use the recordings as backing tracks so that you have something to play along with as you play through the major scale patterns. The mixture of the scale and music creates harmony and gives you a tempo to follow. As a result, you'll really feel and sound like you're making music, which will make practicing the patterns a much more enjoyable experience!

You can use any song with chords that fit into the key of G. Or you can make up your own tracks either by recording yourself strumming a chord progression or by using an audio program that features prerecorded tracks that you can transpose and paste together.

Adding minor notes and patterns

If you're tired of working in G major but still haven't quite mastered the five major scale patterns shown in Figure 12-6, you're in luck! You can practice the same notes and patterns in a minor scale instead. The relative minor to the major scale is always the 6th degree, so in the G scale, the relative minor is the 6th, E (see Chapter 7 for a review of relative major and minor scales). The only difference between the G major and E minor scales is which note is functioning as the tonic and counted as 1; they both have the same notes and patterns. In Figure 12-9, the E notes count as 1 and everything is renumbered from there.

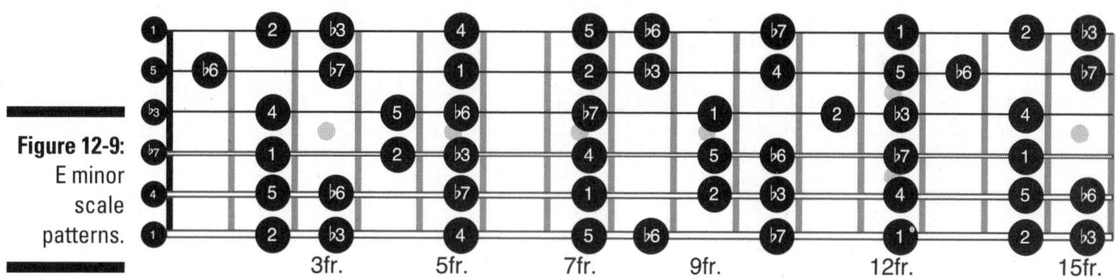

Figure 12-9: E minor scale patterns.

Illustration courtesy of Desi Serna

The E minor scale is broken up into the same five pieces used for the G major scale. So you play the very same patterns you see in Figure 12-6, only with the focus now on E.

Some songs in E minor include "Heart of Gold" by Neil Young, "Livin' on a Prayer" by Bon Jovi, and "Paranoid" by Black Sabbath.

Music can use other degrees of the scale as the tonic, too. When this happens, the music is in a *mode.* You get to know modes in Chapters 7 and 13.

Transposing the major scale to new keys

If you're ready to move past the G major scale onto bigger and better (or at least, different) things, you've come to the right section. Playing major scales in other keys is as simple as starting the patterns in a new position. In Figure 12-10, all the patterns you use in G in the previous sections have been moved up two frets to the key of A. As a result, all the 1s are now A notes. You can continue to connect and play the five patterns until you either run out of fretboard or can't reach any higher (see the section "Connecting the five patterns to cover the whole fretboard" for details).

Practice playing the patterns in Figure 12-10 over any piece of music, song, or track that draws its chords from the A major scale. Don't forget you can use songs in F♯ minor, too. After all, the 6th degree, F♯, is the relative minor to A. Here are the A major chords you have to choose from:

1-2-3-4-5-6-7

A-B-C♯-D-E-F♯-G♯

I-ii-iii-IV-V-vi-vii♭5

A-Bm-C♯m-D-E-F♯m-G♯m♭5

If you need specific song ideas, consider one of these:

"Crazy Train" by Ozzy Osbourne

"Jack and Diane" by John Mellencamp

"Stand by Me" by Ben E. King

"Stir It Up" by Bob Marley

"What's Up?" by 4 Non Blondes

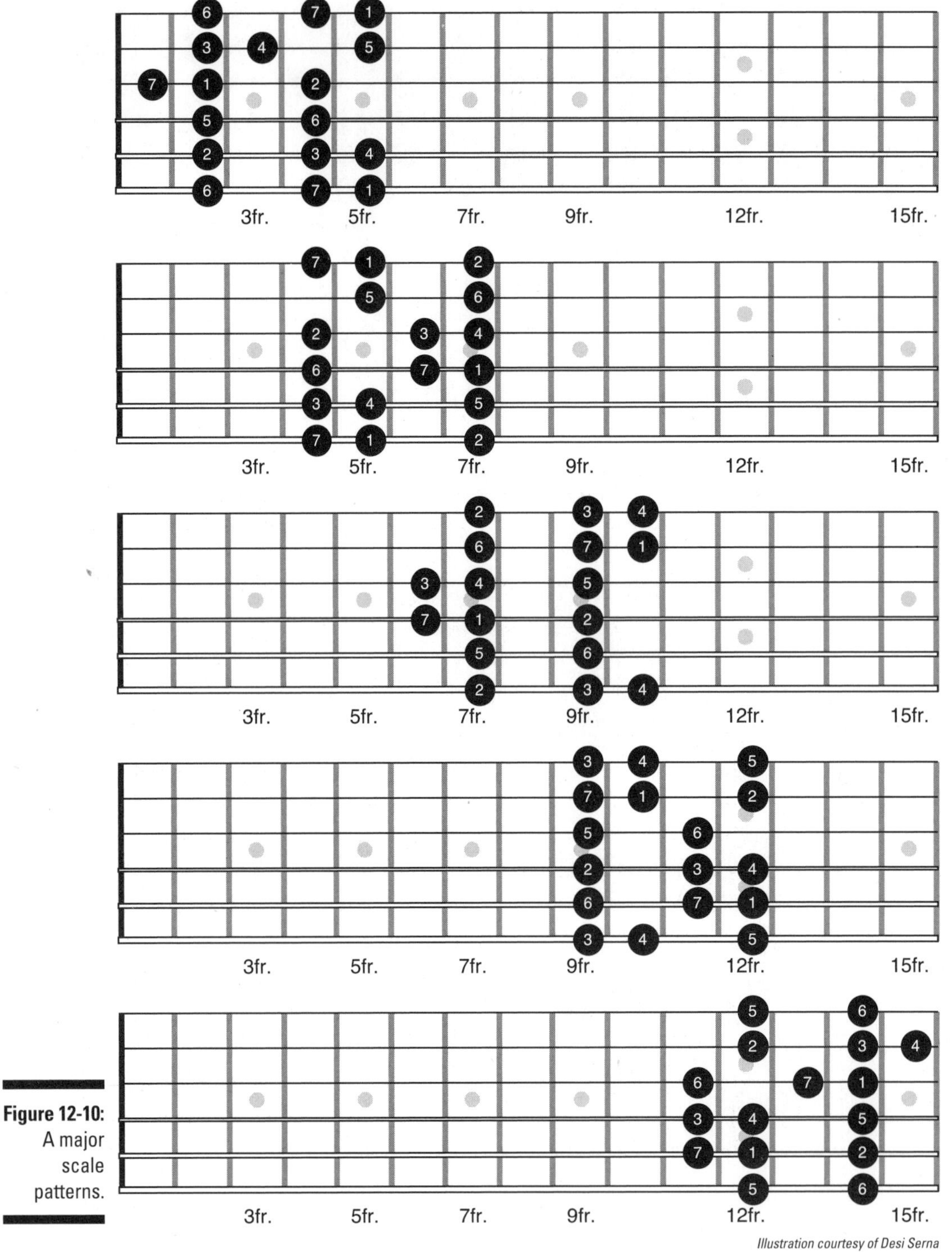

Figure 12-10: A major scale patterns.

You can continue to transpose by moving up from the key of A. For example, you can position the patterns so that 1 is A♯, B, C, C♯, and so on.

Figure 12-11 shows one more sample key, C. Here, all the 1s are C notes. Notice that in this key, you start high enough on the neck that you can come back and fill in the area between the open strings and the 5th fret.

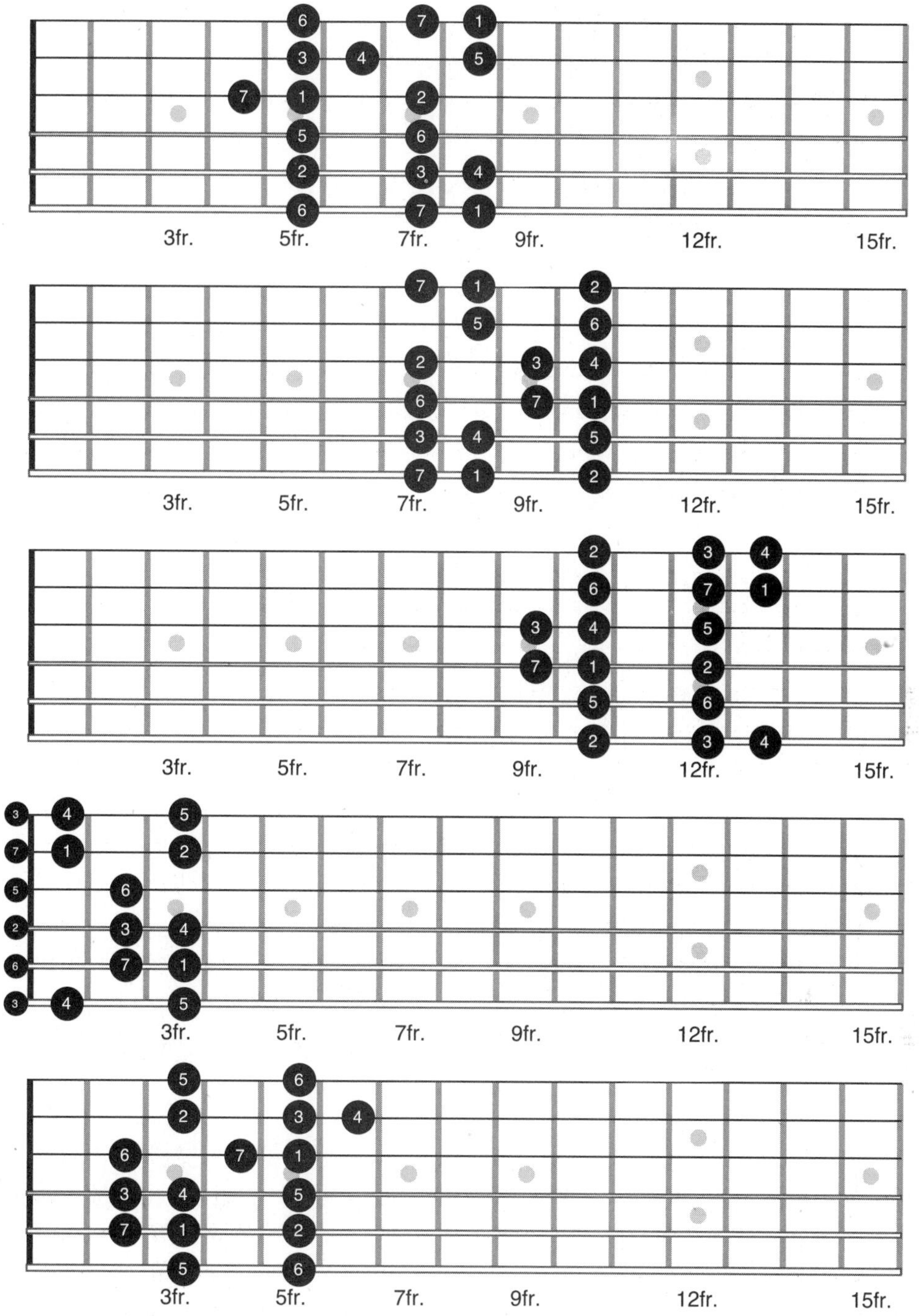

Figure 12-11: C major scale patterns.

Illustration courtesy of Desi Serna

Watch Video Clip 31 to see how to transpose major scale patterns to the key of C.

Practice these patterns over music that draws its chords from the C major scale (see the following list). Feel free to include songs in A minor, too, because the 6th degree, A, is the relative minor to C.

1-2-3-4-5-6-7

C-D-E-F-G-A-B

I-ii-iii-IV-V-vi-vii♭5

C-Dm-Em-F-G-Am-Bm♭5

Some songs based on these chords include the following:

"All the Small Things" by Blink 182

"D'yer Mak'er" by Led Zeppelin

"Fool in the Rain" by Led Zeppelin

"La Bamba" by Los Lobos

"Lean on Me" by Bill Withers

"Let It Be" by The Beatles

"Like a Rolling Stone" by Bob Dylan

"Unchained Melody" by The Righteous Brothers

Songs in A minor include

"Maria, Maria" by Santana

"Mr. Jones" by Counting Crows

You can continue to transpose the major scale to other keys in the same way.

Applying the Major Scale

When applying the major scale to music, you have to pick music that's drawn from the same scale. To determine what scale a song is drawn from, follow these simple steps:

1. **Identify the song's basic chords.**
2. **Fit those chords into a harmonized major scale, better known as the I-ii-iii-IV-V-vi-vii♭5 chord pattern (refer to Chapters 3 and 6).**

For example, say the music in question is based on the chords E, A, and B. When you play these three chords as standard barre chords on the fretboard, you can tell they all fit into an E chord pattern. They're I, IV, and V. They fit into the E chord pattern because they're all drawn together as a progression from the E major scale. So you can play E major scale patterns over the whole progression.

What if a song is based on the chords E, A, and D? It's still E major scale because the music starts on E, right? Wrong! If you play these three chords on the fretboard, they don't all fit together into an E chord pattern. But they do fit into an A chord pattern. In this case, E, A, and D are V, I, and IV in A. So you play A major scale patterns over the whole progression.

Progressions like B-A, C♯m-B-A, and F♯m-B all use the E major scale. Even though E isn't present among the chords, each set of chords is still drawn from the E major scale.

Songs that use major scale patterns

In addition to providing great accompaniment for your major scale practice sessions, many songs also feature melodies, riffs, lead guitar solos, and bass lines that are based in major patterns. You find this true in some of the songs mentioned earlier in this chapter. The following songs all use major scale patterns as an opening, riff, or lead guitar solo:

"Down on the Corner" by Creedence Clearwater Rivival

"Wild World" by Cat Stevens

"Centerfield" by John Fogerty

"Island in the Sun" by Weezer

"Caught Up in You" by 38 Special

"I Love Rock 'n' Roll" by Joan Jett and the Blackhearts

"Mama, I'm Coming Home" by Ozzy Osbourne

"I Want Candy" by Bow Wow Wow

"Lie in Our Graves" by Dave Matthews Band

"Stay Together for the Kids" by Blink 182

"The First Cut Is the Deepest" by Sheryl Crow

"Satellite" by Dave Matthews Band

"I Need a Lover" by John Mellencamp

"Ventura Highway" by America

When applying the major scale, you have to consider the whole chord progression to determine the proper parent major scale from which it's drawn. You can't just go off of the tonic chord in a progression, because the song may use a chord other than I as the tonic. In this case, you have a mode; get to know modes in Chapters 7 and 13.

When using the major scale, you don't have to use all five patterns or touch on every position on the fretboard. Most players settle on a few patterns and positions that they feel most comfortable using. Learning all five patterns is really just a way to explore your options. As long as you can locate a tonic note and play a pattern that corresponds to it, you'll be fine.

Playing Three-Notes-Per-String Patterns

As I mention earlier in this chapter, there's more than one way to break the major scale notes on the fretboard into pattern pieces. In this section, you play through seven major scale patterns that each feature three notes per string. The patterns you see here take on different forms than the five major scale patterns I cover in the rest of this chapter, but they still use the same notes. You don't have to memorize or even use the patterns I describe here, but I recommend that you experiment with them to see how they feel. Consider this section an exercise in exploring your options. If you find that you prefer playing major scales in this way, then go ahead and do so.

What's nice about the seven patterns in Figure 12-12 is that each one starts on a different scale degree on the 6th string, with all seven scale degrees getting touched. This doesn't happen when you divide the neck into five patterns.

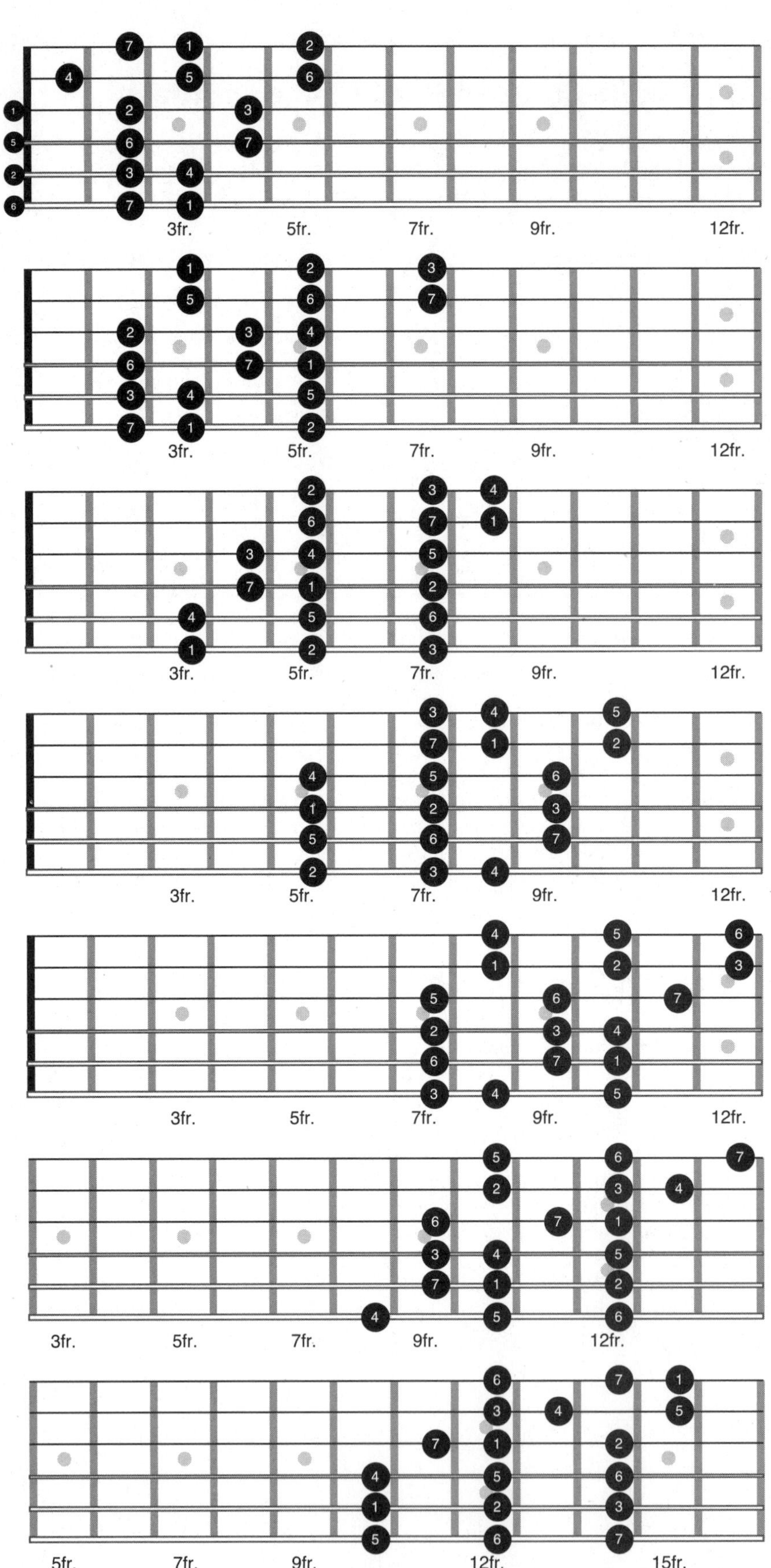

Figure 12-12: Three-notes-per-string patterns in G.

Illustration courtesy of Desi Serna

Just to be absolutely clear, these patterns aren't new scales. They're the very same G major scale notes you play earlier in this chapter as five patterns in Figure 12-6, except that they're arranged in patterns with three notes per string.

Figure 12-13 shows an example of how to finger one of the three-notes-per-string patterns. Here, the numbers represent the four fingers on your fretting hand. Basically, you have three possible three-note groups in all seven patterns. When the notes span four frets, you can use fingers 1-2-4 or 1-3-4. When the notes span five frets, you use 1-2-4, with your first two fingers stretching a whole step.

Don't think of these sample fingerings as strict rules you have to follow; they're really just a starting point. You may find that you can play these patterns better by using a different fingering, and that's perfectly fine. If you don't like the long stretches that three-notes-per-string patterns make, you may choose to use the five patterns I describe earlier in Figure 12-6 instead. That's also fine. Just find what works best for you.

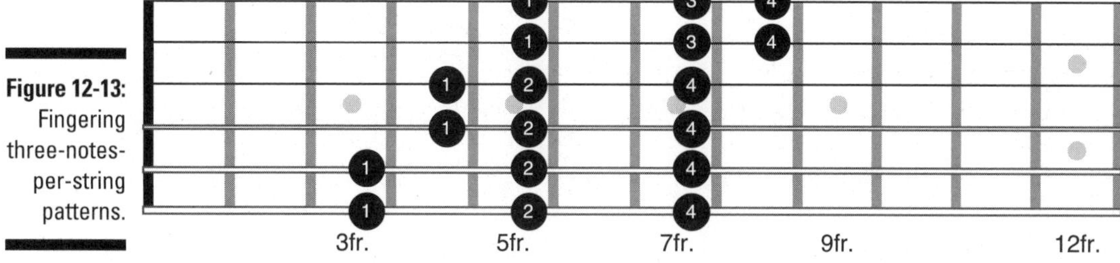

Figure 12-13: Fingering three-notes-per-string patterns.

Illustration courtesy of Desi Serna

Continue to connect the seven three-notes-per-string patterns until you either run out of frets or can't reach any higher. When you're ready to move on, start the seven patterns in other positions and play them in new keys. Don't forget to try playing along with some accompaniment as you go. As you learn guitar riffs and solos based in the major scale, you'll find that some players compose using three notes per string.

Chapter 13

Playing in Modes and Using Modal Scale Patterns

In This Chapter

- Playing the different modes of the major scale
- Using major scale patterns as modal scales
- Comparing modal scales
- Mixing the major scale and its modes with pentatonic scale patterns
- Looking at modal song examples

The concept of modes is based on the different sounds created when music centers on different major scale degrees. In Chapter 7, I introduce you to the basic concept of modes and how they function as key centers for music and chord progressions. In this chapter, you use modes as scales for improvisation. This involves playing through major scale patterns across the fretboard and applying them in contexts that produce the various major and minor mode sounds. Backing tracks are made available to aid you in this process. You take a look at how each mode can be thought of as its own scale. You fit modal scale patterns inside of familiar pentatonic scale patterns to create pattern combinations that are perfect for riffing and soloing. You get to know the popular songs that use modes.

Understanding and applying modes correctly requires you to be familiar with other musical concepts, including

- Building triads and harmonizing the major scale (refer to Chapter 3 for details)
- Chord progressions and playing by numbers (see Chapter 6)
- Keys and modes (turn to Chapter 7)
- Major scale patterns (check out Chapter 12)

These concepts come together to create the modal concept. If you don't already understand these concepts individually, then the material here will be hard to follow.

Listen to Audio Track 13 to hear a demonstration on using modes and find out what this chapter is all about.

Understanding Modes

The major scale has seven degrees, and technically any one of them can function as the *tonic* — the *tonal center,* or *primary pitch,* of the scale. The sound and feel of the scale changes depending on which scale degree is heard as the starting point. The Greek names used to identify the seven modes of the major scale are Ionian, Dorian, Phrygian, Lydian, Mixolydian, Aeolian, and Locrian.

Although the major scale technically has seven modes, one of them, the seventh mode (Locrian), isn't used. (See the sidebar "Playing Locrian mode?" at the end of this chapter if you want the lowdown.) For this reason, you focus on the first six modes in this chapter.

Knowing how modal sounds are made

Making modes is just like mixing colors. With colors, yellow and blue make green, red and blue make purple, and so on. You can't understand what green is like by looking at yellow or blue alone. Only when the two colors are mixed is the new color, green, revealed. The same is true with music modes.

In order to produce modal sounds, you need to mix major scale patterns with the proper accompaniment. The only way you can truly hear a modal sound is by playing a major scale over music that centers on a scale pitch other than 1. You can get the necessary accompaniment by playing along with song recordings, play-along tracks, looping devices, software programs and, of course, other musicians.

Remembering that modes are more than just patterns or starting positions

You don't need to learn new scale patterns in order to play modes. The same patterns that are used to play the major scale on the fretboard also produce all the other modes when applied correctly.

You can't create a complete modal sound by simply starting on a scale degree other than 1 or playing a particular major scale pattern. You really need to hear the scale combined with accompaniment in order to hear the true modal harmony. When you mix the major scale with the right chord, the modal sound is produced even if you don't start on the first modal pitch and regardless of which position or pattern you use on the neck.

Playing Ionian Mode

Ionian mode is the first mode of the major scale. It's the sound that's created when the 1st scale degree is functioning as the tonic. It's better known as the *plain major scale.* In fact, musicians generally don't use the name *Ionian* and don't consider it a mode.

Ionian is the plain major scale. You can think of it as sounding like the "Do-Re-Mi" song. Backward, it sounds like "Joy to the World."

Any time a piece of music uses the major scale and centers on the 1st degree or chord I, it's Ionian mode. This doesn't mean that other scale degrees and chords can't be used; it just means that everything seems to revolve around the 1st degree and come back to it for resolution.

Seeing and hearing Ionian mode in action

Using the G major scale as an example, G Ionian mode looks like this:

> **G major**
>
> 1-2-3-4-5-6-7
>
> G-A-B-C-D-E-F♯
>
> I-i- iii-IV-V-vi-vii♭5
>
> G-Am-Bm-C-D-Em-F♯m♭5

Figure 13-1 shows how to view the fretboard in G Ionian mode. You see all the notes of G major with numbers indicating each scale degree, just for reference. You also see the seven chords of the major scale as both Roman numerals and actual letter names.

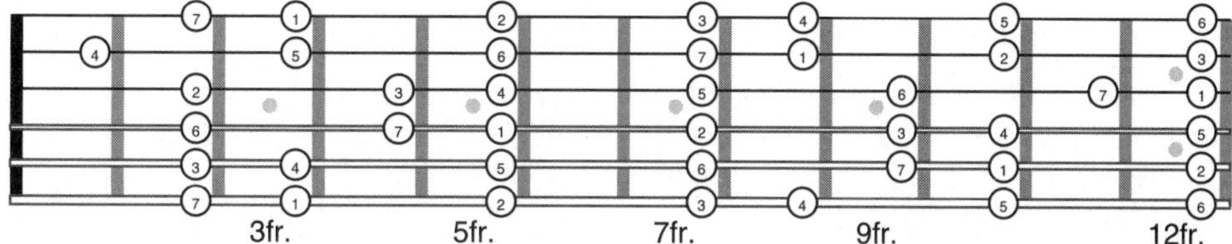

G major scale Roman numerals

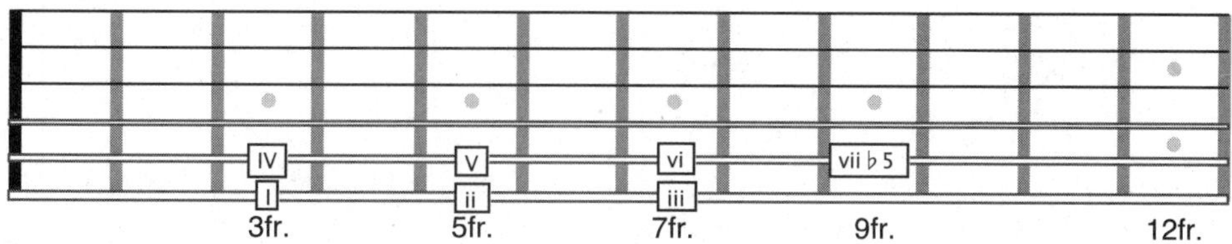

G major scale chords

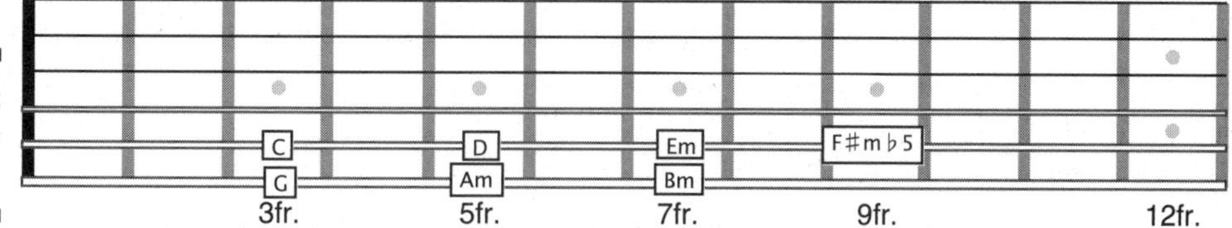

Figure 13-1: G Ionian mode.

Illustration courtesy of Desi Serna

This is just one example of how you can view the fretboard in G Ionian mode. You can play the notes as five separate patterns, as shown in Chapter 12, or make your way through the notes in some other fashion, perhaps just focusing on one small area of the neck. You can play the chords as shown here, which are taken from the chord pattern in Chapter 6, or play the chords elsewhere, even in the open position. Whatever you do, it'll always be G Ionian mode as long as you're using notes and chords from the G major scale and the 1st degree, G, is functioning as the tonic.

In order to properly produce the Ionian sound, you need to hear the G major scale notes played against a chord progression that centers on the 1st degree. In Figure 13-2, you see a sample chord progression that can be used as accompaniment.

Figure 13-2: G Ionian accompaniment.

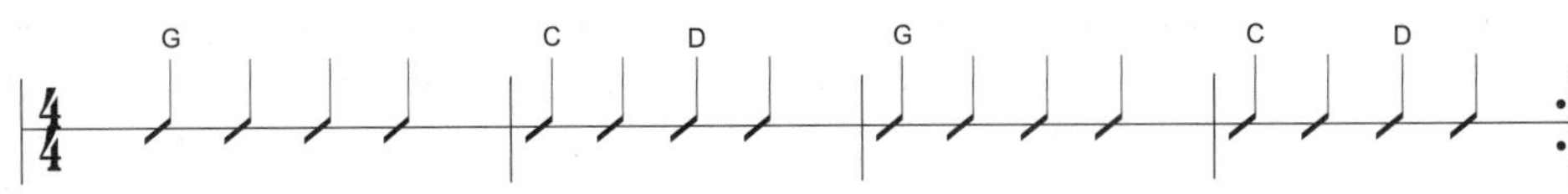

Illustration courtesy of Desi Serna

Play G major scale notes along with Audio Track 14 to produce the sound of G Ionian mode.

Using Ionian mode with the pentatonic scale

Lead guitar players seem to favor playing in pentatonic scale patterns even when they're using something else, like the full major scale. Because Ionian mode centers on a major chord, you can approach it with major pentatonic scale patterns. You can see how to put together the five G major pentatonic patterns with the five G major scale patterns in Figure 13-3. The black dots represent the pentatonic scale. Both the black and gray dots complete the whole major scale.

What's nice about combining patterns this way is that you can stay in familiar pentatonic boxes and use standard pentatonic licks and phrases while at the same time incorporating major scale notes to produce the full major scale sound.

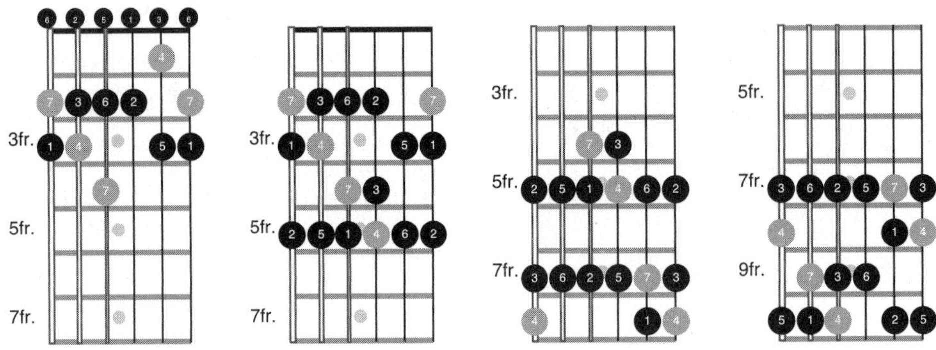

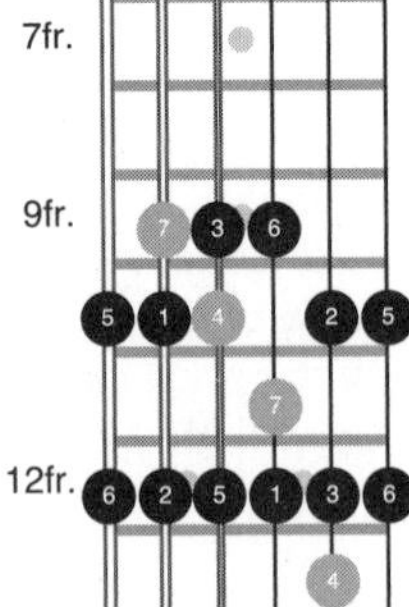

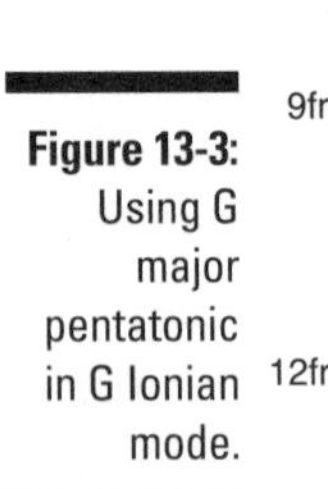

Figure 13-3: Using G major pentatonic in G Ionian mode.

Illustration courtesy of Desi Serna

You don't need to memorize and master every one of these pattern combinations right now. You can work on the idea over time, perhaps with a focus only on the patterns and positions that you prefer to play in. As a starting place, I recommend that you play through pentatonic pattern 1, the go-to pattern of choice for most lead guitarists (the first example in Figure 13-3). Remember that patterns like this repeat at the 12th fret. Try pattern 1 in the 12th position.

The key of G major is just a starting point. You can produce Ionian mode in other keys by moving the scale to new positions and centering your playing on the 1st degree. For example, move up the patterns in Figures 13-1 and 13-3 two frets and play in A Ionian, the A major scale. Move up two more frets for B Ionian, and so on.

A few Ionian mode song examples include

"Wonderful Tonight" by Eric Clapton (G Ionian)

"Stir it Up" by Bob Marley (A Ionian)

"The Lion Sleeps Tonight" by The Tokens (F Ionian)

"Twist and Shout" by The Beatles (D Ionian)

Every song listed in Chapter 6 that starts on chord I.

You can play along with any of these songs using the appropriate major scale patterns to produce the Ionian sound. You can also put together your own tracks by centering a progression around the 1st degree and chord from the major scale.

To see a demonstration on how to play in Ionian mode, watch Video Clip 32.

Playing Dorian Mode

Dorian mode is the second mode of the major scale. It's the sound that's created when the 2nd scale degree is functioning as the tonic. Because it features a ♭3rd and centers on a minor chord, it's considered a minor mode.

Getting the Dorian details

Drawing from the G major scale, Dorian mode looks like this:

G major

1-2-3-4-5-6-7

G-A-B-C-D-E-F♯

I-ii-iii-IV-V-vi-vii♭5

G-Am-Bm-C-D-Em-F♯m♭5

A Dorian

1-2-♭3-4-5-6-♭7

A-B-C-D-E-F♯-G

i-ii-♭III-IV-v-vi♭5-♭VII

Am-Bm-C-D-Em-F♯m♭5-G

Looking at this scale's construction, Dorian mode can be thought of as a natural minor scale with a major 6th. This major 6th makes the fourth chord in Dorian mode major, allowing for a i-IV chord progression in a minor key, which you play in a moment.

In music, you use the major scale as your starting place for naming chords, scale degrees, and intervals. From this perspective, the pattern of whole steps and half steps between the scale degrees of the major scale, or Ionian mode, are what we think of as the naturally occurring ones. If the distance between any two scale degrees is changed for some reason, you can reflect this change with an accidental, typically a sharp or a flat. You use accidentals this way when you're representing the scale degrees of different modes.

Figure 13-4 shows how to view the fretboard in A Dorian mode. Notice that these notes and chords are the very same ones you use for G major. The only difference is that the 2nd degree, A, is now the tonic and counted as number 1. If you want to play a Dorian scale, play 1 to 1.

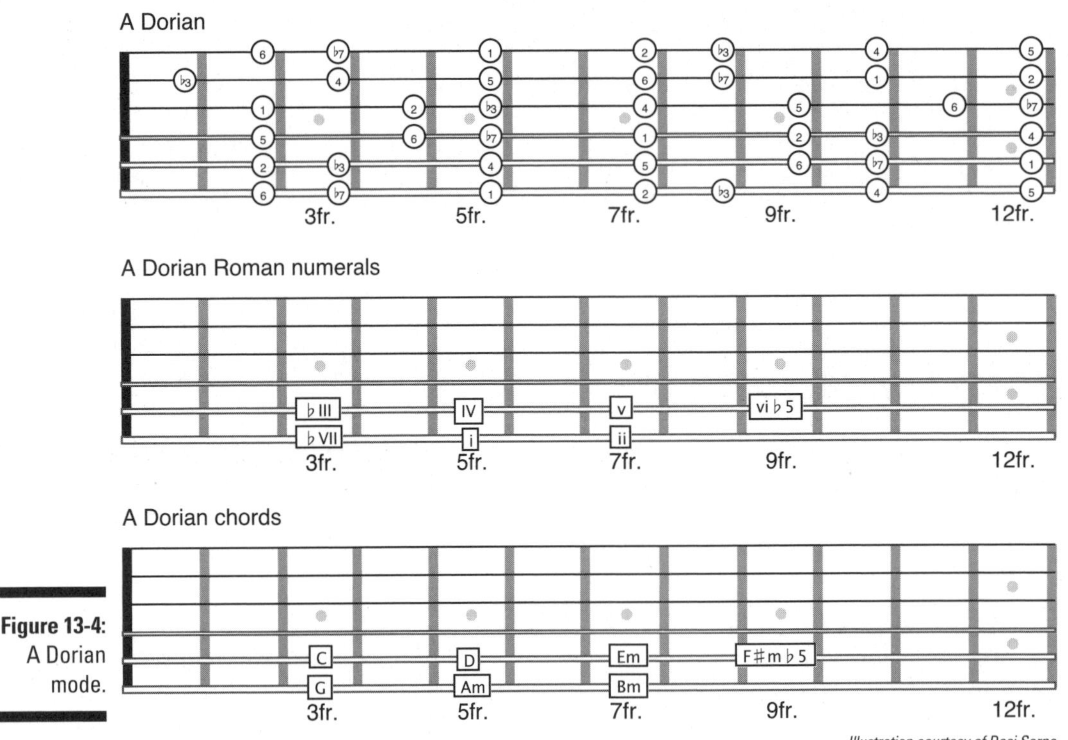

Figure 13-4: A Dorian mode.

Illustration courtesy of Desi Serna

This is just one example of how you can view the fretboard in A Dorian mode. You can play the notes as five separate patterns or make your way through the notes in some other fashion. You can play the chords as shown here, or play the chords elsewhere. Whatever you do, it'll always be A Dorian mode as long as you're using notes and chords from the G major scale and the 2nd degree, A, is functioning as the tonic. You can play in other Dorian keys by centering music on the 2nd degree of other major scales.

In order to properly produce the Dorian sound, you need to hear the G major scale notes played against a chord progression that centers on the 2nd degree, A. In Figure 13-5 you see a sample chord progression that can be used as accompaniment. This is essentially a ii-V chord progression in G major that becomes i-IV when you number from A.

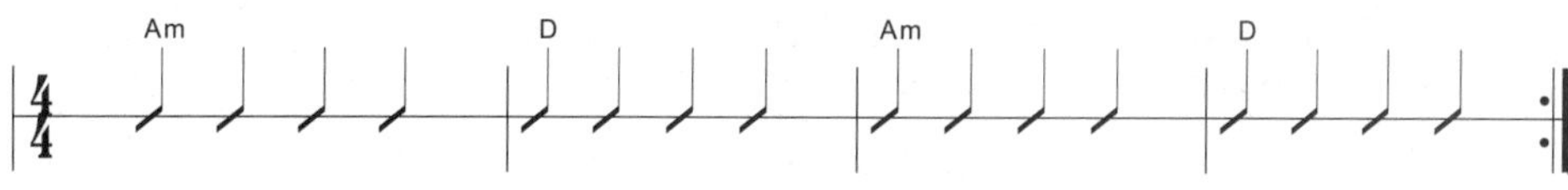

Figure 13-5: A Dorian accompaniment.

Illustration courtesy of Desi Serna

Play G major scale notes along with Audio Track 15 to produce the sound of A Dorian mode.

As you play through the G major scale patterns, you should notice something. The tonic pitch isn't G; it's A. As a result, you change how you play your phrases. Generally speaking, it sounds best to center your playing around the tonic pitch, A. This doesn't mean that you *must* start and end on A — all the other notes in the scale are still fair game — it just means that the scale will sound stable and at rest on A because it's the tonic pitch.

Some say that to play a Dorian scale, you just start on the 2nd degree of the major scale (or play 1 to 1 in Figure 13-4). Although this is true in a sense, it's really misleading. You don't create the true modal sound simply by starting a scale on a different degree. You need to mix the scale with accompaniment to produce the true modal harmony.

When you mix the major scale with the right modal chord, it doesn't even matter what note you start on. In other words, playing G major scale patterns over a piece of music centering on Am produces the A Dorian sound, even if you don't start playing the scale on A. Likewise, playing the same patterns over a piece of music centering on G produces G Ionian, even if you start playing the scale on A or some other note.

The starting place doesn't create the mode. The mixture of the scale and the tonic pitch or tonic chord does.

Using Dorian mode with the pentatonic scale

Because Dorian mode centers on a minor chord, most lead guitar players prefer to approach it with minor pentatonic scale patterns. You can see how to put together A minor pentatonic and G major scale patterns in Figure 13-6.

You can think of Dorian mode as being the minor pentatonic with an added 2nd and major 6th. What's nice about combining patterns this way is that you can stay in familiar pentatonic boxes, while at the same time incorporating major scale notes to produce the full Dorian sound. You don't need to memorize and master every one of these pattern combinations. Most guitarists end up settling on only a few preferred patterns and positions. As a starting place, I recommend that you play through A minor pentatonic pattern 1 beginning at the 5th fret (the first example in Figure 13-6). That's a position all guitarists use. Remember that all the patterns begin to repeat at the 12th fret.

The key of A Dorian is just a starting point. You can produce Dorian mode in other keys by combining the patterns in this way in new positions. For example, move up the patterns in Figure 13-6 two frets to play in B Dorian. Move up another fret for C Dorian, and so on.

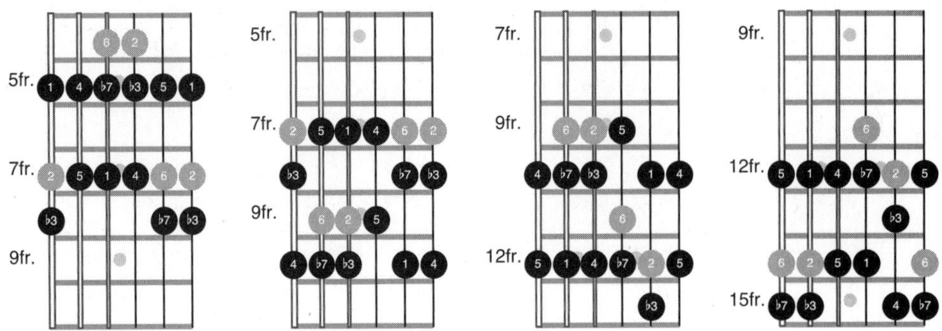

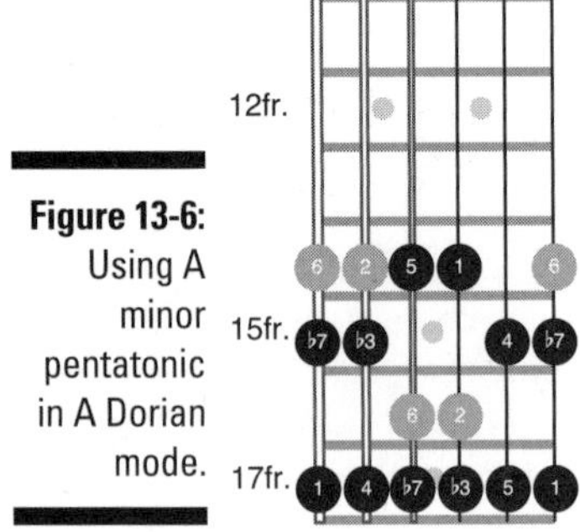

Figure 13-6: Using A minor pentatonic in A Dorian mode.

Illustration courtesy of Desi Serna

Any time a piece of music uses the major scale and centers on the 2nd degree, which is normally chord ii, it's Dorian mode. Some song examples that are either entirely based in Dorian mode or at least have a Dorian section include the following:

"Oye Como Va" by Santana (A Dorian)

"Moondance" by Van Morrison (A Dorian)

"Who Will Save Your Soul" by Jewel (A Dorian)

"It's Too Late" by Carol King (A Dorian)

"Light My Fire" by The Doors (A Dorian and guitars tuned down one half step to E♭)

"Evil Ways" by Santana (G Dorian)

"Another Brick in the Wall (Part II)" by Pink Floyd (D Dorian)

"Your Body Is a Wonderland" by John Mayer (D Dorian)

"Ecstacy" by Rusted Root (D Dorian)

"Spooky" by Atlanta Rhythm Section (E Dorian)

"Horse with No Name" by America (E Dorian)

"I Wish" by Stevie Wonder (E♭ Dorian)

As you can tell from this song list, Dorian has a bit of a jazzy flavor to it. Any one of these songs is good for playing along with and practicing Dorian mode. You can also put together your own tracks by centering a progression around the 2nd degree and chord from the major scale.

Modes are referred to by their tonic pitch and Greek name. *A Dorian* means that the tonic pitch is A and it's the 2nd scale degree in the major scale. If A is 2, then G must be 1 and the parent major scale. *G Dorian* means that the tonic pitch is G and it's the 2nd scale degree in the major scale. If G is 2, then F must be 1 and the parent major scale. Likewise, D Dorian is drawn from C major and E Dorian from D major.

To see a demonstration on how to play in Dorian mode, watch Video Clip 33.

Playing Phrygian Mode

Phrygian is the third mode of the major scale. It's the sound that's created when the 3rd scale degree is functioning as the tonic. Because it features a ♭3rd and centers on a minor chord, it's considered a minor mode.

Drawing from the G major scale, Phrygian mode looks like this:

G major

1-2-3-4-5-6-7

G-A-B-C-D-E-F♯

I-ii-iii-IV-V-vi-vii♭5

G-Am-Bm-C-D-Em-F♯m♭5

B Phrygian

1-♭2-♭3-4-5-♭6-♭7

B-C-D-E-F♯-G-A

i-♭II-♭III-iv-v♭5-♭VI-♭vii

Looking at this scale's construction, Phrygian mode can be thought of as a natural minor scale with a flattened 2nd. In fact, Phrygian's most defining characteristic is its ♭2nd. Most Phrygian progressions use the ♭II chord, as you see in a moment.

Figure 13-7 shows how to view the fretboard in B Phrygian mode. Notice that these notes and chords are the very same ones you use for G major (or A Dorian, for that matter). The only difference is that the 3rd degree, B, is now the tonic and counted as number 1. If you want to play a Phrygian scale, play 1 to 1.

This is just one example of how you can view the fretboard in B Phrygian mode. You can play the notes and chords in any manner you like. Whatever you do, it'll always be B Phrygian mode as long as you use notes and chords from the G major scale and the 3rd scale degree, B, functions as the tonic. You can play in other Phrygian keys by centering music on the 3rd degree of other major scales.

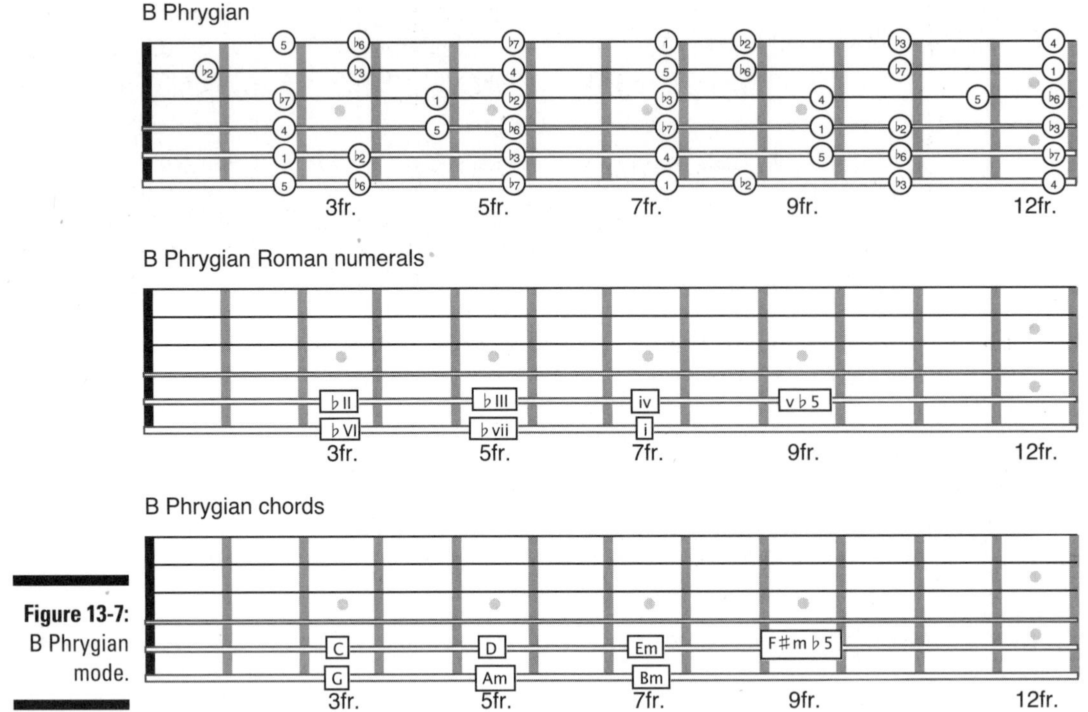

Figure 13-7: B Phrygian mode.

In order to properly produce the Phrygian sound, you need to hear the G major scale notes played against a chord progression that centers on the 3rd degree, B, as you see in Figure 13-8. This iii-IV progression in G major becomes i-♭II when you number from B.

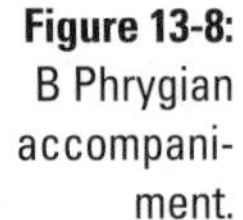

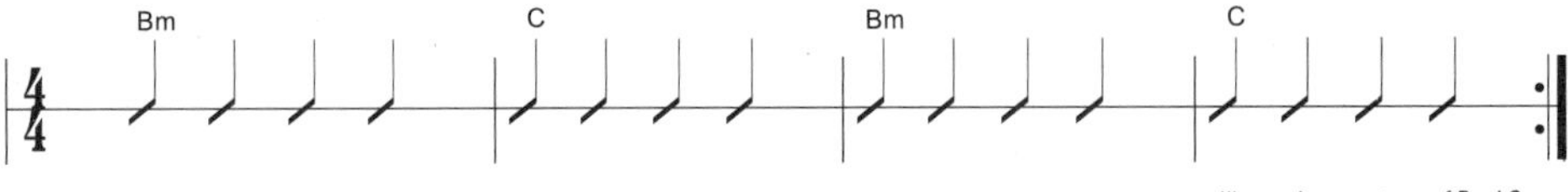

Figure 13-8: B Phrygian accompaniment.

Play G major scale notes along with Audio Track 16 to produce the sound of B Phrygian mode.

Because Phrygian mode centers on a minor chord, most lead guitar players prefer to approach it with minor pentatonic scale patterns. You can see how to put together B minor pentatonic and G major scale patterns in Figure 13-9.

You can think of Phrygian mode as being the minor pentatonic with an added ♭2nd and ♭6th. What's nice about combining patterns this way is that you can stay in familiar pentatonic boxes and simultaneously incorporate major scale notes to produce the full Phrygian sound. Keep in mind that you don't need to memorize and master every one of these pattern combinations. You can settle on just a few that you prefer. As a starting place, I recommend that you play through B minor pentatonic pattern 1, beginning at the 7th fret (the first example in Figure 13-9). Notice that instead of having you play past the 15th fret for pentatonic patterns 4 and 5, I position you an octave lower on the fretboard.

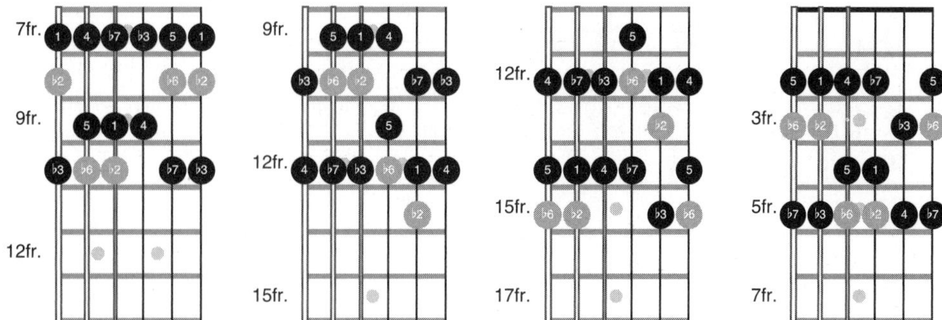

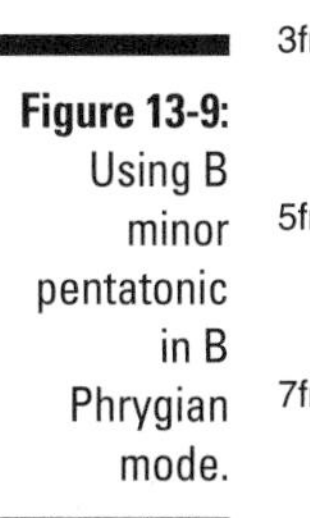

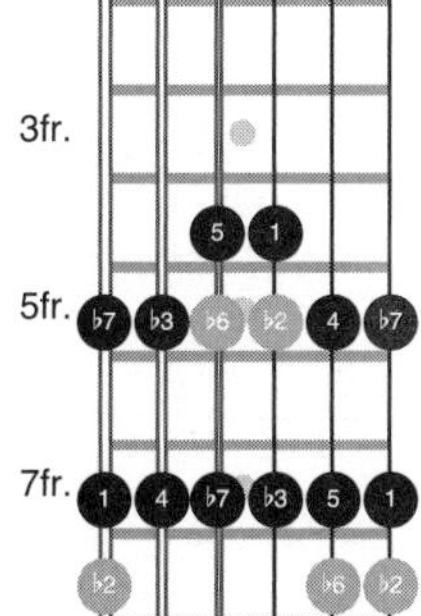

Figure 13-9: Using B minor pentatonic in B Phrygian mode.

Illustration courtesy of Desi Serna

The key of B Phrygian is just a starting point. You can produce Phrygian mode in other keys by combining the patterns in this way in new positions. For example, move up the patterns in Figures 13-9 one fret to play in C Phrygian, then two more for D Phrygian, and so on.

Any time a piece of music uses the major scale and centers on the 3rd degree, chord iii, it's Phrygian mode. Some song examples that are either entirely based in Phrygian mode or at least have a Phrygian section include

"The Sails Of Charon" by Scorpions (B Phrygian)

"Symphony of Destruction" by Megadeath (E Phrygian)

"Remember Tomorrow" by Iron Maiden (E Phrygian)

"Wherever I May Roam" by Metallica (E Phrygian)

"War" by Joe Satriani (E Phrygian with guitars tuned down one half step to E♭)

Note that E Phrygian is drawn from the C major scale. Any one of these songs is good for playing along with and practicing Phrygian mode. You can also put together your own tracks by centering a progression around the 3rd degree and chord from the major scale. As you can tell from the preceding song examples, Phrygian has a dark and slightly Spanish sound quality to it.

Playing Lydian Mode

Lydian, the fourth mode of the major scale, is the sound that's created when the 4th scale degree functions as the tonic. Because it features a major 3rd and centers on a major chord, it's considered a major mode.

Drawing from the G major scale, Lydian mode looks like this:

G major

1-2-3-4-5-6-7

G-A-B-C-D-E-F♯

I-ii-iii-IV-V-vi-vii♭5

G-Am-Bm-C-D-Em-F♯m♭5

C Lydian

1-2-3-♯4-5-6-7

C-D-E-F♯-G-A-B

I-II-iii-♯iv♭5-V-vi-vii

C-D-Em-F♯m♭5-G-Am-Bm

Lydian can be thought of as a major scale with a raised 4th, it's most defining characteristic. This ♯4th causes the 2nd chord to be major. A typical Lydian progression is I-II, two major chords right in a row.

Figure 13-10 shows how to view the fretboard in C Lydian mode, using, of course, the very same notes and chords you use for G major. The only difference is that the 4th degree, C, is now the tonic and counted as number 1. If you want to play a Lydian scale, play 1 to 1.

C Lydian

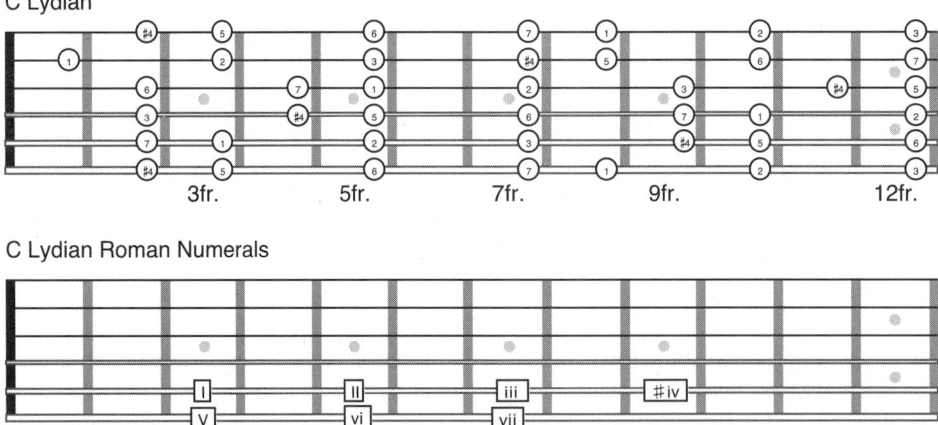

C Lydian chords

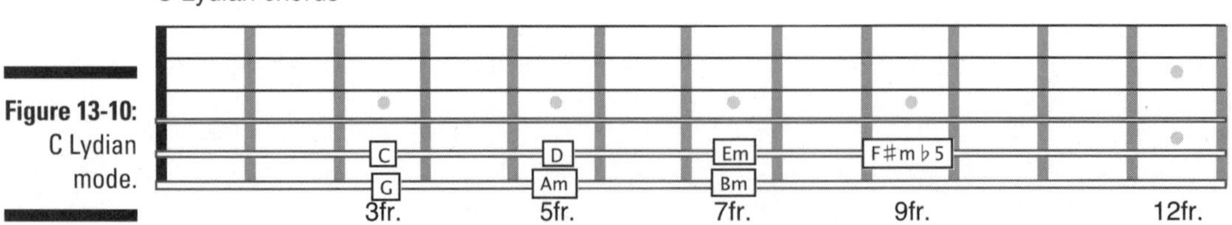

Figure 13-10: C Lydian mode.

Illustration courtesy of Desi Serna

This is just one way to view the fretboard in C Lydian mode. You can certainly use other positions, patterns, and chord shapes to play in this mode too. As long as you use notes and chords from the G major scale and the 4th degree, C, functions as the tonic, the mode is C Lydian. You can play in other Lydian keys by centering music on the 4th degree of other major scales.

In order to properly produce the Lydian sound, you need to use some type of accompaniment, like the one shown in Figure 13-11. This IV-V chord progression in G becomes I-II when you start on C.

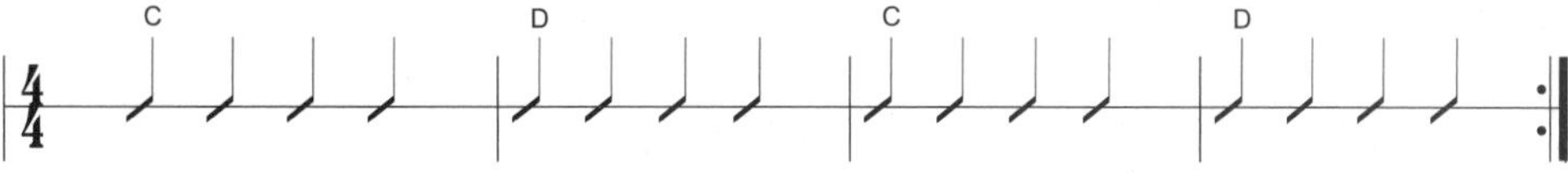

Figure 13-11: C Lydian accompaniment.

Illustration courtesy of Desi Serna

Play G major scale notes along with Audio Track 17 to produce the sound of C Lydian mode.

Because Lydian mode centers on a major chord, most lead guitar players prefer to approach it with major pentatonic scale patterns. You can see how to put together C major pentatonic and G major scale patterns in Figure 13-12.

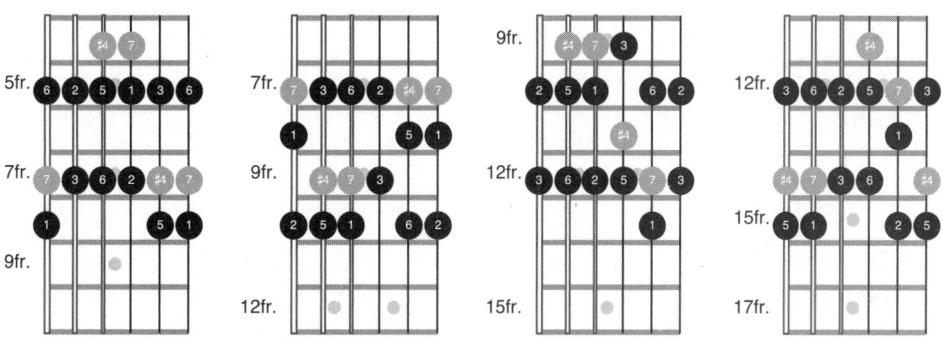

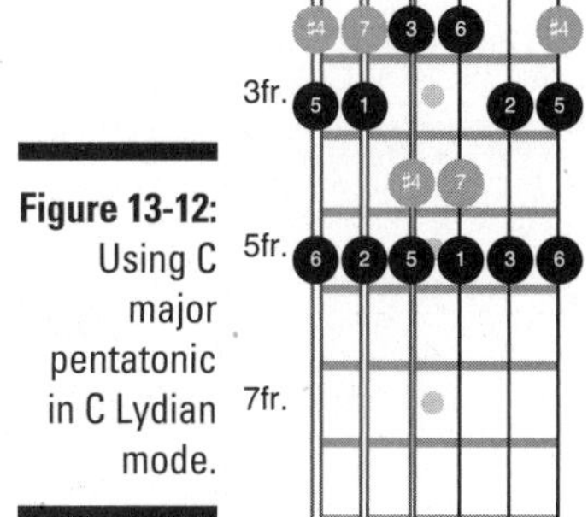

Figure 13-12: Using C major pentatonic in C Lydian mode.

Illustration courtesy of Desi Serna

You can think of Lydian mode as being the major pentatonic with an added ♯4th and 7th. Coincidentally, C Lydian and A Dorian use the same pattern combinations because C major and A minor pentatonic are relative to one another, and they're both mixed with the G major scale. Although you don't need to master all these patterns, I recommend that you at least play through the combination set in C major pentatonic pattern 1 beginning at the 5th fret of the 6th string (it starts on A; C is located at the 8th fret). Notice that instead of having you play past the 15th fret for pentatonic pattern 5, I position you an octave lower on the fretboard. The key of C Lydian is just a starting point. Move the same patterns around to play Lydian mode in other keys.

Any time a piece of music uses the major scale and centers on the 4th degree, chord IV, it's Lydian mode. Some song examples that are either entirely based in Lydian mode or at least have a Lydian section include the following:

"Man on the Moon" by R.E.M. (C Lydian)

"Dreams" by Fleetwood Mac (F Lydian)

"Just Remember I Love You" by Firefall (F Lydian)

"Jane Says" by Jane's Addiction (G Lydian)

"Here Comes My Girl" by Tom Petty (A Lydian)

"Hey Jealousy" by Gin Blossoms (D Lydian)

"Space Oddity" by David Bowie (F Lydian)

"Freewill" by Rush (F Lydian)

Any one of these songs is good for playing along with and practicing Lydian mode. You can also put together your own tracks by centering a progression around the 4th degree and chord from the major scale.

I find that artists often use the Lydian mode only temporarily in their songs. Because of its unresolved sound, the Lydian mode quickly dissipates when you move to a more stable tonic, such as the I chord in the parent major scale. In these songs, it's very common for a section to focus on a major scale's IV chord, creating a Lydian mode, followed by another section that centers on chord I, creating an Ionian mode. This shift from the Lydian to plain major often happens between a verse and chorus.

Playing Mixolydian Mode

Mixolydian is the fifth mode of the major scale. It's the sound you hear when the 5th scale degree is functioning as the tonic. Because it features a major 3rd and centers on a major chord, it's considered a major mode. And because the 5th scale degree of the major scale is named the dominant, the fifth mode is also called the *dominant scale.*

Drawing from the G major scale, Mixolydian mode looks like this:

G major

1-2-3-4-5-6-7

G-A-B-C-D-E-F♯

I-ii-iii-IV-V-vi-vii♭5

G-Am-Bm-C-D-Em-F♯m♭5

D Mixolydian

1-2-3-4-5-6-7

D-E-F♯-G-A-B-C

I-ii-iii♭5-IV-v-vi-♭VII

D-Em-F♯m♭5-G-Am-Bm-C

You can think of Mixolydian as a major scale with a flattened 7th. This ♭7th is the most defining characteristic of Mixolydian mode, both as it occurs in the scale and as a ♭VII chord.

Figure 13-13 shows how to view the fretboard in D Mixolydian mode, using the notes and chords of G major. The only difference is that the 5th degree, D, is now the tonic and counted as number 1. If you want to play a Mixolydian scale, play 1 to 1.

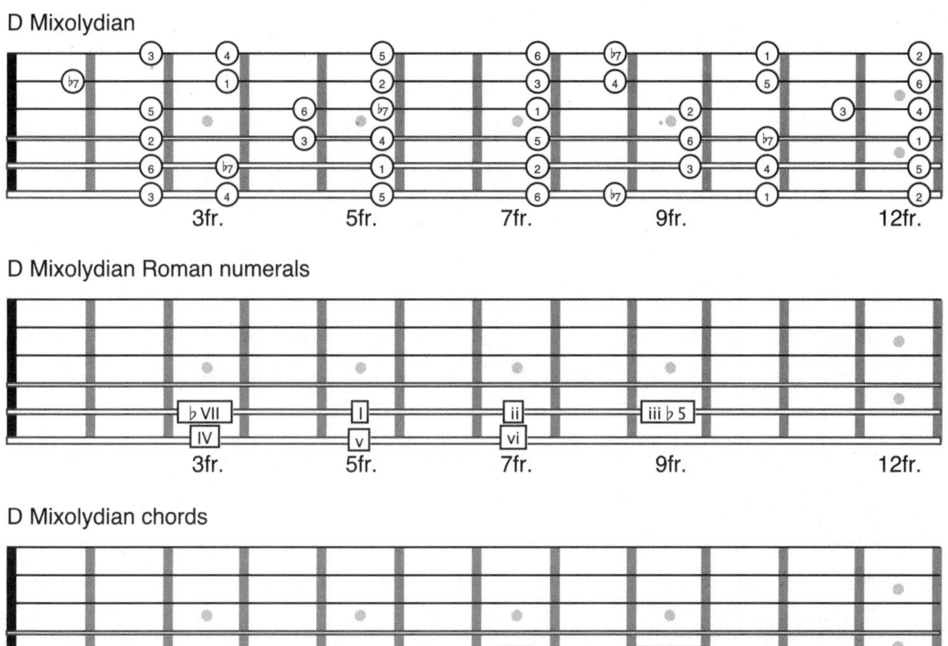

Figure 13-13: D Mixolydian mode.

Illustration courtesy of Desi Serna

This is just one example of how you can view the fretboard in D Mixolydian mode. You can play the notes and chords in any manner you like. Whatever you do, it'll always be D Mixolydian mode as long as you're using notes and chords from the G major scale and the 5th degree, D, is functioning as the tonic. You can play in other Mixolydian keys by centering music on the 5th degree of other major scales.

In order to properly produce the Mixolydian sound, you need to use some type of accompaniment, like the one shown in Figure 13-14. This V-IV-I-V chord progression in G becomes I-♭VII-IV-I when you start on D.

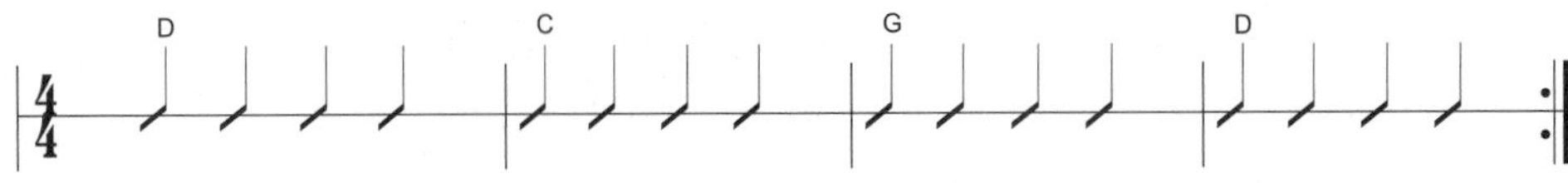

Figure 13-14: D Mixolydian accompaniment.

Illustration courtesy of Desi Serna

Play G major scale notes along with Audio Track 18 to produce the sound of D Mixolydian mode.

Because Mixolydian mode centers on a major chord, most lead guitar players prefer to approach it with major pentatonic scale patterns. You can see how to put together D major pentatonic and G major scale patterns in Figure 13-15.

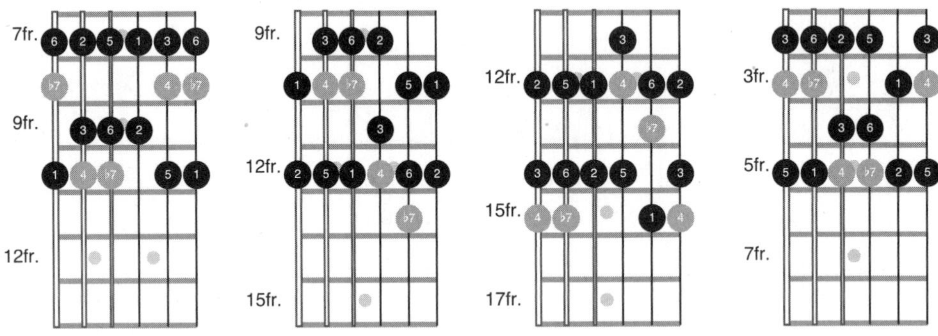

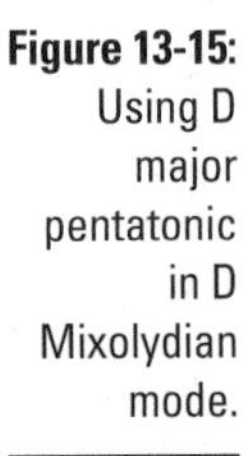

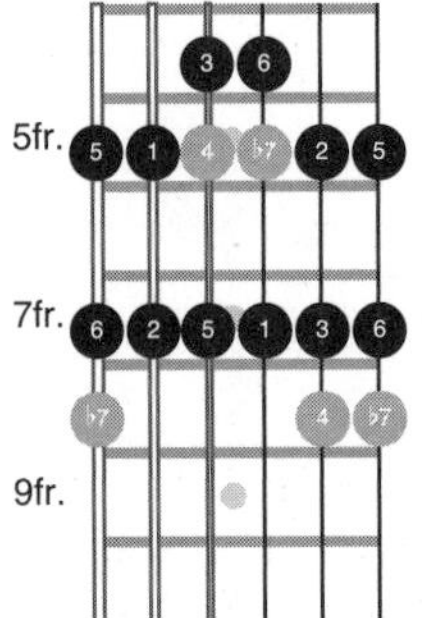

Figure 13-15: Using D major pentatonic in D Mixolydian mode.

Illustration courtesy of Desi Serna

You can think of Mixolydian mode as being the major pentatonic with an added 4th and ♭7th. Coincidentally, D Mixolydian and B Phrygian use the same pattern combinations because D major and B minor pentatonic are relative to one another. I recommend that you at least play through the combination set in D major pentatonic pattern 1 beginning at the 7th fret of the 6th string (it starts on B; D is located at the 10th fret). The key of D Mixolydian is just a starting point. Move the same patterns around to play Mixolydian mode in other keys.

Any time a piece of music uses the major scale and centers on the 5th degree, chord V, it's Mixolydian mode. Some song examples that are either entirely based in Mixolydian mode or at least have a Mixolydian section include the following:

"Seven Bridges Road" by the Eagles (D Mixolydian)

"Southern Cross" by Crosby, Stills and Nash (A Mixolydian)

"Nothing But a Good Time" by Poison (A Mixolydian)

"Louie, Louie" by The Kingsmen (A Mixolydian)

"What I Like About You" by The Romantics (A Mixolydian)

"Franklin's Tower" by Grateful Dead (A Mixolydian)

"Third Stone From the Sun" by Jimi Hendrix (E Mixolydian)

"No Rain" by Blind Melon (E Mixolydian)

"I'm So Glad" by Cream (E Mixolydian)

"Norwegian Wood (This Bird Has Flown)" by The Beatles (E Mixolydian)

"Cinnamon Girl" by Neil Young (D Mixolydian)

"Tequila" by The Champs (F Mixolydian)

"Get Down Tonight" by KC and The Sunshine Band (F Mixolydian)

"Cult of Personality" by Living Colour (G Mixolydian)

"Scarlet Begonias" by The Grateful Dead (B Mixolydian)

"Golden Years" by David Bowie (F♯ Mixolydian)

"Two Tickets to Paradise" by Eddie Money (A Mixolydian)

"Fire on the Mountain" by Grateful Dead (B Mixolydian)

"But Anyway" by Blues Traveler (B Mixolydian)

"On Broadway" by The Drifters (A♭ Mixolydian)

Any one of these songs is good for playing along with and practicing Mixolydian mode. You can also put together your own tracks by centering a progression around the 5th degree and chord from the major scale.

Playing Aeolian Mode

Aeolian, the sixth mode of the major scale, is the sound that's created when the 6th scale degree functions as the tonic. Because it features a minor 3rd and centers on a minor chord, it's a minor mode. It's better known as the *natural* or *relative minor scale.* Rather than being called *Aeolian mode,* it's usually referred to as the *minor scale.*

Drawing from the G major scale, Aeolian mode looks like this:

G major

1-2-3-4-5-6-7

G-A-B-C-D-E-F♯

I-ii-iii-IV-V-vi-vii♭5

G-Am-Bm-C-D-Em-F♯m♭5

E minor

1-2-♭3-4-5-♭6-♭7

E-F♯-G-A-B-C-D

i-ii♭5-♭III-iv-v-♭VI-♭VII

Em-F♯m♭5-G-Am-Bm-C-D

The minor scale can be thought of as a major scale with a flattened 3rd, 6th, and 7th. Figure 13-16 shows how to view the fretboard in E minor, using the notes and chords of G major. The only difference is that the 6th degree, E, is now the tonic and counted as number 1. If you want to play a natural minor scale, play 1 to 1. You can play in other natural minor keys by centering music on the 6th degree of other major scales.

E minor scale

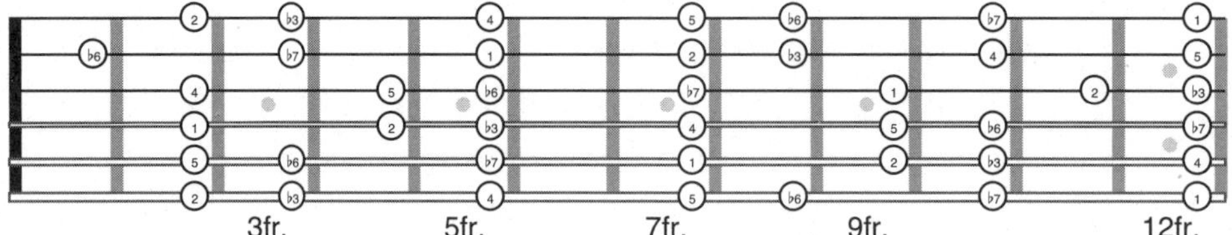

E minor scale Roman Numerals

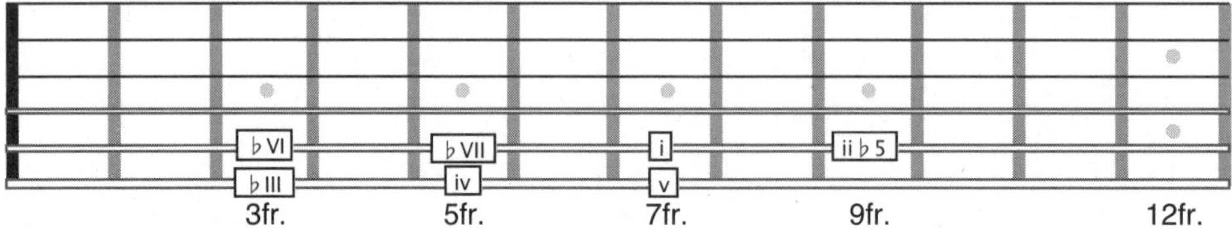

E minor scale chords

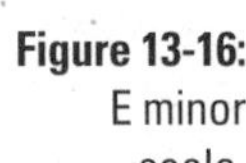

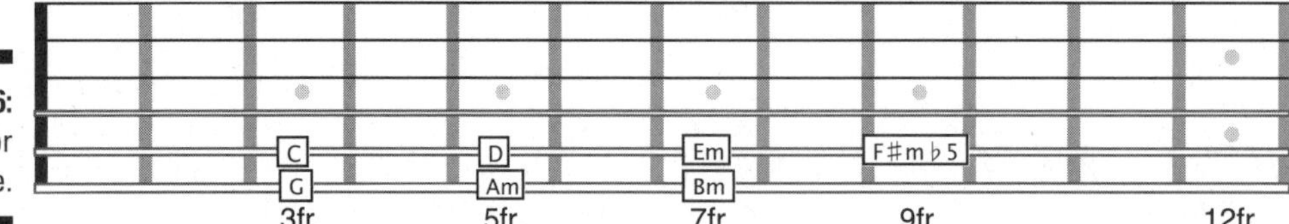

Figure 13-16: E minor scale.

Illustration courtesy of Desi Serna

This is just one example of how you can view the fretboard in E minor. In order to properly produce the natural minor sound, you need to use some type of accompaniment, like the one shown in Figure 13-17. This vi-ii-iii chord progression in G becomes i-iv-v when you center on Em.

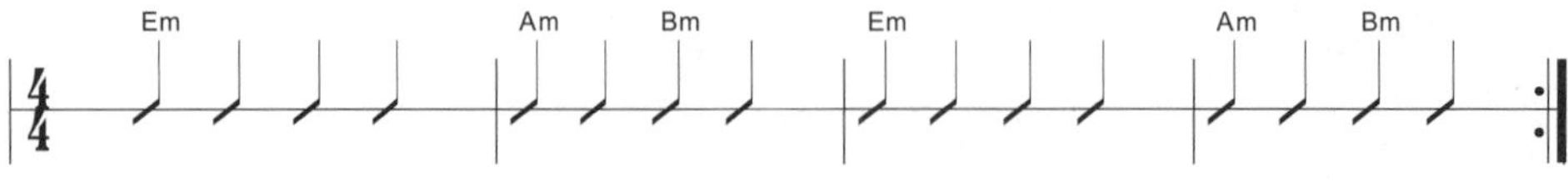

Figure 13-17: E minor scale accompaniment.

Illustration courtesy of Desi Serna

Play G major scale notes along with Audio Track 19 to produce the sound of E Aeolian mode.

Because Aeolian mode centers on a minor chord, you approach it with minor pentatonic scale patterns. You can see how to put together E minor pentatonic and G major scale patterns in Figure 13-18.

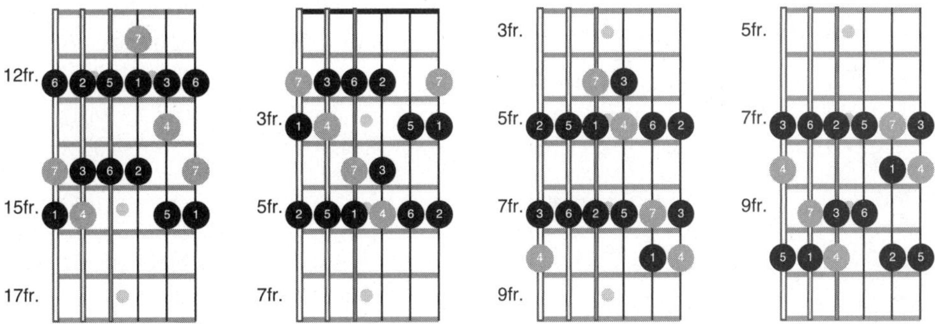

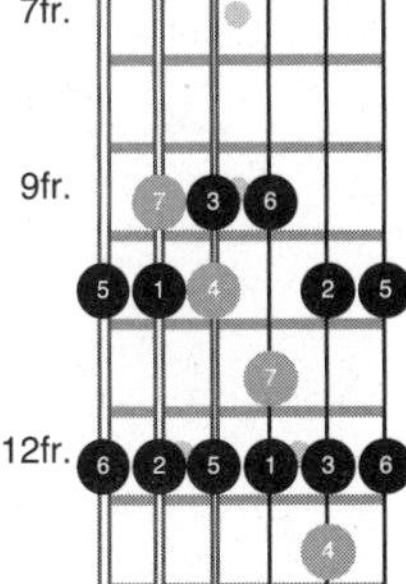

Figure 13-18: Using E minor pentatonic and the E minor scale.

Illustration courtesy of Desi Serna

You can think of the minor scale as being the minor pentatonic with an added 2nd and ♭6th. Because G major and E minor are relative to one another, they both use the same pentatonic and major scale patterns. I recommend that you at least play through the combination set in E minor pentatonic pattern 1 beginning at the 12th fret of the 6th string. Notice that because you start with pentatonic pattern 1 at the 12th fret, I put the remaining patterns an octave lower in order to place you in a more comfortable position on the neck. The key of E minor is just a starting point. Move the same patterns around to play Aeolian mode in other keys.

Any time a piece of music uses the major scale and centers on the 6th degree, chord vi, it's Aeolian mode, better known simply as the minor scale. Some song examples that are either entirely based in Aeolian mode or at least have an Aeolian section include

"Livin' On a Prayer" by Bon Jovi (E minor)

"Maria Maria" by Santana (A minor)

"Black Magic Woman" by Santana (D minor)

"You Give Love a Bad Name" by Bon Jovi (C minor)

"Smells Like Teen Spirit" by Nirvana (F minor)

"Paranoid" by Black Sabbath (E minor)

"The Thrill Is Gone" by B.B. King (B minor)

"I Shot the Sheriff" by Bob Marley/Eric Clapton (G minor)

"Fade to Black" by Metallica (B minor)

"All Along the Watchtower" by Jimi Hendrix (C♯ minor with guitars tuned down one half step to E♭).

Any one of these songs is good for playing along with and practicing Aeolian mode. You can also put together your own tracks by centering a progression around the 6th degree and chord from the major scale.

Playing Locrian mode?

Guess what? Locrian isn't used. You're done!

You really don't need to spend any time on the Locrian mode simply because it isn't used in popular music. You could build Locrian on the 7th degree of its parent major scale. The tonic chord has a minor-flat-five quality (diminished triad), which has a dissonant and unresolved sound. This instability of its sound makes basing a piece of music on it impractical.

If you're curious, feel free to go through the process of renumbering the chords on your own, using the same methods you see with the other modes. You could try F♯ Locrian, whose parent scale is G major.

Chapter 14

Exploring New Patterns with the Harmonic Minor Scale

In This Chapter

- Getting familiar with the harmonic minor scale
- Playing over harmonic minor chord progressions
- Using harmonic minor scale patterns
- Looking at harmonic minor song examples
- Getting introduced to the melodic minor scale

The majority of popular music is based on pentatonic and major scale patterns; however, some types of scales have pitches that fall outside of these patterns. Most of these other scales are rare in popular music, but one — the *harmonic minor* — occurs quite regularly. Understanding this scale can help you better understand both melody and harmony. In this chapter you get to know the harmonic minor scale and how it's used for composition and improvisation. You work on combining the harmonic minor with other types of scales, such as the pentatonic and major scale modes.

Understanding and applying the harmonic minor scale requires you to be familiar with other musical concepts, including

- Pentatonic scale patterns (refer to Chapter 11 for details)
- Major scale patterns (see Chapter 12)
- Relative (or natural) minor scale (turn to Chapter 7)
- Dominant function (check out Chapter 9)

These concepts come together to create the harmonic minor concept. If you don't already understand these concepts individually, the material here will be hard to follow.

Listen to Audio Track 20 for samples of the harmonic minor scale and to get an idea of what this chapter is all about.

Getting to Know the Harmonic Minor Scale

Before you dive into the harmonic minor scale, you need to understand the concept of dominant function, which I cover in detail in Chapter 9. Basically, *dominant function* is the tendency of the dominant chord, chord V, to pull to the tonic, chord I, in a key. Similarly, *secondary dominants* are a way of using the dominant sound to strengthen a progression toward chords other than the tonic. Some examples include II7 leading to V, VI7 leading to ii, and III7 leading to vi.

In the latter example, III7 leading to vi creates the harmonic minor scale. In order to change what is normally a minor iii chord to a major III chord, the 7th note of the relative minor scale is raised.

III7-vi is a very important chord change in music because it uses dominant function to lead to the relative minor — one of the most common types of keys. Because musicians prefer to think of the relative minor tonic as "1," you can also think of III7-vi as V7-i in the relative minor key with the major V chord a result of the harmonic minor scale.

Raising the 7th scale degree

One way to think of the harmonic minor scale is as an altered version of the natural minor with its 7th scale degree raised by a half step. For example, when you play an A minor scale and raise the 7th G to G♯, you're playing an A harmonic minor scale:

A Natural Minor

1-2-♭3-4-5-♭6-♭7

A-B-C-D-E-F-G

A Harmonic Minor

1-2-♭3-4-5-♭6-7

A-B-C-D-E-F-G♯

The chords of the A minor scale are the same as its relative major, C, except that they start on Am:

Am-Bm♭5-C-Dm-Em-F-G

When you renumber these chords with A as the tonic, you get the following sequence:

1-2-3-4-5-6-7
i-ii♭5-♭III-iv-v-♭VI-♭VII

Notice that the dominant chord (the chord built on the 5th scale degree named the dominant) is minor. In A, it's an Em chord: E, G, and B.

Take a look at how the raised 7th of the harmonic minor scale affects the dominant chord. In A harmonic minor, the 7th scale degree is raised from G to G♯. This G♯ changes the Em chord, E-G-B, to E major, E-G♯-B. The v chord becomes V, making a much stronger dominant-tonic V-i chord progression. As with major keys, you can add a 7th (creating a dominant 7th chord) to intensify the movement from dominant to tonic. In our A minor example, this would be E7-Am. Songs in minor keys often use V7 chords.

If you're a soloist, keep in mind that you only need to use the harmonic minor scale temporarily. Typically, you use the natural minor scale until the dominant chord sounds, at which point you need the raised 7th of the harmonic minor. In other words, when the V or V7 chord appears, use the harmonic minor; for all other chords, use the natural minor.

Identifying some harmonic minor chord progressions

This section shows you several examples of typical harmonic minor chord progressions. Notice that the progressions use chords from the A natural minor scale, except for the V7 chord, E7, which comes from the harmonic minor scale.

Figure 14-1 shows an Am-E7 harmonic minor chord progression. Something similar is used in "Istanbul (Not Constantinople)" by Santo & Johnny.

Figure 14-1: Am-E7.

Illustration courtesy of Desi Serna

Figure 14-1 is available as a play-along backing track. Listen to Audio Track 21.

Figure 14-2 shows an Am-Dm-E7-Am harmonic minor chord progression. Some of the same chords are used in "Abracadabra" by Steve Miller Band.

Figure 14-2: Am-Dm-E7-Am.

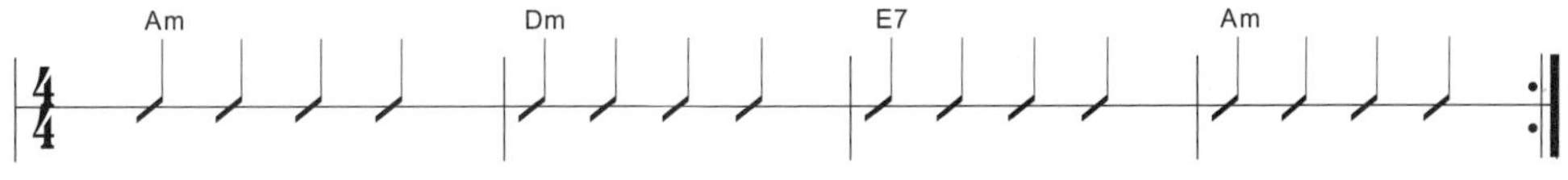

Illustration courtesy of Desi Serna

Figure 14-3 shows an Am-F-E7 harmonic minor chord progression. The main sections to "Smooth" by Santana are based on a nearly identical progression.

Figure 14-3: Am-F-E7.

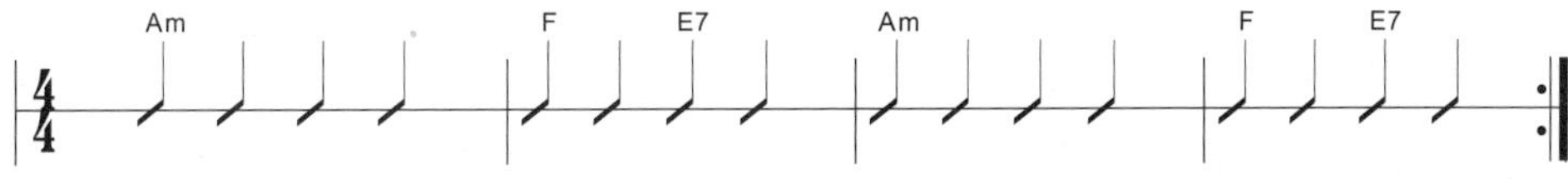

Illustration courtesy of Desi Serna

Figure 14-4 shows an Am-G-F-E7 harmonic minor chord progression. "Walk, Don't Run" by The Ventures starts out with the same chord changes.

Figure 14-4: Am-G-F-E7.

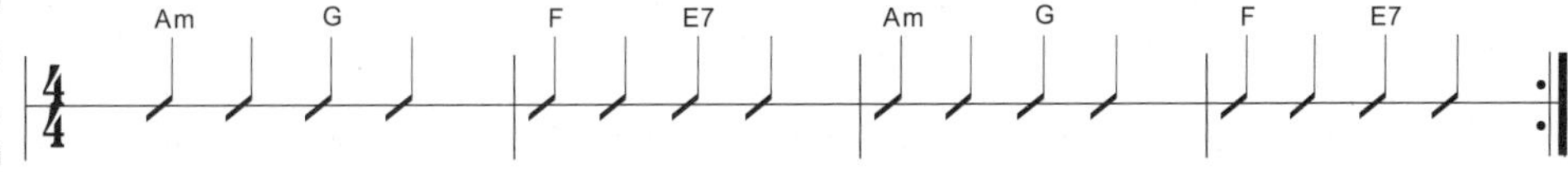

Illustration courtesy of Desi Serna

Figure 14-5 shows an Am-Dm-G-C-F-Bm7♭5-E7 harmonic minor chord progression. Some songs based on similar chord movement include "El Farol" by Santana, "I Will Survive" by Gloria Gaynor, and "Still Got the Blues" by Gary Moore.

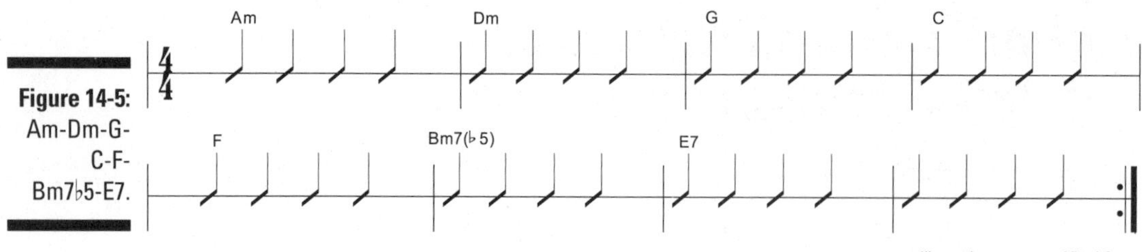

Figure 14-5: Am-Dm-G-C-F-Bm7♭5-E7.

Illustration courtesy of Desi Serna

You can play in other harmonic minor keys simply by playing a minor chord and a dominant 7th chord a 5th above it; for example, Em and B7, Fm and C7, Dm and A7, and so on.

Following is a list of songs in other minor keys that use V7. Rather than showing the complete progressions, which include other chords from the keys in most examples, I have just identified the i and V7 chords.

B♭m and F7

"Runaway" by Del Shannon

Bm and F♯7

"Hotel California" by the Eagles

Cm and G7

"Girl" by The Beatles

"Stray Cat Strut" by Stray Cats

C♯m and G♯7

"California Dreamin'" by The Mamas and the Papas

Dm and A7

"A Hazy Shade of Winter" by Simon and Garfunkel

"Like the Way I Do" by Melissa Etheridge

"The Man Who Sold the World" by Nirvana

"Sultans of Swing" by Dire Straits

"The Thunder Rolls" by Garth Brooks

Em and B7

"Black Horse and the Cherry Tree" by KT Tunstall

"Hanuman" by Rodrigo y Gabriela

"Paint It, Black" by The Rolling Stones

"People Are Strange" by The Doors

"Nothing Else Matters" by Metallica

"Secret Agent Man" by Johnny Rivers

F♯m and C♯7

"The Way" by Fastball

Using Harmonic Minor within a Pentatonic Pattern

Raising the 7th in the minor scale creates whole new scale patterns for lead guitarists to learn. But believe it or not, I don't recommend learning all the patterns of the harmonic minor scales on the fretboard at once. Instead, I suggest that you work on adding harmonic minor to a pentatonic scale pattern. This is how most guitar players use the harmonic minor scale, anyway. After you can incorporate the harmonic minor scale into a pentatonic pattern, you can explore the full harmonic minor patterns that cover the guitar neck (see the later section "Covering the Fretboard with Harmonic Minor Scale Patterns" for details).

To use the harmonic minor scale in a pentatonic pattern, follow this process:

1. **Add a raised 7th to the pentatonic.**
2. **Outline the V7 chord with an arpeggio pattern.**
3. **Fill in the notes that complete the harmonic minor scale within the pentatonic pattern.**

All along the way, work on switching between natural and harmonic minor as you play over chord progressions.

I discuss each step of this process in more detail in the following sections.

In order to follow this process, take a few minutes to record yourself strumming the chords in any one of Figures 14-1 to 14-5. You'll use this recording as a backing track for practice. You can also use a looping device, a program that allows you to assemble pre-recorded tracks; Audio Track 21; or an A minor song example from the previous section, such as "Smooth."

Adding a raised 7th to the pentatonic

The best way to start using the harmonic minor scale in a pentatonic pattern is to play over a simple minor chord progression, using a minor pentatonic pattern and adding a raised 7th over the V7 chord. Start with A minor pentatonic and the chords Am and E7. In Figure 14-6, you see A minor pentatonic followed by the same pattern with the raised 7th scale degrees of the harmonic minor shown in gray. Notice that this isn't a full harmonic minor scale; it's just a raised 7th added to the pentatonic.

In music, the harmonic minor scale appears only for the V7 chord in a minor key progression. You use the natural minor scale over the other chords. For example, in progressions like Am-E7, Am-F-E7, and Am-G-F-E7, you only use the G♯ of the harmonic minor scale over the E7 chord. For the remaining chords, a G-natural works better. Check out "Smooth" by Santana for a great example of this technique. The song's main progression is Am-F-E7, and Carlos Santana uses the A harmonic minor scale only over the E7 chord. He uses the pitches from A natural minor over the Am and F chords.

Play the A minor pentatonic pattern over the recording you create in this section's introduction. Whenever the progression moves to E7, try to play the raised 7th scale degree. If you can, play this note on the first beat of the E7 measure. When the progression returns to Am, leave the raised 7th out of your solo, just using the A minor pentatonic and its ♭7th. If you find that your recording changes chords too fast, either rerecord your play-along track at a slower tempo or increase the number of measures per chord.

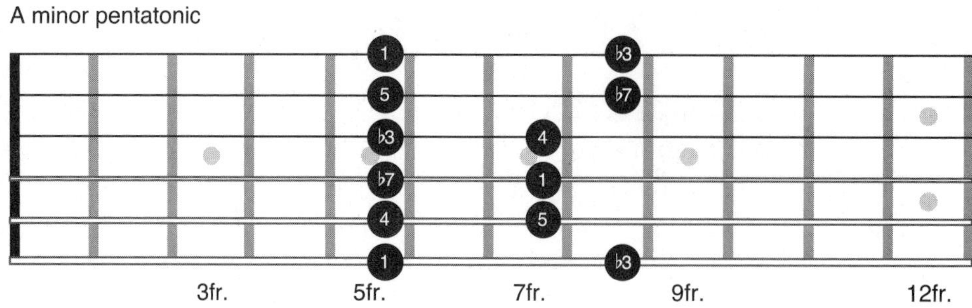

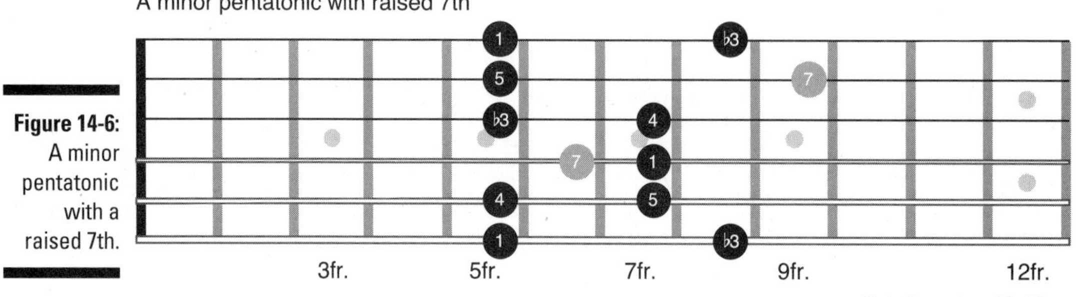

Figure 14-6: A minor pentatonic with a raised 7th.

Illustration courtesy of Desi Serna

As you work through this simple exercise, you begin to hear the sound quality of the harmonic minor. See how you can use this sound — created mostly by the raised 7th degree — without having to learn a whole new set of patterns? Easy as pie!

You can transpose this pentatonic pattern with the added raised 7th to other keys simply by moving it up and down the neck. Whatever key you choose to play in, use both the minor tonic chord and its V7 in your practice progressions. For example, use Em-B7 in the key of E minor, Gm-D7 in G minor, and Dm-A7 in D minor. You can also try playing along with any of the harmonic minor songs listed in the earlier section "Identifying some harmonic minor chord progressions," such as "Smooth" by Santana, "Nothing Else Matters" by Metallica, and "Sultans of Swing" by Dire Straits.

Outlining the V7 chord

The raised 7th in the harmonic minor scale is the same pitch as the 3rd of the V7 chord. For example, in A harmonic minor, the G♯ is also the 3rd of E7. When you play the G♯ over E7, you're *outlining* the E7 chord by emphasizing one of its chord tones, the 3rd. You can also outline E7 by emphasizing any of its other chord tones. To see what I mean, look at an E arpeggio pattern in the pentatonic and practice targeting chord tones of the basic triad: E, G♯, and B.

Figure 14-7 shows an E major arpeggio pattern combined with A minor pentatonic. The CAGED form used here for the E chord is the C form (see Chapter 4 for details on the CAGED system). The arpeggio is shown in black, and the rest of the scale is in white. The numbers identify the root, 3rd, and 5th of the E chord.

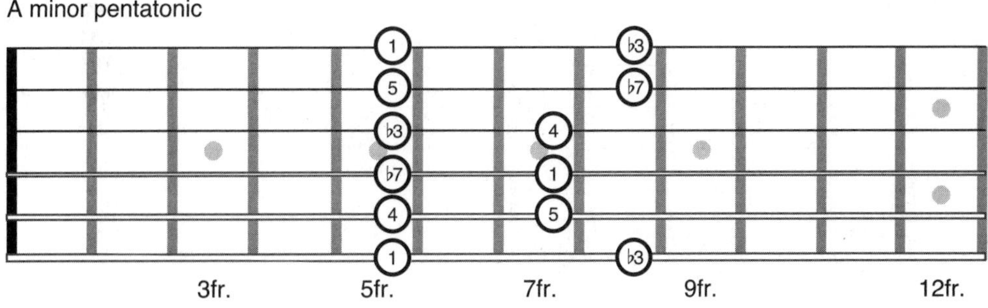

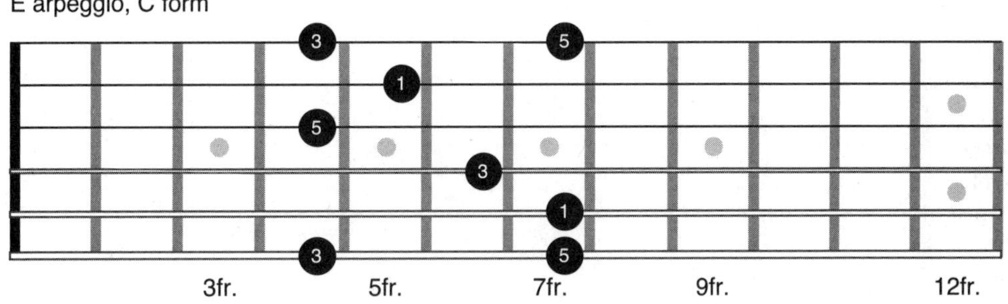

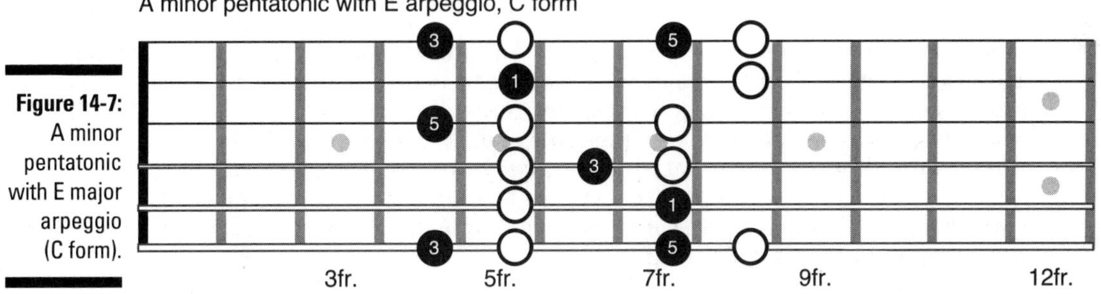

Figure 14-7: A minor pentatonic with E major arpeggio (C form).

Illustration courtesy of Desi Serna

Use any examples or songs that use Am and E7 to practice outlining the complete E major arpeggio over the V7 chord. Try to target one of its chord tones on the first beat of the V7 chord. You can also play several of the chord tones during the measure as time allows. When the progression returns to the Am chord, stick with A minor pentatonic notes and avoid the raised 7th of the harmonic scale, or the G♯.

The root and 5th of E should still work over the Am chord. After all, the note E belongs to A minor pentatonic, and the B belongs to the A natural minor scale. So in some ways, you've just picked up an extra note for your pentatonic patterns — B, in this case — which you can use over both the tonic and dominant chords.

So far, you've used a major triad arpeggio to play over a dominant 7th chord, but you can also use a complete dominant 7th arpeggio. I show you how in Figure 14-8. You need to add only one note, the note D, to an E chord to make E7. D also belongs to both A minor pentatonic and natural minor scales, so you can use it over both the Am and E7 chords.

E7, C form

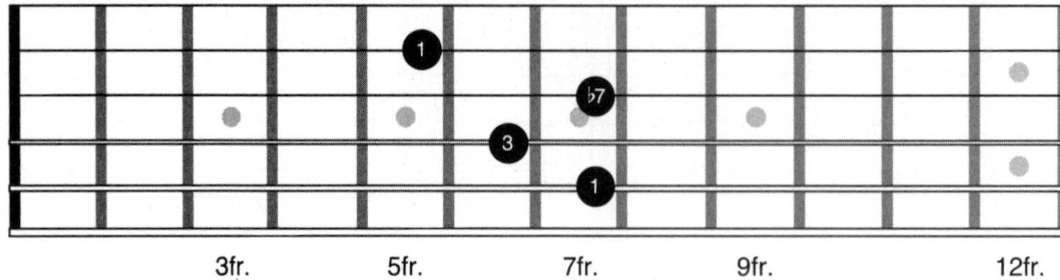

E7 arpeggio, C form

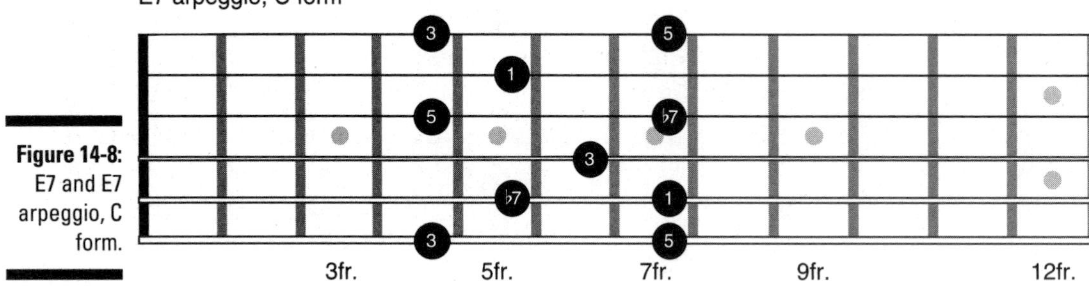

Figure 14-8: E7 and E7 arpeggio, C form.

Illustration courtesy of Desi Serna

At this point in your practice, you may have a hard time keeping track of a full dominant 7th arpeggio. If that's the case, simplify your practice by using just one part of the arpeggio instead of trying to cover all of it. For example, focus on strings 1, 2, and 3. Or skip the dominant 7th for now and just work with the basic triad for a while. Over time, you can gradually add in more notes and transpose to new keys as you become more proficient.

For a demonstration on how to get started with outlining V7 chords while using the minor pentatonic scale, watch Video Clip 34.

Completing the harmonic minor scale

After you add the notes of the V7 chord into the pentatonic pattern, you're just one note away from having complete natural and harmonic minor scales. In A minor, you only need to add in F. Figure 14-9 shows A minor pentatonic, then A natural minor and A harmonic minor with the F note added. Notice that the only difference between natural minor and harmonic minor is the 7th scale degree — G versus G♯.

Guess what you have to do now? Practice, practice, practice! Well, I like to consider it *playing* rather than *practicing*, but whatever you call it, be sure to work with these patterns for a while, taking time to alternate between the natural and harmonic minor scales. You can shift these patterns to new positions in order to play in other keys. As you practice, try playing along with some of the songs listed in the earlier section "Identifying some harmonic minor chord progressions."

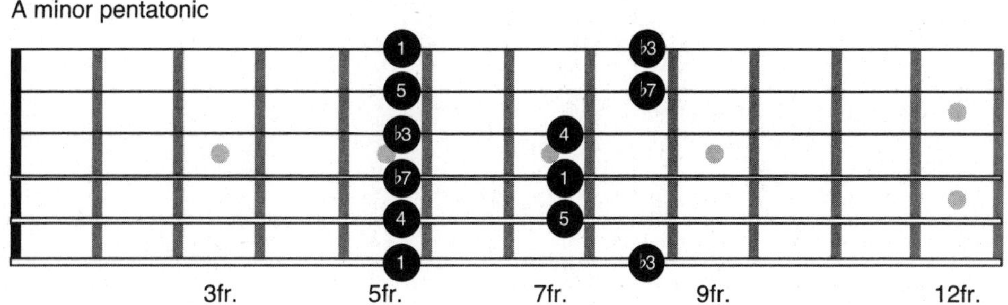

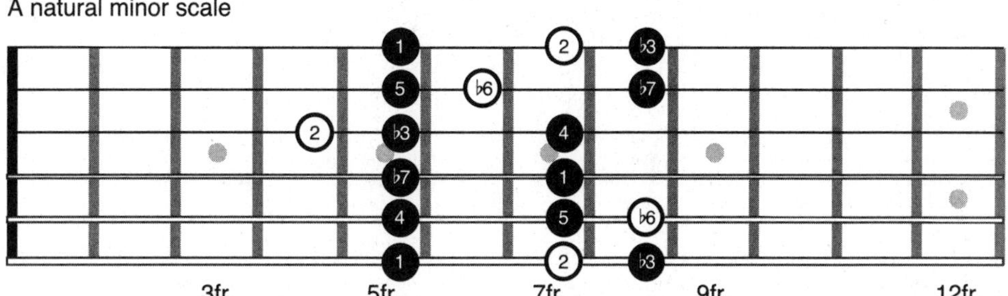

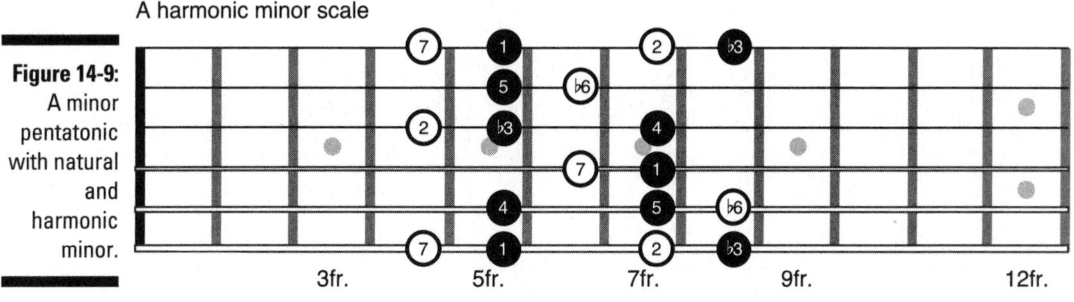

Figure 14-9: A minor pentatonic with natural and harmonic minor.

Illustration courtesy of Desi Serna

REMEMBER

How you choose to play over the V7 chord in minor key chord progressions is a matter of preference. You can play the harmonic minor scale only over the V7 chord by using the raised 7th degree in place of the flat 7th. Or you can use the other notes of the V7 arpeggio and those of the complete harmonic minor scale in addition to the raised 7th.

You don't always have to use the harmonic minor over a V7 chord in a minor key. You can continue to play the natural minor scale or just a minor pentatonic scale. If you go this route, be aware that the minor 7th scale degree will create a dissonance with one of the pitches in the V7 chord, but it'll do so in a musically agreeable way. For example, in the key of A minor, the minor 7th scale degree G sounds against the E7's G♯. But it still works. In music theory terms, the sound you create is an E7♯9 chord (see the nearby sidebar for details on this particular chord). A chord like this can be a big part of a bluesy sound. If, however, you want to get the full effect of the harmonic minor sound, you need to use the raised 7th, as I do in the rest of this chapter.

The E7♯9 chord

An E7♯9 chord is built with the chord tones 1-3-5-♭7-♯9. It's a dominant 7th chord with a sharp 9th added above the 7th. Look at this chord's pitches:

1-3-5-♭7-♯9

E-G♯-B-D-F♯♯ (you read that right, double-sharp)

As you can see, the interval of a 9th is actually a compound 2nd, E-F♯♯, only with an added octave. Although you usually think of this pitch as a sharpened 9th, it's useful to read this pitch enharmonically to understand why it works the way it does. The F♯♯ is actually the same note as G-natural. So the E7♯9 chord contains both a G♯ and a G, a major and minor 3rd in the chord. These two pitches create a dissonance that makes for an edgy, bluesy, even mean type of sound with a lot of musical tension in it.

Various styles of music, including jazz, blues, funk, and rock, employ altered dominant chords like this one as part of their basic sound. Because it was a favorite chord of Jimi Hendrix, it's sometimes nicknamed the "Hendrix Chord" or "Purple Haze Chord" among rock guitarists. You hear an E7♯9 chord in "Born To Be Wild" by Steppenwolf, "The Lemon Song" by Led Zeppelin, "Testify" by Stevie Ray Vaughan, and "Funk #49" by James Gang.

Covering the Fretboard with Harmonic Minor Scale Patterns

When you're ready to cover the entire fretboard with the harmonic minor scale, you have a couple of choices to make. First, you have to decide how you want to organize the notes of the harmonic minor scale into patterns. To keep things simple, I show you five patterns in this section. Over time, these patterns will start to run together, and you'll stop thinking of them in only the five forms shown here.

After you choose which patterns you want to practice with, you need to decide which fingerings to use. You don't have to use all the patterns I show here or even all the parts of each pattern. Most guitarists find a few patterns and positions that they feel most comfortable using. So the process of learning harmonic minor scale patterns is really about exploring your options and deciding what works best for you.

Picking out patterns

The first diagram in Figure 14-10 shows you all the notes of A harmonic minor across the whole fretboard. The second through sixth diagrams break the scale into five different positions or patterns. The last diagram is a variation on the first pattern (the one in the open position in the second diagram). You can continue to connect patterns until you either run out of fretboard or can't reach any higher.

Notice that the patterns in Figure 14-10 don't have numbers assigned to them. If you ever see these patterns paired with numbers, they're arbitrary and simply for reference.

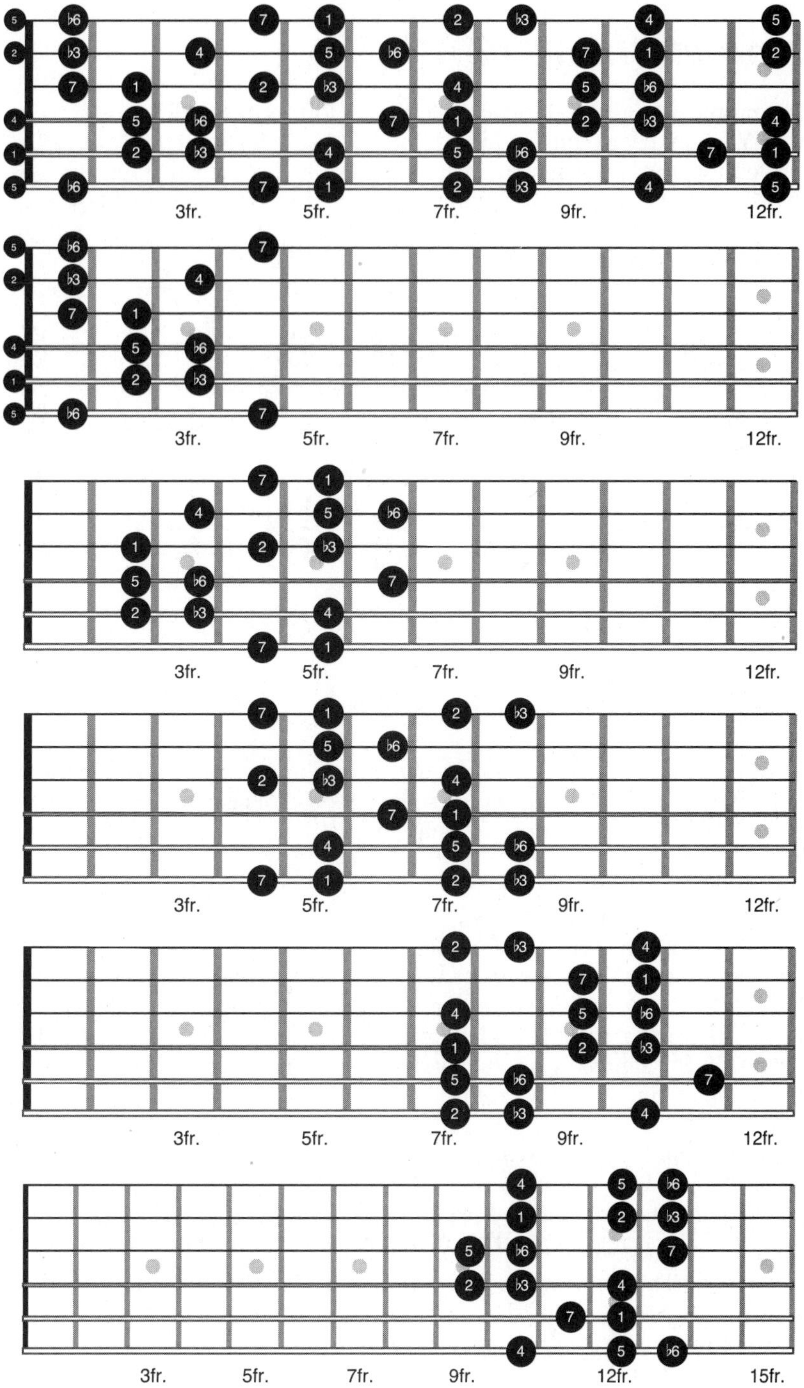

Figure 14-10: Full A harmonic minor scale patterns.

Illustration courtesy of Desi Serna

To see a demonstration on playing full harmonic minor scale patterns, watch Video Clip 35.

Focusing on fingering

With the harmonic minor scale, some strings have four notes on them, as you can see in Figure 14-10. You can try fretting groups of four by using fingers 1-1-3-4, but as with all fingerings, the exact fingering you use is really a matter of preference. So take some time to figure out what works best for you. I give you one fingering example in Figure 14-11. This is the pattern that fits over an Em form barre chord and the pentatonic pattern used throughout this chapter. Numbers here represent the four fingers on your fretting hand.

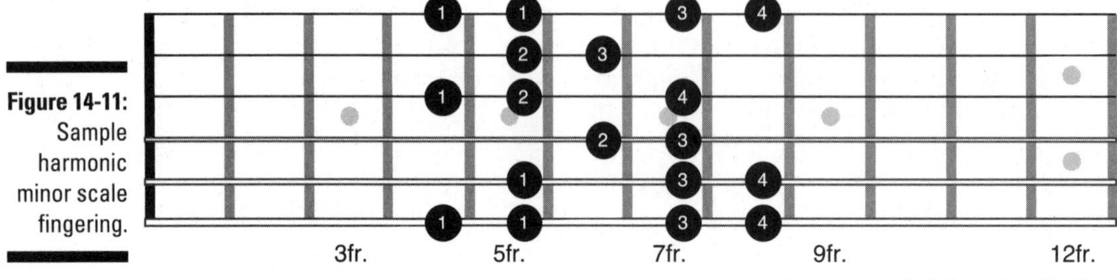

Figure 14-11: Sample harmonic minor scale fingering.

Illustration courtesy of Desi Serna

Practice, practice, practice!

Even after you understand how to play the harmonic minor scale, you may be unsure about how to actually use it to make your solos sound good. This is where practicing different songs that use the harmonic minor can help you.

All the harmonic minor songs that I mention earlier in this chapter (particularly those by Carlos Santana and those listed in the section "Identifying some harmonic minor chord progressions") have melodies, riffs, guitar solos, and bass lines that can help you work on different licks and phrases. Get their recordings and guitar tabs to start working out their various parts. After you learn a particular part, practice playing it along with the song. Mix the licks and phrases up, playing them in different orders. Try similar licks and phrases on different songs in the same key or transpose them to other keys. Just make sure you apply the harmonic minor only to the V7 chord.

Mastering the complete harmonic minor scale is a slow, gradual process that requires a lot of work, so don't give up when the going gets tough! The methods I explain here and throughout this chapter are exactly how most great players develop their skills, build their own repertoire of licks, and create their own style. So just keep playing!

Transposing the harmonic minor scale to new keys

When you're comfortable playing in the key of A harmonic minor, you can start the patterns in a different position and play in other keys. Just keep track of where the scale tonic is in each pattern, specifically the tonics that land on the 6th and 5th strings, the strings most guitarists use to track scales and chords on the fretboard (see Chapter 2 on navigating the fretboard).

I recommend that you start new keys with the pentatonic/harmonic minor combo you play in the section "Using Harmonic Minor within a Pentatonic Pattern." This combo fits together with a standard Em form barre chord. Start with this form and then connect to other patterns from it.

Playing in a Harmonic Minor Mode

Generally speaking, you use only one mode of the harmonic minor scale. In this mode, the 5th degree of the harmonic minor scale functions as the tonic. That's means that the V chord is the tonic chord. Figure 14-12 shows an example of this modal application of the harmonic minor scale — with two major chords a half step apart: E and F. In A harmonic minor, E-F is V-VI. The V chord, E, draws on the harmonic minor for its pitches, and you play A harmonic minor over the progression.

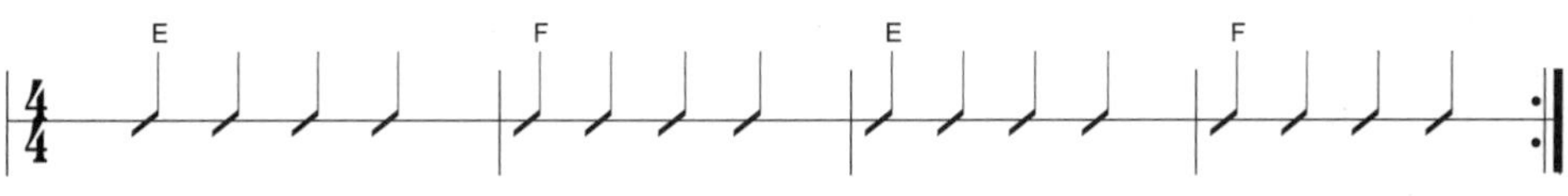

Figure 14-12: Half step major chord progression.

Illustration courtesy of Desi Serna

You can think of the chord progression in Figure 14-12 as a type of Phrygian mode. That would be the third mode of the C major scale, E Phrygian. Now raise the 3rd of E from G to G♯. This altered Phrygian scale has a strong Spanish flavor to it, but it also appears in Jewish, Greek, Turkish, Arabic, and Persian music. This particular mode goes by many different names, including Spanish Phrygian scale, Spanish Gypsy scale, Phrygian major scale, Phrygian dominant scale, and Freygish scale. Though it can be thought of as a type of Phrygian mode, it's really drawn from the 5th degree of the harmonic minor scale, in this case, A harmonic minor.

You hear the fifth mode of harmonic minor in the songs "Misirlou" by Dick Dale and "White Rabbit" by Jefferson Airplane. "Misirlou" is played along the 6th string centering on E but using notes from A harmonic minor. "White Rabbit" opens with an F♯-G chord progression, V and VI of B harmonic minor.

Getting to Know the Melodic Minor Scale

In this section and the one that follows, you get to know some additional theory relating to the melodic minor scale. Fully exploring the use of melodic minor is beyond the scope of this book, but an introduction is needed because of its close relationship to the harmonic minor.

The melodic minor scale is a variation of the harmonic minor scale with a raised 6th in addition to the raised 7th. It's used more often in jazz and classical music than in rock, and its formula looks like this: 1-2-♭3-4-5-6-7. It's also thought of as a major scale with a flattened 3rd or a Dorian scale with a raised 7th.

In classical theory, this scale has an ascending and descending form. They say that you're supposed to play the raised 6th and 7th while ascending the scale but play all natural minor scale degrees while descending the scale. However, this is not how modern musicians use the scale. Instead, they use the raised 6th and 7th degrees in both directions. You can use this scale over V7 chords in a minor key just as you do with harmonic minor.

A really great example of this scale is the Christmas song "Carol of the Bells," which uses the natural minor scale over most of the chord progression but changes to melodic minor over the V7 chord. Another good example is "Yesterday" by The Beatles, which uses part of the D melodic minor scale over the Em-A7-Dm chords during "all my troubles seem so far away" (guitar tuned down one whole step to D).

Using Harmonic Minor in Dorian Mode

The Dorian mode (see Chapter 13 for more on the Dorian mode) is like a natural minor scale with a raised 6th. So if you raise the 7th as well, you end up with a melodic minor scale.

Using a V7 chord in Dorian mode is just as common as using one in natural minor. When a V7 chord occurs in Dorian mode, you have a few options for your solos:

- Ignore the chord completely and keep playing the minor pentatonic scale, or the Dorian scale.
- Target the raised 7th or outline the V7 chord (see the earlier section "Outlining the V7 chord" for details).
- Play the whole Dorian scale with a raised 7th (which produces the melodic minor scale).
- Play the harmonic minor scale, which is the natural minor scale with a raised 7th.

I've heard and used all of these options, so pick whichever ones work best for you.

Practicing Dorian mode songs with a V7 chord can help you learn which options work best in different situations. Two songs that I recommend working with are "Oye Como Va" and "Evil Ways" by Santana, both of which are Dorian songs that feature a V7 chord at some point.

Chapter 15

Playing the Blues

In This Chapter

- Seeing where blues elements fit into popular music
- Making the blues sound with dominant 7th chords
- Playing over the twelve-bar blues chord progression
- Getting familiar with the blues scale

The influence of blues music on popular music is widespread. You hear blues elements in music styles such as rock, alternative, heavy metal, country, folk, and jazz.

Blues music doesn't always follow the rules of traditional music theory and harmony. Specifically, you find *minor* 3rds applied to major chords, and progressions that switch keys on each chord instead of staying in one parent major scale.

If you're a fan of blues music, and you want to find out more about how to play in this style, you've come to the right place. In this chapter, I show you how to play major and pentatonic scale patterns over chords in the way that a blues instrumentalist would do it.

Understanding and playing the blues requires you to be familiar with other musical concepts, including the following:

- Pentatonic scale patterns (Chapter 11)
- Major scale patterns (Chapter 12)
- V7 chords (Chapter 5)
- Chord progressions and playing by number (Chapter 6)
- The dominant scale, also known as Mixolydian mode (Chapters 7 and 13)

These concepts come together to create the blues. If you don't already understand these concepts individually, the material here will be hard to follow.

Listen to Audio Track 22 to hear examples of playing the blues and get an idea of what this chapter is all about.

Recognizing Blues Elements in Popular Music

The three main features of blues music that you hear in popular music, and that I cover in this chapter, are

- All chords with a major 3rd are treated as dominant 7th chords.
- Each 7th chord is a key change — a V7 from a different key.
- Minor 3rds are used over major chords.

Blues players play in both major and minor keys. In minor keys, nothing unusual happens. Depending on what the tonic chord in the progression is, blues players use a corresponding minor pentatonic scale for riffs, melodies, and lead guitar solos. Here are a few examples:

- B.B. King's "The Thrill Is Gone" is based in the key of B minor, and its chords are all drawn from the B natural minor scale. When playing this song, you can use both B minor pentatonic and full B minor scale patterns (relative minor to D major).
- "Green Onions" by Booker T. & the M.G.'s is based on three chords from F minor: Fm, B♭m, and Cm. You can either play F minor pentatonic over the whole thing or follow each chord with its corresponding pentatonic, playing F minor pentatonic over Fm, B♭ minor pentatonic over B♭m, and C minor pentatonic over Cm.
- "Still Got the Blues" by Gary Moore has a chord progression drawn from the A minor scale but with the addition of an E7 chord — V7 in A harmonic minor. You have two options for playing this song. First, you can play A harmonic minor over the E7 and A natural minor (relative to C major) over everything else. Or, because Am is the tonic, you can play A minor pentatonic over the whole thing.

In these examples, the standard rules of theory and harmony apply. But most blues songs aren't in minor keys. Instead, they're based on dominant 7th chords and I-IV-V-type chord progressions. It's in these situations — where blues music is based on chords with major 3rds — that the rules get broken and the blues sound is made.

The remaining sections in this chapter focus on these "broken" rules and how to get that blues sound you're looking for.

Playing Over a Blues V7 Chord

The key to playing blues music is remembering that all the chords used are some type of dominant 7th chord. In other words, blues chords are any type of chord with a major 3rd and ♭7th, such as A7, A9, or A13. Even when the guitar plays chords without ♭7ths, like plain major chords or 6ths, the tonality of each chord is still treated like that of a dominant 7th, and the melodies, lead guitar solos, and bass lines still feature ♭7ths.

Dominant 7th chords are drawn from the 5th degree of the major scale. When you build 7th chords (1-3-5-7) for each degree of the major scale, only the 5th degree produces the major triad and ♭7th necessary for a dominant 7th chord. Blues chords with major 3rds are treated as dominant 7th chords, and all dominant 7th chords are really V7s (turn to Chapter 5 for more info).

Playing the dominant scale

According to traditional theory, the appropriate scale to play over a 7th chord is its parent major scale. To determine the parent major scale of a particular chord, you need to first realize that a dominant 7th chord is based on V and then figure out which chord is I from there. For example, the correct major scale to play over an A7 chord is D because if A7 is V, then D is I. Likewise, you play A major scale over E7 because E is V of A, and you play G major scale over D7 because D is V of G.

When you play a major scale with the 5th degree functioning as the tonic, you're playing in Mixolydian mode, which is also known as the *dominant scale.* (In case you're keeping track, the 5th degree of the major scale is named the *dominant,* the V chord makes a *dominant* 7th, and the fifth mode is called the *dominant* scale. That's a lot of dominants!) Turn to Chapters 7 and 13 for more on modes.

Figure 15-1 shows you two types of A dominant 7th chords (A7 and A9) and two A dominant scale patterns in different positions. The parent major scale here is D because A is V of D. So the patterns are simply D major scale, the same major scale patterns taught in Chapter 12, only with the 5th degree, A, numbered as 1 because it's functioning as the tonic.

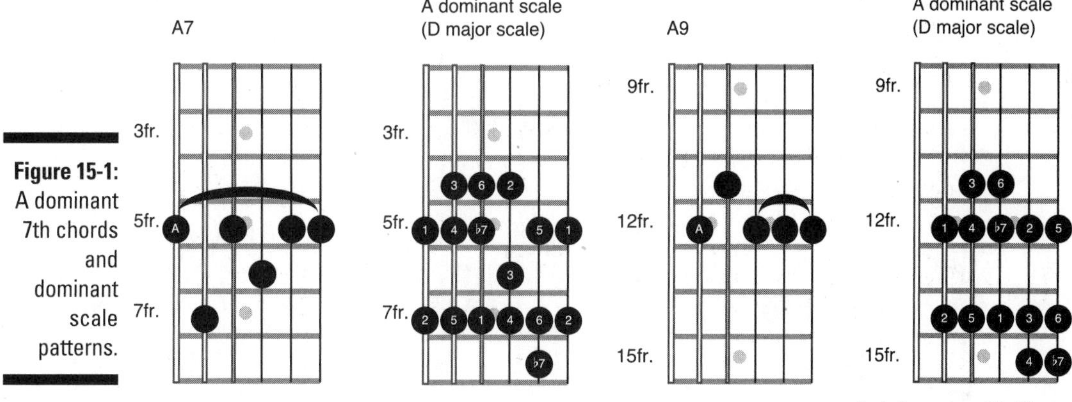

Figure 15-1: A dominant 7th chords and dominant scale patterns.

Illustration courtesy of Desi Serna

Figure 15-1 includes only a few examples to get you started, but of course you can play A7 chords and A dominant scale patterns (D major scale) all over the neck.

One way you're likely to hear the dominant scale used in blues-based music is in the bass. Figure 15-2 gives you an example of how a bass player typically constructs a walking bass line over an A7 chord using notes from the A dominant scale.

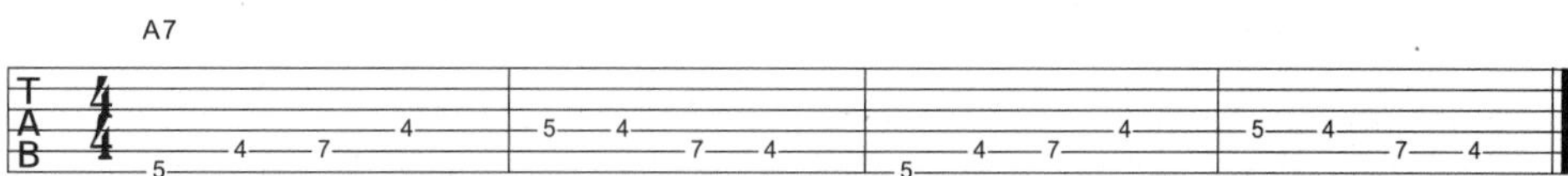

Figure 15-2: Walking dominant scale bass line in A.

Illustration courtesy of Desi Serna

Blues guitarists also use the dominant scale for melodies, riffs, and solos, though they usually use it in combination with some pentatonic scales (see the next section). For example, the guitar in "L.A. Woman" by The Doors uses the A dominant scale but also features a few runs in A minor pentatonic.

Using the major and minor pentatonic

Blues guitar players love to use pentatonic scale patterns, perhaps because of the easy-to-use box-shaped patterns that the pentatonic scale makes.

Normally, you'd use the major pentatonic to play over a chord with a major 3rd. This remains true for dominant 7th chords and, at times, the blues. This means that you can play A major pentatonic over chords like A, A7, A9 and so on. Figure 15-3 shows a reference A7 chord (based on an E form barre chord) and a few A major pentatonic scale patterns. You can play A major pentatonic anywhere, but these patterns are often favored by guitarists because of their proximity to the common A7 chord shape.

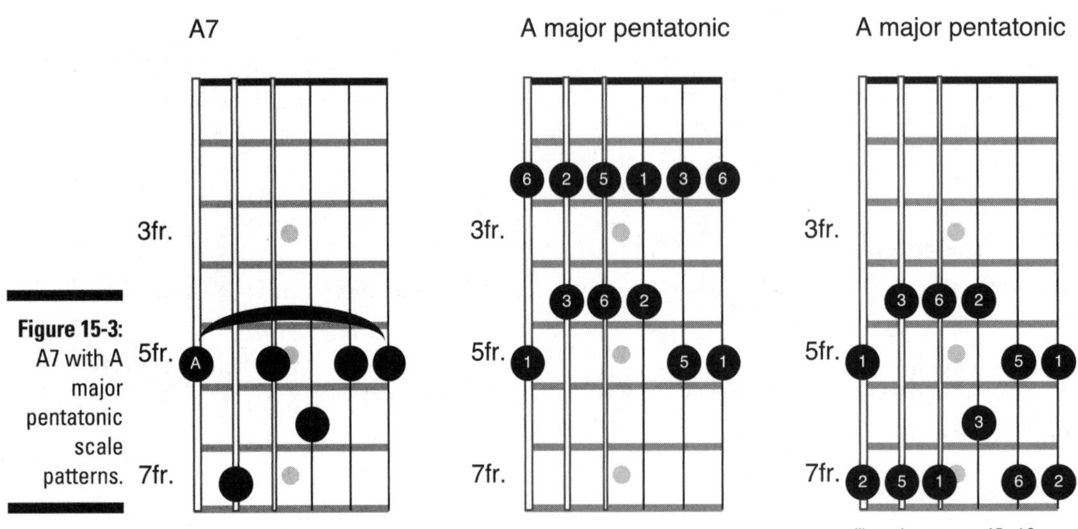

Figure 15-3: A7 with A major pentatonic scale patterns.

While blues players make use of the major pentatonic and the rules of traditional harmony, they usually prefer to break the rules by playing minor over major. This means that the A *minor* pentatonic gets applied to chords like A, A7, A9 and so on. You see a reference A7 chord and a few A minor pentatonic scale patterns in Figure 15-4.

The minor pentatonic scale includes the intervals 1-♭3-4-5-♭7. Dominant chords are built 1-3-5-♭7. The only scale interval here that potentially poses a problem is the ♭3rd. Because a dominant 7th chord has a major 3rd, the ♭3rd is going to conflict. But guess what? It works! In fact, the tension between the major and minor 3rd is the most important feature of the blues sound.

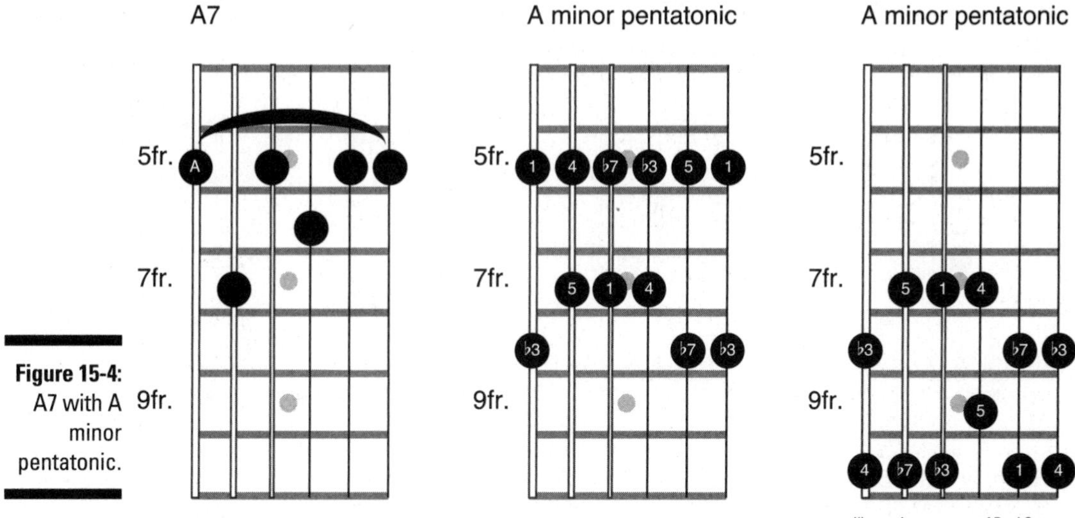

Figure 15-4: A7 with A minor pentatonic.

In blues, a *blue note* is one sung or played at a slightly lower pitch. Sometimes this alteration is a full semitone, as is the case when going from a minor to major 3rd. Blues players often slide or bend from the minor to major 3rd. Here are a few examples of blues songs that use minor over major:

- "Give Me One Reason" by Tracy Chapman is based in the key of F♯ using chords with major 3rds, but the vocal melody and guitar solos primarily use the F♯ minor pentatonic.
- "Sundown" by Gordon Lightfoot centers on an F♯ major chord, but the lead guitar solos play in F♯ minor pentatonic.
- Stevie Ray Vaughan's "Pride and Joy" is based on an E major chord, but the guitar solos primarily use E minor pentatonic (guitars tuned down one half-step to E♭).

Mixing up the scale options

Blues-based music usually applies all three of the scales I cover in the preceding sections (that is, the major and minor pentatonic, as well as the full dominant scale) by mixing them up on the fretboard. To begin this mix, combine the major and minor pentatonic scales, as I do in Figure 15-5.

For a demonstration on how to mix major and minor pentatonic, watch Video Clip 36.

Notice that the mixture of both major and minor pentatonic scales includes all the notes from the dominant scale, too. So you've covered all your bases! You can move these scale patterns around the fretboard to play over other dominant 7th chords. For example, move everything up one fret to play over B♭7. Move everything down two frets to play over G7. You get the idea.

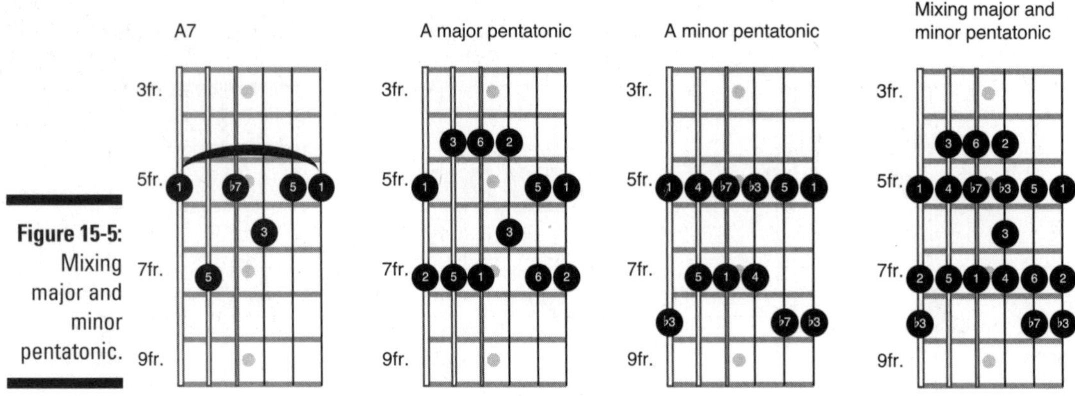

Figure 15-5: Mixing major and minor pentatonic.

Illustration courtesy of Desi Serna

The following songs provide perfect examples of mixing major and minor pentatonic scale patterns over a chord with a dominant 7th tonality:

- In "Johnny B. Goode" by Chuck Berry, most of the guitar solos, including the famous opening to the song, are based in the pentatonic mix from Figure 15-5, except that it's moved up one fret to B♭.
- "Crossroads (Live at Winterland)" by Cream, featuring Eric Clapton, is based in A and uses both A major and A minor pentatonic, sometimes mixed together, and other times used independently.
- In "Sunshine of Your Love," also by Cream, Clapton alternates between D major and D minor pentatonic scales.

Some other songs that feature lead guitarists either mixing or alternating between major and minor pentatonic scales include

"All Right Now" by Free (A)

"Flirtin' with Disaster" by Molly Hatchet (E)

"Get Back" by The Beatles (A)

"Hard to Handle" by The Black Crowes (B)

"Red House" by Jimi Hendrix (B with guitars tuned down one half-step to E♭)

Tackling Whole Chord Progressions with the Twelve-Bar Blues

After you know how to approach a dominant 7th chord in a blues fashion, you're ready to tackle a whole chord progression. The most common type of blues chord progression is the so-called *twelve-bar blues*. It's based on what appears to be the I-IV-V chords of a key, and it's actually one of the most popular chord progressions in all of popular music.

The twelve-bar blues chord progression has many variations. Figure 15-6 presents one very basic example in A. This example has three parts. The first guitar is playing a typical shuffle rhythm, using 5ths and 6ths, while the second guitar is strumming some 7th and 9th chords on the upbeat. The third part is a walking bass line drawn from the dominant scale of each chord.

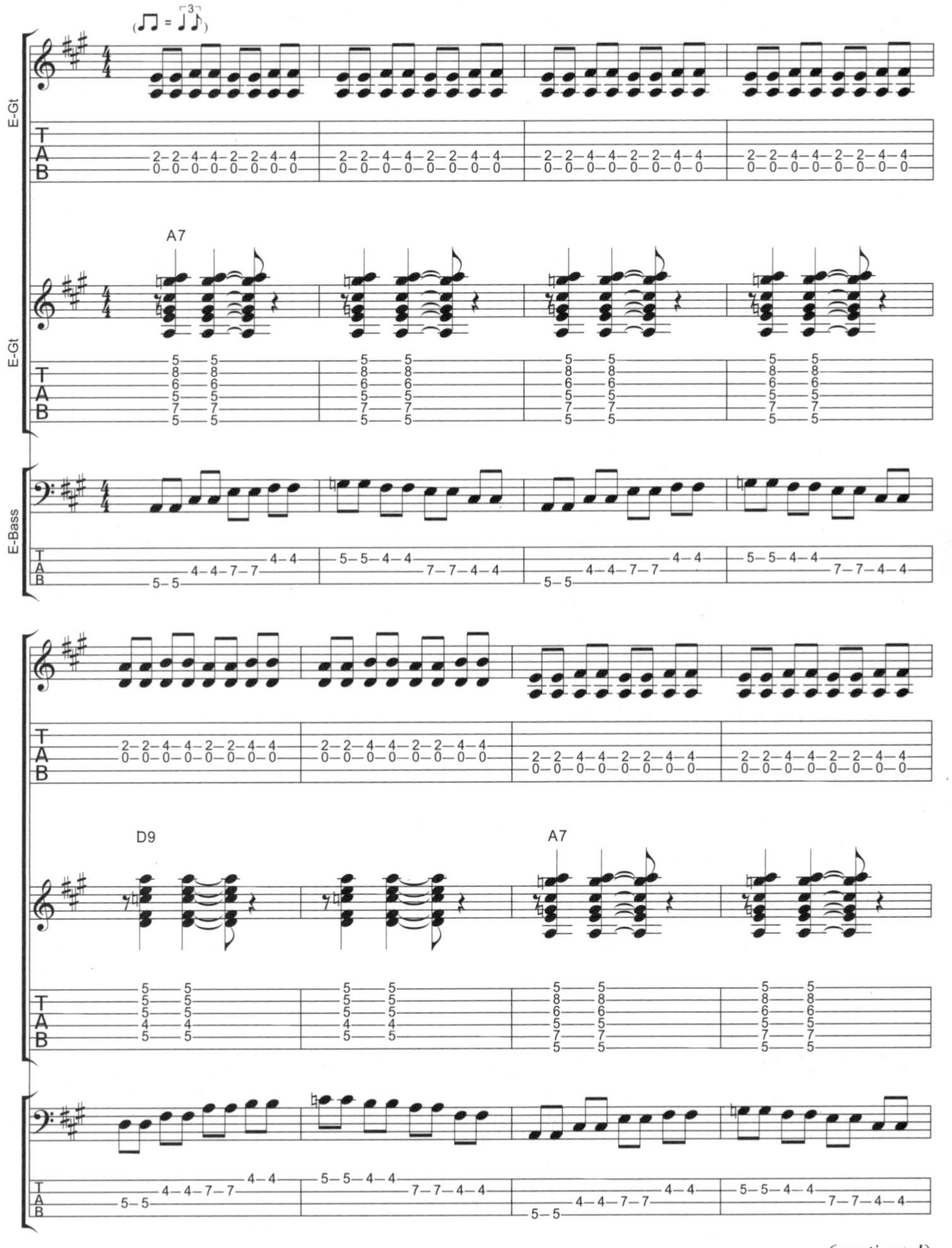

Figure 15-6: Twelve-bar blues in A.

(continued)

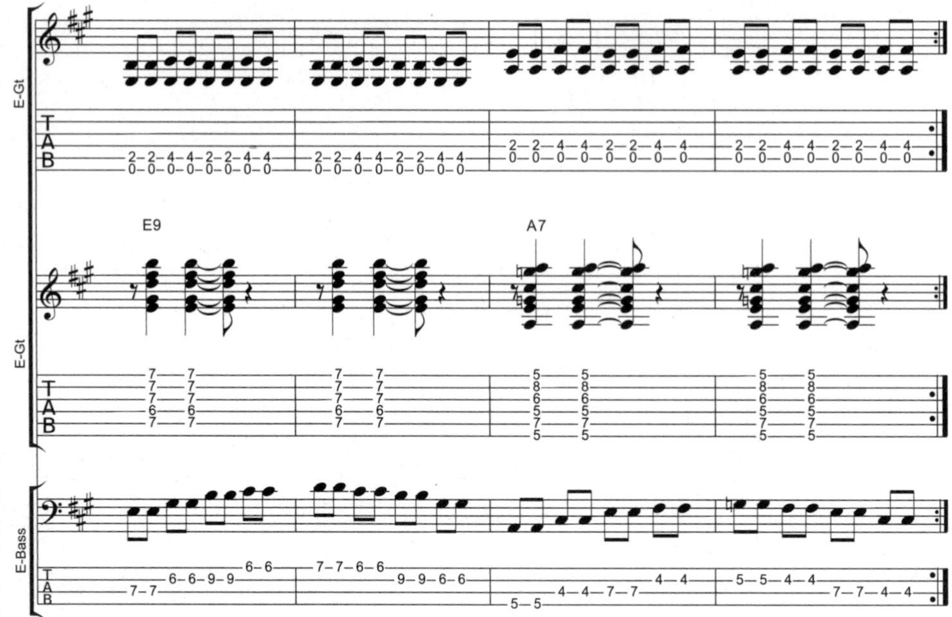

Figure 15-6 *(continued)*: Twelve-bar blues in A.

Illustration courtesy of Desi Serna

You can hear this twelve-bar blues example and play along with it by listening to Audio Track 23. For a demonstration on how to play over this twelve-bar blues example, watch Video Clip 37.

Blues progressions like the one shown in Figure 15-6 are considered to be I-IV-V progressions. However, only one scale degree produces a dominant 7th chord, and that's the 5th, V. So because each chord is some form of dominant 7th, each one is actually a V7 chord from a different scale. In other words, blues progressions are really V7-V7-V7, with each V7 chord representing a different parent major scale.

The chords in Figure 15-6 break down like this:

- A7 is V7 from the D major scale.
- D7 is V7 from the G major scale.
- E7 is V7 from the A major scale.

You can clearly see these chords in the bass line. The bass plays the 1st, 3rd, 5th, 6th, and ♭7th on each chord. These intervals are drawn directly from each chord's parent major. You can also think of each scale as being Mixolydian mode since the 5th is the tonic. Because the 5th mode is better known as the dominant scale, the scales used over each chord are A dominant, D dominant, and E dominant.

Here's another thing to consider: Each chord is drawn from a different parent major scale, so each chord change is technically a key change. But because the tonic chord in the whole progression is A, musicians think of everything as being in the key of A, which is why they still count the chords as I-IV-V. Notice that the key signature in Figure 15-6 is A major throughout and that each chord requires the use of accidentals, except for E7, which is drawn from the A major scale.

The following sections present the different ways to play the twelve-bar blues progression, using the example shown in Figure 15-6. As you experiment with these options, remember to walk before you run. Start with an easy option, like sticking with one pentatonic scale over a whole progression, and gradually add on from there as you become more proficient. Keep in mind that you don't need to master all these options at once. It's more important that you simply understand how blues techniques influence popular music and know what to look for in guitar songs.

Switching dominant scales

As you play over these blues changes, you can switch dominant scales as you go. You don't have to stick to the intervals and patterns that the bass uses. Instead, feel free to play in any position on the neck and use any degrees from the scales. In Figure 15-7, I show you one way to switch scales by staying near the 5th position.

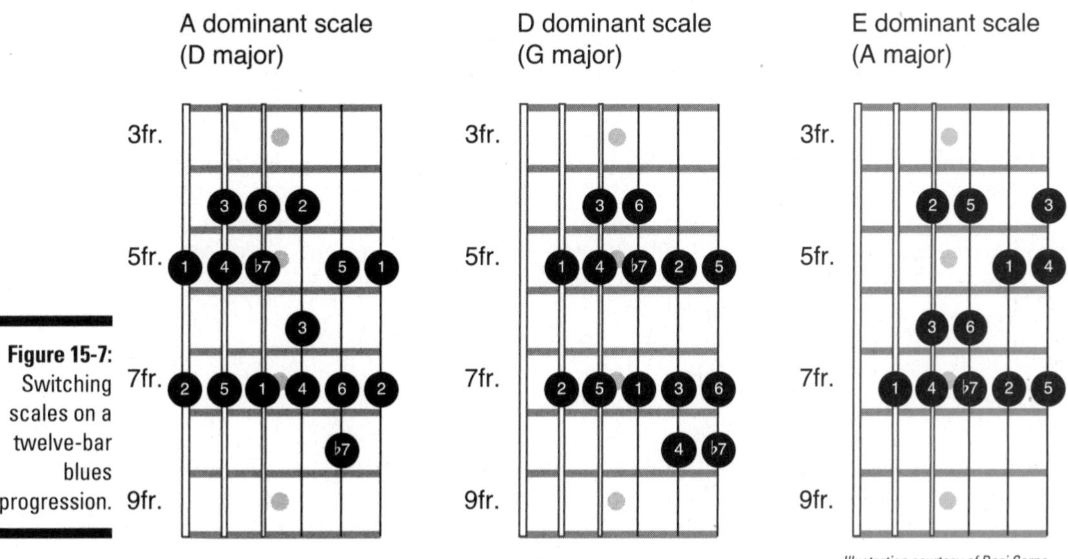

Figure 15-7: Switching scales on a twelve-bar blues progression.

Note: The patterns shown in Figure 15-7 are simply major scale patterns. Just because I label them as *dominant scales* doesn't mean they're new patterns. Refer to the parent major scales in parentheses if you need help identifying them. I start each pattern on the tonic of each dominant scale, but you're free to play any other notes that belong to the scale, including those that may occur below the tonics.

Sticking with minor pentatonic

Knowing how to play and switch full dominant scales like I do in Figure 15-7 is important to understanding how a blues progression is put together and how you can approach such a progression as a soloist. However, blues guitarists usually opt for a different and much simpler approach. The preferred scale among blues players is the minor pentatonic, and instead of switching scales, they stick with one minor pentatonic scale over the whole progression.

For example, you can play A minor pentatonic over all of Figure 15-6. Some of the notes in A minor pentatonic clash a bit with the chords because they're not related to the chords and parent scales, but this edgy sound is a defining characteristic of the blues.

Using a major pentatonic scale

Using minor over major is by far the most common choice among blues soloists, but another option is to play a major pentatonic scale over a whole blues progression. For example, in Figure 15-6, you can use A major pentatonic over everything. The sound isn't quite as bluesy, but it works.

When bluesmen use the major pentatonic, they usually mix it with the minor pentatonic, as you hear in songs like "Johnny B. Goode" by Chuck Berry, "Crossroads" by Cream, and "All Right Now" by Free. Keep in mind that this blues technique is very popular and also applies to other styles of music, especially rock, pop, country, folk, and jazz.

Changing pentatonic scales on each chord

Aside from sticking with one pentatonic scale over a whole blues progression, you can also change pentatonic scales on each chord. So in Figure 15-6, you'd play A pentatonic over A7, D pentatonic over D7, and E pentatonic over E7, with the use of major or minor, or a mix thereof, being your choice.

Generally speaking, rock and blues players like to keep things simple and stick with pentatonic scales that correspond only to the tonic chord in a progression. Changing scales over each chord is far more common in country and jazz. However, a good example of a blues-based song that does some switching over chords with major and minor pentatonic scales is "Keep Your Hands to Yourself" by Georgia Satellites.

Playing the Blues Scale

You can't talk about blues without mentioning the so-called *blues scale,* which is really just a pentatonic scale with a chromatic passing tone. This added scale tone is a ♭5th in the minor pentatonic. When the pattern is applied as major, the same note in the patterns becomes a ♭3rd.

Figure 15-8 includes A minor pentatonic patterns with added ♭5ths shown in gray. These are the same five pentatonic patterns you play in Chapter 11.

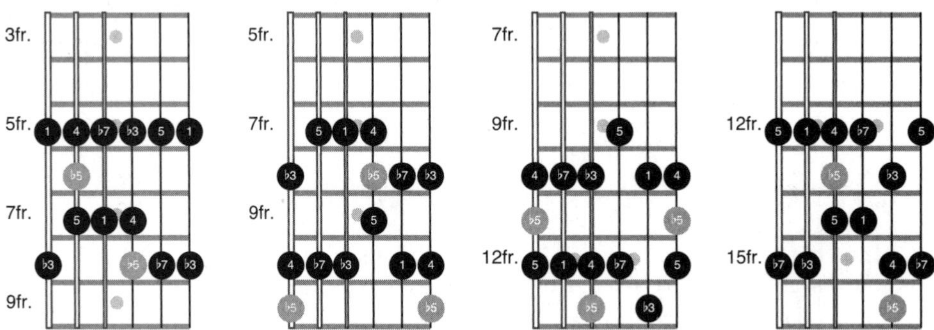

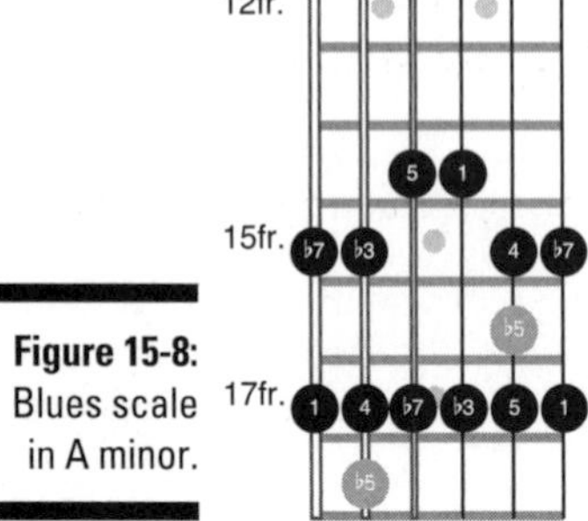

Figure 15-8: Blues scale in A minor.

Illustration courtesy of Desi Serna

To see a demonstration on using the blues scale, watch Video Clip 38.

You don't have to memorize and practice all these blues scale patterns, but I do recommend that you at least try them all and commit the first one to memory. That way, as you work through songs with blues elements in them, you'll be able to make sense of any ♭5ths you see.

Because C is the relative major to A minor, you use the same notes and patterns to play C major pentatonic that you use to play A minor pentatonic. The only difference is which note functions as the tonic and counts as the 1st scale degree. In Figure 15-9, I've redrawn the same patterns from Figure 15-8 but marked the C notes as 1. I've renumbered everything else from there. So what was a ♭5th in the A minor blues scale becomes a ♭3rd in the C major blues scale.

You can transpose the blues scale patterns in Figures 15-8 and 15-9 to play blues scales in other keys. For instance, if you want to play a minor blues scale for a particular note on the 6th string, then put your 1st finger on it and play the 1st pattern. If you want to play a major blues scale for a particular note on the 6th string, then put your 4th finger on it and play the 1st pattern. Putting your 4th finger on a note means that you actually start the 1st pattern three frets lower with your 1st finger. For example, the 1st A minor blues scale pattern starts at the 5th fret with the 1st finger. The 1st A major blues scale pattern starts at the 2nd fret with the 1st finger, putting your 4th finger at the 5th fret on A.

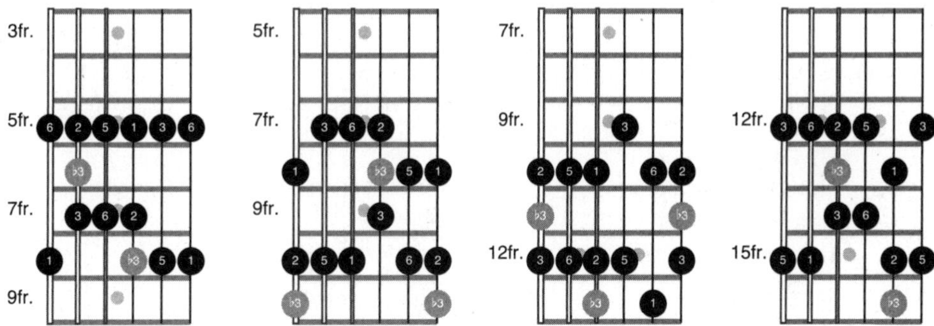

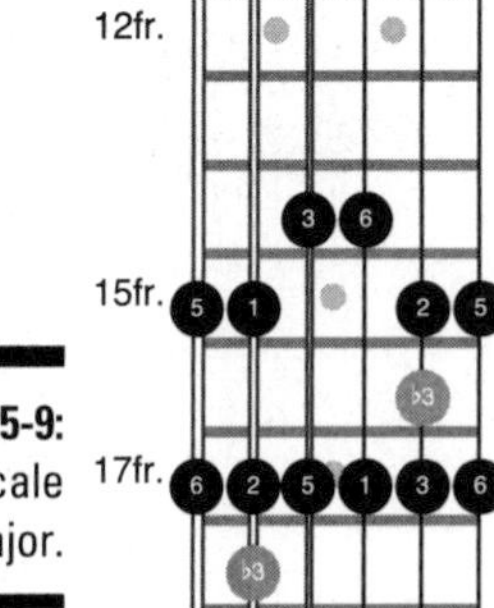

Figure 15-9: Blues scale in C major.

Illustration courtesy of Desi Serna

Songs that make use of the major or minor blues scale at some point include the following:

"Black Dog" by Led Zeppelin

"The Devil Went Down to Georgia" by the Charlie Daniels Band

"Heartbreaker" by Led Zeppelin

"Love Her Madly" by The Doors

"The Old Man Down the Road" by John Fogerty

"Pride and Joy" by Stevie Ray Vaughan

"Roadhouse Blues" by The Doors

"Rock and Roll, Hoochie Koo" by Rick Derringer

"Sir Duke" by Stevie Wonder

"Sunshine of Your Love" by Cream

"Take It Easy" by the Eagles

"Truckin'" by Grateful Dead

Some songs, like "Black Dog" by Led Zeppelin and "Manic Depression" by Jimi Hendrix, make use of an additional chromatic passing tone in the pentatonic scale. Specifically, they add a chromatic step in between ♭7 and 1 in the minor pentatonic, as shown in Figure 15-10.

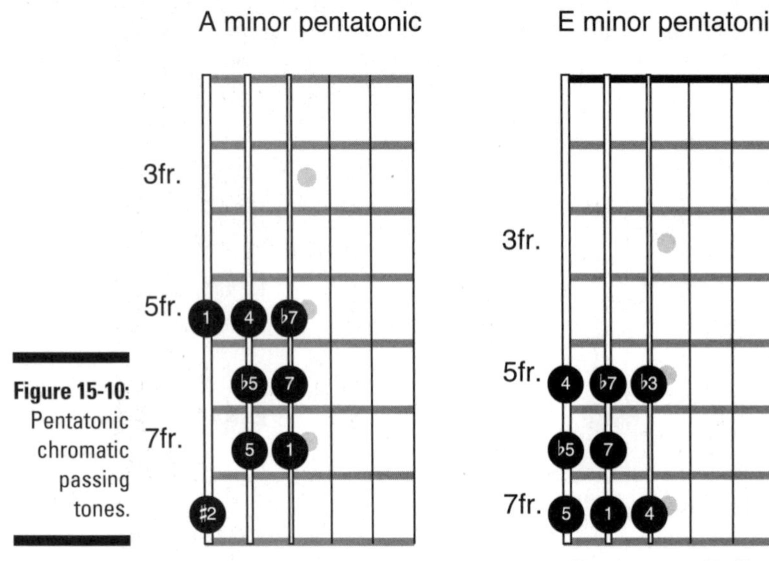

Figure 15-10: Pentatonic chromatic passing tones.

Illustration courtesy of Desi Serna

Whenever you're applying the pentatonic scale, whether it's major or minor and whether you're using it on a blues song or something else, you can always try using chromatic passing tones. If they sound good to your ears, go with them. If they don't, skip them.

Blues music often features chromatic passing tones. Whenever you come across a run of three or more notes in consecutive frets, you're probably just connecting pentatonic scale tones with chromatics.

Part V

Part of Tens

Welcome yourself to the Hotel California with ten steps to applying scales over the Eagles' classic hit. You can find these steps in a free article at www.dummies.com/extras/guitartheory.

In this part . . .

- Unpack the theory to ten popular guitar songs and see how the elements and concepts from the book specifically apply to them.
- Get some practice with pentatonic scales, major scales, modes, and harmonic minor by applying scales to ten sample chord progressions.
- Look at ten steps to help you best apply the information in the book, including practice tips and playing advice.

Chapter 16

Ten Guitar Songs Worth Learning

In This Chapter

- Applying guitar theory to ten popular songs
- Identifying the scales and chords used in some classic guitar songs

Each chapter of this book is full of song references that make great examples of the concepts I cover. Of course, I recommend that you look up and learn as many of these songs as you can. But if you're looking for a shorter list of must-practice songs, you've come to the right place. In this chapter, you get a closer look at ten of the songs I list elsewhere in the book. I've chosen these particular songs because they're very popular, they make exceptional examples of the theory I cover throughout the book, and they're relatively easy to play.

Note: I can't show you exactly how these songs are played. I don't have permission to print the actual notation and guitar tab here. But you can easily purchase the official sheet music and tab so you can learn the parts just as they appear in the original recordings.

While sheet music is great for showing you where to place your fingers on the guitar neck to re-create a certain song, it doesn't explain where the chord shapes come from, why the chord progression works, and what scale the notes belong to. So these are the things I focus on in this chapter.

Speaking of sheet music, I strongly recommend getting your hands on the tab for the following songs and referring to it as you work through this chapter. Some good websites to find complete, accurate, fully licensed, and legal guitar tab are `www.musicnotes.com`, `www.sheetmusicplus.com`, and `www.musicdispatch.com`. I suggest listening to the audio recordings, too.

"Wish You Were Here" by Pink Floyd

"Wish You Were Here" is a great example of using the pentatonic scale patterns from Chapter 10 and the added chord tones as a result of pedal tones from Chapter 5. It's also a good introduction to lead guitar playing.

The song mainly features acoustic guitar playing. It opens with a 12-string guitar playing a combination of chords and melody in the open position. This track becomes the underlying accompaniment for a second acoustic guitar (a standard 6-string) that plays in a more lead-like fashion.

When you're first practicing the 12-string opening to this song, ignore the chords you hear and focus on just the scale melody (which you can play on a regular 6-string guitar). The scale melody starts with a hammer-on from the open 5th string, A, to the 2nd fret of the 5th string, B. These notes and the ones that follow them are all drawn directly from the open position G major pentatonic scale pattern shown in Figure 16-1.

Note: This scale pattern can be either G major or E minor pentatonic, depending on which note functions as the tonic. As you see later in this section, it's played over both the chords G and Em in "Wish You Were Here," so you can think of it in either its major or minor form. To keep things simple, I call it G major pentatonic; the opening resolves on a G chord, anyway.

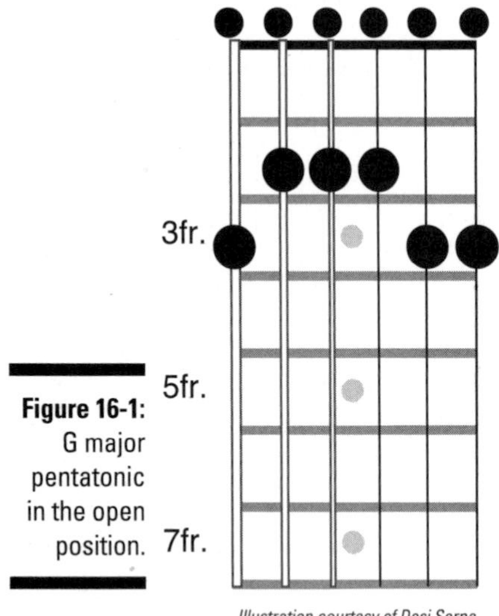

Figure 16-1: G major pentatonic in the open position.

Illustration courtesy of Desi Serna

If you're new to using scales to play melodies, this is a great song to start with. The tempo is nice and slow, you only need a finger or two, you don't need any alternate picking, and the hammer-on articulation is a cinch.

Looking at the chords, the progression is based on Em, G, and A7. But instead of playing standard shapes, the guitar holds and sustains the 3rd fret of the 1st and 2nd strings. This use of pedal tones ends up creating chords with more depth and color. It also gives them more complicated names, as you see here and in Figure 16-2. (The numbers in the figure indicate fingerings.)

- **Em7:** The Em7 chord is a partial shape based on a common open Em chord. The addition of the D note at the 3rd fret of the 2nd string makes the chord Em7.
- **G:** The G is a standard open G. You can play an open G chord by using either the open 2nd string, B, or the 3rd fret of the 2nd string, D. Both notes are part of the G triad, G-B-D. By using the D on the 2nd string, you keep the same notes, D and G, sustaining over all three chords, creating a type of pedal tone.
- **A7sus4:** Keeping the 3rd frets of the 1st and 2nd strings as part of the A chord adds a 7th and 4th and removes the 3rd, hence the name *7sus4.* The open 3rd string, G, is another 7th.

The second guitar that comes in playing lead licks also uses the G major pentatonic scale. It begins by sliding along the 3rd string from the open position pattern to the next position between the 3rd and 5th frets. From there, it uses some standard guitar articulations, including slides, pull-offs, hammer-ons, bends, and double-stops. ***Note:*** Bending on an acoustic guitar is difficult, especially in this position. To play this part properly, use very light-gauge strings with an unwound 3rd string, G, or use an electric guitar.

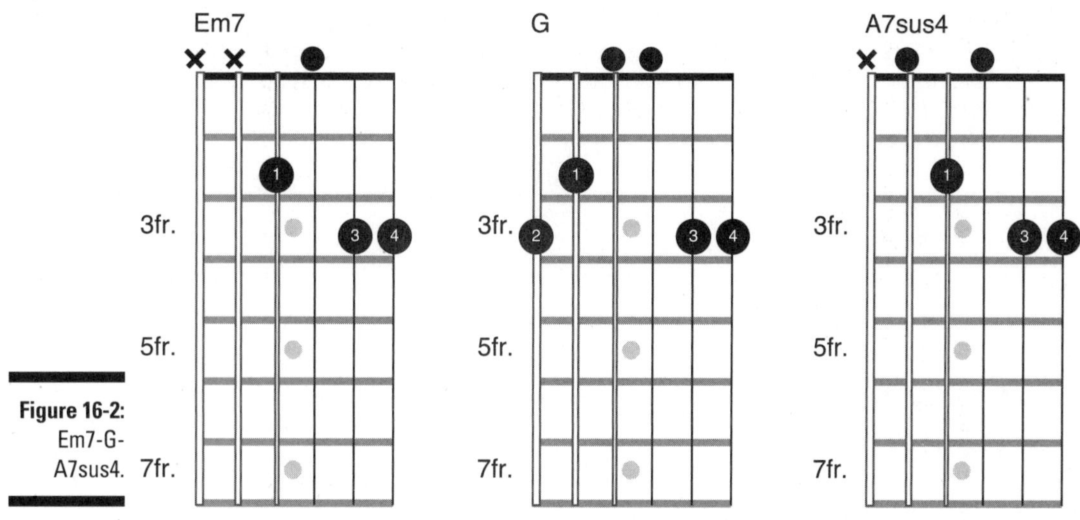

Figure 16-2: Em7-G-A7sus4.

Illustration courtesy of Desi Serna

"La Bamba" by Los Lobos

"La Bamba" is a Mexican folk song first made famous by Ritchie Valens and later by Los Lobos, with the latter being my focus here. It's a great example of the I-IV-V chord progression from Chapter 6, the use of major scale patterns from Chapter 12, and the technique of playing in 3rds from Chapter 2.

The song is very simple from a theory standpoint — key of C, I-IV-V, and major scale patterns. You can't get any more basic than that; however, you may have a hard time keeping up because of the tempo and the techniques involved.

The song opens up by using the C major scale in the open position, as shown in Figure 16-3.

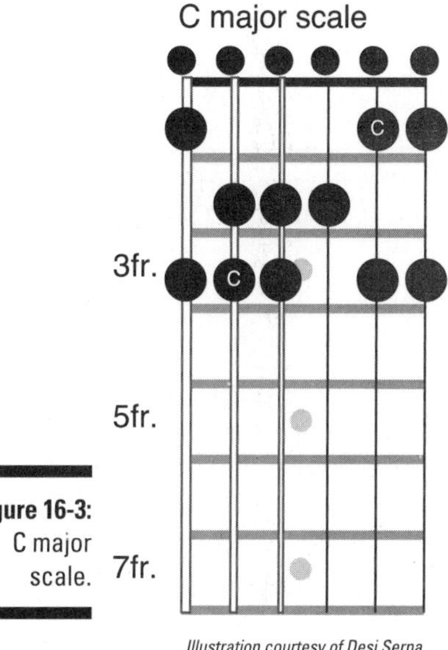

Figure 16-3: C major scale.

Illustration courtesy of Desi Serna

The riff outlines the chord progression C-F-G, which is I-IV-V in the key of C. Double-stops, which are groups of two notes, appear frequently in the form of 3rds (that is, two notes separated by three major scale degrees). You can complete the whole C major scale in 3rds by following the tab in Figure 16-4.

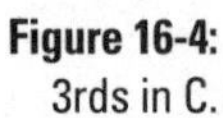

Figure 16-4: 3rds in C.

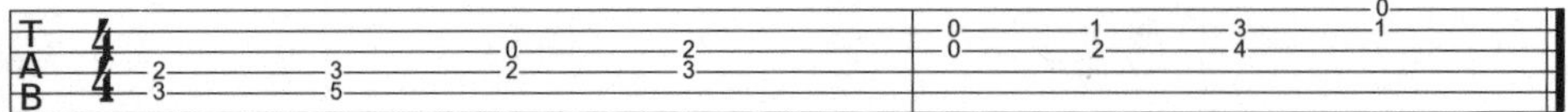

Illustration courtesy of Desi Serna

Later, the guitar solo section makes good use of C major scale patterns, mainly in the open position but also by sliding up the neck into other positions. At points, you hear some very fast alternate picking on single notes, called *tremolo picking*, and even the use of pedal point, applied here by repeatedly returning to the 3rd string open after sounding other scale notes at other frets on the same string. You play an example of pedal point in C in Figure 16-5.

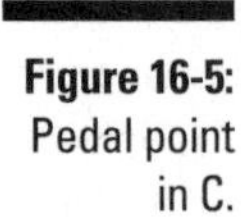

Figure 16-5: Pedal point in C.

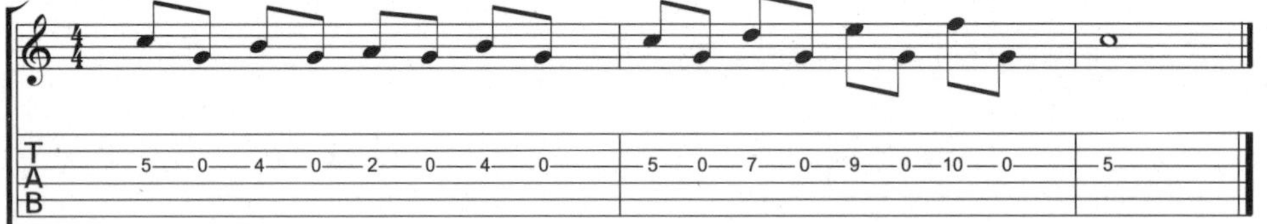

Illustration courtesy of Desi Serna

"Jack and Diane" by John Mellencamp

Here's a little ditty about using partial CAGED form barre chords from Chapter 4 to create unique rhythm guitar parts. Each section of "Jack and Diane" is based on the chords A, D, and E, yet each section sounds different. You see some of the chord voicings used during the song in Figure 16-6.

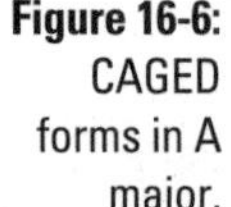

Figure 16-6: CAGED forms in A major.

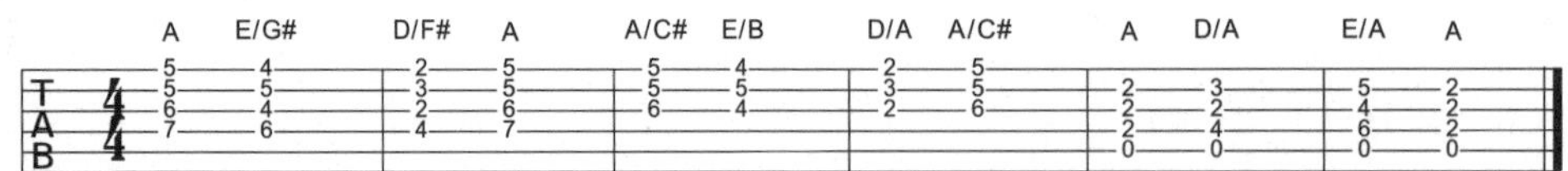

Illustration courtesy of Desi Serna

In addition to using CAGED forms, "Jack and Diane" also features chords with added chord tones (discussed in more detail in Chapter 5), as shown in Figure 16-7. The numbers in the figure indicate fingering.

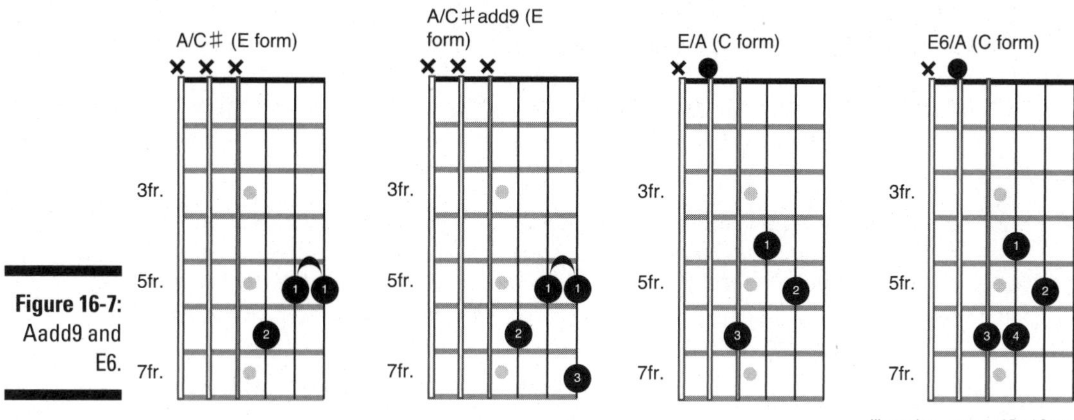

Figure 16-7: Aadd9 and E6.

Illustration courtesy of Desi Serna

"Brown Eyed Girl" by Van Morrison

"Brown Eyed Girl" is another classic example of a I-IV-V chord progression (see Chapter 6) and of using 3rds (see Chapter 2). This song is in the key of G and uses the chord changes G-C-G-D. An Em chord pops up from time to time for a little variation. The trademark guitar riff at the beginning of the song uses both the G and C major scales in 3rds in a way similar to Figure 16-8.

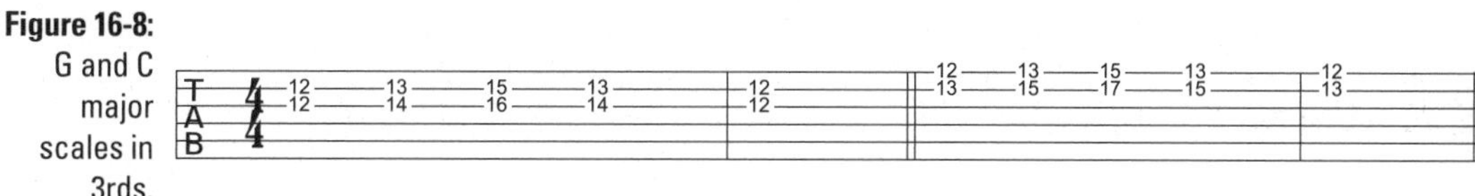

Figure 16-8: G and C major scales in 3rds.

Illustration courtesy of Desi Serna

Inverted 3rds, better known as 6ths, are featured throughout the verses, similar to Figure 16-9.

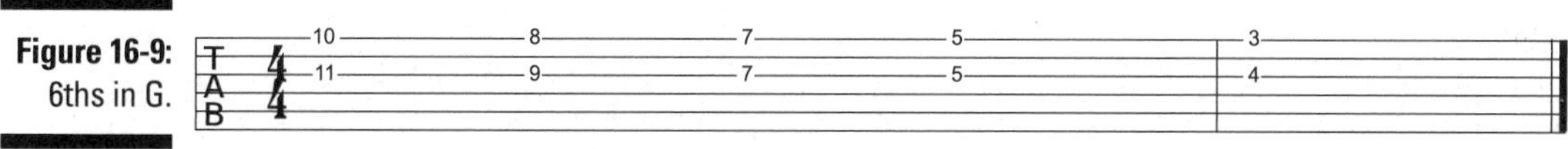

Figure 16-9: 6ths in G.

Illustration courtesy of Desi Serna

Another reason why you absolutely must learn "Brown Eyed Girl" is that it's one of the most popular songs of all time, especially among girls with brown eyes (and among girls with blue eyes who stand right in front of the stage, pointing at their eyes and demanding, "Say blue! Say blue!").

"With or Without You" by U2

"With or Without You" has a few features that make it one of the most important examples of playing contemporary music in this chapter. These features include implied chords, ambient guitar playing, sustained notes, pedal point, and the use of a delay effect.

Starting with the D-A-Bm-G chord progression, the chords are never explicitly played. Instead, they're implied by the root notes played on the bass and the notes featured in the vocal melody and guitar parts. Because all the notes are drawn from the D major scale, you can conclude that the bass notes D, A, B, and G represent I-V-vi-IV from D. (You get to know chord progressions and discover how to play by numbers in Chapter 6.)

The U2 guitarist The Edge intentionally avoided playing plain triads and block chord changes, so the opening guitar track in "With or Without You" is very ambient and features sustained notes using a special guitar that produces an effect similar to an E-bow. Focusing more on sonic texture than composition or rhythm, this style of playing has become quite common in popular styles of contemporary pop music, often supporting other guitar parts that are played in a standard fashion.

One of the song's signature guitar riffs — the one that's introduced around the 1:50 mark — is essentially a Dsus4-D chord change in the 7th position that's played over the regular I-V-vi-IV progression. You see an example composed in a similar way in Figure 16-10. This example is a type of pedal point from Chapter 5 because it repeats a melodic figuration and sustains a D at the 10th fret of the 1st string throughout. When played over the bass note A, the notes of Dsus4 create an A7sus4 sound. This whole riff sounds even bigger thanks to the use of *delay,* a guitar effect that echoes the notes being played.

You have to hear both parts of Figure 16-10 together to get the true effect of the harmony. So I suggest recording one of the parts first and then playing along with it using the other part. You can also play along with a recording of the song itself if you prefer.

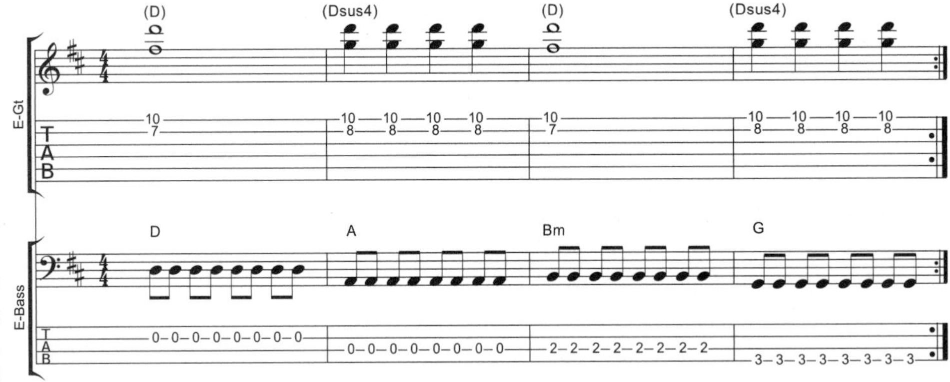

Figure 16-10: Dsus4-D riff.

Illustration courtesy of Desi Serna

Another signature guitar riff occurs just past the 4:00 mark in "With or Without You." This part is drawn from the first two strings in the chords D-Dsus2-D-Dsus4 played in the open position, while the regular I-V-vi-IV progression remains constant. You see an example composed in a similar fashion in Figure 16-11. When played over the bass note A, the notes of Dsus2 create an Asus4 sound. The notes on the 1st string relate to the basic triads in the regular chord progression, and the stationary D note on the 2nd string functions as a type of pedal tone. The use of delay gives this part more depth as well. Eventually, the previous guitar riff is reintroduced to the mix, and you hear both parts together, which creates very rich harmony over what is otherwise a simple chord progression.

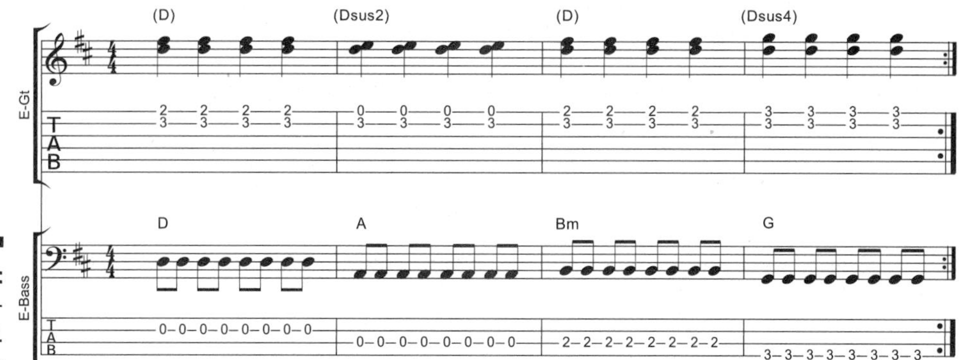

Figure 16-11: D-Dsus2-D-Dsus4 riff.

Illustration courtesy of Desi Serna

"With or Without You" has some moments when the music is very sparse and other moments that feature rich harmony and depth. Through it all, though, the guitars never actually play standard chord changes. This performance technique has become a staple in popular music thanks to the influence of U2.

"Stairway to Heaven" by Led Zeppelin

This is one of the most popular guitar songs of all time and for good reasons. Not only is it a great piece of music to listen to, but it's also a goldmine of guitar chords and techniques. In it, you hear both 6- and 12-string guitars, both acoustic and electric. Some parts are picked and arpeggiated, some are strummed, and still others are fingerpicked. Other features include CAGED chord forms, chord inversions, voice leading, added chord tones, modal interchange, pedal tones, riffs, and guitar solos. My goodness, what more can a guitar player ask for?

The opening features chords connected by descending chromatic voice leading, which I discuss in Chapter 9. On the 4th string beginning at the 7th fret, you move down in half steps to the 2rd fret. This series of changes, which is similar to Figure 16-12, uses some shapes from the CAGED chord system (see Chapter 4).

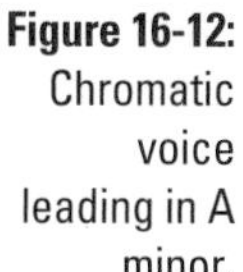

Figure 16-12: Chromatic voice leading in A minor.

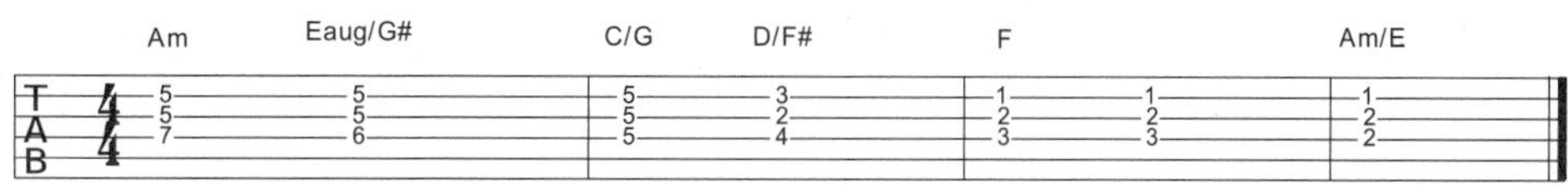

Illustration courtesy of Desi Serna

After a repeat of the intro, the next section of the song features fingerpicked open position chords, including an Fmaj7 and Dsus4, as shown in Figure 16-13. (The numbers in the figure indicate fingers.)

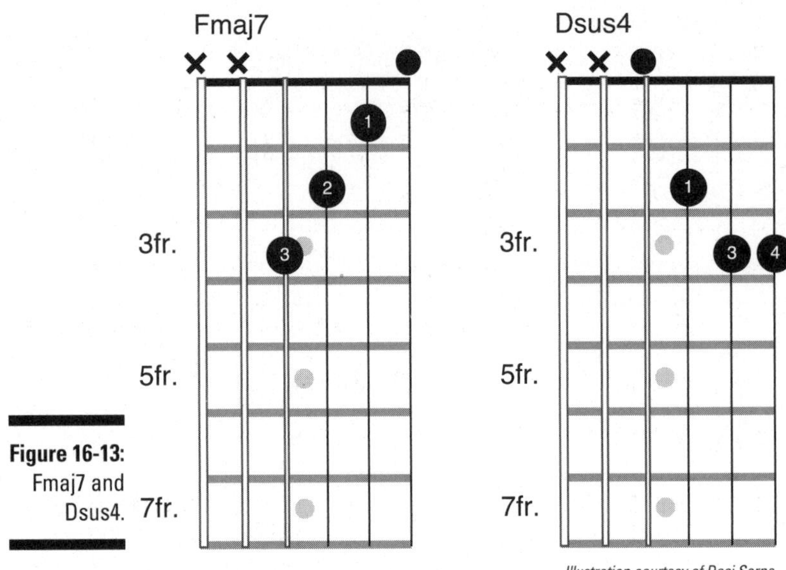

Figure 16-13: Fmaj7 and Dsus4.

Around the 2:14 mark, a new interlude section features layered, strummed guitars, including a 12-string. You also hear some more added chord tones (Chapter 5) and, in the Em/D-D-C/D changes, the use of pedal point (Chapter 5) with D sustained in the bass position of each chord. See Figure 16-14.

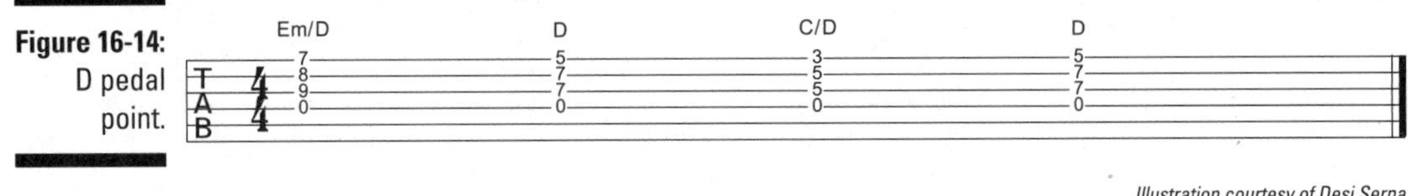

Figure 16-14: D pedal point.

The extended guitar solo section is based on Am-G-F in the key of A minor, as shown in Figure 16-15.

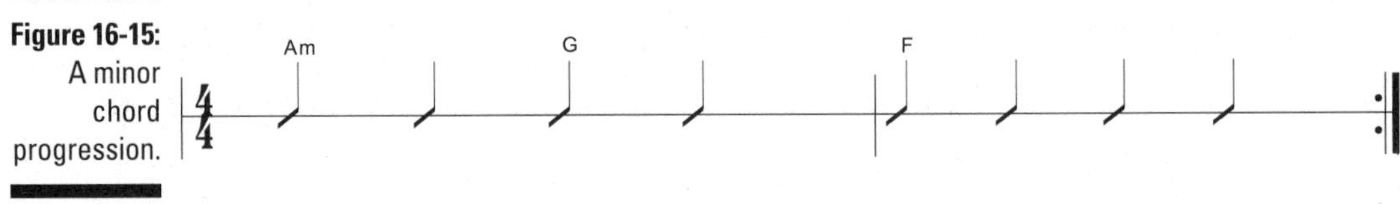

Figure 16-15: A minor chord progression.

Led Zeppelin's guitarist Jimmy Page positions himself in familiar A minor pentatonic patterns but adds a minor 6th, F, to the scale to outline the F chord in the underlying progression (see Figure 16-16).

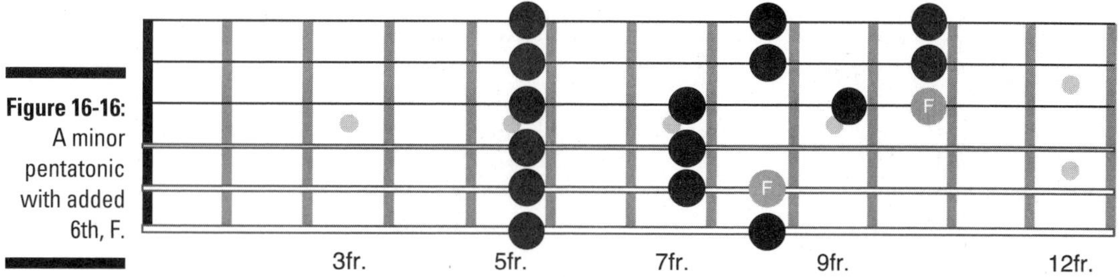

Figure 16-16: A minor pentatonic with added 6th, F.

Illustration courtesy of Desi Serna

"Smooth" by Santana

"Smooth" makes this list for two reasons. First, because the song is a massive chart-topping hit. Second, because it features the harmonic minor scale you play in Chapter 14. The primary chord progression in the song is Am-F-E7. That's i-♭VI-V7 in the key of A minor. Guitarist Carlos Santana plays A minor scale patterns over most of the song, but you can hear him using the raised 7th of harmonic minor during the V7 chord (see Figure 16-17). The harmonic minor scale plays a very important role in popular music and harmony.

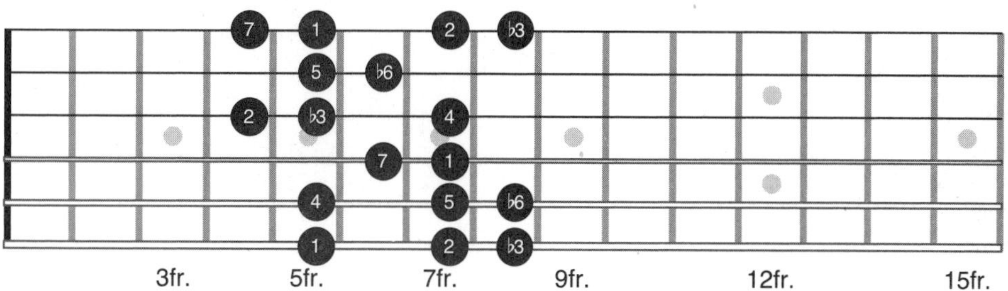

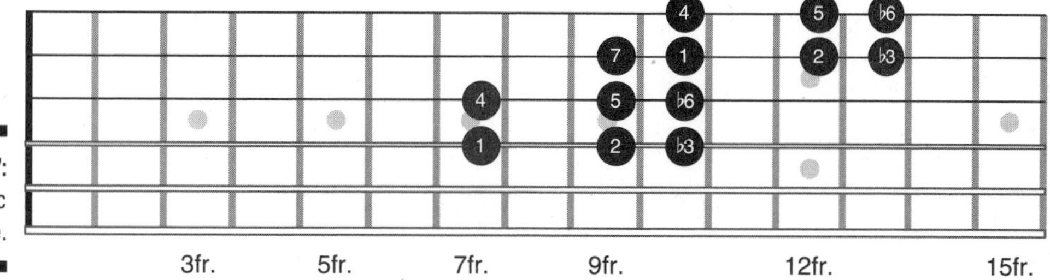

Figure 16-17: A harmonic minor scale.

Illustration courtesy of Desi Serna

"Sunshine of Your Love" by Cream

"Sunshine of Your Love" includes one of the most recognizable guitar riffs of all time. It consists primarily of power chords and pentatonic scale patterns (see Chapter 11), but it's also a great example of using the chromatic passing tones I cover in Chapter 15. Plus, the main parts of the song are simple enough for many beginner guitarists to play.

Figure 16-18 includes an example of D minor and G minor pentatonic, both with an added ♭5th chromatic passing tone. When guitarists use the pentatonic this way, it's often called the *blues scale* (see Chapter 15). Play these patterns backward and you nearly have the "Sunshine of Your Love" riff.

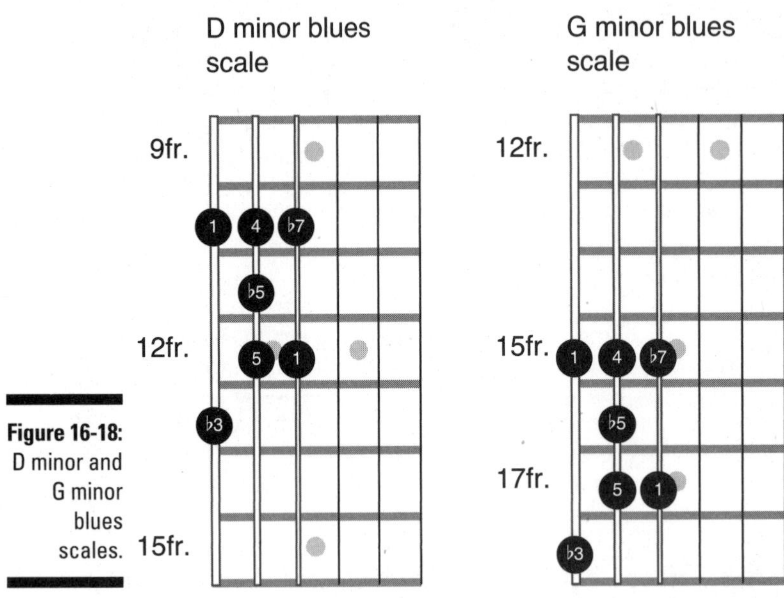

Figure 16-18: D minor and G minor blues scales.

The guitar solo, which is more challenging to play than the main riff, mixes both D major and D minor pentatonic scales. You see both scales in Figure 16-19.

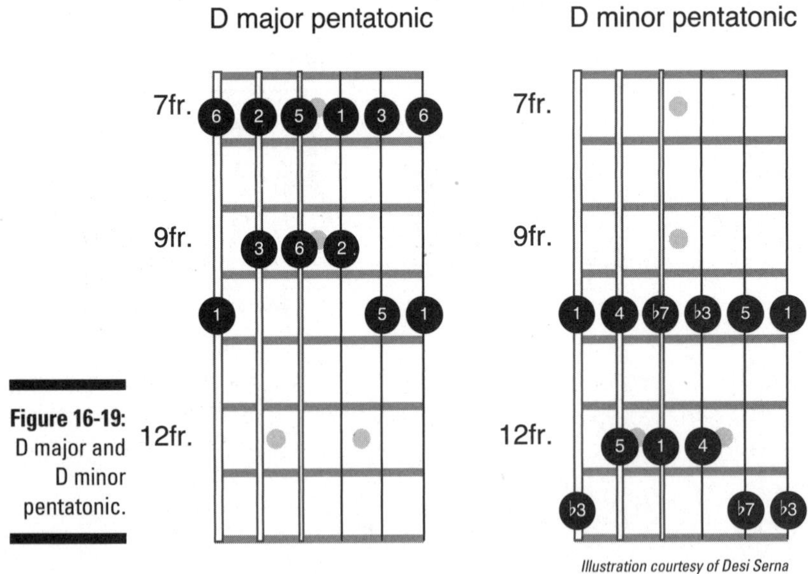

Figure 16-19: D major and D minor pentatonic.

"Johnny B. Goode" by Chuck Berry

"Johnny B. Goode" is one of the most recognizable songs in music history. In fact, a copy of it is currently hurling through space aboard the Voyager spacecraft waiting for any extraterrestrial life to discover and, presumably, boogie woogie to (alien parents aren't ready for it, but their kids are going to love it).

What's so important about the lead guitar parts in this song is the use of both B♭ major and minor pentatonic scale licks. Combining these two scales produces both chromatic passing tones and the dominant scale that you play in Chapter 15. See the sample run in Figure 16-20 and notice the switch from a minor 3rd to a major 3rd at the 6th and 7th frets of the 3rd string. This approach to lead guitar playing has been very influential on the blues, rock, and pop music that has followed this original 1958 hit.

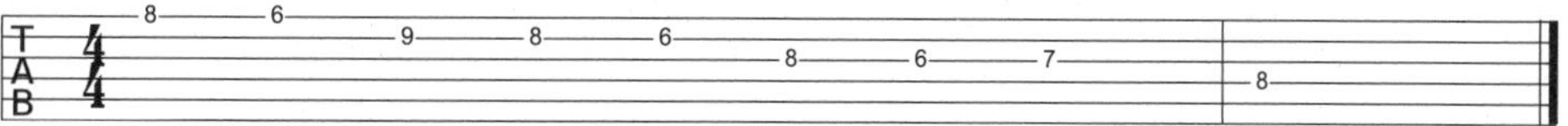

Figure 16-20: Mixing scales in B♭.

Illustration courtesy of Desi Serna

"Jingle Bell Rock" by Bobby Helms

Despite being titled "Jingle Bell *Rock,*" this song was performed in the crossover style known as *rockabilly.* But its jazz elements are what make the song so beneficial to learn. The music features major, minor, and dominant 7th chords (see Chapter 5), voice leading and secondary dominants (see Chapter 9), and diminished chords (see Chapter 10). You can play a chord progression arranged in a similar fashion to it in Figure 16-21.

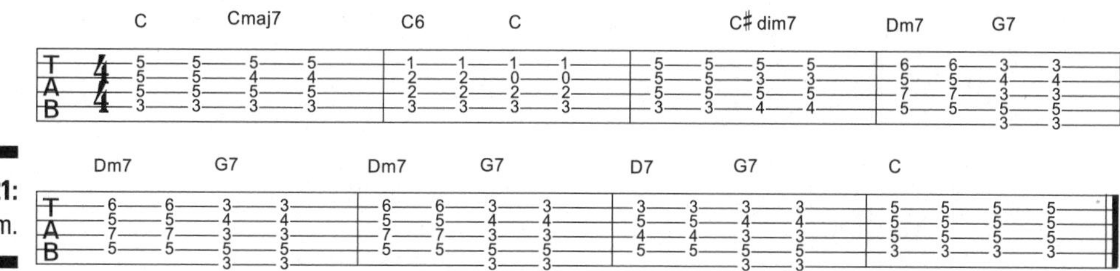

Figure 16-21: Jingle Jam.

Illustration courtesy of Desi Serna

The types of chord changes you encounter in "Jingle Bell Rock" are quite different from what you typically find in a standard blues or rock song. So learning this particular song really broadens your horizon and prepares you to study more complicated types of music like jazz.

Chapter 17

Ten Sample Scale Applications

In This Chapter

- Applying scales to ten sample chord progressions
- Looking at some popular songs that use these progressions

Guitarists use scales to add melody, harmony, riffs, and solos over chords and progressions. In this chapter, you practice applying scales over ten sample chord progressions. These chord changes involve the use of pentatonic scales, major scales, modes, and harmonic minor.

Here are a few general rules to keep in mind as you work through the progressions in this chapter:

- The pentatonic scale follows the tonic chord in a progression. If the tonic chord is major, you play the same major pentatonic scale over it. If the tonic chord is minor, you play the same minor pentatonic scale over it.
- When applying the major scale, you have to consider all the chords and find out which parent major scale they fit into *all together*. To do so, you have to fit the chords into the chord patterns I cover in Chapters 3 and 6.
- When the major scale is in use, the tonic may not always be 1. For example, sometimes the 6th scale degree is the starting point as in the relative or natural minor scale. Other times you see the 2nd, 3rd, 4th, or 5th used as the starting point producing the different modes.
- When a V7 chord leads to a minor tonic chord in a minor key, you have a harmonic minor progression, which requires you to raise the 7th degree of the minor scale.

G-Em-C-D

With this progression, you have a handful of different chords, but one of them, G, is the tonal center of the progression as a whole. Because the G major chord is the tonic, you can play the G major pentatonic scale over the whole progression.

If you were to play all these chords on the fretboard as common barre chords by using the chord patterns I cover in Chapters 3 and 6, then you'd see that they fit into the G major scale as chords I, vi, IV, and V. For this reason, you can play the G major scale over the whole progression. Try it — it's a perfect fit. Most players favor playing in a pentatonic scale pattern and then adding in G major scale notes in the same position (see Ionian mode in Chapter 13). "Last Kiss" by Pearl Jam and "Wonderful Tonight" by Eric Clapton both use the G major pentatonic scale and the G major scale over similar chord changes.

E-B-C♯m-A

Here, you have a chord progression that centers on an E major chord, so you play the E major pentatonic scale over it. An E major chord appears in three different major scales, but the E major scale is the only one that features an E together with a B, C♯m, and A. Play these chords on the fretboard as common barre chords by using the chord patterns in Chapters 3 and 6 and you'll see what I mean: They're I-V-vi-IV. For this reason, you can play the E major scale over the whole progression. "Beast of Burden" by The Rolling Stones follows a similar progression, using the same scales.

E-D-A-E

Here's another progression that revolves around E. So you can play E major pentatonic and the E major scale over it, right? Wrong! E major pentatonic works because the tonic chord is E, but the rest of the progression isn't drawn from the E major scale, so the E major scale doesn't work. All together, these three chords fit into the A major scale. They're V-IV-I-V in A or I-♭VII-IV-I in E if you prefer to renumber. When you play A major scale patterns over this chord progression, the notes fit perfectly. Because the 5th, E, is the tonic, this is E Mixolydian mode (see Chapters 7 and 13). "No Rain" by Blind Melon uses the same chords and scales.

D-C-G-D

Here's an example in D that uses the major pentatonic and Mixolydian mode. D major pentatonic works because the tonic chord is D, but the rest of the progression isn't drawn from the D major scale. All together, these three chords fit into the G major scale. They're V-IV-I-V in G or I-♭VII-IV-I in D if you prefer to renumber. When you play G major scale patterns over this chord progression, you can hear that the notes fit perfectly. Because the 5th, D, is the tonic, this is D Mixolydian mode. "Sweet Child O' Mine" by Guns N' Roses uses the same chords and scales (with guitars tuned down one half step to E♭).

Am-G-F

In this progression, everything centers on the A minor chord. For this reason, you play A minor pentatonic over the whole thing. On the fretboard, these chords fit into a chord pattern that starts on C at the 3rd fret of the 5th string: vi-V-IV in C or i-♭VII-♭VI in A minor if you prefer to renumber. Play C major scale patterns over this progression and hear that they're a perfect fit. Because the tonic in this case is A, not C, you're really playing A minor (that is, A natural minor, A relative minor, or A Aeolian mode). Most players would favor a pentatonic scale pattern and then also play C major scale notes in the same position (see Chapter 13). You hear the same scales applied over a similar progression during the guitar solo section in "Stairway to Heaven" by Led Zeppelin.

Am-D

This type of progression has many variations, including Am7-D, Am7-D7, and Am7-D9. In any case, it's in the key of A minor, so you use the same scales that you use for the preceding progression, Am-G-F, right? Wrong! The C major/A minor scale has a Dm chord, not D major. The only way you can have a minor chord and a major chord opposite each other on different strings in this arrangement is when they're ii and V. If Am is ii, then G must be I. Hence, this is a ii-V chord progression in the G major scale. Because the 2nd scale degree A is functioning as the tonic, it's A Dorian mode. If you prefer to renumber, then the progression is i-IV.

Playing G major scale patterns over this progression produces the A Dorian mode sound. Because the tonic chord is Am, you can also simply use A minor pentatonic. Most players would favor a pentatonic scale pattern and then also play G major scale notes in the same position (see Dorian mode in Chapter 13). Many popular songs, including "Oye Como Va" and "Evil Ways" by Santana (G Dorian), have sections based on this type of progression.

Am-Bm

This progression is very similar to the preceding one in that it centers on Am and is also in A Dorian mode. Two minor chords a whole step apart can only be ii and iii from the major scale (i-ii if you renumber). Playing G major scale patterns over this progression produces the A Dorian mode sound. Because the tonic chord is Am, you can also use A minor pentatonic.

Some songs that have sections featuring this chord progression are "Moondance" by Van Morrison, "Light My Fire" by The Doors, and "Horse with No Name" by America (E Dorian).

Em-D-C-B7

The first thing you need to notice about this progression is that it centers on a minor chord (Em) and has a dominant 7th chord (B7) that's a 5th away. That's harmonic minor! But before you go playing the E harmonic minor scale over these chord changes, remember that you use the harmonic minor only temporarily (refer to Chapter 14 for details). Take out the B7 chord and the rest of the progression fits into the E natural minor scale. E minor is relative to G major. In the G major scale, Em-D-C is vi-V-IV. If you renumber starting on Em, then it's i-♭VII-♭VI. So you can play the E natural minor scale (also known as E Aeolian mode) over Em-D-C. The only chord to which you apply the E harmonic minor, which is an E minor scale with a raised 7th, is the B7. "Nothing Else Matters" by Metallica uses the same chords and scales.

F♯-B-C♯

This progression is similar to the one used in "Give Me One Reason" by Tracy Chapman. It appears to be a I-IV-V progression in F♯ major, but that's not how Chapman treats it. Instead of playing the major pentatonic and major scale, she and her bandmates sing and play primarily the F♯ minor pentatonic, creating a minor-over-major blues sound (see Chapter 15). Many blues-sounding pieces of music include minor pentatonic played over major chords. In this situation, guitarists usually don't apply full major scale patterns.

While playing minor over major sounds great in bluesy styles of music, it can sound totally off in other styles. Be sure to apply this concept only when appropriate.

E5-D5

In this progression, the tonic is E, and the progression as a whole is very sparse since it includes only two chords, incomplete ones at that. You play both chords as power chords, leaving out any type of 3rd. In cases like this, knowing whether the music is major or minor and determining which parent major scale the chords belong to can be tricky.

Because the tonic is E and the E5 has no 3rd, you can treat it as either major or minor by playing the E major or E minor pentatonic. As a whole, both chords E5 and D5 can fit together into four possible major scales because each chord can be either major or minor. These scales include

- E minor (Aeolian): E5-D5 is vi-V from the G major scale
- E Dorian: E5-D5 is ii-I from the D major scale
- E Phrygian: E5-D5 is iii-ii from the C major scale
- E Mixolydian: E5-D5 is V-IV from the A major scale

If you're playing over E5-D5 with no other instrumentation or vocal melodies to fill in the gaps and establish a parent major scale, then you're free to choose any of the preceding options. Which one you choose is a matter of preference. The three minor options are natural minor, Phrygian, and Dorian, and the one major option is Mixolydian. Another option is to play a mix of major and minor pentatonic, even including Mixolydian; this would be a good option if you were going for a bluesy sound (see Chapter 15).

"Cocaine" by Eric Clapton features an E5-D5 chord progression that you can play over in a couple of different ways. Clapton generally uses minor pentatonic scales, but he has been known to take a modal approach. On his live album *Just One Night* at 2:45 into "Cocaine," Clapton interprets the progression as ii-I in D major, playing solos based on E Dorian. You can clearly hear him playing this mode in its entirety in the recording. At 4:33 in this same live recording, Clapton's sideman, Albert Lee, incorporates E Mixolydian mode for his solo, playing over the progression as if it were E-D, V-IV in A major (I-♭VII in E if you renumber).

For the record, E5-D5 can only be a mode that has a ♭7th because if E5 is the tonic, then D5 is the ♭7th. Right away you can rule out any mode with a major 7th like Ionian and Lydian. Also, you can rule out Locrian mode because it features a ♭5th and the E power chord has a perfect 5th.

Chapter 18

Tens Ways to Put Theory into Practice

In This Chapter

- Learning new songs and playing along with music
- Playing with others and in front of an audience
- Focusing more on playing than on practicing
- Setting achievable goals

Knowing music theory is one thing; applying it is another. In order to be a strong guitar player, you have to practice and play!

This chapter includes suggestions to help you transfer your understanding of guitar theory to your playing. Here, you discover some of the best ways to practice, as well as tricks to help you take advantage of every playing opportunity.

Learn and Analyze Songs

Learning songs is the absolute best way to develop as a musician. Every song you learn teaches you something new about using chords, playing progressions, and applying scales (not to mention licks, phrasing, fingering, and overall technique). For each new song you study, identify its components and analyze how it's put together. For example, answer the following ten questions about every song you work on:

- What's the key of the song?
- What's the parent major scale of the music?
- On which major scale degree is the tonic chord based?
- How would you number the chord progression?
- From which CAGED forms are the chord shapes drawn?
- Does the song change keys?
- Which type of scale patterns does the song use?
- How is the music similar to other songs you play?
- What are some other ways that you can play the song?
- How can you borrow ideas from the song to play over other songs or compose your own music?

Learning a song today is as easy as searching its title in a search engine. After all, just about any song you can imagine is available online for download. Plus, you can stream a lot of music for free online, and you can find official, complete, accurate tabs to most popular songs in songbooks or individual scores. You can even download songs off the Internet to play anytime you want.

If you're looking for sheet music, I recommend the following resources:

- www.musicnotes.com
- www.sheetmusicplus.com
- www.musicdispatch.com

Some of these websites also include play-along guitar books and tracks, instructional videos, and software programs that make the song learning and practicing process easier and more enjoyable.

A few resources that catalog songs by their chords and progressions that I found helpful while writing this book include chordmine.com and the books *Money Chords: A Songwriter's Sourcebook of Popular Chord Progressions* and *Chord Progressions For Songwriters* by Richard Scott.

Play Along with Songs

Aside from learning parts from songs, you can also play along with them as you practice. Keeping up with the pace of a recording helps you develop timing and endurance. Plus, it gives you an opportunity to hear your part harmonically mixed with the rest of the music.

Recorded music makes for a great play-along track even when you're not playing parts from that specific song. For example, you can practice G major scale patterns simply by playing them over a piece of music based in the same scale. Hearing how the scale mixes harmonically with the rest of the music really brings it to life. Turn to Chapter 12 to put this practice technique into action.

Record and Listen to Yourself

When you play guitar, your mind can become so focused on the physical tasks of fretting and picking that you fail to properly sense other important aspects of music like pitch, timing, feel, and tone. The way you think you sound while playing is often quite different from how you really sound. The best way to critique your playing is to listen to a recording of yourself. You may be surprised to hear that you speed up or slow down without realizing it. Maybe your touch is too heavy or too light. Maybe your bends are out of tune or you hear too much unwanted string noise. Or — and this is where the process can be very encouraging — you may be pleased to hear that some sounds come out better than you thought!

You don't need a lot of fancy technology to record yourself, and you don't have to make a big production out of it. Most computers, laptops, tablets, smartphones, and other portable devices have features, programs, and apps that you can use to record yourself. For example, I often just set my iPhone on my lap or in front of my amp as I practice and play, using the built-in voice memo. If you want something a little more traditional, you can choose from various types of handheld recorders. Some guitar effects pedals have recording capabilities, too. If you want more visual help, you can make videos of your practice sessions by using a webcam, camcorder, or smartphone.

Become a Super Looper

A *loop* is a repeated section of sound material. You can make loops with a wide range of music technologies, like recording programs, drum machines, and guitar effects pedals.

As a guitarist, you can easily add a *loop pedal* into your signal change so that you can record and play back your playing at the stomp of a foot. The most popular unit for this use is the Boss Loop Station, which is available in different models. However, other manufacturers produce products that do the same thing.

When using a loop pedal, you need to run an electric or acoustic-electric guitar through it. You plug your instrument into the pedal and then connect the pedal to your amp, mixing board, and so on. When you stomp on the pedal, the device starts recording you. When you stomp on it again, it plays back what it just recorded. After it reaches the end of the recorded section, it immediately starts again from the beginning. It continues to loop the recorded material until you stop it. Some models even let you layer multiple recorded parts.

Looping devices, or *loopers,* as they're often called, are great practicing tools that you can use for recording, making play-along tracks, and layering multiple guitar parts all on the fly. They come in handy when you're critiquing your playing, practicing scales and chords, and learning how to harmonize guitar tracks. Loopers have also become a popular performance tool as many players use them in live settings.

Play with Others

More often than not, music is a group effort. While you can perform on some instruments completely solo, nothing compares to groups of musicians playing together. If you know other guitarists or other types of instrumentalists, such as pianists, bassists, or drummers, ask them if you can play together. You can also accompany singers.

Playing with others is good for both practice and play. Other musicians can give you feedback, share ideas, provide accompaniment, and trade licks. Learning and practicing aside, it's fun just to hang out with others doing something you love. After all, we humans are relational beings; we're made to harmonize with one another.

When playing with others, you can have one person play rhythm while another plays melody, sings, or improvises. You can then trade parts.

Play Out

Have you ever wanted to practice more or harder but just lacked the motivation? Well, you'll get motivated really fast when you have to get up and play something in front of others! Finding opportunities to "play out," as musicians say, is a surefire way to make you take your practice time more seriously. Having a live performance scheduled is kind of like a deadline. So, for example, if your gig is next Saturday, you absolutely have to have your parts down by then!

Aside from being terrifying, er, I mean, motivating, playing out can be enjoyable and rewarding, as well. Part of the appeal of playing an instrument is the opportunity to share your love of music with others. Plus, everybody needs to feel appreciated; a little applause now and then is great encouragement. You'll really feel like you've accomplished something after you have a good performance in front of others.

Playing out also gives you more time with your instrument in your hands, which can only make you a better player. I used to play three to five nights a week, usually three one-hour sets each night. That's 9 to 15 hours of guitar playing every week, not including all the other hours I spent learning material, practicing, and teaching.

Practice a Little and Play a Lot

Learning and practicing are very important, but you don't want to overdo it. You need to spend a lot of time just casually playing without always trying to accomplish something. My middle school shop teacher used to tell the class to saw a lot and sand a little. Sanding allows you to refine your edges. I've always told my students to play a lot and practice a little. Although you need plenty of practice to refine your skills and techniques, most of the time, you just need to relax and simply enjoy playing guitar.

I realize that my attitude about practicing goes against what others may say. You often hear stories about virtuoso musicians who spent eight hours a day practicing. I suppose if you want to be a technical virtuoso, then you can follow a rigid practice routine. But most people just want to enjoy the process. There's nothing wrong with spending most of your time playing through familiar songs or improvising just for the fun of it. The more you play, the better you'll get anyway.

Study More Music Theory Resources

One of the best ways to develop your understanding of music and guitar playing is — and I realize this seems strange — to keep on studying! Countless books, DVDs, and websites offer guitar instruction and music theory lessons. You don't need to master everything that's out there, but it's helpful to always have something that you're slowly working your way through. That way, you're always making progress and developing new skills and techniques.

There's more online at `www.dummies.com` from me and other guitar authors for you to check out . You may even enjoy taking a traditional music theory class at a nearby community college or music school. This sort of thing isn't for everyone, but if you're the nerdy, er, I mean, very analytical type, you may really enjoy it.

Learn how to read music. Understanding music notation influences how you play the guitar even when you don't have sheet music in front of you. Plus, you'll be better able to follow charts and lead sheets when the need arises. You don't have to learn to read like a concert violinist; just learn the basics. I recommend that you learn up to at least the point where you can count and play 16th notes. Start with a book like *Mel Bay's Modern Guitar Method Grade 1* or something similar.

Set Reasonable, Realistic Goals

If you're serious about progressing as a guitarist, you need to set some goals. You don't have to set major goals ("I *will* be the next guitar god!") — just something simple that you can work toward. A good goal is to complete this book (if you haven't already). Another is to learn a song or a part of a song. Maybe your goal is to play at an open mic night or at church or to make a YouTube video to share with friends. Whatever the case may be, just set small, achievable goals that give you a target to set your sights on. Then work toward them.

As you set goals, be reasonable and realistic. As the old saying goes, "Everybody is created equal, but some are more equal than others." If you think you're going to be the next Jimi Hendrix, you probably aren't being realistic. Some people are blessed with exceptional guitar-playing skills, and others aren't. In fact, most people aren't. As well as I can play some things, I still watch others who are better and say, "Dang! Why can't I do that?" Accept your limitations, play to your strengths, and enjoy what you're able to do well. You don't need to be a virtuoso to make a contribution to music.

Have a Good Time All the Time

When asked about his philosophy on life, Viv Savage of Spinal Tap replied, ""Have a good time all the time." Whatever you study, however you play, wherever your skills lead you, enjoy what you do and be grateful for the gift of music and the opportunity to play this great instrument, the guitar.

Appendix

Audio Tracks and Video Clips

Sometimes, reading about a concept and trying to practice it just doesn't cut it — you need to see or hear it, too. Wherever you see the "PlayThis!" icon, you find references to audio tracks and video clips that demonstrate various musical techniques. I also provide a few audio tracks that you can use as backing tracks to play over to make your practice sessions more fun and interesting. This appendix provides you with a handy list of all the audio tracks and video clips referenced throughout the book.

If you've purchased the paper or e-book version of *Guitar Theory For Dummies,* you can find the audio tracks and video clips — ready and waiting for you — at `www.dummies.com/go/guitartheory`. (If you don't have Internet access, call 877-762-2974 within the U.S. or 317-572-3993 outside the U.S.)

Discovering What's on the Audio Tracks

Table B-1 lists all the audio tracks that accompany each chapter, along with any figure numbers if applicable. You also find several backing and play-along tracks to help you with your practice.

Table B-1 Audio Tracks

Track Number	*Chapter*	*Description*
1	1	Demonstration of the sound of some the of the material presented throughout this book
2	2	Notes, steps, octaves, and intervals
3	3	Chord construction, triads, chords, and the harmonized major scale
4	4	Examples of the CAGED system in action
5	5	Chord tones, extensions, and pedal point
6	6	Sample chord progressions
7	7	Tonics, keys, and modes
8	8	Key change examples
9	9	Dominant function and voice leading
10	10	Passing chords
11	11	Demonstration of what the pentatonic scale sounds like and how it's used
12	12	Examples of the major scale

(continued)

Table B-1 *(continued)*

Track Number	*Chapter*	*Description*
13	13	Using modes
14	13	Play-along backing track of Figure 13-2 Ionian
15	13	Play-along backing track of Figure 13-5 Dorian
16	13	Play-along backing track of Figure 13-8 Phrygian
17	13	Play-along backing track of Figure 13-11 Lydian
18	13	Play-along backing track of Figure 13-14 Mixolydian
19	13	Play-along backing track of Figure 13-17 Aeolian
20	14	Samples of the harmonic minor scale
21	14	Play-along backing track of Figure 14-1 Am-E7
22	15	Examples of playing the blues
23	15	Play-along backing track of Figure 15-6 12-bar blues

Looking at What's on the Video Clips

Table B-2 lists all the video clips that accompany each chapter, along with corresponding figure numbers when applicable.

Table B-2 Video Clips

Clip Number	*Chapter*	*Description*
1	2	How to finger and play octave shapes
2	2	Playing thirds, as shown in Figure 2-15
3	3	Building and playing triads
4	3	The G major scale chords
5	4	Fingering and playing the first CAGED form, C
6	4	How to connect the CAGED forms shown in Figure 4-21
7	4	How to play through the example of CAGED chord changes, Round 1, shown in Figure 4-27
8	5	7th chords in G
9	5	Playing the 6ths example shown in Figure 5-16
10	5	How to record and play the pedal tone example shown in Figure 5-19
11	6	Playing through the major scale chord pattern shown in Figure 6-2
12	6	How to play by number in the open position
13	7	Brief demonstration on playing in G major and E minor
14	7	Brief demonstration on playing in A Dorian

Clip Number	*Chapter*	*Description*
15	8	Transposed chord progression, as shown in Figure 8-2
16	8	Mixing major and Mixolydian, as shown in Figure 8-4
17	8	"House of the Rising Sun" example, as shown in Figure 8-9
18	8	Playing ascending 5ths, as shown in Figure 8-11
19	9	Closing progression and dominant function as shown in Figure 9-3
20	9	Playing secondary dominants, as shown in Figure 9-6
21	9	An example of voice leading, as shown in Figure 9-10
22	10	Playing a chromatic passing chord example
23	10	Blues progression with chromatic passing chords, as shown in Figure 10-4
24	10	Demonstration of Bdim7 chord fingerings, as shown in Figure 10-8
25	10	Using a diminished passing chord, as shown in Figure 10-10
26	10	Augmented chromatic voice leading, as shown in Figure 10-16
27	11	Playing up and down pentatonic scale patterns, as well as how to finger and connect pentatonic patterns
28	11	A demonstration of the use of E minor and G major pentatonic
29	11	The pentatonic scale transposed to new keys
30	12	How to play the five major scale patterns in G, as shown in Figure 12-6
31	12	Transposing major scale patterns to the key of C, as shown in Figure 12-11
32	13	How to play in Ionian mode
33	13	Demonstration of playing in Dorian mode
34	14	Outlining V7 chords with the minor pentatonic scale
35	14	Playing full harmonic minor scale patterns, as shown in Figure 14-10
36	15	How to mix major and minor pentatonic, as shown in Figure 15-5
37	15	Demonstration on how to play over a 12-bar blues example
38	15	Using the blues scale

Index

• Symbols and Numerics •

• A •

• B •

• C •

• D •

• E •

• F •

• G •

• H •

• I •

• N •

• P •

• R •

• S •

• T •

• U •

• V •

• W •

About the Author

Hailed as a "music-theory expert" by *Rolling Stone* magazine, guitarist **Desi Serna** is the author of the very popular *Fretboard Theory* line of guitar instructional material. He's known for his hands-on approach to music theory and his emphasis on popular music. Desi honed his craft through decades of guitar teaching, performing, and publishing. He operates his own guitar theory website, where he posts online guitar lessons and discusses various music-theory-related topics with his community of followers. He lives near Toledo, Ohio, with his wife and two daughters.

Dedication

For all my friends and family who have supported me throughout the years.

Author's Acknowledgments

I want to extend a very special thanks to David Lutton for initially reaching out to me about this project. I gratefully acknowledge all the folks at John Wiley & Sons, Inc., who had a hand in seeing this book through to completion, including Chrissy Guthrie, Amanda Langferman, and Christy Pingleton, as well as all the folks in Composition Services and Vertical Websites. Thanks also to Sandy Williams for his expert technical review of the content and to Jeff Harris of MadSam Recording for doing the audio tracks. I also need to mention my personal editor, guitarist Thomas Evdokimoff, who was involved in previous work that influenced the writing of this book. Above all else, I thank God for the gift of music!

Publisher's Acknowledgments

Acquisitions Editor: David Lutton

Senior Project Editor: Christina Guthrie

Copy Editors: Amanda Langferman, Christy Pingleton

Technical Editor: Sandy Williams

Project Coordinator: Kristie Rees

Cover Image: ©PRSGuitars.com/Marc Quigley

Math & Science

Algebra I For Dummies, 2nd Edition
978-0-470-55964-2

Anatomy and Physiology For Dummies, 2nd Edition
978-0-470-92326-9

Astronomy For Dummies, 3rd Edition
978-1-118-37697-3

Biology For Dummies, 2nd Edition
978-0-470-59875-7

Chemistry For Dummies, 2nd Edition
978-1-1180-0730-3

Pre-Algebra Essentials For Dummies
978-0-470-61838-7

Microsoft Office

Excel 2013 For Dummies
978-1-118-51012-4

Office 2013 All-in-One For Dummies
978-1-118-51636-2

PowerPoint 2013 For Dummies
978-1-118-50253-2

Word 2013 For Dummies
978-1-118-49123-2

Music

Blues Harmonica For Dummies
978-1-118-25269-7

Guitar For Dummies, 3rd Edition
978-1-118-11554-1

iPod & iTunes For Dummies, 10th Edition
978-1-118-50864-0

Programming

Android Application Development For Dummies, 2nd Edition
978-1-118-38710-8

iOS 6 Application Development For Dummies
978-1-118-50880-0

Java For Dummies, 5th Edition
978-0-470-37173-2

Religion & Inspiration

The Bible For Dummies
978-0-7645-5296-0

Buddhism For Dummies, 2nd Edition
978-1-118-02379-2

Catholicism For Dummies, 2nd Edition
978-1-118-07778-8

Self-Help & Relationships

Bipolar Disorder For Dummies, 2nd Edition
978-1-118-33882-7

Meditation For Dummies, 3rd Edition
978-1-118-29144-3

Seniors

Computers For Seniors For Dummies, 3rd Edition
978-1-118-11553-4

iPad For Seniors For Dummies, 5th Edition
978-1-118-49708-1

Social Security For Dummies
978-1-118-20573-0

Smartphones & Tablets

Android Phones For Dummies
978-1-118-16952-0

Kindle Fire HD For Dummies
978-1-118-42223-6

NOOK HD For Dummies, Portable Edition
978-1-118-39498-4

Surface For Dummies
978-1-118-49634-3

Test Prep

ACT For Dummies, 5th Edition
978-1-118-01259-8

ASVAB For Dummies, 3rd Edition
978-0-470-63760-9

GRE For Dummies, 7th Edition
978-0-470-88921-3

Officer Candidate Tests, For Dummies
978-0-470-59876-4

Physician's Assistant Exa
For Dummies
978-1-118-11556-5

Series 7 Exam For Dummies
978-0-470-09932-2

Windows 8

Windows 8 For Dummies
978-1-118-13461-0

Windows 8 For Dummies, Book + DVD Bundle
978-1-118-27167-4

Windows 8 All-in-One For Dummies
978-1-118-11920-4

Available in print and e-book formats.

Available wherever books are sold. For more information or to order direct: U.S. customers visit www.Dummies.com or call 1-877-762-2974
U.K. customers visit www.Wileyeurope.com or call (0) 1243 843291. Canadian customers visit www.Wiley.ca or call 1-800-567-4797.
Connect with us online at www.facebook.com/fordummies or @fordummies

Take Dummies with you everywhere you go!

Whether you're excited about e-books, want more from the web, must have your mobile apps, or swept up in social media, Dummies makes everything easier .

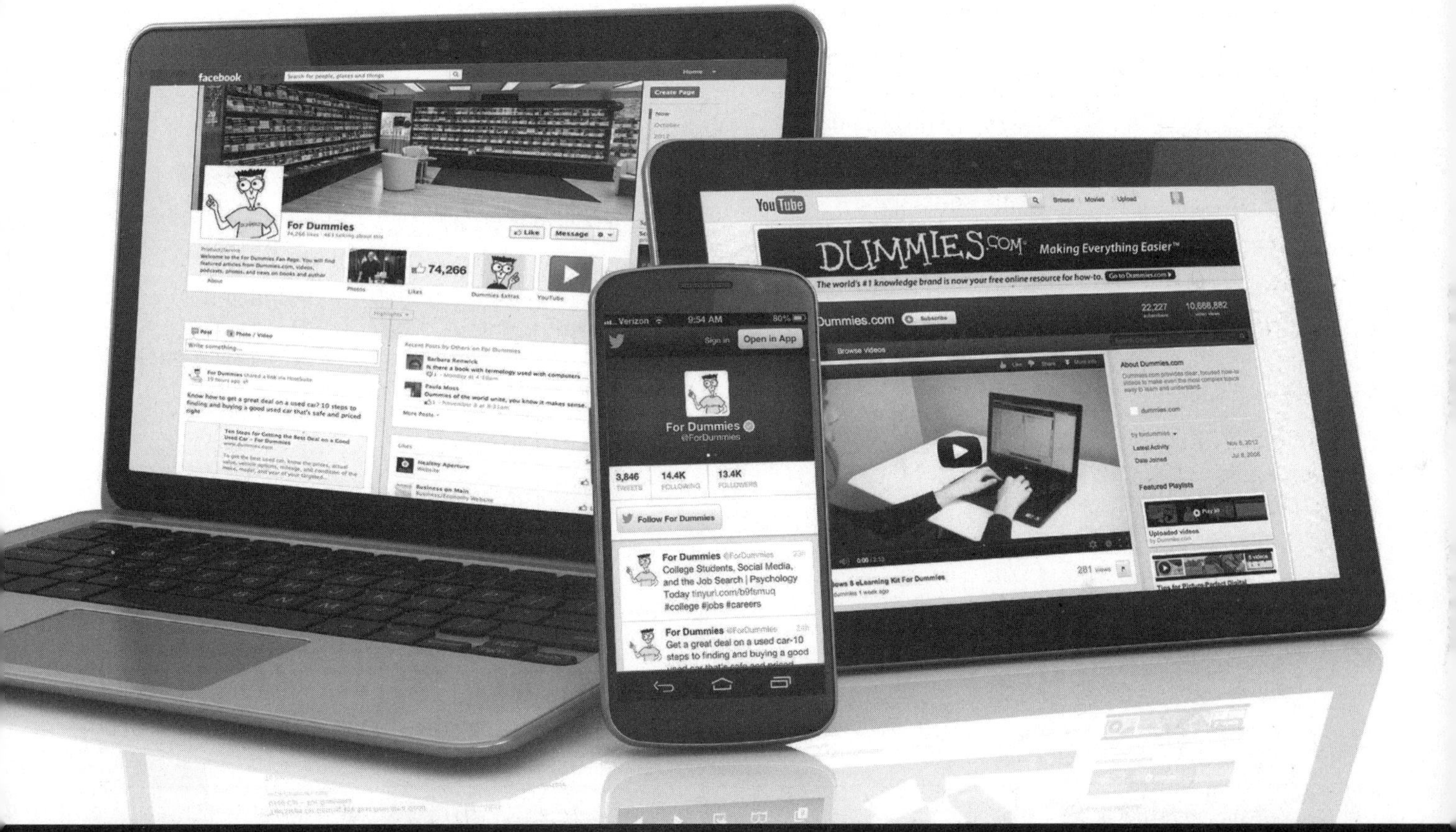

Visit Us	Like Us	Follow Us	Watch Us
Join Us	**Pin Us**	**Circle Us**	**Shop Us**